PSYCHOANALYSIS AND CURRENT BIOLOGICAL THOUGHT

Proceedings of an Interdisciplinary Research Conference Sponsored by the Wisconsin Psychiatric Institute and the Department of Psychiatry of the University of Wisconsin Medical Center, June, 1963

PSYCHOANALYSIS AND CURRENT BIOLOGICAL THOUGHT

EDITED BY
NORMAN S. GREENFIELD
AND WILLIAM C. LEWIS

Madison and Milwaukee, 1965
THE UNIVERSITY OF WISCONSIN PRESS

Published by
The University of Wisconsin Press
Madison and Milwaukee
Mailing address: P.O. Box 1379, Madison, Wisconsin 53701

Printed in the United States of America
by Kingsport Press, Inc., Kingsport, Tennessee

Library of Congress Catalog Card Number 64–8488

CONTRIBUTORS

A. A. ALEXANDER, Ph.D.
Assistant Professor, Department of Psychiatry
Research Associate, Wisconsin Psychiatric Institute
University of Wisconsin Medical Center, Madison, Wisconsin

JOHN D. BENJAMIN, M.D.
Professor of Psychiatry
University of Colorado School of Medicine, Denver, Colorado

NORMAN S. GREENFIELD, Ph.D.
Professor of Psychiatry
Associate Director, Wisconsin Psychiatric Institute
University of Wisconsin Medical Center, Madison, Wisconsin

ROBERT R. HOLT, Ph.D.
Professor of Psychology
Co-Director, Research Center for Mental Health
New York University, New York, N.Y.

GEORGE S. KLEIN, Ph.D.
Professor of Psychology
Co-Director, Research Center for Mental Health
New York University, New York, N.Y.

WILLIAM C. LEWIS, M.D.
Professor of Psychiatry
University of Wisconsin Medical Center, Madison, Wisconsin

SYDNEY G. MARGOLIN, M.D.
Professor of Psychiatry
Director, Human Behavior Laboratory
University of Colorado School of Medicine, Denver, Colorado

MILTON H. MILLER, M.D.
Chairman and Professor, Department of Psychiatry
Director, Wisconsin Psychiatric Institute
University of Wisconsin Medical Center, Madison, Wisconsin

DONALD OKEN, M.D.
Associate Director
Institute for Psychosomatic and Psychiatric Research and Training
Michael Reese Hospital and Medical Center, Chicago, Illinois

MORTIMER OSTOW, M.D.
Private Practice
New York, N.Y.

KARL PRIBRAM, M.D.
Professor of Psychiatry
Stanford University Medical School, Palo Alto, California

BENJAMIN B. RUBINSTEIN, M.D.
Private Practice
New York, N.Y.

SHELDON T. SELESNICK, M.D.
Research Associate, Department of Child Psychiatry
Mount Sinai Hospital, Los Angeles, California

FREDERICK SNYDER, M.D.
Chief, Section of Psychophysiology of Sleep, Adult Psychiatry Branch
National Institute of Mental Health, Bethesda, Maryland

JOSEPH C. SPEISMAN, PH.D.
National Institute of Mental Health
Bethesda, Maryland

ZANWIL SPERBER, PH.D.
Chief Psychologist, Department of Child Psychiatry
Mount Sinai Hospital, Los Angeles, California

RICHARD A. STERNBACH, PH.D.
Assistant in Psychology, Department of Psychiatry
Harvard Medical School
Massachusetts Mental Health Center, Boston, Massachusetts

HERBERT WEINER, M.D.
Associate Professor of Psychiatry
Albert Einstein College of Medicine, New York, N.Y.

PREFACE

Paul Adrian Maurice Dirac, the distinguished English theoretical physicist, recently published an account of physical theory in which he traced past developments and sketched future possibilities in that field.

After reviewing some problems of theory he said:

> . . . quantum theory is an extremely good theory. It gives wonderful agreement with observation over a wide range of phenomena. There is no doubt that it is a good theory, and the only reason physicists talk so much about the difficulties in it is that it is precisely the difficulties that are interesting. The successes of the theory are all taken for granted. One does not get anywhere simply by going over the successes again and again, whereas by talking over the difficulties people can hope to make some progress.[1]

Dirac's comments express exactly the spirit of the papers in this volume, and can apply directly to the conference at which they were presented if one substitutes the term 'psychoanalytic theory' in place of 'physical' or 'quantum' theory. For there is an unusual combination displayed here. The critics of psychoanalytic theory, and even some of its defenders, too often do not display a mastery of that theory and its complex developmental history. And when criticism is advanced, it is often not backed up by evidence, or by efforts to illuminate the difficulty. Here, we have contributions by workers in many fields. Some of these workers owe their research orientation and inspiration to psychoanalytic theory. Others, in advancing theoretical discussion of some problems of the theory, are thoroughly conversant with the theory and its enormous power. All these workers either practice psychoanalysis or are intimately associated with those who do. The result is a rich exploration of an area that is neither psychoanalysis in the narrow sense, nor biology proper, but something in between (here we refer to psychoanalysis as a therapeutic technique, or as a research technique in its own right). This border area, however, properly falls in the broad domain of psychoanalytic theory.

All those who participated in the conference felt a touch of excitement at the prospects and insights offered by the work of others. Perhaps the reader will catch this same stimulation and clarification. Some themes come up again and again in diverse contexts. Among these are the nature of consciousness, the varieties of experiencing and perceiving, and how these relate to the processes of biology. The participants were asked to consider the sorts of phenomena that led Freud to construct the *Project for a Scientific Psychology.*

[1]P.A.M. Dirac, "The evolution of the physicist's picture of nature," *Scientific American 208*:45, 1963.

The mind-body problem looks different in the light of this century's thought and knowledge—of developmental processes, of physiology, and of psychology. We have developed tools and achieved precision in their use; we now have some ways which were not available to Freud to detect subtle properties of living organisms. Examples of this type are scattered through the papers, but we may mention a few. One is the development of the electroencephalograph and allied instruments, making possible some exploration of the relation of dreams to other behavior during sleep. Also, observations of the rapid periodicities of some biological functions depend upon computers and on statistical techniques which were not available until recently. The close interrelationship of psychic events and physiologic processes is capable of demonstration by use of the polygraph and refined instruments of observation. These tools have made possible some insights into order and structure in human events, evident in the papers. Not only the tools of the fields close to psychoanalysis, but also the tools and theories of distant fields have made important changes in our world view. These changes both complicate and simplify some of the problems of psychoanalytic theory.

This volume presents both new data and new attempts to weld the implications of this data to what is already known. In the words of Ernest Jones,

> . . . the preconceptions from the world of contemporary scientific thought . . . with which Freud approached his studies had a visible influence on his theoretic structure, and they necessarily bear the mark of a given period. We must expect that other workers, schooled by different disciplines than his, will be able to effect fresh orientations, to form fresh correlations. In spite of our natural piety we must brace ourselves to welcome some changes, fortifying ourselves with the reflection that to face truth and to hold truth above all other considerations had been Freud's greatest lesson to us and his most precious legacy to psychological science.[2]

This is the spirit of this volume and its contributors.

We wish to thank the American Psychological Association, the publishers of the *Journal of Abnormal and Social Psychology* and *Psychological Monographs,* for permission to reproduce in Dr. Speisman's article figures which originally appeared in those journals (Figs. 12.2 and 12.3 from R. S. Lazarus, J. C. Speisman, A. M. Mordkoff, and L. A. Davison, "A laboratory study of psychological stress produced by a motion picture film," *Psychol. Monogr. 76,* whole no. 553, 1962; and Figs. 2 and 3 from J. C. Speisman, R. S. Lazarus, A. Mordkoff, and L. A. Davison, "The experimental reduction of stress based on ego-defense theory," *J. abnorm. soc. Psychol. 68:367–380,* 1964).

Madison, Wisconsin
May, 1964

N. S. G.
W. C. L.

---

[2]E. Jones, presidential statement, American Psychoanalytic Association, 1936; quoted by S. Rado, R. Grinker, and F. Alexander, *Archives of General Psychiatry* 8:527, 1963.

CONTENTS

PSYCHOANALYSIS AND CURRENT BIOLOGICAL THOUGHT

ONE

On Building Bridges

MILTON H. MILLER, M.D.

This gathering of biological and social scientists from all parts of the continent attests to a growing appreciation of the unity of our diverse efforts. This is to be credited in part to those few who pass knowledgeably between us, thereby forming the rudimentary shape of the bridge, or bridges, to come. In the decade ahead these bridges will be much better traveled, and, hopefully, such travel will be in both directions. It is not enough to say that everything psychological has a biochemical basis or that biochemistry is a necessary step in understanding the phenomenon of experiencing. Rather, an adequate understanding of either psychology or biology requires an appreciation of the unifying closed circle of events which encompasses both.

Developments in biochemistry, neurophysiology, psychopharmacology, social psychology, and the promise of a "science-fiction" era of telemetered psychophysiological studies make obsolete any notions of a purely intuitive science of psychoanalysis or psychotherapy; nor will research in these areas retain the exclusive model of a "he said and then I said" variety. Nevertheless, we must not be afraid to "know" in those realms which presently, and perhaps permanently, will not be amenable to chemical or mathematical analysis. Paradoxically, many of the very matters best and most deeply understood evade tabular compilation.

The technology of our age has advanced at a staggering pace. Our newest computer at the University will complete in twelve minutes what it took our last computer an hour to perform. That computer in turn could complete in an hour an equivalent of work which the old 650 IBM required a week to finish; and the IBM 650 could do in an hour what a skilled operator with a hand calculator could do in 30 years. Restated, our newest computer can perform in an hour the equivalent of 25,000 years of computational work by a skilled operator with a hand calculator. There are comparable advances in the techniques of data collection. New telemetering devices are being developed which may allow a myriad of 24-hours-per-day psychophysiological computations to be received and processed on tape in a central laboratory while the subject being studied goes about his activities within a hospital building. These projected monitors, and the already available television cameras which make any room a "one-way vision setting," will provide for researchers a mass of data, much of which has hitherto been unavailable. No art, no science, no profession will be unaffected by this shift in technology, by this impending mountain of "information." Greenfield warns that the day may not be far away when the raw data will go from telemetered polygraph to multi-channel tape, to computer, and come out in a neatly typed, ready-to-mail, finished publication, accompanied by an estimation of the number of reprints which will be requested.

However, it is precisely in the face of this kind of development that we must be particularly careful not to lose touch with, to bury in data, or to ignore as "unscientific" that uniquely human skill best described as the capacity for intuitive knowing. The acquisition of new knowledge is not simply an additive process. One cannot be taken, by data alone, to those broad leaps which have so enriched mankind and which are, fundamentally, often the richest yield of the whole process of research. Often such contributions represent a stepping out from the scientific data at hand or the hypotheses currently entertained by the majority and represent, instead, a reliance upon what Polanyi describes as "that personal knowledge," that sensing of relationships which, once sensed, may then be verified and elaborated by the ways of analytic science (*10*). Indeed, intuitive knowing often comes long before the technical skills necessary to prove or disprove consequent applications are available to the scientist. Collection of data alone, no matter at what speed, cannot replace such knowledge. Instead, one wonders whether the dazzling computers may not actually tend to obscure and freeze scientific growth to additive patterns. This would be a dreadful development in any science and a lethal one in the mental sciences.

Admittedly, intuition, poetic hypotheses, and speculations based upon non-quantified observations are in a state of current disrepute. The existence of the brand new science of sleep causes us to wonder whether we will ever again believe that cadre of authorities which includes the lovers of all times, the poets, and the "unscientific dreamers" of the world. After all, for how many eons have man and woman slept juxtaposed to each other and how many a lovesick swain has written or professed a line something like this:

> The bluest sky,
> The calmest sea,
> The forest stilled on a windless day,
> The greenest hill,
> The warmest fire,
> The whiteness of a snow piled deep
> Are coarse, uneven, truculent
> Compared to my beloved's sleep.

In required that purest of scientists, a graduate student working toward his Ph.D. thesis, to open the doors to a new understanding of phenomena hitherto undreamed of.

One mystery alone remains
Of my beloved's sleep:
We've solved the movement of her eyes
And why they do repeat;
We know what brings her breath in sighs;
We've tracked her EEG;
The haunting doubt that still remains
Is does she dream of me?

Yet in the face of the facts and figures which will emerge from the new laboratories of sleep, we must be careful not to lose sight of the significance to the individual of his dreams and of his dreaming; nor should we ignore those observations which have collected from the times of Plato through Freud which also speak a truth about the dream and the dreamer.

Nowhere are the achievements of analytic sciences or their present limitations more evident than in the study of thought and of the mind. Speaking to this point, Penfield writes, "How it may be that ganglionic activity is transformed into thinking and how it is that thought is converted into the neural activity of conscious voluntary action we have no knowledge. Here is a fundamental problem. Here, psychology and physiology come face to face" (quoted by John [*4*]). This coming face to face by psychology, psychoanalysis, and biology in an effort to comprehend the nature of our lived life experience has received much attention. Some regard the problem as solved, or as nearly solved, or at least regard the fundamental philosophic question as having been answered. We may hear of Turing's speculation that, if it were possible to maintain sensory input, one might remove all the body and much of the brain, leaving a minimum structure of brain tissue, of the order of a cubic inch, which would adequately provide consciousness yet below which there could be no consciousness (*13*). The same author suggests that the mental activity of the brain might be reproduced in a computer with one billion binary digits of storage working at a speed of 500 elementary instructions per second following 3,000 man years of programing (*13*). Similarly, Hebb notes, "Mind can only be regarded for scientific purposes as the activity of the brain. Conscious processes are primarily neuro-activity" (*2*). And Bailey describes man's mind thus: "It is a mechanism for the transmission of signals which arrive in peripheral sense organs, are transmitted by sensory nerves as pulses of electrical potential to the central nervous system and are variously integrated and reflected over the motor nerves to result in our behavior" (*1*). Conversely, and speaking for psychotherapists generally, Straus maintains: "It is man who is doing the thinking, not the brain" (quoted by Kahn [*5*]).

Indeed, the nature of mind as a subjective phenomenon has persistently evaded an understanding illumination by the techniques of the biological scientist. In the words of the French philosopher, Merleau-Ponty, "The whole universe of science is built upon the lived world and yet science has been least able to illuminate the nature of subjective lived experience" (quoted by Veatch [*14*]). Mechanical systems are notoriously unsatisfactory when offered as explanations of biological phenomena, and both the computer and other proposed models as applied to mental functioning have proved no exception. The complexity of biological systems in general is compounded in efforts to comprehend the problem of mind. Here, the interrelationship of the perceived to the perceiver, of the experience to the experiencer, is most intricate and variable. In the words of Whitehead, "The status of life in nature is the standing problem of philosophy and of science" (*15*). Rogers (*11*), Heidegger (*3*), Polanyi (*10*), Langer (*6, 7*), Scher (*12*), Lyons (*9*), and others emphasize the inseparability of subjective man from the data and nature of his world.

These complex interrelationships have not always been adequately understood, either by biological sciences or by a psychiatry which, following the lead of Descartes, began "after the fact" with study of a hypothesized independent nature of an independent world of perceiving man. Man's awareness of himself was simply assumed, leading to the trap of the body and the mind and to a failure to consider not only the products of consciousness but consciousness per se. Narrowing, reductionist theories, whether of biological or psychological stripe, fail equally to engage with the true complexity of the system studied. Man, biology, causality, "objects in the independent world" must be viewed as part of a unified experiental totality. We have moved far enough in the clinician's office as well as in the scientist's laboratory to view more clearly the necessity for study which recognizes this unity. To date, even at a time when a computer can perform so many of the overt behaviors ordinarily ascribed to man, the royal road to his subjective world (and, for him, his only world) remains that bumpy, long, dusty, somewhat circuitous span traversed through the years by the priests, philosophers, poets, psychologists, and therapists who not only listened but heard.

The task of building bridges, as in all construction work, is vigorous labor, and the importance of recruiting the young while they are still young and of providing them with the necessary tools and inspiration for such endeavor cannot be overstated. Generally, we the teachers of those who will build the future bridges do not have an auspicious record in fulfilling this mandate. Opportunities for our students to be trained in settings where the best of various traditions are represented are remarkably few and far between. Even when varied training opportunities do exist in physical proximity within a campus or a building, estrangement among them, of remarkably pervasive degree, can occur. By and large, psychoanalytic-psychotherapeutic clinicians go to schools which are totally separate from those attended by students in the mental sciences. Rare it is that a biologist can ever "see a patient."[1] Equally rare it is that the clinician who finishes his classical training is young enough, open enough, or financially unencumbered enough to study and appreciate the broad tactical strategy and techniques of the scientist. Most graduating clinicians today know little or nothing of the recent advances in the mental sciences, of the developments in brain chemistry, of the reticular activating system, of the research on sleep, or genetics, of psychophysiology; not one biological scientist in ten will ever acquire an appreciation of clinical phenomena which delineate fear from anxiety, fright from bewilderment, or pain which is pleasure and pleasure which is pain. In short, our present educational techniques, philosophies, and settings do not suffice. They are ordinarily parochial, isolating, and unimaginatively conceived. Consider the young physician: too often, in the past, his decision in the early years of college to pursue a medical education served to estrange him from the art, literature, music, history, anthropology, the ethics and culture of his society. Once in a medical school he is ordinarily subjected to a most orthodox, tightly scheduled curriculum, one which rarely allows an opportunity for the development of his own ideas or even an opportunity for deeper study in areas of particular interest. In many respects medical education may compare unfavorably with the educational practices in the best divisions of a good "graduate school." All too often residency training in psychiatry has served to perpetuate or accentuate, rather than to correct, deficits in general medical training. Psychiatric residents are often shielded from an awarenes of the lack of specific information in certain areas in our field; they may be presented with a sense of "truth" regarding currently favored hypotheses which are actually highly tentative and speculative in nature. Obviously, the resident will learn a great deal during his training. At times, however, he learns by rote, by memory, by acquiescence to authority, by estrangement from intuition, and, worst of all, by group assent. Savant in his home terrain, when abroad he may be lost, confused, without real guidelines, and thereby strongly opinionated and defensive.

No less parochial is the training of a great many biologists within the mental sciences, many of whom share a smug belief in the ultimate reducibility of all human experience to simple chemical, physiological, or behavioral psychological formula. For such individuals psychoanalysis and all clinical psychological theories pertaining to human behavior represent some form of

[1]"Seeing a patient" takes as much time for a biologist as it does for a young clinician and not only requires a patient and an atmosphere where real encounter is possible but requires, as well, the diligent teaching of a clinician teacher.

opulently sustained, modern-day, phlogiston theory. That whole area of human experience is "bracketed" by them as lacking pertinence for the scientist.

There are many problems in fusing an image which is coherent upon a collective retina. By and large, neither the clinicians nor the biological scientists are "men of the renaissance." They are bound by limitations of their parochial languages, handicapped by their failure to acquire the kind of background that now seems so vital to those who will carry forth their work. The task of providing scientific training for some of today's gifted clinicians and of providing a clinical appreciation in some of the biological scientists is a significant responsibility for all of us. There are not many good institutional models. Many of the "interdisciplinary" efforts of the last decade proved disappointing. Neither "take a scientist to lunch week" nor "interdisciplinary coffee breaks at 10 A.M. and 3 P.M. each day" will do the job—for, in the normal course of things, we tend to associate with individuals whose training and experience is most like our own, people able to understand and appreciate our efforts. This is not surprising. In the words of J. M. Thorburn, "All the genuine, deep delight of life is in showing people the mud-pies you have made; and life is at its best when we confidingly recommend our mud-pies to each other's sympathetic consideration" (Langer [*8*]). Nevertheless, the growing magnitude of our knowledge and of our awareness of the complexity of many phenomena which have hitherto been studied only in part has begun to disrupt hierarchial barriers separating psychology, psychiatry, the social and analytic biological sciences. We need to be more attuned to the question "What can this co-worker do?"—rather than to the question "What degree has he?"

The scaffolding of tomorrow's bridges can be visualized if we look closely. The architecture is on the drawing boards. An interdisciplinary awareness within the single investigator rather than an interdisciplinary liaison among investigators may become a more prevalent model. This puts greater responsibility upon today's teachers than ever before, and upon their students as well. We cannot simply train our students in our own image. They must take from us and take as well from those who live across the bridge.

REFERENCES

1 BAILEY, P. "Cortex and Mind." In *Theories of the Mind,* edited by J. Scher. New York, The Free Press of Glencoe, 1962, p. 3.

2 HEBB, D. O. *The Organization of Behavior.* New York, Wiley, 1949, p. 422.

3 HEIDEGGER, M. *Being and Time,* translated by J. Macquarrie and E. Robinson. London, SCM Press, 1962.

4 JOHN, R. E. "Some Speculations on the Psychophysiology of Mind." In *Theories of the Mind,* edited by J. Scher. New York, The Free Press of Glencoe, 1962, p. 117.

5 KAHN, E. "Some Thoughts on the Mind." In *Theories of the Mind,* edited by J. Scher. New York, The Free Press of Glencoe, 1962, p. 422.

6 LANGER, SUSANNE KATHERINA (KNAUTH). *An Introduction to Symbolic Logic.* 2nd edition (revised). New York, Dover Publications, 1953.

7 LANGER, SUSANNE KATHERINA (KNAUTH). *Philosophy in a New Key: A Study in the Symbolism of Reason, Rite and Art.* 3rd edition. Cambridge, Harvard Univ. Press, 1957.

8 LANGER, SUSANNE KATHERINA (KNAUTH). *Philosophy in a New Key: A Study in the Symbolism of Reason, Rite and Art.* New York, New American Library of World Literature, 1961, p. ix.

9 LYONS, J. The problem of existential inquiry. *J. existent, Psychiat. 4*(14):141, 1963.

10 POLANYI, M. *Personal Knowledge: Towards a Post-Critical Philosophy.* Chicago, Univ. of Chicago Press, 1958.

11 ROGERS, C. R. *On Becoming a Person: A Therapist's View of Psychotherapy.* Boston, Houghton Mifflin, 1961.

12 SCHER, J. M. The concept of the self in schizophrenia. *J. existent. Psychiat. 1*:1, 1960.

13 TURING, A. N. Computing machinery and intelligence. *Mind 59*:443–460, 1950. Reprinted as "Can a Machine Think?" in *The World of Mathematics,* Vol. IV. New York, Simon and Schuster, 1956.

14 VEATCH, H. B. "Minds: What and Where in the World Are They?" In *Theories of the Mind,* edited by J. Scher. New York, The Free Press of Glencoe, 1962, p. 316.

15 WHITEHEAD, A. N. *Alfred North Whitehead: His Reflections on Man and Nature.* Selected by Ruth Nanda Anshen. New York, Harper, 1963. World Perspectives, Vol. XXVII, p. 10.

TWO

Psychoanalysis as a Biological Science

HERBERT WEINER, M.D.

In living organisms physical integration and psychical integration represent two aspects, corresponding to two mutually complementary sets of factors of one and the same fundamental biological process.

R. S. Lillie (*82*)

"Purpose" is not imported into nature, and need not be puzzled over as a strange or divine something else that gets inside and makes life go; it is no more an added force than mind is something in addition to brain. It is simply implicit in the fact of organization, and it is to be studied rather than admired or "explained."

H. J. Muller (*95*)

In the past forty years many eminent biologists with various professional interests have come to recognize that organization is the distinctive feature of life, of form and structure, of directiveness, and of development (*114*). Since directiveness is possible in lower forms without a nervous system, it is argued that the nervous system, which controls behavior in higher forms, is but a special instance of biological organization and a special means by which self-regulation and adaptation toward a goal are achieved.

It is curious, then, that certain psychoanalysts—who are, above all, students of behavior—have been from the beginning more prone to build physicalist models and theories, at the highest level of their explanatory hypotheses, than biological ones (*33, 35, 38, 39*). Yet psychoanalysis is, of course, replete with statements concerning the biological implications of many concepts of behavioral phenomena which psychoanalysts study, such as self-preservation (*34, 36, 37*), anxiety (*42*), and adaptation (*54*).

The concept of instinctual drives is said by psychoanalysts to be biological;

Supported in part by a Public Health Service Research Career Program Award (MH–K3–18448) from the National Institute of Mental Health.

but it is never stated in what sense the concept is biological, except that it is "borderline" between the somatic and the psychic according to Freud's well-known definition.

There are other psychoanalysts, however, who object to these physicalist theories and to the biological implications of human behavior. They emphasize the differences between man and animals and eschew the theory that man is a species of animal understandable only in biological terms and comprehensible ultimately in nonliving terms.

Notwithstanding these objections, one must inquire whether all biological concepts must necessarily be patterned after physical ones—or whether there are specifically biological concepts which deal with the observable complexity, organization, historical character, and directiveness of organisms (*12, 53, 108, 112, 113, 130*). If we agree that biology concerns itself with more than just the natural history of organisms, its claim to independence as a discipline must, as Beckner (*4*) has said, rest "on the fact that its historical, functional and polytypic concepts are distinctive, in that they are defined by means of properties which are of intrinsic interest only to biologists. The utility of these concepts rests in the very fact that they attempt to deal with the over-all properties of organisms mentioned."

Furthermore, questions such as "What for?" and "How come?" typically asked by many biologists and psychoanalysts concerning their own data (*112*) are not generally asked by physicists (*112*). The physicist who inquires into differences in the behavior of quantum particles would probably phrase the answers not in terms of their past histories but rather in terms of mass and energy. Similarly, differences in conduction rates of nerve fibers are generally couched in terms of physical properties, such as fiber diameter, or of biochemical ones—e.g., the presence or absence of myelin, etc. However, if we ask what the origins of an organism are, our answer—depending on the time scale we have in mind—cuts across all levels of organization from the macro-molecular to that of the evolution of populations (*112*). Again, a statement describing the biological differences of organisms in terms, for example, of "selection," "adaptation," or "mutation" carries with it clear-cut historical implications.

In certain areas of physics the time-span of phenomena under investigation has been progressively reduced; when it is prolonged, as in astronomy, the phenomena under investigation deal with change, not evolution. Biological and psychological phenomena, however, share another property: we may study the operations of organisms occurring over brief periods of time, changes involving months and years which occur from fertilization of the ovum to its maturity and death, hereditary phenomena requiring the span of many lifetimes, and also speciation—the process of biological or cultural evolution—which necessitates many generations of study.

Thus, the kinds of questions biologists and psychoanalysts ask about the observable phenomena in organisms are not equivalent or even analogous to those which physicists ask. Realizing that many biologists and even psychologists would disagree with such a statement increases one's awareness of the kind of discomfort such a conclusion generates, because it does not answer two questions:

1. Are the properties ascribed to living organisms—i.e., complexity, organization, historicity, and directiveness—exclusive only to them? or are they also characteristic of nonbiological phenomena? If such a claim of exclusiveness were made for organisms and found to be untrue, the biological position would become seriously weakened or untenable. There is evidence to date that directiveness characterizes certain activities of viruses: e.g., certain bacteriophages always attach themselves tail first to a specific area of the cell wall of *E. coli* (*94*). This directed manner of attachment is 100 per cent effective once the virus and the bacterium are brought sufficiently close together and despite the fact that the bacteriophage may have been placed randomly in space prior to attachment. However, Mora inquires whether the molecular and statistical concept of such directed phenomena is adequate "to explain the actual phenomenon of directiveness."

2. To what extent should biology or psychology rely on physics and chemistry? To do so totally would mean that all the phenomena of life can be accounted for in terms of those processes which can be discovered among nonliving things.

If physics and chemistry are not relied on at all, we may incline to one or the other of two points of view: the first being vitalism, the postulate of a nonmaterial, nonmechanistic unifying principle (such as "entelechy"); or, second, if we are more moderate, in dualism, in which case we would find ourselves in the company of Adrian (*2*), Schrödinger (*110*), or Sherrington (*111*).

Another escape from this dilemma was, of course, first traversed by Whitehead (*128*). One starts with the observable and builds models or concepts constituted of simpler elements which, in combination, may wholly or partly account for the observed. Yet we do not know much more about these simpler elements, once we have identified them, than we did on observing the phenomena for which they are supposed to account. There is nothing about the number of electrons of a potassium atom which will tell us that, when potassium combines with chlorine, a salt is formed; or that, when a shift occurs in the specific relationship of sodium and potassium ions lying on opposite sides of a complex membrane, an electrical impulse will flow. (It is, of course, true that the study of an element in some contexts may provide the basis for predicting its behavior in other contexts—e.g., knowledge of the valence and atomic weights of potassium and chlorine allows us to predict their combined atomic weights.) Such diverse behavior simply points up a new range of facts about potassium. The apparent mystery of these new properties, however, is a function of arrangement, architecture, and surrounding; every time we discover a new structured entity in which potassium partakes, more of its properties are revealed.

Thus, there is nothing mysterious about "organization," and certainly statements such as "organization is a matter of complexity" or "the whole is greater than the sum of its parts" are mere evasions. In fact, it appears that the more complex the structural arrangement is, the less likely that its basic constituents reveal their character and properties (*123*). Nerve net models made of "hardware," e.g., may have all the functional characteristics of the actual nets which they simulate. No implication is intended that the arrangement is of prepotent or determinant significance. Clearly, the arrangement depends in part on the properties of its constituent elements, but neither can be neglected.

I have argued, then, that there are certain requirements for our study of living organisms which are not fully met by a resort to physics and chemistry or by accounting for phenomena in terms of self-contained entities. The fact that we are liable to do so may in part be a result of the current and perennial paradigms of science (*78*) and the fact that our techniques and methodologies best lend themselves to isolating and analyzing such entities and their properties. Yet it is curious that even in physics two general types of theories exist: an atomistic or particle theory and one that accounts for phenomena in terms of sets of relations—the wave theory.

In summary, many of the phenomena which biology and psychoanalysis seek to study and explain share certain common characteristics. These should be considered not only in terms of their constituent entities but also in terms of organization relations at different levels of complexity. The questions that biologists and psychoanalysts ask about the phenomena they encounter are of an analogous order and differ from those that physicists and chemists ask. Specifically, the former wish to know about events, the latter properties.

My aim is, therefore, to examine what is meant by the statement that psychoanalytic concepts and propositions are biological. I am not interested here in examining the correctness of these ideas. I hope that I will not strain the analogies. I do not mean to take any position about the Mind-Brain controversy, since I am not competent to do so, but will deal with the concepts of the historical nature, directiveness, and organization of living organisms about which biologists have written and which appear and reappear in psychoanalysis. Finally, I shall try to determine whether it is at all possible, given these common properties, to arrive at some way in which psychoanalytic observations and hypotheses may be investigated by neurophysiological techniques.

II

The next questions to be asked are: In what way is the psychoanalytic model of development biological? and can some of the developmental concepts in biology be used as necessary, if not sufficient, correctives for some of the concepts of psychoanalysis and psychoanalytically inspired developmental psychology? Obviously, the subject matter of the two fields does differ radically, as indeed does the manner in which the data are collected. Only when observation is used alone or combined with reconstruction do the methods for studying development approach one another (*30, 31, 75, 76*).

There are, of course, inherent dangers in using biology as a yardstick, in that concepts in biology change as more data become available or that the concept and model may be wrong. Illustrative of this is the fact that Haeckel's biogenetic law, coupled with a Darwinian model and a curious Lamarckian view of evolution, indubitably had an influence on Freud's thinking in the area of human development and on his formulation of the "genetic" principle (*106*).

Haeckel's "law" has encountered many difficulties, both empirical and logical. DeBeer (*14*) has, for instance, gathered much evidence that the early stages of ontogeny do not at all resemble the adults of the ancestors, except on a very superficial plane, and that specific fetal adaptations occur (e.g., birth membranes) which have no counterpart in the adult. However, this does not mean that other genuine recapitulations do not occur in ontogeny. On a logical level the "law" does not hold in view of the fact that Haeckel believed that phylogeny is a mechanical cause of ontogeny. However, differences in adult morphology over several generations cannot be deemed a cause of ontogeny, in the usual sense of a cause (*4*). Freud's Lamarckian views have often been discussed as being quaint; yet, such views might seem much less absurd today in the light of the recent work with Planaria (*127*) than they did several years ago.

To return to the point I wish to make and to illustrate: biologists today consider the genotype as consisting of a collection of potentialities. The phenotype consists of all the characteristics—elicited potentialities—that an organism may develop, depending on those specific circumstances under which he may happen to grow up. Any one genotype may, in different environments, give rise, within certain limits, to different phenotypes.

The biologist does not, of course, speak of phylogeny as if it were the direct result of ontogenetic development. Rather, he would say that it is the type of ontogenetic development which changes in the course of phylogeny. The biologist is interested in the manner in which an organism acquires particular properties—such as reaction tendencies, disposition, and attributes—which enable it to carry out the functions of life which subserve reproduction. If phylogeny were the direct outcome of ontogeny there could be no natural selection, and adaptation would be impossible.

Psychoanalysis has from its beginnings avoided the uncritical assumption that adult characters are the direct "effects" of causes present in the germ—

an asumption which is in direct contrast to the views of those schools associated with the names of Kretschmer, Morel, and Magnan, who have their contemporary counterparts (*105, 106*).

The biologist's definition of genotypes and phenotypes requires further specification. Ginsburg (*45*) has reported that the members of one of three strains of inbred mice are markedly superior to members of the other strains in terms of interstrain aggressiveness in fighting. All members of all strains had been isolated from weaning to sexual maturity. However, this superiority in fighting in this particular strain also depended on whether the animals had been handled during the pre-isolation period. When they were handled they became submissive to members of other strains; when not, they dominated. The other two strains were unaffected by handling or not handling.

This experiment exemplifies two developmental principles in biology: first, that early experience determines sensitivity to later specific experiences rather than determining sustained behavior; second, that similar behavior patterns may have a considerably different ontogeny and phylogeny. The same developmental end may be reached by various routes. The only manner of differentiating the same behavioral end-results is by a historical review of the steps by which the behavior occurred (*59, 106*). Here, psychoanalytic propositions are in line with Driesch's principle of equifinality shorn of its teleologic overtones.

Ginsburg's elegant experiment does not, however, exhaust the types of developmental questions which psychoanalysis asks. Developmental propositions go far beyond the discovery and isolation of the childhood prototypes of reaction tendencies. Psychoanalysis interests itself in the nature of the problem, why it was not solved in childhood (a question that requires specification of what phase the child was in), why it was solved in a particular manner, how this solution affected later development. A complete answer to such questions requires knowledge of what problem-solving and adaptive functions were available and how the environment responded to the problem—i.e., the nature of the experience (*57, 59*).

The answer to each one of the interdependent questions clearly does not depend on any single factor. Here I do not want to retrace the development of ideas about the innate and the acquired in psychoanalysis. This has been done much more ably by Benjamin (*5*), Hartmann and Kris (*59*), and others. Suffice it to say that the history of ideas about the articulation of nature and nurture bespeaks the difficulty, both within and outside of psychoanalysis, with which this topic is fraught. This articulation has in the past years been extended, clarified, and explicated, so that an over-all view of personality development emerges.

The genotype obviously resists investigation by psychological means. It may first be manifested, however, by individual differences at birth (*5, 6, 12, 79, 92, 129*). These individual differences enter as independent variables into the development sequence. The other variables are those of the maturation and development[1] of instinctual drives, the maturation and development of the potentialities and capabilities for perception, motility, anxiety, memory, for responding to stimuli, for discrimination (*11*), etc., which at first are rudimentary. However, as development proceeds, interactions between need and drive expression, on the one hand, and controlling structures, on the other, and the environment proceed. At the same time experience shapes the maturing adaptive functions. Problem-solving and conflict-solving are continuous and in themselves result in new functions (*54, 56*). Adaptive tasks face the organism and are handled according to the age, phase, and predispositions of the child. Thus, culture and biology are clearly interdependent (*17*). The unfolding of "psychic sructure" goes through an orderly, stepwise series of transformations and crises which become more and more complex: it is epigenetic. The details of this epigenetic sequence have been portrayed by Erickson (*21, 25*), who also documented the articulation between endowment, maturation, and interactions of the child and the parent who is prepared by his culture to respond adaptively to the child. "Whatever reaction patterns are given biologically and whatever schedule is predetermined developmentally must be considered to be a series of potentialities for changing patterns of mutual regulation" (*24*).

By studying infants who differed in endowment, Escalona (*28*) has documented the fact that different actions of mothers may lead to "very similar consequences in terms of the impact upon the child's experience as reflected in behavior" and vice versa. She has provided us with crucial observations of what experience entails. In her words:

> Experience is not the outer stimuli as such, not inborn reaction tendencies, not these in simple summation—but the manner in which these factors alter what the baby feels with his senses, what he does with his body, and the content and quality of successive events in his life. Both the universals of development and the extraordinary variations may be said to consist of experience. A person cannot do, or feel, or think or be anything except as these verbs are derived from the events in time and space, unified by the fact that the organism remains continuous; that we call experience. By the same token, development may be regarded as the result of experience.[2]

It is almost banal, or course, to state that "experience" in Escalona's sense is of a different order than the kind that weaning or handling of a young animal entails, with well-known results (*81*).

Without succumbing to environmentalism, but to emphasize the crucial nature of development and experience in determining behavior, one might

---

[1]These terms are used according to Hartmann, Kris, and Loewenstein's definition (*60*).

[2]I wish to thank Dr. Escalona for permission to quote from her paper which is in press.

note that gender, role, and sexual identity seem experientially co-determined in human hermaphrodites (see, e.g., *93*).

The factors that are, nowadays, necessary postulates in human development and the biological conceptualization of the genotype and phenotype do, of course, account for individual variability without having to implicate any single, or prepotent factor. The model is broadly enough based to account for the well-known "magnifying effect" of development and, particularly, of differentiation (*50*). In biology the magnifying effect of development refers to the observation that the earlier genes with deleterious effects exert themselves the more detrimental they are likely to be. Infant observation is rendered even more difficult by the possibility that genetically determined factors do not have to manifest themselves at birth but may do so at any time during development, thus introducing another variable into a multidetermined process. It is doubly difficult to ascertain whether the results of devastating early experiences, such as Spitz (*116, 117*) has described, are not also partly predicated on genetic factors. The biologist's concept of a "magnifying effect" might, however, also be applied to human postnatal development: the earlier very deleterious experiences occur or genetically determined deleterious effects obtain, the more detrimental are the ensuing results (*85, 116, 117*).

Psychoanalysis has often been accused of the fact that its genetic propositions are not predictive but lay claim to "sufficiency." In view of the multiplicity of factors involved in development it is hard to see how they could be predictive. Furthermore, genetic explanations fall in the category of model explanations, and models from a logical point of view cannot be predictive (*4*).

III

For many the word "biological" connotes biophysics, biochemistry, and physiology; all else is unscientific. Inevitably, therefore, the answer to all living processes lies in reductionism. However, nothing that has so far been said should be construed as an argument for or against reductionism. There is nothing intrinsically wrong *qua* theory in reductionism; it is simply that reductionist models or theories are at times inadequate as descriptions or explanations of some complex phenomena. Biological phenomena may at times be considered in reductionistic terms, at other times, in organismic (*123*). Biology, and perhaps psychoanalysis, are or might be reinforced by the mutual interplay of atomistic and organismic theories. For instance, embryonic development cannot be understood without knowledge of the biochemical mechanisms of heredity, any more than human post-natal development can be understood without life experience. Nevertheless, such a statement still begs the question: which biological phenomena can be analyzed in terms of atomistic theories and which cannot?

The revolutionary analytic revelations begun by Mendel in the field of genetics emphasize the success of the atomistic approach in the analysis of biological phenomena despite the fact that present-day geneticists would no longer support the concept that each particular potentiality for development is controlled by a separate, discontinuous hereditary factor. Rather, the view would be that many interacting factors, or reactions between units, control such potentialities. Yet nothing that has been discovered since Mendel's time vitiates the point of view that genes and their chemical structures represent discrete units. If we are interested only in how nucleotide sequences relate to amino acid sequences—i.e., in how genes effect the production of definite chemical substances—then the atomistic level of analysis is sufficiently descriptive. However such data, reveal nothing of the process by which a normal cell may result in certain binucleated fungi which contain an *abnormal* set of nucleotides ("cistrons") separated from one another by cytoplasm (*29*); nor how morphological pattern or shape is determined. Thus, Pontecorvo (*100*) has suggested that the morphological pattern is determined by the interaction of groups of subgenic units ("cistrons"). Yet, clearly, not even this is sufficient to explain morphology. The surroundings in which usual morphological differentiation occurs will in part determine whether it occurs, as evidenced by the fact that, if cartilage cells are tissue-cultured for periods as brief as five days, they lose their morphological characteristics as well as their characteristic chemical capacity to secrete sulfated mucopolysaccharides (*62*). In addition to this *in vitro* phenomenon, *in vivo* analysis of the process of differentiation inclines biologists to the view that it depends on interaction among tissues (*50*).

The problem of organization, at whatever level, which seemed so mysterious even fifteen years ago (*113*) may involve nothing more, it would seem, than spatiotemporal continuity and the interaction, or "organizing relations," between parts (*4, 96*); and clearly no atomistic theory per se will account for these. That both contiguity and interaction are requisite to organization has been more than adequately demonstrated for embryonic development, especially morphogenesis, by Waddington (*122*) and Needham (*97*). The fact that the inducer may be RNA (*98*) does not vitiate the earlier facts.

This statement may be reassuring except for the disquiet engendered by the fact that some logicians might say that organization emerges as a problem only because of the complexity of the phenomena: too much knowledge in one direction and too little in another, so that "organization is only a methodological question" (*4*).

In other words, the fact that induction may be accomplished by many different chemical substances does not mean that there is not one basic substance in nature, but tells more about the response than the stimulus. The initial response which leads to organ differentiation occurs during a critical period and is most probably under the control of many interrelated genes;

but, in view of the fact that organs are distinctly constituted, the gene groups must be organized into mutually exclusive, interacting complexes (*123*). Differentiation and individuation are not limitless, and organogenesis does not proceed simultaneously. Another kind of interaction—that of a whole set of genes—is at work which determines the pathways of progressive development. The models used to explain interaction and inhibitions are usually of a cybernetic nature.

A leading biologist thus writes, "Biological phenomena exist in interlocked superordinacy and subordinacy," requiring techniques appropriate to each level of analysis but also those appropriate for the level above and below. The "interlocking" referred to is a function of interactions betwen levels (*50*). (The biologist's range of interest from the level of DNA to those of natural selection and evolution requires then considerable technical virtuosity.)

What of psychoanalytic propositions? It is curious that perhaps only Rapaport (*106*) has systematically dealt with the question of organization, although the question of organization, in the sense of "psychic sructure," was first discussed by Freud (*41, 42*) and clarified by Hartmann, Kris, and Loewenstein (*60*). From the basis of any observable behavior, one is impressed by its coherent, integrated quality, even if the behavior is irrational. The fact that one can then discover that there are many components—often conflicting—of this particular behavior (*10, 124*) only begs the question of how behavior achieves coherence and organization. How do motivational, affective, cognitive, defensive, moral, ethical, or other considerations interact so that the end-behavior has this organized quality? Obviously, these components are not separate behaviors (*106*), and the particular behavior cannot be divorced from a larger organization—that of personality. As Rapaport has written:

> What this organismic point of view asserts is not that each behavior is a microcosm which reflects the macrocosm of the personality but rather that an explanation of behavior, in order to have any claim to completeness, must specify its place within the functional and structural framework of the total personality and therefore, must include statements about the degree and kind of involvement in the behavior in question, of all the relevant aspects of the personality.

It is clearly not only motive which gives behavior its organized quality (*42*) and its directed quality (*24, 54*). Yet the hidden assumption in much of the psychoanalytic literature is that personality organization is a function of drive derivatives. Clearly such an "atomistic" point of view is inadequate.

These are inherent in psychoanalysis multiple levels of behavior analysis; each, however, reveals functional interactions. If much has been made of conflict, this is because it is a special example of the fact that interactions (even if contradictory or exclusive) occur among functions (*56*). One might mention the interaction between reality-testing and attitudes, motive and memory, defense and memory, defense and perception, between identifications

(*54, 56*). In addition, organization has, so to speak, a "vertical" aspect to it—formalized in the topographic point of view—in terms of derivative motivations, controlling functions and defenses, which occur and are re-represented at several heirarchic levels (*38, 42, 58, 68, 106*). Unfortunately, we are still ignorant of the full range of interactions between functions (for example, those which are subsumed under the generic name of the "ego"). The organization of the "ego" is given conceptual treatment by the postulation of a synthetic function or principle (*42, 54, 99*), of which the coherence of behavior is the product, while the organization of behavior is in turn under the control of a coordinated, integrated coterie of ego functions (*56, 106*).

At each step during personality development and maturation a reorganization is necessary, as has been exemplified by the effects of maturation of the locomotor system on the interaction of the mother and child (*88*), leading to new tasks, anxieties, new developments, differentiations, and integrations; the development of language behavior (*72*) and the changes of adolescence (*69*) also bring about such reorganization, none of which can be understood except in terms of the interactions of the component functions operative at the time. The question of organization can, therefore, never be answered except in terms of the relations between components, whether on the psychological or the biological level.

Further recognition of this has been given very clear-cut demonstration in another area through the analysis of eating and drinking behavior in the rat. Rather than trying to localize eating and drinking to an anatomical site in the nervous system, Stellar (*118*) and Teitelbaum (*119*) used lesions in known integrating sites to analyze the components of these motivated behavior patterns. They discovered that such lesions bring out the components of this behavior, which includes peripheral sensory stimuli emanating from taste, tactile, and temperature receptors in the mucosa of the upper gastrointestinal tract. For example, lesions in the ventromedial hypothalamus heighten the rat's sensitivity to stimuli impinging on these receptors. In addition to these factors, these investigators found that the kind of food, central neural factors, and previous experience (learning) all play a role in the understanding of eating and drinking behavior (*118*).

IV

Psychoanalysts have not been averse to trying to explain psychological function in terms of neural function: witness, for instance, Freud's abandoned attempts at neurodynamic formulation of psychology and his statement that correlations were to be made between physiological and psychological organization and that physiological terminology could eventually be substituted for psychological terms (*32*). As long as this was not possible, he felt that psychological terminology must still be adhered to without substitution (*40*). However, Woodger (*131*) has pointed out that such a linguistic substitution is not logically possible, even if it were methodologically possible to make psychology directly translatable into neurophysiology.

The problem of such translation has often been misstated; to attempt to specify, for instance, what thought processes are in anatomical or physiological terms is clearly not possible. Rather, perhaps, starting from a behavioral manifestation, we should first specify what the components of thought processes are and then analyze their functional properties and organization, but in psychological terms. During such an attempt one is impressed by the fact that, whatever the neural substrate of such a behavior pattern might be, it clearly cannot be specifically located in any one position in the nervous system, any more than one can locate or identify the source or nature of a computer's output in any one of its electronic units. Having then made a first-level analysis of the behavior in question, one might specify the kinds of functional and organizational properties which could account for the known characteristics of this behavior. At the same time one would ask what kind of known neural organization has such properties. Probably these could be the resultant only of highly complex unit interactions which initially resist detailed specification, and one could not accomplish this translation by postulating an explanation of the behavior in terms of physics and then expect to use it as a link to a neural phenomenon. Concretely, it is absurd to inquire where the location of the "ego" is in the nervous system if one really takes its definition seriously (that it is a generic name for a complex series of interacting functions which, in an integrated, organized manner, are involved in adaptive, defensive, and self-regulatory behavior, etc. [*56*]). We might rather attempt a molar level of analysis of these part-functions of the "ego" in the hope of refining their properties. From them we may derive testable principles of their functioning and organization and look for their physiological referents, no matter how vague. Surely what we know about memory or learning processes makes it doubtful that any one specific locus in the nervous system subserves them. Perhaps a clear demonstration of this is that neural activity during the establishment of a conditioned response—classical or avoidance—is widely distributed throughout the nervous system (*44, 70*).

We should attempt to refine our behavioral observations, and the intervening variables which are derived from them, not with the idea of substituting for them purely physiological ones, but with the hope of learning more about their inherent properties which are obscured by the very nature of their complexity (*61*). What we may find if we then test them may be something which was unpredictable and surprising but does not alter at all the original behavior phenomenon or dispense with it.

To exemplify: In the auditory cortex of the cat 66 per cent of the units recorded by a microelectrode could be activated by sounds (*26*). This observation was confirmed by Hubel, Henson, Rupert, and Galambos (*63*) in the unrestrained cat. In this latter series 10 per cent of all the units examined were not firing when repeated stimuli such as clicks or tones were used. However, as soon as the animal turned its head and became attentive to the voice of the experimenter, the source of the click, or the squeak of a mouse, these inactive units became active. Obviously, this experiment does not reveal much about the phenomenon of attention; but the finding that certain cortical units in specific systems actively fire only during periods of attention is both surprising and illuminating.

It is doubtful whether whole segments of psychoanalytic theory of various explanatory levels can be translated into neurophysiological or anatomical terms or that these can tell us everything concerning behavior, consciousness, or mind. It is not only a matter of making the language more operational (*19*) but rather of proceeding in the outlined manner. The problem is a methodological, rather than a linguistic, one.

In this manner one may be able to arrive at some of the necessary or even sufficient mechanisms for the phenomena underlying adaptive or self-regulatory functioning. The only excuse for what follows, most of which is highly hypothetical, is that the spirit guiding this group of papers is exploratory.

Some aspects of the model outlined[3] should be ascribed to Freud (*32*), Hebb (*61*), Mirsky (*91*), Pribram (*101*), and Engel (*20*). Psychoanalysis may also be the source of rich behavioral hypotheses; it has not overlooked the complexity of behavior, and it has implicitly or explicitly had something to say in psychological terms about many facets of behavior and their functional properties.

To illustrate further the main thesis of this section, the following examples are suggested.

One of the most complex and certainly most important processes which has been studied by psychoanalysts is that of the progressive differentiation of the ability to tell self from object. It is not necessary to mention all the factors that enter into the development of this function—e.g., deprivation (*60*)—or the consequences of a failure in its development. Suffice it to say that it does not seem unlikely that one of the necessary conditions and substrates at its inception may be the maturation of distance receptors, plus the further maturation of the discriminative capacity of these, which according to the data of Bridger (*11*) and Lipton (*84*) are already present at birth. Yet developmental neurophysiology is just in its infancy (see, however, *7, 18, 46, 51, 65, 90, 102, 107, 109, 120*).

There is a second behavioral observation which may lend itself to further

[3]So much of modern neuropsychology is oppositely oriented: its model is to build up a picture of integrated behavior by the addition of lower-level neural properties or constructs, a point made by Pribram (*101*).

analysis and neurophysiological observation. As is well known, infants vary in their behavioral responses to sensory stimuli, some becoming excitable, some showing no response, others being unduly sensitive to the stimuli—the latter response being inferred from the infants' behavioral response (*6*). These observations are valid even when factors concerning the state of the organism at the time of stimulation are taken into account (*27*) and are not due to "adaptation" or "habituation."

These observations suggest certain ways in which the individual may vary in his capacity to respond to input. The behavioral referents further suggest that, in addition to inter-individual variability, the organism, at an early age, has available a way of actively "gating out" or modulating and "dampening"—i.e., of regulating—sensory stimuli impinging on receptors and impulses transmitted from them up sensory pathways. Even if such mechanisms were identified, it still would not alter the fact that stimuli would be "experienced" differently by an unusually sensitive child.

A brief review of some of the known neural mechanisms meeting the proposed conditions follows. It is derived, of course, from work on *adult* animals. It would be necessary to identify these mechanisms in young animals, preferably primates, in order to verify the suggested hypothesis. However, there is evidence that sensory input patterns may be actively "inhibited" or modified not only at the point of origin at receptors but also at synapses all the way to the sensory cortex. Such modulation and regulation of activity also depend on factors such as the animal's directed attention to objects. Autonomic, that is, sympathetic, influences (both neural and humoral) have facilitatory effects on touch receptors (*85*). Other peripheral (stretch) receptors either are regulated by their own reflex activity (*77, 80*) or are facilitated by stimulation of the brain stem reticular facilitatory region (*49*) and inhibited by stimulation of the cerebellum and the brain stem inhibitory region (*47*). Inhibitory effects emanating from centrally placed pathways on ongoing cochlear (*43*), retinal (*47*), and olfactory bulb activity (*73*) have been demonstrated.

At other levels the reticular formation appears to have inhibitory descending influences on impulses passing up the specific sensory, spinal pathways (*52*). Similar effects emanate from the anterior cingulate gyrus, the anterior cerebellar vermis, and the sensorimotor cortex. Not only specific pathways but also relay nuclei are thus affected by descending influences (*71*). At other levels it can be demonstrated that the cortex modifies activity in the cephalic brain stem (*1*) and that sensory evoked responses in the cortex may be influenced by activities initiated from within various other regions in the brain, including the cortex (*13*). Furthermore, it is well known that previous experience (habituation) and shifts in attention to external stimuli influence the activities within sensory systems.

It is clear, then, that there is no one place where sensory integration occurs but that interacting mechanisms obtain which modulate, or even eliminate, impinging sensory stimuli.

Becoming even more hypothetical, I would like to suggest some functional properties of certain "defenses." The behavioral referents from which a defense such as denial is inferred demands that the recognition of complex percepts, which carry with them a valence of threat or danger, be attenuated, inhibited, or modified. Other "defenses" are characterized by changes in directed activity (in "aim" or "object"), whereas still others act to inhibit motor discharge if the motive (defined by Freud [*32*] as directing ongoing processes, linking drive with object) is signaled as dangerous. In the first case, the functional processes suggest mechanisms that again modulate sensory impulses which are the physical basis of perception. In the latter case, modulation and inhibition of motor activity should occur before it is initiated, or while ongoing (cf. investigations in animals by Delgado [*15, 16*], Hunter and Jasper [*66*], Lilly [*83*], Ward and Lequire [*125*]). I hope I am not straining observation or definition in psychoanalysis: when we say that a defense is a "structure," we do not refer to anatomy (such as muscle or sensory receptors, or to cell bodies or axons) or to something static, but to the stable, psychological regulation of motility and perception. The question remains whether such regulators have been or can be demonstrated neurophysiologically.

One of the basic postulates of psychoanalysis is the linking of motive and memory (*103, 104*). In addition to this "drive organization" of memories, there is said to be a "conceptual-organization" of memory. The functional characteristics of these two memory systems have not been fully analyzed. One of the reasons for the failure of analysis is that memory consists of an aggregate of behavior constituents characterized by a similarity in *effect,* with the result that many so-called memory processes have really nothing in common but this functional effect. Further delineation of the differences involved in memory processes and the functional characteristics of each should be attempted before plunging into a search for chemical or physiological explanations of a fallacious class of processes.

In addition, the clinical study of memory processes has been retarded by a tendency to particularize it—to divide memory into processes of registration, retention or storage, and recall, and to study some of the factors and conditions which influence these. Such a particulate approach has heuristic value but reveals little about functional characteristics. Second, the search for a single *mechanism* to account for memory processes has not been fruitful. Thus, for instance, the empirical evidence for RNA as being the chemical basis for memory is not convincing; yet the question of whether RNA can account for short-term memory, long-term memory, or for the various forms—visual or verbal—in which a memory may be retrieved, is hardly ever asked.

There may be more than one kind of memory system with different functional properties. Hunt and Brady's research in animals suggests that there may be two distinct memory systems (*64*). Might there not be more than two? What single system can account for "imprinting," which may also account for short-term memory; the kind of memories which have continuing long-term and covert influence on ongoing behaviors, such as the memory system for body image, self-concepts, or self-representations; or those which underlie skills? Is there not also evidence that, depending on the state of consciousness and the form of retrieval of the memory and its content, differs from that when another state obtains? Here the referents are dreams (*33*), delirious (*8*) or hypnagogic states (*67*). Furthermore, it is possible that memories recorded in certain states of consciousness can best be recovered during the same or similar states of consciousness at a later point in time.

If this were so, it would imply that no single memory system could account for all the known functional properties of memory. Perhaps it is of interest that seven different kinds of automatic storage and retrieval systems (each having characteristics of "memory") are known to biomathematicians (*86*), and even if we knew the neural or chemical basis of memory we still would not have accounted for memories (*74*).

V

In summary, it is suggested that we begin by analyzing the functional and organizational properties of behavior and its molar components and that we bring these together "from above," so to speak, with neural systems which display similar properties, in an attempt to ascertain whether they correlate or correspond. In view of the organized nature of psychological phenomena, which in turn appears to be a function of interacting systems, we would expect to seek interactions at the neural level of analysis as well.

I have tried in this essay to indicate certain directions in which both psychoanalysis and biology point, because, if psychoanalysis is a science of human behavior (with its own methods which are the source of rich hypotheses), then it is a part of biology (*115*).

The fact that there is a tendency among psychoanalysts to emphasize the difference between human and animal behavior (*55, 56*) does not place psychoanalysis outside of the biological arena; it only tells us something about the evolution of behavior.

I do not believe that it is derisive to point out the analogy between psychoanalysis and biology, as some might think. The so-called weakness of biology as a science is said to occur in those areas (e.g., ecology, systematics, population genetics, biogeography) for which no physico-chemical tools are provided (or may ever be). Though curiosity, interest, and contemporary fashion may lead one to study the physical and chemical components of organisms, though deductive explanations from a relatively small number of fundamental principles may be devoutly to be hoped for, the "ultimate scientific explanation of life must indeed be biological. Both historically and functionally, live organisms share a number of basic organizational and behavioral properties not known in the non-living world" (*126*).

REFERENCES

1 Adey, W. R., Segundo, J. P., and Livingston, R. B. Corticofugal influences on intrinsic brainstem conduction in cat and monkey. *J. Neurophysiol. 20:*1–16, 1957.

2 Adrian, E. D. The mental and physical origins of behavior. *Int. J. Psycho-Anal. 27:*1–6, 1946.

3 Alpert, A., Neubauer, P. B., and Weil, A. P. Unusual variations in drive endowment. *Psychoanal. Stud. Child 11:*125–163, 1956.

4 Beckner, M. *The Biological Way of Thought.* New York, Columbia Univ. Press, 1959.

5 Benjamin, J. D. "The Innate and Experiential in Child Development" (first published in 1959). In *Lectures in Experimental Psychiatry,* edited by H. W. Brosin. Pittsburgh, Univ. of Pittsburgh Press, 1961.

6 Bergman, P., and Escalona, S. Unusual sensitivities in very young children. *Psychoanal. Stud. Child 3/4:*333–352, 1949.

7 Bernhard, C. G., Kaiser, I. H., and Kolmodin, G. M. On the development of cortical activity in foetal sheep. *Acta physiol. Scand. 47:*333–349, 1959.

8 Betlheim, S., and Hartmann, H. Ueber fehlreaktionen bei der korsakowschen psychose. *Arch. Psychiat. Nervenkn. 72:*275–286, 1924.

9 Brady, J. V. The effect of electroconvulsive shock on a conditioned emotional response: The permanence of the effect. *J. comp. physiol. Psychol. 44:*507–511, 1951.

10 Breuer, J., and Freud, S. *Studies in Hysteria* (first published in 1895). New York, Nervous and Mental Disease Publications, 1937.

11 Bridger, W. H. Sensory habituation and discrimination in the human neonate. *Amer. J. Psychiat. 117:*991–996, 1961.

12 Bridger, W. H., and Reiser, M. F. Psychophysiologic studies of the neonate: An approach toward the methodological and theoretical problems involved. *Psychosom. Med. 21:*265–276, 1959.

13 Chang, H.-T. Interaction of evoked cortical responses. *J. Neurophysiol. 16:* 133–144, 1953.

14 DeBeer, G. R. *Embryology and Evolution.* Oxford, Clarendon Press, 1930.

15 Delgado, J. M. R. Responses evoked in waking cat by electrical stimulation of motor cortex. *Amer. J. Physiol. 171:*436–446, 1952.

16 Delgado, J. M. R. "Emotional Behavior in Animals and Man." In *Explorations in the Physiology of Emotions,* edited by L. J. West and M. Greenblatt. Psych. Res. Reports, No. 12, 1960, pp. 259–266.

17 Dobzhansky, T. *Mankind Evolving.* New Haven & London, Yale Univ. Press, 1962.

18 Ellingson, R. J., and Wilcott, R. C. Development of evoked responses in visual and auditory cortices of kittens. *J. Neurophysiol. 23:*363–375, 1960.

19 Ellis, A. "An Operational Reformulation of Some of the Basic Principles of Psychoanalysis." In *Minnesota Studies in the Philosophy of Science,* Vol. I, edited by H. Feigl and M. Scriven. Minneapolis, Univ. of Minnesota Press, 1956.

20 Engel, G. L. *Psychological Development in Health and Disease.* Philadelphia, Saunders, 1962.

21 Erikson, E. H. "Problems of Infancy and Childhood." In *Cyclopedia of Medicine.* Philadelphia, Davis, 1940, pp. 714–730.

22 Erikson, E. H. Childhood and tradition in two American Indian tribes. *Psychoanal. Stud. Child 1:*319–350, 1945.

23 Erikson, E. H. Ego development and historical change. *Psychoanal. Stud. Child 2:*359–396, 1946.

24 Erikson, E. H. *Childhood and Society.* New York, Norton, 1950.

25 Erikson, E. H. Growth and crises of the healthy personality. *Psychol. Issues 1*(1):Monograph 1, pp. 50–100, 1959.

26 Erulkar, S. D., Rose, J. E., and Davies, W. P. Single unit activity in the auditory cortex of the cat. *Bull. Hopkins Hosp. 99:*55–86, 1956.

27 Escalona, S. K. The study of individual differences and the problem of state. *J. Amer. Acad. Child Psychiat. 1:*11–37, 1962.

28 Escalona, S. K. Patterns of infantile experience and the developmental process. *Psychoanal. Stud. Child 18:* 1963.

29 Fincham, J. R. S., and Pateman, J. A. Formation of an enzyme through complementary action of mutant "alleles" in separate nuclei in a heterocaryon. *Nature, London 179:*741–742, 1957.

30 Freud, Anna. Observations on child development. *Psychoanal. Stud. Child 6:*18–30, 1951.

31 Freud, Anna. Some remarks on infant observation. *Psychoanal. Stud. Child 8:*9–19, 1953.

32 Freud, S. *The Origins of Psychoanalysis; Letters to Wilhelm Fliess, Drafts and Notes, 1887–1902.* New York, Basic Books, 1954.

33 Freud, S. *The Interpretation of Dreams* (first published in 1900). New York, Basic Books, 1955.

34 Freud, S. *Three Essays on the Theory of Sexuality* (first published in 1905). London, Imago, 1949.

35 Freud, S. "Formulations Regarding Two Principles of Mental Functioning" (first published in 1911). *Collected Papers,* Vol. IV. London, Hogarth, 1948, pp. 13–21.

36 Freud, S. "On Narcissism: An Introduction" (first published in 1914). *Collected Papers,* Vol. IV. London, Hogarth, 1948, pp. 30–59.

37 Freud, S. "Instincts and Their Vicissitudes" (first published in 1915). *Collected Papers,* Vol. IV. London, Hogarth, 1948, pp. 60–83.

38 Freud, S. "Repression" (first published in 1915). *Collected Papers,* Vol. IV. London, Hogarth, 1948, pp. 84–97.

39 FREUD, S. "The Unconscious" (first published in 1915). *Collected Papers,* Vol. IV. London, Hogarth, 1948, pp. 98–136.
40 FREUD, S. *Beyond the Pleasure Principle* (first published in 1920). London, Hogarth, 1948.
41 FREUD, S. *The Ego and the Id* (first published in 1923). London, Hogarth, 1947.
42 FREUD, S. *The Problem of Anxiety* (first published in 1926). New York, Norton, 1936.
43 GALAMBOS, R. Suppression of auditory nerve activity by stimulation of efferent fibers to cochlea. *J. Neurophysiol. 19:*424–437, 1956.
44 GALAMBOS, R. "Changing Concepts of the Learning Mechanism." In *Brain Mechanisms and Learning,* edited by J. F. Delafresnaye. Oxford, Blackwell, 1961, pp. 231–242.
45 GINSBURG, B. E. Genetic control of the ontogeny of stress behavior. Symposium on "Evocation mechanisms of genetic potentialities in behavior." Amer. Psychol. Ass. New York, Sept. 7, 1960.
46 GRAFSTEIN, B. Postnatal development of the transcallosal evoked response in the cerebral cortex of the cat. *J. Neurophysiol.* 26:79–99, 1963.
47 GRANIT, R. Centrifugal and antidromic effects on ganglion cells of the retina. *J. Neurophysiol. 18:*388–411, 1955.
48 GRANIT, R. *Receptors and Sensory Perception.* New Haven, Yale Univ. Press, 1955.
49 GRANIT, R., AND KAADA, B. R. Influence of stimulation of central nervous structures on muscle spindles in cat. *Acta physiol. Scand.* 27:130–160, 1952.
50 GROBSTEIN, C. Levels and ontogeny. *Amer. Scientist 50:*46–58, 1962.
51 GROSSMAN, C. Electro-ontogenesis of cerebral activity. *Arch. Neurol., Chicago 74:*186–202, 1955.
52 HAGBARTH, K. E., AND KERR, D. I. B. Central influences on spinal afferent conduction. *J. Neurophysiol. 17:*295, 1954.
53 HALDANE, J. S. *Mechanism, Life and Personality.* 2nd ed., New York, Dutton, 1923.
54 HARTMANN, H. *Ego Psychology and the Problem of Adaptation* (first published in 1939). New York, Int. Univ. Press, 1958.
55 HARTMANN, H. Comments on the psychoanalytic theory of instinctual drives. *Psychoanal. Quart. 17:*368–388, 1948.
56 HARTMANN, H. Comments on the psychoanalytic theory of the ego. *Psychoanal. Stud. Child 5:*74–96, 1950.
57 HARTMANN, H. Psychoanalysis and developmental psychology. *Psychoanal. Study. Child 5:*7–17, 1950.
58 HARTMANN, H. Mutual influences in the development of the ego and id. *Psychoanal. Stud. Child 7:*9–30, 1952.
59 HARTMANN, H., AND KRIS, E. The genetic approach in psychoanalysis. *Psychoanal. Stud. Child 1:*11–30, 1945.
60 HARTMANN, H., KRIS, E., AND LOWENSTEIN, R. M. Comments on the formation of psychic structure. *Psychoanal. Stud. Child 2:*11–38, 1946.
61 HEBB, D. O. *The Organization of Behavior.* New York, Wiley, 1949.

62 HOTZER, H., ABBOT, J., LASH, J., AND HOLTZER, S. The loss of phenotypic traits by differentiated cells in vitro. I. Dedifferentiation of cartilage cells. *Proc. Nat. Acad. Sci. USA 46:*1533–1542, 1960

63 HUBEL, D. H., HENSON, C. O., RUPERT, A., AND GALAMBOS, R. "Attention" units in the auditory cortex. *Science 129:*1279–1280, 1959.

64 HUNT, H. F., AND BRADY, J. V. Some effects of electroconvulsive shock on a conditioned emotional response ("anxiety"). *J. comp. physiol. Psychol. 44:*88–98, 1951.

65 HUNT, W. E., AND GOLDRING, S. Maturation of evoked response of the visual cortex in the postnatal rabbit. *EEG clin. Neurophysiol. 3:*465–471, 1951.

66 HUNTER, J., AND JASPER, H. H. Effects of thalamic stimulation in unanesthetized animals. *EEG clin. Neurophysiol. 1:*305–324, 1949.

67 ISAKOWER, O. A contribution to the pathopsychology of phenomena associated with falling asleep. *Int. J. Psycho-Anal. 19:*331–345, 1938.

68 JACOBSON, E. Denial and repression. *J. Amer. Psychoanal. Ass. 5:*61–92, 1957.

69 JACOBSON, E. Adolescent moods and the remodeling of psychic structures in adolescence. *Psychoanal. Stud. Child 16:*164–183, 1961.

70 JOHN, E. R., AND KILIAM, K. F. Electrophysiological correlates of avoidance conditioning in the cat. *J. Pharmacol. exp. Ther. 125:*252–274, 1959.

71 JOUVET, M., AND DESMEDT, J. E. Controle central des messages acoustiques afferents. *C. R. Acad. Sci., Paris 243:*1916, 1956.

72 KATAN, A. Some thoughts about the role of verbalization in early childhood. *Psychoanal. Stud. Child 16:*189–205, 1961.

73 KERR, D. I. B., AND HAGBARTH, D. E. An investigation of olfactory centrifugal fiber system. *J. Neurophysiol. 18:*362–374, 1955.

74 KETY, S. S. A biologist examines the mind and behavior. *Science 132:*1861–1870, 1960.

75 KRIS, E. Opening remarks on psychoanalytic child psychology. *Psychoanal. Stud. Child 6:*9–17, 1951.

76 KRIS, E. The recovery of childhood memories in psychoanalysis. *Psychoanal. Stud. Child 11:*54–88, 1956.

77 KUFFLER, S. W., AND HUNT, C. C. The mammalian small nerve fibers: A system for efferent nervous regulation of muscle spindle discharge. *Res. Publ. Ass. Nerv. Ment. Dis. 30:*24–47, 1952.

78 KUHN, T. S. "The Structure of Scientific Revolutions." In *International Encyclopedia of Unified Science,* Vol. II, edited by O. Neurath. Foundations of the Unity of Science. Chicago, Univ. of Chicago Press, 1962.

79 LEITCH, M., AND ESCALONA, S. The reactions of infants to stress. *Psychoanal. Stud. Child 3/4:*121–140, 1949.

80 LEKSELL, L. The action potential and excitatory effects of the small ventral root fibers to skeletal muscles. *Acta physiol. Scand. 10:*Suppl. 31 (84 p.), 1945.

81 LEVINE, S. "The Effects of Infantile Experience on Adult Behavior." In *Experimental Foundations of Clinical Psychology,* edited by A. J. Bachrach. New York, Basic Books, 1962, pp. 139–169.

82 LILLIE, R. S. *General Biology and Philosophy of Organism.* Chicago, Univ. of Chicago Press, 1945.

83 Lilly, J. C. "Learning Motivated by Subcortical Stimulation: The Start and Stop Patterns of Behavior." In Henry Ford Hospital Symposium, *Reticular Formation of the Brain.* Boston, Little, Brown & Co., 1958.
84 Lipton, E. H., Steinschneider, A., and Richmond, J. B. Auditory discrimination in the newborn infant. Paper presented at Annual Meeting of Amer. Psychosomatic Soc., Atlantic City, N.J., April 27, 1963.
85 Loewenstein, W. R. Modulation of cutaneous mechanoreceptors by sympathetic stimulation. *J. Physiol., London 132:*40–60, 1956.
86 Macy, J. Personal communication.
87 Mahler, M. S., and Gosliner, B. J. On symbiotic child psychosis: Genetic, dynamic and restitutive aspects. *Psychoanal. Stud. Child 10:*195–212, 1955.
88 Mahler, M. S. On sadness and grief in infancy and childhood. *Psychoanal. Stud. Child 16:*332–351, 1961.
89 Mahler, M. S. "Thoughts on Development and Individuation." A. A. Brill Memorial Lecture, 1962. In press.
90 Marty, R., Contamin, F., and Scherrer, J. La double-response electrocorticale à la stimulation lumineuse chez le chat nouveau-né. *C. R. Soc. Biol., Paris 153:*198–201, 1959.
91 Mirsky, I. A. "Psychoanalysis and the Biological Sciences." In *Twenty Years of Psychoanalysis,* edited by F. Alexander and H. Ross. New York, Norton, 1953, pp. 155–176.
92 Mirsky, I. A. Physiologic, psychologic and social determinants in the etiology of duodenal ulcer. *Amer. J. digest. Dis. 3:*285, 1958.
93 Money, J. Cytogenetic and psychosexual incongruities with a note on space-form blindness. *Amer. J. Psychiat. 119:*820–827, 1963.
94 Mora, P. T. Directiveness in biology on the molecular level. *Amer. Scientist 50:*570–575, 1962.
95 Muller, H. J. *Science and Criticism.* New Haven, Yale Univ. Press, 1943.
96 Needham, J. *Order and Life.* New Haven, Yale Univ. Press, 1936.
97 Needham, J. *Biochemistry and Morphogenesis.* Cambridge, Cambridge Univ. Press, 1942.
98 Niu, M. C. "Current Evidence Concerning Chemical Inducers." In *Evolution of Nervous Control from Primitive Organisms to Man,* edited by A. D. Bass. Washington, D.C., A.A.A.S., Publication No. 52, 1959.
99 Nunberg, H. "The Synthetic Function of the Ego" (first published in 1931). *In Practice and Theory of Psychoanalysis.* New York, Int. Univ. Press, 1955.
100 Pontecorvo, G. *Trends in Genetic Analysis.* New York, Columbia Univ. Press, 1958.
101 Pribram, K. H. "The Neuropsychology of Sigmund Freud." Chapt. 13. In *Experimental Foundations of Clinical Psychology,* edited by A. J. Bachrach. New York, Basic Books, 1962, pp. 442–468.
102 Purpura, D. P., Carmichael, M. D., and Housepian, E. M. Physiological and anatomical studies of development of superficial axodendritic synaptic pathways in neocortex. *Exp. Neurol. 2:*324–347, 1960.
103 Rapaport, D. *Emotions and Memory.* 2nd edition. New York, Int. Univ. Press, 1950.

104 Rapaport, D. *Organization and Pathology of Thought.* New York, Columbia Univ. Press, 1951.

105 Rapaport, D. The theory of ego autonomy. *Bull. Menninger Clin. 22:*13–35, 1958.

106 Rapaport, D. The structure of psychoanalytic theory: A systematizing attempt. *Psychol. Issues 2*(2): Monograph 6, 1960.

107 Rose, J. E., Adrian, H., and Santibañez, G. Electrical signs of maturation in the auditory system of the kitten. *Acta neurol. Lat. Amer. 3:*133–143, 1957.

108 Russell, E. S. *The Directiveness of Organic Activities.* Cambridge, Cambridge Univ. Press, 1945.

109 Scherrer, J., and Oeconomos, D. "Responses Evoquees Corticales Somesthesiques des Manniferes Adulte et Nouveau-ne." In *Les grandes Activities du Lobe Temporal.* Paris, Masson, 1955, pp. 249–268.

110 Schrödinger, E. *What Is Life?* (first published in 1944). New York, Doubleday, 1956.

111 Sherrington, C. *Man on His Nature.* Cambridge, Cambridge Univ. Press, 1951.

112 Simpson, G. G. The status of the study of organisms. *Amer. Scientist 50:*36–45, 1962.

113 Sinnott, E. W. *Cell and Psyche: The Biology of Purpose* (first published in 1950). New York, Harper Torchbooks, 1961.

114 Sinnott, E. W. "A Common Basis for Development and Behavior in Organisms." In *Evolution of Nervous Control from Primitive Organisms to Man,* edited by A. D. Bass. Washington, D.C., A.A.A.S., Publication No. 52, 1959.

115 Skinner, B. F. Behaviorism at fifty. *Science 140:*951–958, 1963.

116 Spitz, R. A. Hospitalism: An inquiry into the genesis of psychiatric conditions in early childhood. *Psychoanal. Stud. Child 1:*53–74, 1945.

117 Spitz, R. A. Hospitalism: A follow-up report. *Psychoanal. Stud. Child 2:*113–117, 1946.

118 Stellar, E. "Drive and Motivation." Chapt. 57 in *Handbook of Physiology,* edited by J. Field *et al.,* Vol. III. Washington, D.C., Amer. Physiol. Soc., 1960, pp. 1501–1527.

119 Teitelbaum, P. Sensory control of hypothalamic hyperphagia. *J. comp. physiol. Psychol. 48:*156–163, 1955.

120 Ulett, G., Dow, R. S., and Larsell, O. The inception of conductivity in the corpus callosum and the cortico-pontocerebellar pathway of young rabbits with reference to myelinization. *J. comp. Neurol. 40:*1–10, 1944.

121 Von Bertalanffy, L. *Modern Theories of Development* (first published in 1933). New York, Harper Torchbooks, 1962.

122 Waddington, C. H. *Organizers and Genes.* Cambridge, Cambridge Univ. Press, 1940.

123 Waddington, C. H. *The Nature of Life.* New York, Atheneum, 1962.

124 Waelder, R. The principle of multiple function: Observations on overdetermination. *Psychoanal. Quart. 5:*45–62, 1936.

125 WARD, J. W., AND LEQUIRE, V. Responses elicited by electrical stimulation of the gyrus cingulus in unanesthetized cats. *Anat. Rec. 106:*256–257, 1950.
126 WATERMAN, T. H. Revolution for biology. *Amer. Scientist 50:*548–569, 1962.
127 WESTERMAN, R. A. Somatic inheritance of habituation of responses to light in planarians. *Science 140:*676, 1963.
128 WHITEHEAD, A. N. *The Concept of Nature.* Cambridge, Cambridge Univ. Press, 1920.
129 WOLF, K. M. "Observation of Individual Tendencies in the First Year of Life." *Problems of Infancy and Childhood,* edited by M. J. E. Senn. New York, Josiah Macy, Jr., Foundation. Sixth Conf., 1952, pp. 97–137.
130 WOODGER, J. H. *Biological Principles.* London, Routledge and Kegan, Paul, 1948.
131 WOODGER, J. H. *Biology and Language.* Cambridge, Cambridge Univ. Press, 1952.

THREE

Psychoanalytic Theory and the Mind-Body Problem

BENJAMIN B. RUBINSTEIN, M.D.

The mind-body problem is generally regarded as a philosophical rather than a scientific problem; hence, with few exceptions, psychologists including psychoanalysts have felt free to ignore it. However, when pushed to its final consequences every form of psychology will be seen to have implications bearing on this problem. There are no disembodied minds. Accordingly, no psychological theory is completely independent of physiology and, specifically, of neurophysiology. Hebb (*23*) has strongly emphasized this point. If they make no allowance for whatever physiological knowledge we have, psychologists risk seriously limiting the validity of their theories. In some instances such disregard has led to seemingly unresolvable confusion.

In the following I will try to show that many of the ambiguities of current psychoanalytic theory—ambiguities of which psychoanalysts are by no means unaware—stem from an ambiguous stand on the mind-body problem implicit in the theory. It is to be expected that an explication of this implicit stand will lead to a clearer understanding of the theory itself and eventually to less ambiguous reformulations.

Traditionally, the mind-body problem is formulated in terms of the relationship between conscious mental events—i.e., events of immediate experience—and neurophysiological events. We must also consider unconscious mental events, however. We cannot simply assume that the two varieties of mental events are related to neurophysiological events in the same manner. There is, on the other hand, no reason to distinguish in this connection between unconscious and preconscious events. Both are, as Freud (*10*) put it, "descriptively unconscious" and hence, in this respect, not distinguishable from each other.

The term 'unconscious mental event' refers to a hypothetical entity or event. Terms of this type have been called theoretical terms (*1, 3*). Other psychoanalytic theoretical terms are 'defense,' 'psychic energy,' 'ego,' 'id,' 'superego.' The ambiguity inherent in psychoanalytic theory concerning the mind-body problem becomes apparent in the ways these and similar terms are used.

I can discuss these uses only in a very general way. The mind-body problem is one of great generality, and hence only the most general psychoanalytic formulations are relevant. Before entering on this discussion, however, one must consider in some detail the more traditional aspects of the mind-body problem. Without an understanding of these aspects one cannot ascertain the specific problems that psychoanalytic theory presents.

PHENOMENAL EVENTS

Events of immediate experience will be referred to as phenomenal events. Examples are such events as wishing, thinking, perceiving, dreaming, imaging, fantasying, and feeling. Their most peculiar characteristic is a commonplace. Directly, each of us knows them only from his own experience. Ordinarily, however, we do not hesitate to infer phenomenal events in others. For instance, the sadness of another person we infer from observing that he looks sad, that he says he is sad, and that he generally speaks and acts in certain typical ways. Heider (*24*), who speaks about *perceiving* phenomenal events in other people, nevertheless admits that unconscious inference may be involved.

It is important to note that the data mentioned allow still another inference. When we assert that an individual is sad we do not expect him to look sad continually and to say only that he is sad, nor do we expect him to speak and act continually in the typical ways. It suffices if he does some of these things at least some of the time. According to Ryle (*36*), we can account for this state of affairs most unequivocally by saying that the individual in question has a *disposition* to display the expressions and perform the activities that are characteristic of sadness. Ryle maintains that, from the point of view of an observer, this disposition is the essence of the state of being sad.

This disposition, however, is related not merely to the outward manifestations of sadness but more intimately still to the actual experience itself. As Ryle sees it, this experience is not a global event, but a composite—partly of certain bodily sensations such as a feeling of heaviness, and partly of a *felt inclination* to perform precisely the activities the inferred disposition is for. We may regard as indirect evidence for the last assertion the fact that if we are sad we feel no inclination to laugh, to tell jokes, or to say that we are having a wonderful time. We may also surmise that at least some of the bodily sensations a sad person experiences are related to the characteristic postural and other expressive manifestations by which an observer (at least tentatively) identifies the sadness of the sad person. It thus seems that there is a strict correlation between the felt inclination and the bodily sensations, on the one hand, and the inferred disposition, on the other.

In the present connection I am not concerned with whether this analysis is accurate in detail. I have cited it only because, appropriately modified, it can be used as a model of the mind-body relationship.

Even though Ryle does not himself take this step, his dispositions are readily interpreted as neurophysiological events. The term 'disposition,' because of its vagueness, may be referred to as a protoneurophysiological term. It obviously belongs to the class of theoretical terms. By interpreting this term neurophysiologically we have in fact, as is easily seen, constructed a simple model of the mind-body relationship. The usefulness of the model is immediately apparent. It allows us to conclude that, since a phenomenal event like sadness is inferred from the same data as the corresponding disposition, from the point of view of an observer it can be an actual state of affairs only if the disposition is also an actual state of affairs. The two events, the phenomenal and the neurophysiological, are thus in this sense correlated.[1]

Clinical as well as experimental neurological findings accumulated over the years strongly indicate that every phenomenal event is correlated with a neurophysiological event. We will refer to this relationship between the two sets of events as the *hypothesis of empirical parallelism.* We will now take a further step: Expressed in terms of statements about the events, rather than in terms of the events themselves, empirical parallelism implies that statements about any two correlated events are also correlated; but they are not translatable to one another. Translation means transposition *without change of reference* of a sentence in one language into a sentence in another. Phenomenal and neurophysiological (or protoneurophysiological) statements belong to different languages. The difference between correlated statements is, however, not merely one of language: empirically, the referents of these statements are also different—a phenomenal event in the one case and a neurophysiological in the other. Hence, any given statement in one of the languages is not translatable to its correlated statement in the other.

To avoid misunderstanding: the term 'neurophysiological statement' refers to statements that mostly have not yet been formulated but that we, presumably, will be in a position to formulate some time in the future.

It is thus evident that two statements may be said to be correlated when, *if* one of them is true, the other one is true also. We can assume this to imply that correlated statements are logically but not empirically equivalent. This

[1]Another conclusion that emerges from the model is that at least some correlated phenomenal and neurophysiological events are probably isomorphic. Köhler (*28*) bases his view of the mind-body relationship on the assumption of isomorphism. In the present connection, however, I will not pursue this theory further.

is not the only possible reading of this definition of the correlation of statements, but it is helpful for our present purpose.

If we accept the indicated reading, the various solutions of the mind-body problem may be regarded as different means of resolving the contradiction between logical equivalence and empirical disparity. According to the double-aspect theory, phenomenal and neurophysiological events are merely different aspects of an underlying unknown and unknowable reality. The dualistic theories posit two disparate realms of existence, the mental and the physical; the events of these realms are regarded either as independent but nevertheless perfectly synchronized (metaphysical parallelism) or as causally related, in the physical-to-mental direction only (epi-phenomenalism) or in both directions (interactionism). These theories thus interpret empirical as transempirical—i.e., metaphysical—disparity. The monistic theory, on the other hand, interprets empirical disparity as transempirical identity. According to this theory two correlated events are fundamentally one, but appear in one way to the experiencing individual himself and in another to an outside observer. The transempirical identity of correlated events evidently does not contradict the logical equivalence of the corresponding correlated statements.

The significant point is that these theories are all compatible with the hypothesis of empirical parallelism. Each of them is based on this hypothesis, i.e., on the empirically found (or surmised) correlation between phenomenal and neurophysiological events; but each interprets in its own way the *nature of the relationship* underlying the correlation. As we have seen, the empirical disparity is interpreted differently, and, with the exception of identity theory, more or less related notions are substituted for the logical equivalence of correlated statements. Thus in all cases the basic contradiction is removed. The choice between these theories, as Feigl (*5*) has stressed, is thus a matter of interpretation: it depends exclusively on which philosophical (i.e., transempirical, metaphysical) presuppositions we bring to bear on it.

The most commonly accepted theories today are epiphenomenalism and identity theory. Interactionism is closest to common sense; but it is rejected by philosophers and scientists alike, primarily because it implies a break in the causality of the physical world (*5*).[2] Schematically, a causal chain according to the interactionist theory looks something like this: physiological-to-mental-to-mental-to-physiological. At least as ordinarily formulated certain basic psychoanalytic statements have precisely this form.

It is hardly possible to discuss the mind-body problem without mentioning the influence that the spectacular achievements of certain machines have had on the attitude of many people to this problem. The facts that servo-mechanisms stimulate goal-directed behavior and that computers can stimulate think-

[2]See also Gellhorn (*15*) and, for a defense of interactionism, Ducasse (*4*).

ing have been interpreted as indicating that the functions we commonly attribute to mind can very well be performed without mind—i.e., by brain, working somewhat after the fashion of the mentioned machines. In a brilliant exposition of this question Anatol Rapoport (*35*) has compared the ordinary use of the concept of mind with the use of the now obsolete concept of vital force. These findings obviously do not imply that mental events and, specifically, events of immediate experience can be safely ruled out of existence or even ignored. What they imply is merely that there is no necessity to posit mind as a causative agent in its own right. The argument is, in other words, directed specifically against interactionism; it hardly touches the other solutions to the mind-body problem. It seems clear, however, that the machine model of brain functioning is best compatible with epiphenomenalism and identity theory. The metaphysics involved in these theories seems to be the least offensive to modern scientific minds.

We find perhaps the most telling evidence for the last two assertions in the somewhat extravagant claim made by Scriven (*38*) and others that thinking machines may conceivably think in the literal sense of this word, i.e., phenomenally, with awareness of what they are doing. The significant implication of this claim is evidently that we could not tell the difference between machines that are and machines that are not endowed with awareness (which shows primarily the hazards of an inference to mentality on the basis of performance only and also the compatibility of the machine model of brain functioning with certain theories of the mind-body relationship—mainly, epiphenomenalism and identity theory). Clearly, it is logically conceivable that man-built machines may be capable of somehow generating awareness only on the two assumptions (*a*) that brain is a machine and (*b*) that it is capable of somehow generating awareness.

If we want to take a definite stand on the mind-body problem our choice is thus essentially between epiphenomenalism and the identity theory. Partly because it is more parsimonious, Feigl (*5*) chooses the latter. Roughly speaking, the core of his view is that correlated phenomenal and neurophysiological terms have the same denotation but widely differing connotations. I will not try to summarize his essentially logical argument. Instead I will borrow a simile from von Bonin (*42*) that puts the matter very simply: a person looking at a circle from the inside sees only the concavity while a person looking at the same circle from the outside sees only the convexity. I may add, without discussing this question further, that on the identity theory mind is no less a mystery than on any dualistic theory; but it is a different kind of mystery, a mystery that concerns the properties of what we generally refer to as matter.

There is, however, no need to commit ourselves to any one of the philosophical positions that the mind-body theories entail. We can stand aloof and simply be content with the hypothesis of empirical parallelism. This hypothesis, as

I have said, is compatible with every one of the theories. With the exception primarily of interactionism, from a practical scientific standpoint if we do choose a theory it makes no difference which one we choose. Even though the remaining theories are philosophically (i.e., metaphysically) incompatible, their empirical consequences are the same. The main point of the above discussion is that, whichever of these philosophical positions we choose or if we choose none of them but stay uncommitted, phenomenal and neurophysiological (or protoneurophysiological) statements may nevertheless be correlated but are not translatable to each other. Correlated events, in other words, can never be said to be *empirically* identical, even though transempirically they may be. This, as far as I can see, is the only strictly empirical general formulation of the mind-body relationship.[3]

PSYCHOANALYTIC THEORETICAL TERMS

We are now prepared to consider psychoanalytic theory in relation to the mind-body problem. Within the scope of the present paper I can deal with this question only in broad outline. A convenient short cut is to focus not on the theory per se but on some of the key theoretical terms it makes use of and on statements including these terms.

I have already given examples of psychoanalytic theoretical terms. These may be divided into two broad classes: (*a*) terms referring to unconscious mental events such as unconscious wishes, unconscious fantasies, the process of repression, etc., and (*b*) terms like 'psychic energy,' 'ego,' 'system *Ucs*.' These two types of theoretical terms will be discussed separately, following a general comment.

I will refer to statements including theoretical terms as theoretical statements. A theoretical statement may be a postulate, an assumption, or a hypothesis. We will assume that psychoanalytic statements of this type are correlated with neurophysiological statements in the previously indicated sense of statement correlation—namely, in the sense that if, and only if, a given theoretical statement is true then there is a particular neurophysiological statement, whether presently known or unknown, that is also true. If we assume that a phenomenal statement like "P is aware of wanting O" is in this sense correlated with a neurophysiological statement, then we can hardly avoid the further assumption that a theoretical statement like "P has an unconscious desire for O" is in the same sense correlated with a neurophysiological statement. We found that phenomenal statements are not translatable to their correlated neurophysiological statements. The question is then: is this also true of theoretical statements?

---

[3]*Autocerebroscopy*, if possible, would appear not to go beyond the establishment of correlations. For a discussion of this question see Feigl (5).

We will note that phenomenal and theoretical statements behave differently in this respect. As we have seen, the fact that phenomenal statements are not translatable to their correlated neurophysiological statements is compatible with both monistic and dualistic interpretations of the mind-body problem. This does not hold for theoretical statements. If we decide that theoretical statements are not translatable, then we have automatically committed ourselves to a dualistic interpretation. A given statement is not translatable to another if the two statements have different referents. Now, *taken in their literal meanings* psychoanalytic theoretical statements have no observable referents. Hence, *empirically* we cannot say that they and their correlated neurophysiological statements have *different* referents. If we say it notwithstanding, then we have clearly postulated that their referents belong to a realm of existence that is not neurophysiological; since it is not phenomenal either, it must be psychological in some other sense—for example, in the parallelistic sense of being pure, only transitorily embodied, unself-conscious mind. The postulate of a realm of existence of this type is evidently compatible only with a dualistic theory of the mind-body relationship.

For the same reason we also cannot say that *empirically* theoretical statements have the *same* referents as their correlated neurophysiological statements. We can say this only on the basis of a transempirical decision—namely, if we decide *not* to postulate a set of events that are neither phenomenal nor neurophysiological. Only if we do not primarily assume a specific realm of existence relevant to mind can we conclude that, since the referents of theoretical statements are not phenomenal, they must be neurophysiological.

The significant point is that only the second but not the first interpretation of psychoanalytic theoretical terms and statements is compatible with the hypothesis of empirical parallelism and, hence, with both monistic and dualistic theories of the mind-body relationship. I mentioned that to regard theoretical statements as not translatable to neurophysiological statements commits us to a dualistic theory. On the other hand, to regard theoretical statements as translatable to neurophysiological statements does not, as we might expect, commit us to a monistic theory. The view that theoretical statements are translatable to neurophysiological statements (the view, in other words, that the referents of theoretical statements are in fact neurophysiological events) is perfectly compatible with the assumption that *some* neurophysiological events may relate to phenomenal events either as envisioned by epiphenomenalism or by the identity theory. We can thus remain uncommitted in regard to the mind-body problem as traditionally formulated only if we choose a monistic interpretation of unconscious mental events and, of course, of theoretical psychoanalytic terms and statements in general.

Even though the view that the referents of psychoanalytic terms and statements are neurophysiological events is ultimately based on a transempirical assumption, it is closer to empirical thinking than the opposite view. I will therefore refer to it as the *empiricist* view or interpretation.[4]

What is the stand of psychoanalytic theory as this theory is actually understood? There is no easy answer to this question. To find an answer we must examine a number of psychoanalytic theoretical terms as these terms are commonly used.

We will begin with terms referring to unconscious mental events. If we adopt the empiricist interpretation, then in what sense can these events be said to be mental? Let me say at once that Freud, apparently without hesitation, accepted the empiricist view. In his early "Project for a Scientific Psychology" (*7*), this was his explicit assumption. His aim was "to represent psychical processes as quantitatively determined states of specifiable material particles . . ." (*7,* p. 355). More than 40 years later he stated that "physical or somatic processes" accompany the conscious ones but are more complete than these; and he concluded that it therefore ". . . seems natural to lay stress in psychology upon these somatic processes, to see in *them* the true essence of what is mental . . ." (*13,* p. 34; italics in text). In the intervening years Freud did not have much to say about the essential somatic—i.e., neurophysiological—nature of mental events and specifically of unconscious mental events. Instead, he repeatedly emphasized the mental nature of the latter. We thus come back to our question: if unconscious mental events are in reality neurophysiological events, then in what sense can they be said to be mental?

Freud did not explicitly raise this question, and, accordingly, he did not explicitly answer it. His answer, however, is implicit in some of his formulations. Thus, he emphasized that we know nothing about the neurophysiological processes as such and that it hence is not very helpful to refer to them. The unconscious mental processes, on the other hand, ". . . have abundant points of contact with conscious mental processes; . . . they can be transformed into, or replaced by, conscious mental processes, and all the categories which we employ to describe conscious mental acts, such as ideas, purposes, resolutions and so on, can be applied to them" (*10,* p. 168). This clearly amounts to a functional definition of unconscious mental events: They can be transformed into conscious events, and they have similar behavioral effects. Hence, regardless of their actual nature, they may be spoken about in the same language and referred to by the same words as the corresponding conscious events. To make his point unmistakably clear Freud added in the same paragraph that ". . . the only respect in which they [i.e., the unconscious events] differ from conscious ones is precisely in the absence of consciousness."

[4]We should note that some psychoanalytic theoretical terms may be related not to neurophysiological events but rather to neuroanatomical entities. The above remarks should be read as referring both to events in the strict sense and to entitles.

Even though Freud's formulations of the distinction between neurophysiological and unconscious mental events are not always unambiguous, it seems fair to say that, according to psychoanalytic theory, unconscious mental events are neurophysiological events which are classified as mental on the two assumptions (*a*) that observed phenomena resembling the effects of such phenomenal events as wishing, intending, fantasying, etc., are in fact the effects of these neurophysiological events, and (*b*) that the latter are in some ways transformable to the particular neurophysiological events that are correlated with the phenomenal events, the effects of which their effects resemble. These are the two criterial—albeit entirely hypothetical—attributes on the basis of which a neurophysiological event is classifiable as an unconscious mental event.

This functional definition makes it possible to describe, say, an unconscious wish in protoneurophysiological terms as a *disposition* for conscious (i.e., phenomenal) wishing and, in addition, as a *part disposition* for certain specific dream contents, character traits, and neurotic symptoms. Similarly, an unconscious fantasy is describable protoneurophysiologically as a *disposition* for the corresponding conscious fantasy and as a *part disposition* for other phenomenal as well as for certain directly observable events. *Empirically* both sets of terms (i.e., dispositions on the one hand and unconscious wishes, fantasies, etc., on the other) have the same meanings; for instance, even in psychoanalytic practice an unconscious wish is spoken about not in terms of what it is but in terms of what it does. To account for psychoanalytic clinical observations we must assume that a disposition may be actual or potential and, further, that an actual disposition under certain circumstances may not become manifest. The question how the various dispositions and part dispositions can be identified will not concern us here; this is primarily a problem of the logic and validation of clinical inference.

As yet the confrontation of psychoanalytic theory with the mind-body problem has not gotten us into serious trouble. We may regard the above conjectures as hypotheses that are confirmable, at least in principle. The difficulties, however, begin to mount as soon as we pose the question *how* unconscious events are transformed into conscious events. According to Freud, an unconscious event is under certain specific circumstances *perceived* by consciousness, which thus functions as an "organ of perception" (*8,* p. 615; *10,* p. 171). This concept is not necessarily as psychophysically ambiguous as it may seem. In the "Project," Freud envisioned the process of perception of unconscious materials as essentially a propagation of excitations to a specific neuronal system the functioning of which is asociated with conscious experience. The decisive difficulties started only when Freud abandoned his attempt at a neurophysiological description in favor of a purely psychological description and to this end introduced a set of high-level theoretical terms such as 'system *Ucs*,' 'psychic energy,' and 'attention cathexis.' We need not examine in detail the ways in which he employed these terms (and later the terms 'id' and 'ego') to describe the transition of mental events from the unconscious to the conscious condition. The ambiguity in regard to the mind-body problem is as much in the terms themselves as in these descriptions.

The concept of psychic energy Freud clearly derived from his early neurophysiological concept of a quantity that is propagated along neuronal pathways (*7*). That he continued (at least implicitly) to think of psychic energy as physiologically definable is evidenced by the fact that he also occasionally referred to it as *nervous* energy (*13*, p. 36). Rapaport (*34*), similarly, has explicitly stated that psychic energy may eventually turn out to be a form of physico-chemical energy. This is one point at which the ambiguity becomes apparent. Physico-chemical energy is nondirectional and, Rapaport's assertion to the contrary notwithstanding, psychic energy, as the term is *actually* used, is unequivocally considered strictly directional. The classification of psychic energies into libidinal and aggressive according to the *aim* of the energy (*22*) is obviously based on directionality as the decisive criterial attribute; and directionality is as obviously implicit in Hartmann's (*18*) conception of energy neutralization as involving transformation of energy into more or less aim-free modes—i.e., transformation toward more or less complete nondirectionality. If taken in its literal meaning, the term 'psychic energy' stands not for a physico-chemical but for a vitalistic concept (see Holt, *26*). Presumably because of these difficulties, a number of years ago Hartmann (*17*) reached the conclusion that the concept of psychic energy is best interpreted as an operational concept. We may note that, despite the merits of this conception, it has not influenced subsequent psychoanalytic theorizing.[5]

Freud (*8*, p. 610) originally conceived of the systems *Ucs*, *Pcs*, and *Cs* merely as conceptual devices for easier descriptions of complex relationships. Essentially they are classificatory systems which, if described in spatial terms, must be conceived of as existing not in actual physical but in a purely abstract geometrical space. Freud once explicitly warned against thinking of these systems in terms of actual neuroanatomical localization (*10*). Nevertheless, in describing the transition of a mental event from the unconscious through the preconscious to the conscious condition he not only used spatial images and expressions but also raised problems in relation to these images and expressions which suggest that he, at least at times, regarded the systems as concrete spatial entities. We find a similar vacillation between abstract and concrete conceptions in the ways the so-called structural terms 'id,' 'ego,' and 'superego' are

[5]We may also note that Kubie's (*29*) criticism of the use of quantitative concepts in psychoanalysis has similarly failed to influence the theory. As Braithwaite (*1*) has observed, scientific theories, even though known to be unsatisfactory, are generally retained until new, more satisfactory theories to replace them have been advanced.

used. Basically these terms, like the terms 'system *Ucs*,' 'system *Pcs*,' and 'system *Cs*,' which they replace, stand for functionally defined classes of events defining, in addition, typical event-relationships. This view is clearly indicated by Hartmann, Kris, and Loewenstein (*21*). As a rule, however, id, ego, and superego are spoken of as if they were more or less concrete entities. Hartmann describes the ego as an "organ of adaptation" (*20*), and, according to him, id and ego have developed from a "common matrix" (*18*, *21*). At times Freud was even more concrete. He thought, for instance, that perceptions become conscious "in the outermost cortex of the ego" (*13*, p. 41)—thus by implication identifying the ego with (at least parts of) the cerebral hemispheres. He also vaguely alluded to a possible localization of the superego in or around the acoustic center in the temporal lobe (*12*, p. 25).

It is sometimes said that such concrete expressions are merely metaphorical. This brings us to the heart of our problem. Generally speaking, a metaphor is the use of one image or meaning to suggest another usually analogous image or meaning. In this sense, for example, description of the ego as an organ of adaptation is metaphorical if this expression is intended to suggest merely that the mental events we classify as ego-events have adaptive effects; but, if one assumes that the term 'psychic energy' and the terms describing the two classificatory systems are in fact metaphorical, what then are these metaphors metaphors of? This is rarely made explicit. Are all the terms metaphorical in the same sense as the description of the ego as an organ of adaptation?

Our answer to this question will depend on the way we interpret the high-level terms in relation to the mind-body problem. It would appear that there are three conceivable interpretations:

1. Psychoanalytic theory as a purely psychological theory.—We can understand this to mean that the high-level theoretical terms have as referents purely psychological entities. The terms 'id,' 'ego,' and 'superego' would thus signify *actual* subdivisions of an *actual* mental apparatus. Accordingly, they would not be translatable into neurophysiological terms. If we regard the mental apparatus, its subdivisions, and the energies operating within it as psychological entities and processes—i.e., if we take the corresponding terms in their literal meanings—then we have obviously cast our vote for a dualistic theory of the mind-body relationship. Obviously, also, we are not using these terms in any metaphorical sense. To refer, as is sometimes done, to the id-ego-superego classification as the "structural hypothesis" is clearly compatible with this view. We generally do not regard a mere classification as a hypothesis; a hypothesis is thought of as having existential implications—i.e., as referring to something that may actually be the case. I doubt that many psychoanalysts who speak as if they used the high-level theoretical terms in this manner are willing to accept the dualistic implication of their usage.

2. The metaphorical interpretation.—We could, of course, say that the terms are used merely metaphorically. We speak in a dualistic language but maintain simultaneously that, since a purely psychological realm of existence cannot be presumed to exist, the terms have *no actual referents*. The dualism is merely apparent, an as-if dualism or *pseudodualism*. Since the terms have no referents, the question of their translatability does not even arise. With this interpretation, if we speak about a "structural hypothesis" we can only mean that the id-ego-superego classification exhaustively categorizes mental events and event-relationships and possibly also that the classification is in some sense relevant, for instance, by bringing out in relief important aspects of behavior. The terms would thus be metaphorical in the same sense as Hartmann's description of the ego as an organ of adaptation.

This interpretation, as is readily seen, successfully avoids the mind-body problem; but in so doing it reduces itself at best to a low-level theory. The theoretical terms, having no actual referents, are definable more or less exclusively in terms of the inferred relationships between observed and/or inferred psychological (i.e., phenomenal and behavioral) events; that is, they point to empirical or hypothetical relationships that could probably be indicated more directly and hence more transparently in other ways. Hartmann's view of the concept of psychic energy as an operational concept would be consistent with this interpretation, and so would be the view that the spatial representation of id, ego, and superego as contiguous "mental provinces" is to be interpreted in terms of abstract and not of physical space. In its core meaning the pseudodualistic interpretation is thus describable as a modified, very much "liberalized" (to borrow an expression from Feigl) form of behaviorism or of operationism. Obviously, psychoanalytic theory can be said to be a "purely psychological" theory according this interpretation as well.

The situation is somewhat reminiscent of one in physics a few years ago. Schlick (*37*) and other philosophers of science maintained in essence that high-level physical hypotheses (e.g., Bohr's atomic model) are not to be taken in their literal meanings; in fact, their meanings were supposed to be exhaustively defined by the meaning of the directly verifiable low-level hypotheses that are deducible in accordance with them and, by the verification of which, they can be themselves indirectly verified. Ryle (*36*) went even further. He regarded high-level hypotheses as "inference tickets"—i.e., as statements the sole function of which is to permit us to draw certain inferences. In a somewhat similar vein Toulmin (*40*) declared that high-level hypotheses are essentially inference rules. They no doubt have these functions. In recent years, however, this concept has changed radically: it is now conceded that high-level hypotheses and the theoretical terms they include may *also* be understood literally, i.e., as actually referring to existential entities or processes (*16, 25, 27, 41*). Both positions are defensible. Whereas the first, equating meaning and verifiability, sees in the low-level hypotheses the only meaning, the second sees in them not the only meaning but rather the only *verification* of the meaning of the high-level hypotheses. The empirical consequences of these positions are the same. Accordingly, Nagel (*30*) has suggested that the two positions essentially represent preferred modes of speech.

The point that interests us in the present connection is that in physics one can adopt either view without committing oneself to an impossible metaphysical position. In the case of psychoanalytic theory the situation is different. We cannot regard the dualistic and the pseudodualistic interpretations of high-level psychoanalytic statements and theoretical terms simply as preferred modes of speech. The two interpretations are not in this sense equivalent, since the ones does, whereas the other does not, commit us to a dualistic theory of the mind-body relationship. If our choice were only between these two interpretations and if we did not want to stray too far from empiricism we obviously would have to decide for pseudodualism. This would, however, leave us with a badly truncated theory.

3. The neurophysiological interpretation.—The third of the three possible interpretations of high-level psychoanalytic theoretical terms is to regard them as referring to neurophysiological events or entities. By this interpretation the terms would, in other words, be completely translatable to neurophysiological terms—i.e., they would be protoneurophysiological. Freud, as I have indicated, alluded to this possibility. It is obviously part of what I referred to above as the empiricist view of psychoanalytic theoretical terms.

It is clearly feasible to combine this interpretation with what I identified as the core meaning of pseudodualism. On this combined view the high-level theoretical terms would be definable *both* neurophysiologically *and* in terms of psychological relationships. Statements including these terms would thus be verifiable in two directions: physiologically and psychologically. Accordingly, explications of the two sets of meanings of psychoanalytic theoretical statements would be more than merely preferred modes of speech. In physics there is no tangible reality that stands in the same relationship to observable physical phenomena as the brain stands to observable (and experienceable) psychological phenomena. Thus interpreted, psychoanalytic theory would be *in part* a metaphorical expression of neurophysiological theory, or, as I would prefer to say, it would be a *protoneurophysiological model.*

Is this interpretation possible? Are the high-level terms actually translatable to neurophysiological terms? The answer is simply that they are not. Psychic energy in the literal, i.e., existential, meaning of the term is a vitalistic concept. Since there is no room for vitalism in present-day physiology the term is evidently not translatable. According to this interpretation the "structural hypothesis" is an anatomical hypothesis. At least at the present there is no indication that id, ego, and superego may one day be definable in strictly neuroanatomical terms. This being so, psychoanalytic theoreticians have vacillated uneasily between the three indicated positions—dualism, pseudodualism, and empiricism—shying away from each when pressed to face its consequences. It is this dilemma that accounts for the ambiguity of psychoanalytic theory as presently formulated in regard to the mind-body problem.

THE EMPIRICIST INTERPRETATION OF PSYCHOANALYTIC THEORY

Both the pseudodualistic and the empiricist interpretations of psychoanalytic theory are compatible with the hypothesis of empirical parallelism. The pseudodualistic interpretation, however, omits any consideration of the nervous system and is thus at best an incomplete theory. The empiricist interpretation does not work. The question is: can it be made to work?

Let us ask first why it does not work. We have assumed that neurophysiological events somehow generate psychological (i.e., phenomenal and behavioral) events. We would expect, accordingly, to be able, from the observation of psychological events, to infer the corresponding neurophysiological events, at least in sufficient approximation to express the inference in appropriate protoneurophysiological terms. It is possible that some psychoanalytic theoreticians have in fact evaluated the situation this way—taking it for granted that as protoneurophysiological terms the psychoanalytic theoretical terms are close-enough approximations; hence, we have only to wait for neurophysiology to develop sufficiently to enable us to translate our theoretical terms into true neurophysiological terms.

This argument does not take into account that, although derived from observation, theoretical terms are derived *not only* from observation. Freud was fully aware of this fact. In a well-known passage he stated that concepts like the concept of drive are derived in part from clinical observation but in part from other sources as well (*9*). Aside from linguistic conventions and the influence of pre-existing theory we can recognize among the determiners of theoretical terms certain explicitly stated, or merely implicit, preconceived ideas. We may regard these ideas as postulates. It is important to note that the same set of observations in conjunction with different postulates will generate different theoretical terms (even though the same words may be used to express the terms). In the present connection the following more specific point is at least as important: if the postulates are physiological or if they have physiological implications, and if the physiology is unsound, then the resulting theoretical terms will evidently be untranslatable to currently accepted physiological language.

I will briefly discuss some of the postulates that are relevant to the high-level theoretical terms we have been discussing. One is the constancy principle. In the "Project" Freud referred to it as "neuronic inertia" (*7*, p. 356); he explained that the process of discharge is the primary function of neuronic systems. Several years later (*9*) he referred to a tendency inherent in the nervous system to maintain its state of excitation at the lowest possible level. Accordingly, since somatic stimuli continually impinge on the system, continually raising its level of excitation, the system is continually at work to discharge the excitation. In Freud's conception, these two processes, the increase and discharge of excitation, constitute the essence of mental events. Sexual excitation and its discharge through coitus are paradigmatic.[6]

The notion of psychic energy clearly derives from this physiological concept. It is true that the constancy principle, particularly in Freud's neurophysiological formulation, hardly has a place in current psychoanalytic theory. Even though today most analysts may not think of action generally as ultimately determined by a striving for maximal tranquility, this idea (the "Nirvana principle" [*11*]) still survives in the ways the terms 'psychic energy,' 'tension,' and 'energy discharge' are used. Despite all the reservations that recent emendations of the theory have brought with them, everything that happens within the mental apparatus is still basically regarded as being made to happen by energy pressing, wildly or mildly as the case may be, toward its ultimate discharge. This notion has no counterpart in present-day physiological thinking. Accordingly, however well in its various uses it may describe psychological data, the term 'psychic energy' is not translatable to neurophysiological terms. The directionality of psychic energy, as I have indicated, makes it even less translatable than it conceivably might have been otherwise. Nevertheless, psychoanalytic writers often speak about the discharge of psychic energy into bodily innervation, using the words 'discharge' and 'energy' as if they had the same meaning in the physiological as in the psychological context, which clearly they have not.

I will briefly indicate some of the problems which the id-ego-superego classification presents. The basis of this classification is motivational in the sense that not only motives, but also factors influencing motives and the instrumentalities by which motives operate (such as perception, thinking, etc.), are included. Since the classification reflects a theory of motivation, it relates to drive theory and to the theories of the containment and channeling of drive. As formulated by Freud (*9, 12*) the concept of drive, like the concept of energy, is ultimately derived from the constancy principle. In fact, the two concepts are used largely correlatively. By and large, whereas the id represents "unbridled" drives and unneutralized energy, the ego represents (among other things) "tamed" drive derivatives and neutralized energy. One postulate underlying this construction is that the id-ego-superego classification reflects not merely an important point of view but a division that is actually inherent in the nature of things. Accordingly, some psychoanalysts, at least

[6]I may mention that this description is readily interpreted so as to fit the interactionist sequence model: physiological-to-mental-to-mental-to-physiological (see above).

implicitly, hold that id, ego, and superego may one day turn out to be neuroanatomical realities.

The classification is generally understood to be all-inclusive—i.e., it is taken for granted that all mental phenomena can be squeezed into the three classes. This is of course possible if the criterial attributes are defined broadly enough; but if they are defined too broadly the classification easily becomes meaningless. Such a broad, all-inclusive classification is justifiable only if it actually reflects either an anatomico-physiological state of affairs or, on the dualistic interpretation of the theory, the subdivisions of an *actual,* i.e., nonmetaphorical, mental apparatus.

Apart from these postulates there is another reason why the id-ego-superego classification is not always clearly seen as a classification. I have in mind the fact that the classification derives in part from the immediate experience of *me-ness* and of *inner conflict,* the ego corresponding to the rational, the id to the irrational, and the superego to the moral self. Often these two concepts are not kept strictly apart. The terms 'id,' 'ego,' and 'superego' are seen, now from the point of view of an observer as class names and now from the point of view of the experiencing individual himself, as pointing to his actual experience of being torn by irreconcilable demands and urges. No doubt some interclass event-relationships reflect this experience; but the classes themselves, except through their names, do not.

We can hardly avoid the conclusion that, if the empiricist interpretation is to work, psychoanalytic theory must rid itself of its obsolete postulates.[7] This may be accomplished by reducing the high-level psychoanalytic theoretical terms to lower-level terms, chiefly to what Carnap (*3*) calls disposition terms (i.e., terms defined exclusively in terms of relevant relationships between observable events).[8] This eliminates any physiological or other "surplus meaning" of the theoretical terms while preserving their empirically testable psychological meanings. The theory is thus cut down to what I referred to above as the core meaning of the pseudodualistic interpretation. Evidently, this is the empirical psychological meaning of all three interpretations. As I have indicated, Hartmann's concept of energy as an operational concept and the interpretation of the terms 'id,' 'ego,' and 'superego' as class names are compatible with this meaning; and so is, obviously, the interpretation

[7]Hartmann's work has weakened the force of these postulates but without removing them. Hence, the ambiguity of psychoanalytic theory in regard to the mind-body problem remains essentially unchanged. His most important contributions in this respect are: (*a*) the concept of a conflict-free ego sphere including the hypothesis of innate ego apparatuses; (*b*) the concept of secondary autonomy; (*c*) the concept of primarily neutral ego energy; (*d*) the suggestion that the ego may set its own goals independently of the drives; and (*e*) the distinction between ego and self (or self-representation) (*18, 19, 20*).

[8]Presumably not all psychoanalytic theoretical terms are reducible to what Carnap calls *pure* disposition terms. This question I cannot, however, discuss here.

of the referents of low-level terms, such as 'unconscious wish' and 'unconscious fantasy,' as particular dispositions and part dispositions. By this view, to speak about the discharge of psychic energy into bodily innervation is to indicate by the use of metaphor a specific relationship, for example, between certain phenomenal and certain musculo-vegetative events. Similarly, we can only metaphorically say, for instance, that the ego develops; if we want to be taken literally we must speak about the differential development of the dispositions constituting the ego-class and about the development of their interrelationships and of their relationships to id- and superego-dispositions.

The next step is to construct on this basis new theoretical terms by adducing as postulates currently accepted neurophysiological conceptions. It is evident that only by this method can we formulate psychoanalytic theoretical terms that will be translatable to neurophysiological terms. Just what these new postulates will look like I cannot say at present. I will only mention a few points. Brazier, among others, has suggested that the concept of information may be more fruitful for neurophysiology than the concept of energy. Functional changes in the brain, she states, are related to "rerouting of nerve impulses, a change in the informational coupling" rather than to changes in energy-coupling. She points out that "to effect a coupling of parts within the nervous system there does not have to be a great interchange of energy—only the infinitesimal transfer concomitant with the passage of the nerve impulse" (*2,* p. 231). Suddenly the discussion of whether psychic energy is a form of physico-chemical energy becomes irrelevant. Defined as referring to functional relationships between dispositions, and between dispositions and disposition manifestations, the term 'psychic energy' lends itself to being interpreted in terms of informational coupling—which means that the term, at least as it occurs in some contexts, has come close to being translatable to neurophysiological terms.

I will merely list, but without discussing them further, the following additional points. It seems probable that the machine models of thinking and of goal-directed behavior will some day also be of assistance in the formulation of psychoanalytic terms and hypotheses. A number of more specifically neurophysiological hypotheses may likewise become relevant—for instance, hypotheses concerning the functions of the ascending reticular formation and of the limbic system; Olds' (*31*) hypothesis of primary reward systems; Fessard's (*6*) hypothesis regarding the relationship between nervous integration and conscious experience, a hypothesis that brings to mind Freud's contention that the preconscious condition of a mental event is brought about through a "synthesis of different processes" (*13,* p. 45); and Sokolov's (*39*) hypothesis of the significance for the release of the orienting reflex of a mismatch between perception and a neuronal model formed by previous perceptions. As Pribram (*32,* p. 196f) has pointed out, Sokolov's hypothesis may elucidate the problem of expectation. It may also provide a helpful analogy for the formulation of a theory of the relationship between wishing, on the one hand, and wish-fulfillment, anticipation, and fantasy, on the other.

To return to psychoanalytic formulations, I may mention that Rapaport's (*33, 34*) concept of *particular* psychological structures seems equivalent to the concept of disposition as I have used this concept above. Thus understood, the term 'structure' evidently qualifies as a protoneurophysiological term. This is presumably also true of the specific dispositions Klein (*14*) refers to as cognitive controls; these dispositions are, however, of a different order than unconscious wishes and fantasies (see also Rapaport [*34,* p. 71]).

PSYCHOLOGICAL AND NEUROPHYSIOLOGICAL ASPECTS

It follows from the above considerations that, if we want an empirical theory but do not intend to disregard the mind-body problem, psychoanalytic theory must be formulated in a way that it will function both as a psychological theory and as a neurophysiological model. To this end its theoretical terms must fulfill two requirements: (*a*) they must be reducible to terms describing observable and/or directly inferable psychological relationships and (*b*) they must be translatable to neurophysiological terms. In other words, they must be both high-level psychological terms and protoneurophysiological terms. It is important to remember that the referents of psychoanalytic theoretical terms are not psychological but neurophysiological events. I cannot here substantiate this statement,[9] but it seems that only if these terms are also physiologically meaningful can the high-level psychological hypotheses in which they are included function as *clinical* "inference tickets" (see above). For instance, when we apply the means-end rule of clinical inference to a strictly "intrapsychic" event (as when we speak about defense) we tacitly assume a neurophysiological mechanism that operates in accordance with this rule or in some analogous fashion.

The following point is important: Since acceptable psychoanalytic theoretical terms are protoneurophysiological does this mean that, as our knowledge advances, they must be replaced by true neurophysiological terms? I do not think so. In a *strict* physiological language we can only relate neurophysiological events to one another and to peripheral organismic events. We encounter a peculiar dichotomy which in part parallels the one between molar and molecular description. To account for behavior intelligibly we need a terminology that, although ideally completely translatable to the language of neurophysiology, must yet be sufficiently gross and may thus, at least occasionally, become virtually void of concrete neurophysiological meaning. A more important point is that a psychoanalytic theoretical term and its corre-

[9] I hope to do so in a monograph on clinical inference (in preparation).

lated neurophysiological term, even though they denote the same event, are reducible, the one to a psychological, the other to a physiological, set of observables. Hence, they are not strictly synonymous; they belong to different languages, and, accordingly, they cannot substitute for each other in the same sentence. Assume that an unconscious wish, W, is physiologically definable as a particular neuronal configuration, C. Although it makes sense to say, for instance, that a specific dream content is the expression of the unconscious wish W, it would not be sensible to say that it is the expression of the neuronal configuration C. However true it may be in fact, the second statement exemplifies a confusion of languages. When we thus stipulate that psychoanalytic theoretical terms must be translatable to neurophysiological terms this stipulation is meant to be taken literally: they must be translatable, but this does not mean that as soon as it is feasible we should go ahead and translate them.

Obviously, we have a long way to go before translatability will be achieved; and on the way it will presumably happen that a term (or set of terms), thought to be translatable, will have lost its translatability as physiological knowledge advances. This, as far as I can see, is precisely the point at which psychoanalytic theory stands today. It seems clear, however, that until new, better translatable terms have been invented we must use the theory as it is. We can do this, of course, only if we keep in mind that in so doing we use the theory exclusively in its somewhat shadowy pseudodualistic meaning.

Finally, although I referred above to two languages, actually we have to recognize still a third language. In this language we may also speak about unconscious wishes; but here the term is not definable protoneurophysiologically or in terms of observable (and experienceable) psychological events. This is the language of everyday life, literature, and also of clinical practice. When we speak about unconscious wishes in this language we conceive of them as being strictly on a par with conscious wishes except that they, as Freud put it, are not conscious. We may refer to this language as the language of psychological or clinical understanding (Verstehen). It is perhaps more appropriate to regard it not just as a third language: in effect it represents a different *meaning system.* Within this meaning system we are concerned with individuals and with their modes of being-in-the-world, not with brains or mental apparatuses. These last concern us within the meaning system constituted by the languages I discussed above—the theoretical language of psychology and the language of neurophysiology. We may say about the two meaning systems that they unfold, as it were, in different dimensions involving different modes of understanding. Both are psychologically relevant, but each in its own way and in its specific embeddedness. Obviously, they cannot be completely unrelated; their relationship is, however, not one of translatability. Within the meaning system of psychological understanding a term like 'unconscious wish' is not denotative; it merely connotes, alludes, suggests. We may refer to terms of this type as *as-if phenomenal terms.* A further discussion of this question is outside the scope of the present paper.

REFERENCES

1 BRAITHWAITE, R. B. *Scientific Explanation.* Cambridge, Cambridge Univ. Press, 1955.

2 BRAZIER, M. A. B. "How Can Models from Information Theory Be Used in Neurophysiology?" In *Information Storage and Neural Control,* edited by W. S. Fields and W. Abbott. Springfield, Ill., Charles C Thomas, 1963, pp. 230–242.

3 CARNAP, R. "The Methodological Character of Theoretical Concepts." In *Minnesota Studies in the Philosophy of Science,* Vol. I, edited by H. Feigl and M. Scriven. Minneapolis, Univ. of Minnesota Press, 1956, pp. 38–76.

4 DUCASSE, C. "In Defense of Dualism." In *Dimensions of Mind,* edited by S. Hook. New York, New York Univ. Press, 1960, pp. 85–90.

5 FEIGL, H. "The 'Mental' and the 'Physical.'" In *Minnesota Studies in the Philosophy of Science,* Vol. II, edited by H. Feigl, M. Scriven, and G. Maxwell. Minneapolis, Univ. of Minnesota Press, 1958, pp. 370–497. (See also Feigl, in *Dimensions of Mind,* edited by S. Hook [ref. 4]; and in *Theories of the Mind,* edited by J. M. Scher [ref. 35].)

6 FESSARD, A. "Mechanisms of Nervous Integration and Conscious Experience." In *Brain Mechanisms and Consciousness,* edited by J. F. Delafresnaye. Springfield, Ill., Charles C Thomas, 1954.

7 FREUD, S. "Project for a Scientific Psychology" (first published in 1895). *The Origins of Psychoanalysis: Letters to Wilhelm Fliess, Drafts and Notes, 1887–1902,* edited by M. Bonaparte, A. Freud, and E. Kris. New York, Basic Books, 1954, pp. 355–445.

8 FREUD, S. "The Interpretation of Dreams" (first published in 1900). *Standard Edition of the Complete Psychological Works of Sigmund Freud,* edited by J. Strachey, Vols. IV & V. London, Hogarth, 1953.

9 FREUD, S. "Instincts and Their Vicissitudes" (first published in 1915). *Standard Edition,* Vol. XIV. London, Hogarth, 1957.

10 FREUD, S. "The Unconscious" (first published in 1915). *Standard Edition,* Vol. XIV. London, Hogarth, 1957.

11 FREUD, S. "Beyond the Pleasure Principle" (first published in 1920). *Standard Edition,* Vol. XVIII. London, Hogarth, 1955.

12 FREUD, S. "The Ego and the Id" (first published in 1923). *Standard Edition,* Vol. XIX. London, Hogarth, 1961.

13 FREUD, S. *An Outline of Psychoanalysis* (first published in 1940). New York, Norton, 1949.

14 GARDNER, R., HOLZMAN, P., KLEIN, G. S., LINTON, HARRIET, AND SPENCE, D. P. Cognitive control. *Psychol. Issues, 1*(4):Monograph 4, 1959.

15 GELLHORN, E., AND LOOFBOURROW, G. N. *Emotions and Emotional Disorders.* New York, Hoeber, 1963.

16 Hanson, N. R. *Patterns of Discovery.* Cambridge, Cambridge Univ. Press, 1961.

17 Hartmann, H. Comments on the psychoanalytic theory of instinctual drives. *Psychoanal. Quart. 17:*368–388, 1948.

18 Hartmann, H. Comments on the psychoanalytic theory of the ego. *Psychoanal. Stud. Child 5:*74–96, 1950.

19 Hartmann, H. Notes on the theory of sublimation. *Psychoanal. Stud. Child 10:*9–29, 1955.

20 Hartmann, H. *Ego Psychology and the Problem of Adaptation* (first published in 1939). New York, Int. Univ. Press, 1958.

21 Hartmann, H., Kris, E., and Loewenstein, R. M. Comments on the formation of psychic structure. *Psychoanal. Stud. Child 2:*11–38, 1946.

22 Hartmann, H., Kris, E., and Loewenstein, R. M. Notes on the theory of aggression. *Psychoanal. Stud. Child 3/4:*9–36, 1949.

23 Hebb, D. O. Drives and the C.N.S. (conceptual nervous system). *Psychol. Rev. 62:*243–254, 1955.

24 Heider, F. *The Psychology of Interpersonal Relations.* New York, Wiley, 1958.

25 Hempel, C. G. "The Theoretician's Dilemma." In *Minnesota Studies in the Philosophy of Science,* edited by H. Feigl, M. Scriven, and G. Maxwell, Vol. II. Minneapolis, Univ. of Minnesota Press, 1958, pp. 37–98.

26 Holt, R. R. Beyond vitalism and mechanism: Contribution to a discussion of "psychic energy." Paper presented at the Mid-Winter Meeting of the American Psychoanalytic Association, December 1962.

27 Kneale, W. "Induction, Explanation and Transcendent Hypotheses." In *Readings in the Philosophy of Science,* edited by H. Feigl and M. Brodbeck. New York, Appleton-Century-Crofts, 1953, pp. 353–367.

28 Köhler, W. "The Mind-Body Problem. In *Dimensions of Mind,* edited by S. Hook. New York, New York Univ. Press, 1960, pp. 3–23.

29 Kubie, L. S. The fallacious use of quantitative concepts in dynamic psychology. *Psychoanal. Quart. 16:*507–518, 1947.

30 Nagel, E. *The Structure of Science.* New York, Harcourt, Brace and World, 1961.

31 Olds, J. Self-stimulation of the brain. *Science 127:*315–324, 1958.

32 Pribram, K. H. Discussion in *Brain and Behavior,* Vol. I, edited by M. A. B. Brazier. Washington, D.C., American Institute of Biological Sciences, 1961.

33 Rapaport, D. "On the Psychoanalytic Theory of Motivation." In *Nebraska Symposium on Motivation,* edited by M. R. Jones. Lincoln, Univ. of Nebraska Press, 1960.

34 Rapaport, D. The structure of psychoanalytic theory: A systematizing attempt. *Psychol. Issues 2*(2):Monograph 6, 1960.

35 Rapoport, A. "An Essay on Mind." In *Theories of the Mind,* edited by J. M. Scher. Illinois, The Free Press of Glencoe, 1962, pp. 271–304.

36 Ryle, G. *The Concept of Mind.* New York, Barnes & Noble, 1949.

37 Schlick, M. "Positivism and Realism" (first published in 1932–33). In *Logical Positivism,* edited by A. J. Ayer. Illinois, The Free Press of Glencoe, 1959, pp. 82–107.

38 Scriven, M. "The Compleat Robot: A Prolegomena to Androidology." In *Dimensions of Mind,* edited by S. Hook. New York, New York Univ. Press, 1960, pp. 118–142.

39 Sokolov, E. N. "Neuronal Models and the Orienting Reflex." In *The Central Nervous System and Behavior,* edited by M. A. B. Brazier. New York, Third Conference, Josiah Macy, Jr., Foundation, 1960, pp. 187–276.

40 Toulmin, S. *The Philosophy of Science.* London, Hutchinson, 1953; New York, Harper Torchbooks, 1960.

41 Toulmin, S. *Foresight and Understanding.* Bloomington, Indiana Univ. Press, 1961.

42 Von Bonin, G. "Brain and Mind." In *Psychology: A Study of a Science,* Vol. IV, edited by S. Koch. New York, McGraw-Hill, 1962, pp. 100–118.

FOUR

Developmental Biology and Psychoanalysis

JOHN D. BENJAMIN, M.D.

The topic I have chosen is one that delimits both sides of the over-all subject of our conference: psychoanalysis and current biological thought. To the extent that psychoanalysis is a developmental psychology, both historically and in terms of current foci of interest, the topic is directly pertinent. There are, of course, many aspects of clinical and general psychoanalytic theory that demand conceptualization and empiric investigation from points of view other than the genetic (*86*)[1]—but developmental studies can help in bringing clarification and necessary revision to these, too. The restriction on the psychoanalytic side, then, is given not so much by our topic itself as by what I shall actually be bringing in the way of data and discussion. I shall be confining myself largely to some aspects of very early development—to stages and contents that are not directly accessible to psychoanalytic reconstruction; and I shall concentrate on relatively simple and easily communicable data.

The limitation of my title as such is even greater on the biological side than on the psychoanalytic, if for no other reason than that developmental biology occupies a relatively subordinate position in the current exciting biological scene. Rather than discuss this statement, and certain important exceptions to it, in the abstract, I shall try to exemplify it.

Greenacre once stated: "It is . . . extremely difficult to say exactly at what time the human organism develops from a biological to a psychobiological

The work reported here was supported in large part by the Scottish Rite Committee on Research in Schizophrenia and by the Field Foundation.

[1]There is no reasonable way to avoid the rather awkward and sometimes confusing use of one word, *genetic,* to denote two quite different things: in biology, the area of heredity and its mechanisms; in psychoanalysis, as in psychology in general, the modes and levels of development of psychological phenomena. I hope that the mere mention of this potential confusion will preclude its actual occurrence.

organization" (*58*). As I commented at the time, "It is indeed difficult, yet crucial to much in developmental theory" (*7*). Subsequent consideration and investigation have led me to the conclusion that it is not only extremely difficult but, in principle, impossible, without arbitrary definitions of what is meant by the psychological level of organization (*4*). Does one mean the capacity to distinguish between inside and outside, between the I and the non-I (*95*)? or the beginnings of reliable discrimination in various sensory modalities? or the much later point of sufficient ego development to establish one or more fully differentiated drive objects, and object constancy (*12*)? or the capacity to internalize? Does one mean, in general, the first appearance of presumably uniquely *human* psychological characteristics? All one can really say is that to the extent that it is possible to draw a meaningful distinction between the biological and the psychological, there is less of this distinction in the first few weeks of life than there ever will be again (*7*). For my present purpose it is sufficient to say that one of the chief potentials of developmental psychobiology, as I see it, lies precisely in the opportunity it affords to follow bio-behavioral relationships as they emerge over time in increasing complexity and differentiation.

THE THREE TO FOUR WEEKS "MATURATIONAL CRISIS" AND THE "STIMULUS BARRIER"

As previously reported (*7,* pp. 659–60; *8,* pp. 27–28; *12,* pp. 127–29), we noted that full-term infants show a marked and relatively sudden increase in sensitivity to external and internal stimulation at the age of 3–4 weeks. The behavioral criteria are increased crying and other motor manifestations of negative affect, of unpleasure. The phenomenon is most easily accessible to naturalistic observation whenever, for one reason or another, the usual physiological needs of the infant are not well met.[2] In all other cases, it is clearly demonstrable only when sensory stimulation in different modalities is experimentally introduced.

We need not be concerned here with a more rigorous and systematic demonstration of this behavioral phenomenon (currently under way), nor with the hypothesized implications of variability in the mother's handling of the "crisis" for the future development of the child, as discussed elsewhere (*8, 12*). I wish, rather, to report on our efforts, in association with Dr. David Metcalf, to find evidence bearing on our assumption that the relatively sudden appearance of the behavioral change is a function of the state of neuroanatomical and physiological maturation at this particular time. Initial examination of our

[2] Although the tension reduction paradigm of psychoanalysis seems to me, as to others, to be an inadequate general explanatory concept in the light of both behavioral and neurophysiological data, it remains an operationally useful and apparently valid one for the restricted field of neonatal and very early infantile behavior.

longitudinal and cross-sectional EEG records between birth and 3 months of age led Metcalf to the statement, independently of my findings, that "there is a rather abrupt change in awake, drowsy, and sleep EEG's some time around the age of 3 weeks, with relatively little change taking place in the period between 3–4 weeks and 7–8 weeks. What change does take place in awake and drowsy recordings in this interval is in the direction of further development of periodicity without major change in types of frequencies" (*79*). The results of subsequent more detailed study on a small sample of 45 records between birth and 5 weeks can be summarized by saying that at 2½–4 weeks of age in the full-term infant there is a regularly occurring shift from the relatively flat undifferentiated neonatal awake EEG to distinct periodicity, maximally expressed in the 3–4 and 4–6/second range, and associated with an increase in amplitude.[3]

Systematic confirmation of these behavioral and EEG findings is being sought by means of the study of a larger number of infants at 2 and 4 weeks of age. In the meantime, in addition to the work of David and Appell in institutionalized infants reported previously (*7, 8*), other clinical-observational confirmation of an informal but perhaps equally convincing sort has been forthcoming—for example, a nurse with long experience in the care of young infants who, being told of this 3–4 week finding, commented: "Any damn fool knows that!"[4]

To return to our own data, when we ask ourselves just what structures and functions are maturing sufficiently at this point in time to account for these changing behavioral and EEG phenomena in the human infant, we find no easy answer; or, rather, we find a plethora of possible and plausible answers, involving cortex, brain stem and reticular system, thalamus, and thalamo-cortical and other pathways. The simple fact is that we do not yet know enough about the details of neuroanatomical and neurophysiological maturation at this particular age to answer the question we have posed. The major contributions of Conel (*21*) and others (cf. *24*) in this area, immensely valuable as they are in understanding developing behavioral potentials in infancy, are on a grosser time scale than is needed in this instance. Thus it

[3]Details of this work, including necessary quantification of the EEG parameters in order to be able to estimate the degree of "abruptness" of these changes, will appear in another publication.

[4]An interesting sidelight on this finding has been reported by Eiduson, Marschak, Getter, and Eiduson (*26*). In a pilot study on some behavioral and biochemical aspects of development in the first 3 months of life, carried out on one infant, they found that the period of 4–8 weeks represented a peak in "fussiness." In studying levels of ketosteroids in the urine, they found that the highest levels and greatest variability were between 4 and 8 weeks, with values as high as 150 mg/mg creatinine, in contrast to average levels of 20 mg/mg creatinine, as in the first week, and corresponding values after the eighth week. If confirmable on more subjects, this finding would be a challenging beginning in studying some early developmental aspects of neuro-endocrine relationships.

is not only in developmental psychology and psychoanalysis that there remains much basic and elementary work to be done, but also in developmental biology, including anatomy. The obstacles to obtaining much of this basic anatomical knowledge in the human species are obvious and formidable, but not insurmountable.

The "stimulus barrier."—We consider that our findings point rather strongly to the conclusion that the so-called stimulus barrier, or protective shield against stimulation, of the very young infant (which is, of course, only a relative and in no sense an absolute "barrier") is, as I have stated, "a purely passive mechanism, due to relative lack of functioning connections. In contrast, we see later how the older infant and young child (as well as the adult) often exerts *active* efforts to protect himself from excessive stimulation" (*12*). Before proceeding to a brief consideration of the stimulus barrier concept and its role in psychoanalytic theory, we must ask whether there are known physiological mechanisms pertinent to the concept of a more "active" stimulus barrier, arising later in infancy and requiring further neural maturation than our early neonatal example. The answer here is an unequivocal "yes." The whole topic of central influences on afferent transmission (*22, 31, 52, 54, 55, 60, 75, 76, 78, 83*), the focus of many neurophysiological investigations in recent years, seems directly applicable. Much is at present being learned about different mechanisms subsumable under this general heading. Rather than attempting to review the details of this work, I must content myself here with a merely paradigmatic statement about one aspect of it. It has been demonstrated in a large number of species that stimulation to the sensorimotor cortex or to the reticular formation can suppress or inhibit peripherally evoked responses in dorsal column nuclei, such as the nucleus gracilis or the cuneate nucleus (*23, 77, 88–90*). It is obvious that these and other comparable mechanisms are applicable to the concept of an "active stimulus barrier." Once again we find that *developmental* work in this area has been sparse, in this case for the very good reason that it was first necessary to study and demonstrate the mechanisms themselves, a recent and still on-going achievement, before their developmental course could usefully be made the object of systematic investigation.

We are not yet in a position to state with any certainty at what approximate point in time the human infant manifests the beginning of this ability to shut out stimuli actively. Our impression from many observations is that this capacity exists to a slight degree as early as 8 to 10 weeks and matures rapidly thereafter. Behaviorally, we have for a long time been rating infants and young children on a variable which we have termed "active mastery of the environment versus passive acceptance of it." As I have stated elsewhere, this not very clearly defined rating scale, making use of a variety of behavioral indices, has proved one of our more accurate predictors of later ego development (*6, 12*).

Psychoanalytic considerations.—Freud's attribution of major importance to his concept of the protective shield (*43, 46, 48, 50, 51*) was a logical consequence of his views of the essential noxiousness of stimulation. Already foreshadowed in some passages in the Project (*34,* pp. 367, 374), the existence of a *Reizschutz* was seen as a necessity for an organism living in "an external world charged with the most powerful energies . . . it would be killed by the stimulation emanating from these if it were not provided with a protective shield against stimuli. . . . *Protection against* stimuli is an almost more important function for the living organism than *reception* of stimuli" (*43,* p. 27). As Freud saw it, "the nervous system is an apparatus which has the function of getting rid of the stimuli that reach it, or of reducing them to the lowest possible level; or which, if it were feasible, would maintain itself in an altogether unstimulated condition" (*40,* p. 120). In one form or another, this statement of the constancy principle (neuronic inertia, Nirvana principle, stability principle) was repeatedly advanced by Freud, with only minor variations in substance; and played a major role in his metapsychological theorizing and speculation.[5]

This is not an appropriate point for a detailed discussion of the historical roots of this basic "postulate" (*40,* p. 120) of Freud's (cf. Bernfeld [*17*], Jones [*69*], Amacher [*2*], Holt [*68*]), nor for an analysis of its impacts on many of his theoretical constructs—as, for example, the pleasure principle, instinct theory and the economic point of view in general, and the death instinct in particular. Nor do I wish to spend much time here on the obvious fact that most of the findings of modern neuroanatomy and neurophysiology speak strongly against any general validity for this particular thesis of Freud's. The fact that there is spontaneous activity not only in the brain, but also in the sense organs themselves,[6] the discovery of positive reinforcement as well as aversive centers in the limbic system (Olds and Milner [*82*]; Delgado, Roberts, and Miller [*25*]); and, following Hebb's original work, the results of many behavioral studies of the effects of partial afferent isolation (*18, 74, 91*) are sufficient evidence, to which much more could be added, that the concept that the organism strives to keep stimulation at a minimum, or if possible at a zero level, is without biological foundation.[7]

Yet none of this alters the fact that sensory stimulation can be noxious

---

[5]E.g., *On the Psychical Mechanisms of Hysterical Phenomena* (*33,* p. 36), *Project for a Scientific Psychology* (*34,* pp. 357–58), *Studies in Hysteria* (*35,* p. 197), *The Interpretation of Dreams* (*36,* pp. 565–66, 598), *On Narcissism: An Introduction* (*39,* p. 85), *Instincts and Their Vicissitudes* (*40,* pp. 120–21), *Beyond the Pleasure Principle* (*43,* pp. 8–9, 55–56, 62), *The Economic Problem of Masochism* (*45,* pp. 151–61).

[6]See Granit (*54,* pp. 81–103) for a clarifying review of earlier and later work on the functional significance of spontaneous activity in sense organs.

[7]Cf. also Holt's contribution to this volume (Paper 6). For a somewhat different viewpoint see Pribram (*84*).

as well as necessary, and obnoxious as well as pleasing, as anyone living in this age of transistor radios and captive audiences can testify. It remains a biological fact that the nervous system is equipped to reduce the impact of excessive stimulation through the mechanisms alluded to above. In a broad sense of the term defense, then, we are dealing here with a defense *mechanism,* albeit one directed against external rather than internal stimuli, and one that clearly serves adaptive purposes. It should be noted, moreover, that it functions not only in the infant (from 2–3 months on?), but in the same way, if more effectively, in the older child and adult. Putting this in another way, the "active infantile stimulus barrier," thus defined, may or may not in any meaningful sense be a precursor of later developing defenses against drives; but it most certainly is a "precursor" of itself in a more advanced stage of neural maturation. In contrast to this, another major way of dealing with excessive external stimulation, through *motor action,* is not available until much later. Its protective function must in these months be taken over by the mother, undoubtedly the best of all potential "stimulus barriers" for the young infant, though by no means always a successful one in practice; a fact of considerable clinical significance, in my opinion, though not necessarily implying anything "wrong" with the mother.

Precursor, prototype, and predisposition.—The concept of the stimulus barrier has been widely used in psychoanalytic literature, in both literal and figurative senses, not only by Freud, but by many others subsequently (e.g., *16, 27, 30, 62–64, 81, 92, 93, 96, 97*). Bergman and Escalona described it nicely as "a baffling, ambiguous, yet provocative concept, that Freud applied to a variety of related but not identical phenomena" (*16,* p. 343). Others (e.g., Nunberg [*81*]) have used it in an even wider and more figurative sense than did Freud. Its present-day empirical and theoretical status must be evaluated in its own right, since its intimate relationship with the biologically untenable Nirvana principle does not necessarily deprive it either of heuristic usefulness or of a restricted but important validity. For that matter, it was equally closely connected with one of Freud's most creative and useful developmental conceptualizations, that of the perception of "inside" and "outside," with its major implications for instinctual drive theory and for ego development (e.g., *37,* p. 168; *40,* pp. 134–36; *43,* p. 29; *47,* pp. 237–38; *49,* pp. 66–68). Nor is it of any particular interest that Freud's literal models of the "shield" show little correspondence with what is known today about the mechanisms of receiving or warding off stimuli, despite the extraordinary anticipation of some modern neurophysiological concepts occasionally shown by him in the Project (*34, 84*). What is more important for us in the context of this discussion is that the mature organism has developed a variety of ways of receiving, processing, and warding off stimulation. The repertoire of the young infant is much more limited with respect to all of these. We have described two "barriers" against external stimulation in early infancy: the one, which we have termed "passive," being a function of lack of neural maturation; the other, "active," being dependent upon a sufficient degree of such maturation having been attained. (As far as we can ascertain behaviorally, the first of these functions in part against internal stimulation also.) That both can be "broken through" is obvious, demonstrable, and of considerable clinical significance (*8, 16, 64*), but not of immediate pertinence to our present topic. At this point, rather, I would ask what, if any, implications this distinction has for the frequently expressed concept of the stimulus barrier as a precursor, or prototype, or nucleus, of defense mechanisms proper.

The concepts of precursor, prototype, and the like are clearly of importance for developmental psychoanalysis, especially for the conceptualization and investigation of the relationships between physiological and psychological development. The actual usages of these terms, however, has often been bewilderingly unclear and undifferentiated, and their impact on theory and theoretically based empiric investigation has accordingly been distinctly uneven. Without attempting to deal with these problems in any generality here, I should like to illustrate them specifically in terms of the stimulus barrier. (For a more general treatment, see my discussions of separation anxiety as a *precursor* of castration anxiety (*6,* pp. 47–49), and of the experience of birth as a *prototype* of anxiety (*48*) or as a codeterminant of a variable *predisposition* to anxiety (*7,* pp. 654–58; *56*); also my discussion of Spitz's ideas about rooting behavior as a prototype of the head shaking "no" (*15, 95*).

In *Beyond the Pleasure Principle,* the work in which he first delineated the stimulus barrier under that name (*Reizschutz*), Freud identified its function as one that would be taken over by the ego, and treated it implicitly as a "potential ego" (*87*), or an ego root, or nucleus, although none of these terms was used by him in this particular connection. Later he stated this same idea much more explicitly (*50,* pp. 105–6; *51,* pp. 15, 110). This concept of the *Reizschutz* as a prototypic homologue of some defensive and adaptive functions of the ego, or perhaps even a true precursor in the sense of a codeterminant of one important but limited ego function, seems entirely plausible or even probable with respect to our "active stimulus barrier,"[8] but much less so with respect to the "passive neonatal barrier." In the latter case one is at best dealing with an analogy without genetic continuity; in the former, with a phenomenon that, in one respect at least, is a true precursor, and beyond that may conceivably have value as an *indicator* of other defensive and adaptive aspects of ego functioning. Specifically, individual variability in the degree of success with which the young infant

[8]Cf. my comments above about this same mechanism functioning in the adult, along with many newly acquired ones.

masters external stimulation by this means may turn out, on the basis of our experience to date, to have some demonstrable predictive value as a co-determinant along with other organismic and experiential variables of defensive and adaptive ego functioning as a whole.[9]

I have digressed for a moment to the subject of individual variability not only or primarily because of its very great clinical significance, but because studies of variability seem to offer us by far the best method for distinguishing between various types of speculative theorizing in this and other areas. All of these may have usefulness of one or another sort (*6, 7, 12*), but they vary greatly in their potential contribution to basic theory building and revision in psychoanalysis.

It was in the same work, *Beyond the Pleasure Principle,* that Freud also assigned a much more specific precursor role to the stimulus barrier. In the course of a discussion on differences between external and internal stimulation, in which some of the ideas he had so creatively expressed in the Project and elsewhere were restated and expanded, Freud wrote:

> Towards the outside it (the mental apparatus) is shielded against stimuli, and the amounts of excitation impinging on it have only a reduced effect. Toward the inside there can be no such shield; . . . This state of affairs produces two definite results. First, the feelings of pleasure and unpleasure (. . . an index to what is happening in the interior of the apparatus) predominate over all external stimuli. And secondly, a particular way is adopted of dealing with any internal excitations which produce too great an increase of unpleasure: there is a tendency to treat them as though they were acting, not from the inside, but from the outside, *so that it may be possible to bring the shield against stimuli into operation as a means of defence against them. This is the origin of projection* [italics mine], which is destined to play such a large part in the causation of pathological processes (*43,* p. 29).

Leaving aside the already emphasized creativity shown by Freud in this as in his many other passages dealing with the "inside" and the "outside," the pertinent question in the context of our topic is what he meant by the words "origin of projection" (*Herkunft der Projection* in the original German).

On the basis of everything else that he wrote about this mechanism, it seems clear that Freud could not have meant that the concept of the protective barrier "explains" projection directly; nor does he imply that pathological projection is a resultant of abnormalities in the development of the barrier as such. On the other hand, his use of the term "origin" shows plainly that he was not thinking in terms of mere analogy. I think the possible meanings of this passage can be reduced to the following propositions:

1. *Projection as a defense at any given point in time occurs in order to*

---

[9]Our data are not yet sufficiently extensive or well ordered to permit isolating this one variable from the larger number subsumed under the ratings on "active mastery" mentioned above.

make use of the stimulus barrier as it exists at that time. (As stated above, it seems clear that Freud could not have meant this. Apart from previously mentioned objections to it, it would broaden the concept of the barrier to an extent that would be incompatible with his use of it.)

2. *Because in the course of development the infant has so often treated internal stimuli as external, in order to invoke the protection of the barrier, there exists a "readiness" to do the same with unacceptable impulses, ideas, and conflicts at a later stage.* (This concept would treat the stimulus barrier as an homologous prototype of a particular defense and would not involve regression as being necessary for projection. It assumes that we know that the infant does in fact "project" *in order* to invoke the stimulus barrier.)

3. *It is a necessary condition for projection that there be a distinction between inside and outside.* (This is unquestionably true, although in severely regressive projection it sometimes seems to be the case that the distinction is cognitively blurred, that the patient has partially regressed to a period *before* the distinction was a sharp one.)

4. *The assumption of a "shield" that is effective against external but not against internal stimulation is necessary to account for the development of the outside-inside differentiation itself.* (This is an ingenious and plausible but by no means validated thesis. Too little is actually known about any neurophysiological differences in this respect. Our "passive" neonatal stimulus barrier seems to be relatively effective against all sorts of stimulation, and it is no more than relatively effective against any. Less is known about possible active inhibition of internal stimulation. It is established, however, that the processing and inhibition of external stimuli is by no means identical for all sensory modalties [*54*], either qualitatively or in the degree to which suppression and inhibition can be achieved. Moreover, other means for distinguishing between the inside and the outside are available, as discussed by Freud and others. In particular, we would emphasize with Freud [*47*], Fenichel [*30*], Spitz [*97*], and others the disappearance and reappearance of the need fulfilling "object" [pre-object] as one such mechanism, and point out that *differential inhibition* of external and internal stimuli, whether or not it exists, is not a conceptual necessity for this process.)

Of authors other than Freud who have dealt with the topic of the stimulus barrier and other similar early infantile behaviors in relation to later defensive and adaptive ego functions, I shall mention only three: Hartmann, Greenacre, and Spitz. The whole of Hartmann's ego-psychological work from 1937 (*61*) on, with its emphasis on adaptation, change of function, and primary and secondary autonomy, contains some explicit and many implicit references to relationships of this sort. He specifically emphasizes the possible direct or indirect genetic (causal) nature of some of these relationships, and the value, therefore, of studying variability and individual differences (e.g., *62*, pp.

82–83; *63,* pp. 12–13).[10] Hartmann also discussed the stimulus barrier specifically. "It is likely," he states, "that the methods by which infants deal with stimuli are later used by the ego in an active way, and especially for defense" (*63,* p. 13).

> . . . I want to emphasize that it seems . . . suggestive to consider very early processes in the autonomous area as fore-stages of later defense against the within as well as the without. . . . I want to point to Freud's statements about what he calls protective barrier against stimuli, in its possible relation to later ego-development. . . . It might well be that the ways in which infants deal with stimuli . . . are later used by the ego in an active way. This active use by the ego of primordial forms of reaction we consider . . . a rather general characteristic of the developed ego. This hypothesis of a genetic correlation between individual differences in primary factors of this kind and the later defense mechanisms . . . is intended as an appeal to further investigation . . . I think that it should be accessible to direct verification or refutation (*62,* p. 83).

To summarize some of Hartmann's views in this area in my own terms, he shows little interest in analogical prototypes of individual defense mechanisms but seeks, rather, for possible homologies and true, if indirect, precursors (developmental codeterminants) of defensive and adaptive ego *functions.* He stresses the importance of potential verifiability or refutability, particularly through the study of individual differences. While not denying (any more than I do) the values of analogy and metaphor, especially in the hands of genius, he tries, as do his coworkers (*66, 67*), to separate these values from those of semantic as well as systematic clarification of theory (*3, 65*). His specific references to the protective barrier are largely in terms of a "passive" mechanism (as with Freud's literal model) ; but he gives indications that some sort of active "use" of it is made by the infant, again as with Freud; but not, of course, in terms corresponding to our distinction of the two models. The assumed duration of the infantile stimulus barrier is not discussed. There is one reference in Hartmann to the possible pathological implications of an inadequate protective shield, in the course of a discussion of the work of Berg-

[10]Parenthetically, it might be useful to expand Hartmann's own terminology by distinguishing change of function from "change of apparatus." The former concept, a major contribution of Hartmann despite its occasional and inevitable misuse in the literature, derives in part from fields other than psychoanalysis, in part from Anna Freud's discussion of defenses (*32*). It leads directly to Hartmann's concept of secondary ego autonomy, although not identical with it (cf. also Rapaport [*85*]). The simplest way to define it paradigmatically is as the use of an already existing "apparatus" (physiological, intrapsychic, or overt behavioral) for a new and different function (cf. Spitz [*95*]). "Change of apparatus," on the contrary, would denote the use of *different* apparatuses to fulfill the same or nearly the same function. This phenomenon is directly pertinent to the topic of prototype and precursor, is mentioned frequently by Hartmann, and was implicitly suggested by Freud when he stated: "It may well be that before its sharp cleavage into an ego and an id . . . the mental apparatus makes use of different methods of defence from those which it employs after it has reached these stages of organization" (*48,* p. 164).

man and Escalona (*64*). It is evident that in many respects these views are similar to mine.

Greenacre's developmental writings deal frequently and richly with the subject of external and internal stimulation, with the infant's responses to these, and with the mother's role as both a protector and a stimulator (*56–59*). Her originality of thought, clinical psychoanalytic perceptivity, and developmental biological interests combine to offer us a wealth of stimulation themselves—against which it is only occasionally necessary to erect a protective barrier of some reserve and skepticism! (*7,* p. 655). With her particular interest in the birth process as a variable source of stimulation or overstimulation, it is not surprising that Greenacre's concept of the stimulus barrier is directly related to the experience of birth and is considered a defense against its overstimulating effects. In her paper on the physical nuclei of some defense reactions she states that "the reduction of responsiveness to external stimulation, varying in degree and duration according to the severity of the individual birth, may be regarded as the first (physical) individual intra-organismic defence reaction" (*59,* p. 70). Although, as we have previously reported (*7,* pp. 654–58), some of our data lend a degree of support to this author's high estimation of the general importance of variability in the birth process, and although we have additional data from twin studies that point in this direction (*9, 10*), we have no empiric support for the thesis that the duration of the "passive" stimulus barrier is a function of this variability. Perhaps there would be such a relationship in cases with sufficient perinatal damage to the nervous system to affect maturational rates directly. Since we have no such cases in our group, we are not in a position to answer this question empirically. In such instances, however, the effect might also be the opposite to that predicated by Greenacre, in that there could be delayed maturation of the second "active" barrier, and thus a longer rather than a shorter time *without* effective protection against stimuli. Purely speculatively, it seems possible that this latter mechanism might be a link connecting the frequency with which signs of C.N.S. damage are found in certain types of so-called childhood schizophrenia with the findings of Bergman and Escalona (*16*) on unusual sensory sensitivities in some such children.

Spitz has used the concepts of precursor and prototype extensively in his developmental theorizing (e.g., *92, 93, 95–97*). Although he specifically disclaims more than analogical purpose in his delineation of prototypes of ego defenses (*97,* p. 639), some of his examples in this paper and elsewhere (e.g., *92; 97,* pp. 639–40, 649) seem to be aimed at the demonstration of homology and perhaps of genetic continuity in the sense of precursors. Moreover, he discusses them not only in relation to defensive and other *functions,* but in terms of the defense *mechanisms* proper; i.e., repression, denial, projection, and so forth. Despite my great appreciation of Spitz's major contributions to the field of psychoanalytic developmental theory (cf. *12*), I do not think that this analogical approach furthers our understanding of either the developmental psychology of defense, or the actual biological antecedents and concomitants of the defense mechanisms.

Spitz is unequivocal, however, in his conception of the neonatal stimulus barrier as a manifestation of neural immaturity. He refers to it in a number of publications (e.g., *92,* p. 138; *93,* p. 67; *95,* p. 105; *97,* pp. 632–35, 645) and states, for example, "It is a manifestation of a maturational state . . . at birth the sensorium is not cathected. . . . The stimulus barrier recedes progressively as the pathways mature . . ." (*95,* p. 105). ". . . This process takes several months" (*92,* p. 138). Accordingly, he is critical of Greenacre's view of the barrier as a *withdrawal* of cathexis (*97,* p. 633), a critique with which I fully agree. Yet at the same time he considers this neonatal barrier to be a meaningful prototype of repression as contrasted to other defense mechanisms (*97,* pp. 632–35) and also speaks of it as functioning "at the level of the primary process" (*95,* p. 105).

I have questioned the significance of the *neonatal* stimulus barrier as a meaningful prototype or precursor of anything in later development; but I am not for that reason discounting its importance in other directions. On the contrary, I think it of high significance by virtue of its negative—our finding of its relative and apparently sharp diminution at about 3–4 weeks of age. This means that there is a period of uncertain length, which we shall provisionally place between 3–4 weeks or a little earlier and 8–10 weeks or later, when the infant has neither of the two described mechanisms for warding off external (and internal?) stimulation at his disposal. The resultant enhanced vulnerability of this period, in turn, makes greater demands upon the mother or mother substitutes. Usually these are well met, with or without conscious awareness on the mother's part that the infant has become more sensitive to stimuli. Sometimes these needs for additional protection against stimulation are less well handled, probably most frequently in some institutional settings, but also in those instances where the mother, for whatever reasons, is less than usually skillful in meeting them. On the basis of a few such observations in our series of longitudinally studied chidren, I have hypothesized that failure to meet these needs of the infant is one important factor out of many that may lead to a heightened *predisposition* to anxiety (*7,* pp. 659–60; *9,* pp. 27–28). Subsequent observations seem to support this idea, although we cannot yet consider it confirmed (*9*). It is an entirely testable hypothesis, but in practice extremely difficult to test! Because of the multiplicity of other determinants of variability in anxiety levels, a much larger population than we can follow longitudinally would be necessary for rigorous statistical confirmation. If it is confirmed, however, there might be some meaning in speaking of the *absence* of the stimulus barrier as one precursor of anxiety, as I expressed it originally (*7,* p. 660). Although couched in different terms, and on the basis of different data, this general point of view is compatible, as I see it, with some of Greenacre's views on the predisposition to anxiety (*56, 58*).

I would add one more comment to what I have said. There is no theoretical reason to expect that the sequelae of overstimulation during this "critical period" (*7, 8, 96*) should be limited to an increased potential anxiety level in the future. On the contrary, one would anticipate other immediate somatic results in addition to the behavioral manifestations I have reported (*7, 8, 12*). It has occurred to me that the so-called "three month's colic" of infancy, which is unquestionably of varied origin (*19, 99*), may in some instances be a direct reflection of this vulnerability, rather than related to any *specific* psychological aspects of the mother-child relationship.[11] In favor of this hypothesis are the typical age of onset, between 3 and 4 weeks, sometimes as early as 2 weeks; the later onset in prematures; and the typical age of disappearance between 2 and 4 months, when our second "barrier" is becoming effective. Against it are these observations that claim a significantly lower incidence of colic in institutionalized infants (*94,* and references cited there). Even if these observations are generally confirmable, however, they would have to be systematically related to the great variability between institutions in terms of over- and understimulation of infants before they could be evaluated in this direction. Plans are now under way to subject this speculative hypothesis to empirical tests.

I have discussed the stimulus barrier concept and our data bearing on it at such length because I think it illustrates rather well some few of the many theoretical, conceptual, and empiric problems in early developmental bio-psychoanalytic research. What follows in the way of data and discussion will have to be presented much more briefly on this occasion.

THE DEVELOPMENT OF SLEEP SPINDLES IN PREMATURE AND FULL-TERM INFANTS

A transition to our next topic, an investigation of the development of sleep spindles, is given by the fact that at 3–4 weeks EEG recordings in sleep show the beginnings of the higher magnitude slow-wave activity that will shortly thereafter regularly accompany sleep spindles in their early form. Since there is some reason to believe that the neural maturation necessary for spindling is itself accelerated by stimulation, the possible connection with what we have reported on the neonatal stimulus barrier is obvious.

This study was undertaken to test an idea that the sensory experiences of

[11]Spitz's finding of "anxious overpermissiveness" with underlying hostility (*94,* pp. 262ff.) is one I have been unable to confirm with any regularity in my own observations (cf. also Gifford [*53*] and Deutsch [cited in *53*]).

extra-uterine life would probably interact with relatively autonomous neural maturation in such a way as to result in the appearance of sleep spindles at an earlier *post-conceptional* (although later post-natal) age in prematures than in full-term infants. Although this investigation has been briefly mentioned previously in the course of discussion of the over-all topic of interactions between innate and experiential variables and constants (*8,* pp. 28–30; *11,* p. 62), it has not been completed until recently. The final results (*14*) confirm that there is a distinct though not outstanding contribution of sensory experience to this development, in that the prematures do show a significantly accelerated development of spindling.[12]

The pertinence of the findings of this study to developmental psychoanalysis is perhaps tenuous, and surely indirect. I bring it nevertheless not only as a paradigm of one sort of interaction of innate maturational factors with experience, but because early patterns of sleep, and particularly the differences between neonatal, later infantile, and childhood sleep, are of such direct significance to dream theory, regression theory, and the theory of ego development (cf. Fenichel [*28, 29*], Gifford [*53*], Lewin [*73*], Spitz *97,* pp. 642–47] and others [*15*]). At this point, however, I wish merely to present the finding for your consideration, rather than discuss these major issues. Nor shall I attempt to relate it to the exciting current work of many investigators on the neurophysiology of sleep and on the association of dreaming with rapid eye movements (see the contribution of Snyder to this volume, Paper 14).

STRANGER AND SEPARATION ANXIETY IN INFANCY

In contrast to the two foregoing studies, our investigations of some early developmental aspects of anxiety[13] have dealt extensively with more advanced and differentiated stages of infant and child development—from about 3 months on at the earliest, and especially from 5 to 6 months on (*6–8, 12, 98*). Moreover, they have not been primarily focused on biological maturation as such, but rather on the shifting genetics and dynamics of fear responses accompanying such maturation in conjunction with the developmental relationships to one another of fear of strangers, fear of separation, fear of object loss, the establishment of object constancy, fear of loss of love, fear of castration, and so forth. I shall assume the results of these investigations, as far as they have gone, to be known to you; at any rate, I shall not repeat them here. In the context of our topic of developmental biopsychological relationships, I wish

[12]Although the hypothesis itself and the design of the study were mine, the electroencephalographic competence necessary for undertaking it was that of my co-authors Metcalf and Levy.

[13]In association with Katherine Tennes, Esther Lampl, and others in the Child Research Council, University of Colorado School of Medicine.

only to point out the number and varying nature of biological maturational elements entering into these early fear manifestations: for example, those early points of sufficient tactile and auditory discrimination necessary to evoke fear of strangeness as such; the point at which visual development is sufficient to permit discrimination of the face from the non-face, as in the early stages of the smiling response; the much more advanced visual development that allows well-known faces, particularly the mother's, to be reliably distinguished from all others—a necessary but not sufficient condition for *stranger anxiety* and for the full development of discriminating smiling; the development of memory, and with it the *anticipatory* function of the ego, which adds a new dimension to anxiety—all of these constitute discrete although only relatively autonomous biological ego roots. A good deal is known about some of them, but much more remains to be learned; and all of them are in principle subjects for further experimental investigation (*12*). When I add, however, that one of the chief dynamic sources of variability in both stranger anxiety proper and the somewhat later appearing infantile separation anxiety seems, on the basis of our data, to lie in the degree and balance of libidinal and aggressive cathexes of the mother, it is clear that here the question of discrete biological determinants and concomitants is of a different order of complexity both conceptually and in terms of empirical investigation. Further discussion of this would lead us directly into problems of the psychoanalytic theories of instinctual drives and of psychic energy, in themselves as *psychological* theories, as well as in their relationships to current biological knowledge (cf. *13, 72, 80*). Although clearly of major relevance to the general topic of this symposium, the presentation of data pertinent to these issues would far exceed the limited scope of these introductory remarks.

STUDIES IN GENETIC-ENVIRONMENTAL INTERACTION

What follows will deal more with method than with data, since the results of our twin studies, initiated fairly recently, are in general more suggestive than demonstrative at this time.

From the beginnings of our longitudinal studies of a non-twin population, we have been directly concerned with problems of conceptualizing and investigating the ways in which variable hereditary and nonhereditary constitutional factors interact with, as well as codetermine, variable experiences in the course of development (*3,* p. 151; *4,* pp. 6–7; *5,* pp. 430–32; *6,* pp. 28–29, 69–70; *8–10*). Having discussed some of the issues and presented some of our data in previous communications, I shall not repeat myself here; nor shall I again review in any detail the fascinating history of Freud's own thinking on the subject of heredity and experience (cf. *8,* pp. 21–27), beyond restating what seems to be an essential and often overlooked point in its development. I refer to the paradoxical impact of his famous and much discussed discovery that he had made a "momentous error" in viewing actual seductions by parents and others as constituting the "specific aetiology" of hysteria. On the one hand, there can be no question that this insight contributed directly to Freud's major discoveries of unconscious fantasies, of infantile sexuality, of the Oedipus, and of the role played by fantasies and the drive organization they reflect in shaping individual experience to a significant degree (cf. *8,* pp. 21–23, and references cited there). On the other hand, I interpret the data as showing that the same discovery led Freud to relegate variability in individual experience to a secondary position, to displace "the role of highly specific experiences from the ontogenetic to the phylogenetic" to such an extent that "the innate *was* the experiential." Thus, as I see it, his Lamarckian views on heredity, never revised, were at the least strongly reinforced, if not actually importantly determined, by this major event in the history of psychoanalysis (*8,* p 23).

In more recent years we have attempted to go further in empiric research in this area by applying some of the observational methods and specific findings of our long-term developmental studies to a small but growing population of twins, sometimes in conjunction with therapeutic investigation also (*9; 10,* pp. 102–8).[14]

I conceive of twin studies as serving at least four interrelated but separate goals (cf. *10,* pp. 99–102). The first and classic method is of course that of comparing concordance-discordance ratios in monozygotic and dizygotic twins. This method is in principle applicable not only to disease entities, where it has been most widely used, but also to any reliably assessable overt behavioral or intrapsychic phenomena. I have discussed elsewhere (*5,* pp. 431–32; *10,* pp. 91, 98–99), as have many others, the limitations inherent in the method itself, apart from any biases in its application; but I have also emphasized its values and the fact that these have by no means been fully exploited to date. The maximum attainable goal of this method by itself is the demonstration of the relative importance or unimportance of genetic factors for any given phenomenon. The number and nature of these factors, their modes of transmission, the enzymes involved, and the pathways through which they work must all be studied by other means.

A second approach to the study of twins, and one of more immediate pertinence to psychoanalytic psychology, focuses on the psychological aspects of being a twin, or a parent of twins. The nature of the inter-twin relationship and its impacts on the development and handling of aggression, on cognitive development, and particularly on identifications and identity formation are of major interest to us, as to many other investigators (cf. *9, 10,* and references there). Since they do not involve problems of discrete biopsychologi-

[14]In association with G. E. Blom, K. Tennes, S. Santostefano, and others.

cal relationships, however, I shall omit further discussion of them here.

A third method, and the one we are most heavily involved in at present, takes advantage of the phenomenon of monozygotic twinning to study the impact of *experience* on personality development in a somewhat more controlled fashion than is otherwise possible. Similarities and differences between members of monozygotic twin pairs are assessed, and an attempt made to relate the latter to independently assessed differences in parental attitudes, fantasies, and handling. Ideally these pairs would be followed from birth on; but we have not yet started this planned phase of our investigations. At present most of our subjects are of pre-school ages, and we are thus in part dependent upon retrospection as well as upon objective data from baby diaries, pediatric records, and the like.

The major conceptual fallacy that must be avoided in using this method is the tendency to attribute all significant personality differences to differences in psychosocial experiences alone. Although our findings to date strongly support the overriding significance of such experiences in many areas (*6, 8*), we cannot disregard the important fact of *congenital physiological differences* in twin pairs. These vary greatly from one monozygotic twin pair to another, depending upon intra-uterine factors (placentation) as well as upon occasional major variability in natal and perinatal experience. That they can have direct effects on later personality development (e.g., differential brain damage) has been demonstrated by others. That they can also have indirect effects by contributing to differential perceptions of the twins by the parents has been shown by us (*9*). Only thorough knowledge of these congenital differences as well as of the developmental course and timing of the behavioral and intrapsychic differences can clarify some of these relationships in the individual case. And sometimes they remain unclarified.

Of our provisional results from the application of this method, I shall mention only two: (*a*) As in the case of our intensively studied twins Jimmy and Charlie (*9, 10*), we have also found in a few other pairs major differences in overt behavioral "masculinity" and "femininity," in parental identifications, and in sexual identity formation. These variables, while highly intercorrelated, are by no means in perfect correlation with each other;[15] nor from a theoretical point of view, should they be. (*b*) In apparent but not yet fully confirmed association with the differences in identifications and sexual identity formation, there are equally firmly established differences in cognitive and perceptive styles in some of our twin pairs.[16]

I bring these data not only because of their psychological interest,

[15]This statement is based not only on our small twin population, but on an unpublished study of these phenomena in our intensive longitudinal series, carried out in association with K. Tennes (cf. also *6* and *8*).

[16]These studies are being undertaken in association with S. Santostefano and R. Crager.

which seems great to me, but also to demonstrate the limitations of this method. What we have shown, and I think it important, is that experiences alone can account for major differences in the areas cited. But this would in no way justify a generalization that "masculinity," or sexual identity, or cognitive style is not importantly a function of genetic variability in many instances. For the method as outlined neglects genetic variability in order to take advantage of genetic identity for the purpose of studying experience. For this reason it can contribute relatively little, by itself, to the finer delineation of genetic-experiential *interactions* as such, in elaboration of Freud's original *complemental series* concept (*6,* p. 70; *8,* pp. 23–24). This constitutes a major long-term goal of our twin studies, although it is unlikely that we shall achieve it ourselves. In this fourth method, which is essentially an expansion of the sort of studies we have just described, the emphasis would be as much on inter-twin pairs as on intra-twin pair comparisons; and on similarities as much as on differences. The genetic variability would be given by the different genetic constitutions of the twin pairs; and similarities and differences in congenital physiological behaviors, psychosocial experience, and behavior would all have to be assessed between as well as within pairs. The design is actually much simpler than it sounds, and we are attempting just this sort of analysis on our small sample. But apart from the increased uncertainty of some of the assessments, the number of pairs needed to fulfill the requirements for similarities and differences in all the variables involved is sufficiently large that perhaps this will turn out to be a fantasy rather than a research!

In the meantime, the application of our second and third methods to a variety of *specific* developmental phenomena may give us some partial answers to a number of questions. In fact, I can think of few of our developmental findings and hypotheses that would not be enriched by being undertaken on a twin population, even a small one. Beyond the data from early infancy that I have brought, I would mention in this connection such studies as those on "vectors and modes" (*6,* pp. 40–44; sensory-motor behavior in relation to the development of adaptive and defensive ego functions (*6,* pp. 36–37; *8,* pp. 31–32); and autonomous and nonautonomous roots of cognitive development (*8,* pp. 32–34).

CONCLUDING COMMENTS

The phrase "Current Biological Thought" in the title of this symposium would, I believe, suggest to many biologists, and certainly does to this nonbiologist, the truly exciting and revolutionary discoveries and theoretical advances of the last twenty years or so in cellular and molecular biology, including basic genetics. Although I feel sure that these findings will eventually prove to have both direct and indirect pertinence to psychoanalysis as a general psychology, there is a long way to go in theory revision and in data accumulation before these potential relationships can be meaningfully discussed, at least by me.

To others, the phrase might suggest the major advances of recent years in neurophysiology, and in information and communication theory, with their direct and immediate implications for psychoanalysis (cf. *1, 72, 84*). I have touched on only one aspect of current neurophysiological investigation, and not at all on information theory—not only because of my lack of professional competence in these fields, but because I wish to shape my comments around a few data connecting developmental psychoanalysis with developmental biology. Even within the limits of this restriction, I have had to omit much in the way of data and theory, and have not attempted any sort of systematic analysis of the different types of biopsychological relationships we encounter. Rather than attempting to make up for these and many other omissions in what would have to be an overly condensed fashion (*13*), I shall conclude with still another quotation from *Beyond the Pleasure Principle* (*43,* p. 60) : "Biology is truly a land of unlimited possibilities. We may expect it to give us the most surprising information and we cannot guess what answers it will return in a few dozen years to the questions we have put to it."

REFERENCES

1 ADRIAN, E. D. The mental and the physical origins of behavior. *Int. J. Psycho-Anal. 27:*1–6, 1946.

2 AMACHER, M. P. The influence of the neuroanatomy, neurophysiology and psychiatry of Freud's teachers on his psychoanalytic theories. Unpublished doctoral thesis, Univ. of Washington, Seattle, 1962. Cited by Holt (*68*).

3 BENJAMIN, J. D. Methodological considerations in the validation and elaboration of psycoanalytical personality theory. *Amer. J. Orthopsychiat. 20:*139–156, 1950.

4 BENJAMIN, J. D. Directions and problems in psychiatric research. *Psychosom. Med. 14:*1–9, 1952.

5 BENJAMIN, J. D. Some considerations in biological research in schizophrenia. *Psychosom. Med. 20:*427–445, 1958.

6 BENJAMIN, J. D. "Prediction and Psychopathological Theory." In *Dynamic Psychopathology in Childhood,* edited by L. Jessner and E. Pavenstedt. New York, Grune & Stratton, 1959, pp. 6–77.

7 BENJAMIN, J. D. Some developmental observations relating to the theory of anxiety. *J. Amer. Psychoanal. Ass. 9:*652–668, 1961.

8 BENJAMIN, J. D. "The Innate and the Experiential in Development." In *Lectures in Experimental Psychiatry,* edited by H. W. Brosin. Pennsylvania, Univ. of Pittsburgh Press, 1961, pp. 19–42.

9 BENJAMIN, J. D. An interim report on a twin research. As quoted in A. Z. Pfeffer, Research in psychoanalysis, *J. Amer. Psychoanal. Ass. 9*:564–565, 1961.

10 BENJAMIN, J. D. "Some Comments on Twin Research in Psychiatry." In *Research Approaches to Psychiatric Problems,* edited by T. T. Tourlentes, S. L. Pollack, and H. E. Himwich. New York, Grune & Stratton, 1962, pp. 92–112.

11 BENJAMIN, J. D. Panel discussions. *J. Amer. Acad. Child Psychiat. 1*:59–66, 182–195, 1962.

12 BENJAMIN, J. D. "Further Comments on some Developmental Aspects of Anxiety." In *Counterpoint: Libidinal Object and Subject,* edited by H. S. Gaskill. New York, Int. Univ. Press, 1963, pp. 121–153.

13 BENJAMIN, J. D. Theory, method, and data in psychoanalysis. Paper given at panel on "Psychoanalytic methodology" at Meeting of the American Psychoanalytic Association, December 1963.

14 BENJAMIN, J. D., METCALF, D. R., AND LEVY, I. B. The development of sleep spindles in premature and full-term infants. Submitted for publication, 1964.

15 BENJAMIN, J. D., AND TENNES, K. A case of pathological head nodding. Paper read at December 1958 Meeting of the American Psychoanalytic Association. To be published.

16 BERGMAN, P., AND ESCALONA, S. K. Unusual sensitivities in very young children. *Psychoanal. Stud. Child 3/4*:333–352, 1949.

17 BERNFELD, S. Freud's earliest theories and the school of Helmholtz. *Psychoanal. Quart. 13*:341–362, 1944.

18 BEXTON, W. H., HERON, W., AND SCOTT, T. H. Effects of decreased variation in the sensory environment. *Canad. J. Psychol. 8*:70–76, 1954.

19 BRAZELTON, T. B. Crying in infancy. *Pediatrics 29*:579–588, 1962.

20 BRONSON, G. A neurological perspective on ego development in infancy. *J. Amer. Psychoanal Ass. 11*:55–65, 1963.

21 CONEL, J. L. *The Postnatal Development of the Human Cerebral Cortex.* Cambridge, Harvard Univ. Press, Vol. I, 1939; Vol. II, 1941; Vol. VI, 1959.

22 DAWSON, G. D. The central control of sensory inflow. *Proc. Roy. Soc. Med. 51*:531–535, 1958.

23 DAWSON, G. D. The effect of cortical stimulation on transmission through the cuneate nucleus in the anesthetized rat. *J. Physiol., London 142*:2P–3P, 1958.

24 DEKABAN, A. *Neurology of Infancy.* Baltimore, Williams & Wilkins, 1959.

25 DELGADO, J. M. R., ROBERTS, W. W., AND MILLER, N. E. Learning maturated by electrical stimulation of the brain. *Amer. J. Physiol. 179*:587–593, 1954.

26 EIDUSON, B. T., MARSCHAK, M., GETTER, E., AND EIDUSON, S. An exploratory study of the development of the human infant from birth through three months. Paper given at symposium on "Behavior and biochemistry" at Meeting of the American Psychological Association, St. Louis, September 1962.

27 ENGEL, G. L. *Psychological Development in Health and Disease.* Philadelphia, Saunders, 1962.

28 FENICHEL, O. "A Critique of the Death Instinct" (first published in 1935). *Collected Papers.* New York, Norton, 1953, pp. 363–372.

29 Fenichel, O. "Early Stages of Ego Development" (first published in 1937). *Collected Papers.* New York, Norton, 1954, pp. 25–48.

30 Fenichel, O. *The Psychoanalytic Theory of Neurosis.* New York, Norton, 1945.

31 French, J. D. The reticular formation. *Handbook of Physiology II,* Washington, D.C., American Physiological Society, 1960, pp. 1281–1305 (pp. 1300–1301).

32 Freud, A. *The Ego and the Mechanisms of Defense* (first published in 1936). New York, Int. Univ. Press, 1946.

33 Freud, S. "On the Psychical Mechanisms of Hysterical Phenomena" (first published in 1893). *Standard Edition of the Complete Psychological Works of Sigmund Freud,* edited by J. Strachey, Vol. III. London, Hogarth, 1962, pp. 27–39.

34 Freud, S. "Project for a Scientific Psychology" (first published in 1895). *The Origins of Psychoanalysis; Letters to Wilhelm Fliess, Drafts and Notes 1887–1902,* edited by M. Bonaparte, A. Freud, and E. Kris. New York, Basic Books, 1954, pp. 355–404.

35 Freud, S. (with J. Breuer). "Studies in Hysteria" (first published in 1895). *Standard Edition,* Vol. II. London, Hogarth, 1955.

36 Freud, S. "The Interpretation of Dreams" (first published in 1900). *Standard Edition,* Vols. IV & V. London, Hogarth, 1953.

37 Freud, S. "Three Essays on the Theory of Sexuality" (first published in 1905). *Standard Edition,* Vol. VII. London, Hogarth, 1953, pp. 135–243.

38 Freud, S. "Formulations Regarding the Two Principles in Mental Functioning" (first published in 1911). *Standard Edition,* Vol. XII. London, Hogarth, 1958, pp. 218–226.

39 Freud, S. "On Narcissism: An Introduction" (first published in 1914). *Standard Edition,* Vol. XIV. London, Hogarth, 1957, pp. 73–102.

40 Freud, S. "Instincts and Their Vicissitudes" (first published in 1915). *Standard Edition,* Vol. XIV. London, Hogarth, 1957, pp. 117–140.

41 Freud, S. "The Unconscious" (first published in 1915). *Standard Edition,* Vol. XIV. London, Hogarth, 1957, pp. 166–204.

42 Freud, S. "A Metapsychological Supplement to the Theory of Dreams" (first published in 1917). *Standard Edition,* Vol. XIV. London, Hogarth, 1957, pp. 222–235.

43 Freud, S. "Beyond the Pleasure Principle" (first published in 1920). *Standard Edition,* Vol. XVIII. London, Hogarth, 1955, pp. 7–64.

44 Freud, S. "The Ego and the Id" (first published in 1923). *Standard Edition,* Vol. XIX. London, Hogarth, 1961, pp. 12–59.

45 Freud, S. "The Economic Problem of Masochism" (first published in 1924). *Standard Edition,* Vol. XIX. London, Hogarth, pp. 159–170.

46 Freud, S. "A Note Upon the 'Mystic Writing-Pad' " (first published in 1925). *Standard Edition,* Vol. XIX. London, Hogarth, 1961, pp. 227–232.

47 Freud, S. "Negation" (first published in 1925). *Standard Edition,* Vol. XIX. London, Hogarth, 1961, pp. 235–239.

48 Freud, S. "Inhibitions, Symptoms, and Anxiety" (first published in 1926). *Standard Edition,* Vol. XX. London, Hogarth, 1959, pp. 87–172.

49 Freud, S. "Civilization and Its Discontents" (first published in 1930). *Standard Edition,* Vol. XXI. London, Hogarth, 1961, pp. 64–145.

50 Freud, S. *New Introductory Lectures on Psychoanalysis.* New York, Norton, 1933.

51 Freud, S. *An Outline of Psychoanalysis* (first published in 1940). New York, Norton, 1949.

52 Galambos, R. Suppression of auditory nerve activity by stimulation of efferent fibers to the cochlea. *Fed. Proc. 14:*53, 1955.

53 Gifford, S. Sleep, time and the early ego: Comments on the development of the 24-hour sleep-wakefulness pattern as a precursor of ego functioning. *J. Amer. Psychoanal. Ass. 8:*5–42, 1960.

54 Granit, R. "Centrifugal Control of Sensory Measures." *Receptors and Sensory Perception.* New Haven and London, Yale Univ. Press, 1955, pp. 103–112.

55 Granit, R., and Kadda, B. R. Influence of stimulation of central nervous structures on muscle spindles in cat. *Acta Physiol. Scand. 27:*130–160, 1952.

56 Greenacre, P. The predisposition of anxiety. *Psychoanal. Quart. 10:*66–94, 610–638, 1941.

57 Greenacre, P. Infant reactions to restraint; problems in fate of infantile aggression. *Amer. J. Orthopsychiat. 14:*204–218, 1944.

58 Greenacre, P. The biological economy of birth. *Psychoanal. Stud. Child 1:*31–51, 1945.

59 Greenacre, P. Toward an understanding of the physical nucleus of some defence reactions. *Int. J. Psycho-Anal. 39:*69–76, 1958.

60 Hagbarth, K. E., and Kerr, D. I. B. Central influences on spinal afferent conduction. *J. Neurophysiol. 17:*295–307, 1954.

61 Hartmann, H. *Ego Psychology and the Problem of Adaptation* (first published in 1939). New York, Int. Univ. Press, 1958.

62 Hartmann, H. Comments on the psychoanalytic theory of the ego. *Psychoanal. Stud. Child 5:*74–95, 1950.

63 Hartmann, H. Psychoanalysis and developmental psychology. *Psychoanal. Stud. Child 5:*7–17, 1950.

64 Hartmann, H. Contribution to the metapsychology of schizophrenia. *Psychoanal. Stud. Child 8:*177–198, 1953.

65 Hartmann, H., and Kris, E. The genetic approach in psychoanalysis. *Psychoanal. Stud. Child 1:*11–29, 1945.

66 Hartmann, H., Kris, E., and Loewenstein, R. M. Comments on the formation of psychic structure. *Psychoanal. Stud. Child 2:*11–38, 1946.

67 Hartmann, H., Kris, E., and Loewenstein, R. M. Notes on the theory of aggression. *Psychoanal. Stud. Child 3/4:*9–36, 1949.

68 Holt, R. R. Beyond vitalism and mechanism: A contribution to a discussion of psychic energy. Unpublished manuscript, 1962. Abstract in *J. Amer. Psychoanal Ass. 11:*608–609, 1963.

69 Jones, E. *The Life and Work of Sigmund Freud,* Vol. I. New York, Basic Books, 1953.

70 Kris, E. The significance of Freud's earliest discoveries. *Int. J. Psycho-Anal. 31:*108–116, 1950.

71 Kris, E. Introduction to S. Freud, *Origins of Psychoanalysis.* New York, Basic Books, 1954, pp. 3–47.

72 Kubie, L. S. Some implications for psychoanalysis of modern concepts of the organization of the brain. *Psychoanal. Quart. 22:*21–68, 1953.

73 Lewin, B. Sleep, the mouth and the dream screen. *Psychoanal. Quart. 15:*419–434, 1946.

74 Lilly, J. C. Mental effects of reduction of ordinary levels of physical stimuli on intact, healthy persons. *Psychiat. res. Rep. 5:*1–9, 1956.

75 Lindsley, D. B. Physiological psychology. *Annu. Rev. Psychol. 7:*323–348, 1956.

76 Livingston, R. B. "Central Control of Afferent Activity." In *Reticular Formation of the Brain,* edited by H. H. Jasper *et al.* Boston, Little, Brown & Co., 1958, pp. 177–185.

77 Magni, F., Melyak, R., Moruzzi, G., and Smith, C. J. Direct pyramidal influences on the dorsal column nuclei. *Arch. Ital. Biol. 97:*357–377, 1959.

78 Magoun, H. W. "Non-specific Brain Mechanisms." In *Biological and Biochemical Bases of Behavior,* edited by H. F. Harlow and C. N. Woolsey. Madison, Univ. of Wisconsin Press, 1958, pp. 25–36 (pp. 29–33).

79 Metcalf, D. R. Personal communications, 1962–63.

80 Modell, A. H. In report of panel on "The concept of psychic energy." *J. Amer. Psychoanal. Ass. 11:*605–618, 1963.

81 Nunberg, H. *Principles of Psychoanalysis.* New York, Int. Univ. Press, 1955.

82 Olds, J. and Milner, P. Positive reinforcement prdouced by electrical stimulation of septal area and other regions of rat brain. *J. comp. physiol. Psychol. 47:*419–427, 1954.

83 Perl, E. R., Whitlock, D. G., and Gentry, J. R. Cutaneous projection to second-order neurons of the dorsal column system. *J. Neurophysiol. 25:*337–358, 1962.

84 Pribram, K. H. "The Neuropsychology of Sigmund Freud." In *Experimental Foundations of Clinical Psychology,* edited by A. J. Bachrach. New York, Basic Books, 1962, pp. 442–468.

85 Rapaport, D. The theory of ego autonomy: A generalization. *Bull. Menninger Clin. 22:*13–35, 1958.

86 Rapaport, D., and Gill, M. M. The points of view and assumptions of metapsychology. *Int. J. Psycho-Anal. 40:*153–162, 1959.

87 Rubinfine, D. L. A survey of Freud's writings on earliest psychic functioning. *J. Amer. Psychoanal. Ass. 9:*610–625, 1961.

88 Satterfield, J. H. Effect of sensorimotor cortical stimulation upon cuneate nuclear output through medial lemniscus in cat. *J. nerv. ment. Dis. 135:*507–512, 1962.

89 Scherrer, H., and Hernández-Peón, R. Inhibitory influence of reticular formation upon synaptic transmission in gracilis nucleus. *Fed. Proc. 14:*132, 1955.

90 Scherrer, H., and Hernández-Peón, R. Hemmung postsynaptischer po-

tentiale im nucleus gracilis. *Pflüger's Arch. ges. Physiol. 267:*434–445, 1958.
91 Solomon, P., *et al. Sensory Deprivation.* Cambridge, Harvard Univ. Press, 1961.
92 Spitz, R. A. Anxiety in infancy: A study of its manifestations in the first year of life. *Int. J. Psycho-Anal. 31:*138–143, 1950.
93 Spitz, R. A. Relevancy of direct infant observation. *Psychoanal. Stud. Child 5:*66–73, 1950.
94 Spitz, R. A. The psychogenic diseases in infancy: An attempt at their etiologic classification. *Psychoanal. Stud. Child 6:*255–275, 1951.
95 Spitz, R. A. *No and Yes: On the Genesis of Human Communication.* New York, Int. Univ. Press, 1957.
96 Spitz, R. A. *A Genetic Field Theory of Ego Formation; Its Implications for Pathology.* New York, Int. Univ. Press, 1959.
97 Spitz, R. A. Some early prototypes of ego defenses. *J. Amer. Psychoanal. Ass. 9:*626–651, 1961.
98 Tennes, K., and Lampl, E. Stranger and separation anxiety. *J. nerv. ment. Dis. 139:*247–254, 1964.
99 Wessel, M. A., *et al.* Paroxysmal fussing in infancy, sometimes called "colic." *Pediatrics 14:*421–434, 1954.

FIVE

Freud's Project: An Open, Biologically Based Model for Psychoanalysis

KARL PRIBRAM, M.D.

Biological matters in psychiatry are perceived in several ways. For the most part, biochemical etiologies are called to mind, inherited individual differences are sought, or the effect of some psychological process (e.g., stress) on the physiology of the organism is evaluated. Generally in contrast to these "biological" and "organic" approaches are those which concentrate on the psychological and social determinants of mental health and illness.

There is another biology, however, a biology which shows a special kinship to just these nonorganic, seemingly nonbiologic psychologies and psychiatries. This other biology is *neuro*biology—the study of the organic system whose office it is to organize, to structure the psychological and social functions of such concern to nonorganicists. Paradoxically, it was this other biology that spawned today's nonorganic views. It is my opinion that advances in research methods make it probable that neurobiology can again contribute substantially to psychiatry if permitted, i.e., if readmitted for serious consideration.

I have pointed out elsewhere (*16*) that the psychoanalytic model from which much of today's psychological (*20*) and psychiatric (*7*) theory derives is fundamentally a *neuro*psychological model. The neurological aspects of the model were abandoned by Freud and therefore failed to motivate neurophysiological research. Despite this, many of the neurological conceptions

This manuscript was prepared by the author during tenure on career grant No. MH–15,214–02 from the U.S. Public Health Service. For the past two years he has worked on the analysis of Freud's 1895 Project with someone who has expressed the wish to remain anonymous. Needless to say, the present manuscript owes much to this collaboration.

contained in his model have a current ring to them—the technical advances of the past half-century make the neurophysiological hypotheses derived from the model now testable. Further, specification of the neurological detail of the model, by producing a "real world" referent, can considerably clarify issues hitherto limited to metapsychological analysis.

My proposal is that we take seriously the detail—in its *structured* combination of the neurological and psychological—with which the psychoanalytic model is replete. The richness which the model provides is lost as long as its verbal currency fails to be tested against experimental standards; and today's available neurophysiological, neurobehavioral, and experimental behavioral techniques leave no excuse for failure to make such tests.

CATHEXIS—AN EXAMPLE

Let me illustrate: Freud bases his construction on the concept of a unitary quantity of neural excitation and the tendency of nerve tissues to discharge this quantity—i.e., on the all-or-none characteristic of the transmitted nerve impulse. However, he recognizes (as did most other neurologists of the 1890's) that this is not the whole story. Nerve tissue shows local, nontransmitted waxing and waning—graded changes—of excitatory potential: in axons electronic phenomena occur; at synaptic junctions and in dendrites potential changes are preponderantly graded. These graded mechanisms of neural excitation have recently become the focus of a great deal of neuropsychological research as the tools for precise investigation have become available. It has become recognized that the graded mechanisms are intrinsically important—that they are to be viewed as more than subthreshold phenomena which, when summed, lead to nerve impulses. Bishop (*3*), a leading investigator of dendritic mechanisms, has gone so far as to suggest that the graded mechanisms represent *the* important functional states of the central nervous system, that nerve impulses merely transmit information about such states from one part of the nervous system to another. The psychoanalytic model recognizes graded, local excitations of neural tissue as cathexes:

> If we combine this account of neurones with an approach on the lines of quantity theory we arrive at the idea of a "cathected" neurone (*N*) filled with a certain quantity (*Q'n*) though at other times it may be empty.[1]

And further:

> The principle of inertial finds expression in the hypothesis of a current passing from the cell processes of dendrites to the axone. Each single neurone is thus a model

[1]Sigmund Freud, "Project for a Scientific Psychology," *The Origins of Psychoanalysis: Letters to Wilhelm Fliess, Drafts and Notes, 1887–1902,* edited by M. Bonaparte, A. Freud, and E. Kris (N.Y., Basic Books, 1954), p. 358. Subsequent quotations from Freud identified only by page number are from this source.

of the nervous system as a whole, with its division into two classes of neurones—the axone being its organ of discharge.—(p. 359)

By implication dendrites (and somata) are the organs primarily responsible for cathexis.

Freud's 1895 model attributed delay to core-brain mechanisms—his nuclear "psi" system:

The system phi might be the group of neurones which receive external stimuli, while the system psi might contain the neurones which receive endogenous excitations. . . . And in fact we know from anatomy that there is a system of neurones (the grey matter of the spinal cord) which is alone in contact with the external world, and a superimposed system (the grey matter of the brain) which has no direct peripheral contacts but which is responsible for the development of the nervous system and for the psychical functions. The primary [primitive] brain gives no bad picture of the characteristics we have attributed to the system psi, if we may assume that paths lead directly, and independently of phi, from the brain to the interior of the body. The derivation and original significance of the primary brain is unknown to anatomists; on our theory it must have been neither more nor less than a sympathetic ganglion.

Further on:

In this way psi is cathected from phi with quantities which, in the normal course of things, are small. While the *quantity* of the phi excitation is expressed in psi as complexity, the *quality* is expressed topographically, since, in accordance with the anatomical relations, the different sense organs communicate only with particular psi neurones. But psi also receives cathexes from the interior of the body, and it seems reasonable to divide the psi-neurones into two groups; the neurones of the pallium which are cathected from phi, and the nuclear neurones which are cathected from the endogenous paths of conduction.—(p. 377)

Neurophysiological tests.—Cathexis and current are opposed in the model. Cathexis accounts for the process of delay, current for the processes of discharge. On the neurological level the concept "delay" has never been put to test. True enough, when excitation fails to produce nerve impulses, delay in discharge is what occurs. In an experiment by Gloor (*8*), for instance, stimulation within one limbic structure (amygdala) increased the graded potential changes recorded from another (the dendritic layer of the hippocampus), and no nerve impulses were generated there (i.e., there was no increase in discharge from the fornix, the major output system from the hippocampus) ; and Eccles (*6*) has found that excitation reaching dendrites of the hippocampus very often fails to generate sufficient depolarization to result in a propagated nerve discharge. These experimental results are compatible with the neurological rudiments of the psychoanalytic model, but experimental support for functional significance is lacking to date. Does the graded response mechanism really function to *delay* discharge, or is it merely an indication that discharge failed of achievement? The psychoanalytic model demands "delay"; more ordinary neurophysiology is satisfied when it can be shown that graded response mechanisms, when appropriately integrated, do result in discharge. Techniques *are* available to test the delay hypothesis. Adey (*1*) and his collaborators have devised methods to study the impedance, and therefore the capacitance and resistance, of central nervous system structures in the awake, performing organism. What, if any, correlations can be demonstrated among changes in capacitance of a neural structure in situations that demand delay? Specifically, is the capacitance of cerebral tissue involved when the organism performs delay tasks, such as delayed reaction or delayed alternation, but not when simple discrimination choices are required? Already we know that removal of certain parts of the cerebral cortex selectively impairs performance of delay tasks, leaving simple discriminations uninfluenced (*15, 19*). Do removals of these areas alter cerebral capacitance?

Psychoanalytic formulation.—Taken seriously, therefore, the concept cathexis in the psychoanalytic model leads to some interesting neurobehavioral and neurophysiological experiments. Perhaps of equal interest would be a consequence that could be attained only by attention to the neural detail of the model. Psychoanalytic theory has had considerable difficulty with the concept of "binding," and here a neurological contribution to metapsychology could prove rewarding.

Freud meets the problem for the first time, because he has constructed a neurological model in which cathexis and discharge are opposed. Yet ordinarily, when two neurones are highly cathected, discharge betewen them is facilitated: "A process of this kind is termed 'summation.' The psi-paths of conductance are filled by summation until they become permeable. It is evidently the smallness of the separate stimuli that enables summation to occur" (p. 378). But now, more specifically:

> Every psi neurone must in general be presumed to have several paths of connection with other neurones—that is, several contact-barriers (synapses). It is on this point that the possibility depends of the excitation having a choice of path, determined by facilitation. This being so, it is quite clear that the condition of facilitation of each contact-barrier must be independent of that of all the others in the same psi neurone. Otherwise, there would once again be no possibility of one path being preferred to another—no motive, that is. From this we can draw the negative inference as to the nature of the condition of "facilitation." If we imagine a neurone filled with quantity (*Q'n*)—i.e., cathected—we can only suppose that this quantity is uniformly distributed over all regions of the neurone, including all its contact barriers. On the other hand, there is no difficulty in supposing that, in the case of a quantity (*Q'n*) in a condition of flow (the nerve impulse), it will take only one particular path through the neurone; so that only one of the contact-barriers will be influenced by that quantity (*Q'n*) and acquire facilitation from it. Therefore facilitation cannot be based upon a cathexis that is retained. . .—(p. 362)

Note that these passages again oppose cathexis and the nerve impulse, current in flow; and note also that facilitation of a current in flow is produced through summation of excitation in the psi *paths of conduction.* This does *not* mean that facilitation is produced by summation of excitation in psi *neurones,* since excitation retained in psi neurones (i.e., retained cathexis) does *not* lead to facilitation. Only when quantity is absorbed by the synapse (as a consequence of use) does facilitation result.

> Our first idea might be that [facilitation] consists in an absorption of quantity (*Q'n*) by the contact barriers . . . we cannot yet tell whether any equivalent effect is produced by the passage of a given quantity (*Q'n*) three times and by the passage of a quantity (*Q'n*) three times as great once only.—(p. 363)

The result of the fact that quantity can be "absorbed" by the synapse suggests that it may be absorbed by the remainder of the neuron as well—that when this occurs, cathexes are retained—and this is later made explicit:

> We must conclude that matters are so constituted that when there is a lateral cathexis [cathexis of a network of neurons in psi, tangential to, i.e., branching out from, the main paths of conducted discharge] small quantities (*Q'n*) can flow through facilitations which could normally be passed only by large ones. The lateral cathexis, as it were, "binds" a certain amount of the quantity passing through the neurone.—(p. 396)

Binding in Freud's original model is thus conceived as the major mechanism through which large quantities of excitation are prevented from immediately discharging through motor action. Binding of these large quantities makes possible selective, appropriately timed, discharge by *small* quantities much as charged condensor-resistor networks can be selectively activated by small quantities of electric current. The binding of excitation by neurons is therefore the mechanism basic to the secondary process. (The quotation above from p. 396 is preceded by the sentence: "Thus, *the secondary process is a recapitulation of the original course of excitation in psi, but at a lower level, with smaller quantities.*") Again, it must be emphasized that the *course* of excitation proceeds at a lower level, with smaller quantities—that this course is taken only when larger quantities are *bound* by lateral cathexis.

What then is nonbound, i.e., free, excitation? Freud repeatedly refers to shifting cathexes, displacement of excitation, and the like. Passages from a description of the development of the ego are illuminating:

> The . . . nuclear neurones abut ultimately upon the paths of conduction from the interior of the body . . . continuously filled with quantity; and since the nuclear neurones are prolongations of these paths of conduction, they too must remain filled with quantity. The quantity in them will flow away in proportion to the resistances met with in its course, until the next resistances are greater than the quotient of quantity (*Q'n*) available for the current. But at this point the whole cathectic mass is in a state of equilibrium. . . . In the inside of this structure which constitutes the

ego, the cathexis will by no means be everywhere equal; it need only be *proportionally* equal—that is, in relation to the facilitations.

If the level of the cathexis in the nucleus of the ego rises, the ego will be able to extend its area; if it sinks, the ego will narrow concentrically. At a given level and a given extension of the ego there will be no obstacle to displacement taking place within the region of its cathexis.—(p. 427)

Now, what about this "displacement"? It occurs most readily in dreams: "... characteristic of dreams is *the ease with which quantity (Q'n) is displaced* in them and thus the way in which B is replaced by a C which is superior to it quantitatively" (p. 404). Displacement also occurs in psychopathology: "... only the distribution of quantity has been altered. Something has been added to A that has been substracted from B. The pathological process is one of *displacement,* such as we have come to know in dreams, and is hence a primary process" (p. 407).

On superficial reading these passages may appear to be full of contradictions. The ego, an equilibrated mass of cathected neurons, makes possible secondary processes (such as thinking) which depend on paths being facilitated by small quantities of discharge. Yet within this same ego a primary process, *displacement* of quantity, can occur, albeit only during dreams and in psychopathology.

What is important to note is that displacement, a shift in quantity, is conceived to occur via a primary process, i.e., a process of sudden discharge. When complete discharge is restricted, as by the presence of a powerful ego (i.e., a set of neurons with ability to bind excitation), the result is the sudden displacement of quantity via nerve impulse activity from one neuronal pool to another. Cathexes have thus been shifted, but not in some mysterious way—shift has resulted from a circumscribed localized discharge to neighboring neurones.

ATTENTION AND REINFORCEMENT ANOTHER EXAMPLE

What then determines the difference between this pathological psi process and a normal one? Freud answers this explicitly: "... the mechanism of attention will regulate the displacement of ego cathexes" (p. 428).

Attention, in the psychoanalytic model, results from progressively developed comparison and feedback process which produce a match between an expectation and indications of reality. Again, the detail of this process is replete with neurological referents which can be directly tested with today's available neurophysiological and neurobehavioral techniques.

Comparison, which determines attention, results from the operation of a series of heirarchically arranged feedback loops which Freud calls the process of satisfaction—a fundamental mechanism in determining the construction of the individual:

The filling of nuclear neurones in psi has as its consequence an effort to discharge, an impetus which is released along motor pathways. Experience shows that the first path to be followed is that leading to internal change (e.g., emotional expression, screaming, or vascular innervation). But, as we showed at the beginning of the discussion [p. 357], no discharge of this kind can bring about any relief of tension, because endogenous stimuli continue to be received in spite of it and the psi-tension is re-established. Here a removal of the stimulus can only be affected by an intervention which will temporarily stop the release of quantity (*Q'n*) in the interior of the body, and an intervention of this kind requires an alteration in the external world (e.g., the supply of nourishment or the proximity of the sexual object), and this as a "specific action," can only be brought about in particular ways. At early stages the human organism is incapable of achieving this action. It is brought about by extraneous help, when the attention of an experienced person has been drawn to the child's condition by a discharge taking place along the path of internal change (e.g., by the child's screaming). This path of discharge thus acquires an extremely important secondary function—viz., of bringing about an understanding with other people; and the original helplessness of human beings is thus the primal source of all moral motives. [Cf. pp. 422–23.]

When the extraneous helper has carried out the specific action in the external world on behalf of the helpless subject, the latter is in a position, by means of reflex contrivances, immediately to perform what is necessary in the interior of his body in order to remove the endogenous stimulus. This total event even then constitutes an "experience of satisfaction," which has the most momentous consequences in the functional development of the individual. For three things occur in this psi-system: (1) A lasting discharge is effected, so that the urgency which had generated unpleasure in *W* is brought to an end. (2) A cathexis corresponding to the perception of an object occurs in one or more neurones of the pallium [p. 377]. (3) At other points of the pallium a report is received of the discharge brought about by the release of the reflex movement which followed the specific action. A facilitation is then established between these cathexes [2, 3] and the nuclear neurones [which were being cathected from endogenous sources during the state of urgency].

The report of the reflex discharge comes about owing to the fact that every movement, as a result of its collateral consequences, gives rise to fresh sensory excitations—of the skin and muscles—which produce a *motor* [*or kinesthetic*] *image*.—(pp. 379–80)

Note here that Freud attributes the origins of satisfying experiences to intervention by a care-taking person. Only by such intervention can wishes develop sufficient complexity; only by such intervention can the psychological structure become organized. As Strachey points out: "In none of Freud's later formulations of this idea has the present one [quoted above] been equalled or surpassed: it indicates the part played by object-relations in the transition from the pleasure to the reality principle" (p. 379).

According to this model wishes are the "residues," i.e., the memory traces, of satisfactory experiences (p. 383), and attention becomes possible when states of craving, having been, through experience, altered into states of wishing, become further modified into states of expecting—states that allow thinking and reality-testing:

This state of attention has a prototype in the "experience of satisfaction" [p. 380] (which is of such importance for the whole course of development) and the repetitions of that experience—states of craving which develop into states of wishing and states of expecting. I have shown [Part 1, Sections 16–18] that these states contain biological justification of all thought. The psychical situation in these states is as follows. The craving involves a state of tension in the ego; and as a result of it the idea of the loved object (the "wishful idea") is cathected. Biological experience has taught us that this idea must not be cathected so intensely that it might be confused with a perception, and that its discharge must be postponed till indications of quality arise from it which prove that it is real—that the cathexis is a perceptual one. If a perception arises which is identical with or similar to the wishful idea, the perception finds its neurones precathected by the wish—that is to say, some or all of them are cathected, according to the degree to which the idea and the perception tally. The difference between the idea and the perception then gives rise to the process of thought; and this reaches its conclusion when a path has been found by which the discordant perceptual cathexes can be merged into ideational cathexes. Identity is then attained.—(pp. 417–18)

Neurophysiological tests.—Neurologically the model proposed by Freud the project is sophisticated: (1) Memory traces are conceived to be hierarchically organized. (2) *Each* memory is at least triply determined—events initiated within (drive stimuli), external to (sensory stimuli), and by (motor stimuli) the organism, compose each trace. (3) Operations (behavior and thought) are carried out by the organism as long as activated memory traces fail to be matched by current inputs.

There is a good deal of behavioral evidence in support of these propositions—e.g., see *Plans and the Structure of Behavior* (*13*). Neurological techniques are just beginning to allow an approach at this level. Doty (*5*) has produced evidence for the multiple determination of the engram, and Sharpless and Jasper (*21*) have shown that habituation involves changes in the neural apparatus which are highly specific to the inputs that have been experienced. Sokolov (*22*) in addition, has demonstrated that orienting occurs whenever there is a mismatch between an input and this habituated neural "model" of prior experience. His experiment is a simple one. He habituated persons to a tone beep of a certain intensity, duration, and frequency, irregularly presented. When habituation had occurred, as gauged by such physiological indices as the galvanic skin response, plethysmography, and alerting responses in the electroencephalogram, he diminished the intensity of the tone. Immediately the person again oriented. Sokolov reasoned therefore that habituation did not indicate some increased neural threshold or loss of neural sensitivity. He suggested that the habituated neural "model" served as a template against which inputs were matched. He tested his suggestion by again habituating his subject; then, instead of diminishing intensity, he *shortened* the tone beep. Orienting again took place—but now at the point when the tone ceased. In other words, the person oriented to the unexpected *silence*.

Habituation, then, can be taken as an indicator that specific changes are occurring in the central nervous system, changes that will influence subsequent reactions to stimuli. Yet these changes are not so simply brought about as these initial experiments would lead us to believe. Experiments performed in my laboratory (*10*) have shown that the probability of orienting is dependent on another set of variables which Lacey and Lacey (*11*) have related to the stability of the person's autonomic effector mechanisms. Further, some indicators of orienting (such as the galvanic skin response) seem to signal that a process is taking place which is not directly involved in alerting (as measured by the electroencephalogram) : the galvanic skin response and electroencephalographic components of the orienting reaction can be dissociated by central nervous system lesions (*9*). These lesions do not alter simple discrimination learning or performance; some of the lesions do, however, interfere with tasks that involve delay, and others alter the ability to transfer what the subject has learned in one situation to another (*2*). The suggestion is that whenever a galvanic skin response is obtained a more complex registration of inputs is being achieved, a registration that allows flexibility in subsequent use beyond some simple match-mismatch mechanism necessary to discriminative performances. The studies have not proceeded to the point where the details of Freud's richly specified psychoanalytic model of reality testing can be brought under experimental scrutiny—but a direction of research has been spelled out which brings such an accomplishment within range.

Psychoanalytic formulations.—I have presented elsewhere (*17, 18*) a model based on the laboratory procedures used in experimental psychology. The suggestion was made that reinforcement (i.e., satisfaction) was a neural process which acted to progressively organize the more or less haphazard sequences of occurrences which make up the life of an organism. This neural process is rooted in habituation—inputs derived from within the organism, from its environment, and from its own actions form a neural model which is the context within which subsequent occurrences can provide *information*. Subsequent events thus become consequent—i.e., meaningful. The organism is learning. Consequences, in turn, are habituated, and, when this occurs, the context itself has been altered. Now events comparable to earlier ones no longer provide information; they match the model. However, these events may still guide performance (perceptual, motor, or thought) ; they *value* the execution of performance, they are part of the contextual matrix within which performance takes place. Other novel occurrences become informative, and the process is repeated. When information becomes organized through learning, satisfaction is experienced; when performances attain adequacy, gratification results (*14*).

This model is in some respects consonant with Freud's; it differs from the psychoanalytic mainly in that it contains no prescription for precedence of drive, perceptual, and motor occurrences and in its emphasis of the distinction between learning and performance and thus between satisfaction and gratification. Some experimental psychologists have suggested that their data fit Freud's model even more closely (e.g., Dollard and Miller [*4*]). However, these similarities are apt to prove sterile if they do not point to specific lacunae in our experimental approach to the problem at issue. One such specification can be made: Both psychoanalysis and experimental psychology have for some time focused on the problem of learning. The problem faced in the clinic, and even in the laboratory, however, is often one that involves not learning but effective unlearning. Specifically, a patient or experimental subject must restructure, reorganize, the psychic set, i.e., the neural apparatus with which he approaches occurrences. Stated in terms of the model of the process of reinforcement, the task is not so much one of acquiring information as one of changing values. This can be accomplished through learning, but experience tells us that this is not the whole story. The learner must somehow be made receptive to a change in values which allows a greater amount of gratification to result from his actions. To date, although both learning theory and psychoanalytic theory are aware of this problem, neither has had much that is testable to say about it. Questions remain to be posed in experimental terms. For the most part these would center about the problem of extinction, which until recently has received only cursory development in the experimental literature (see Lawrence and Festinger [*2*] for a review of the main problem areas). How much true "forgetting" takes place? What factors determine the persistence of behavior (perception, thought) in the face of changed conditions? Does attention per se, as suggested by Freud's model, really alter the persisting behavior? What takes place in the central nervous system when input conditions change but performance remains the same? Are the neural antecedents to such actions indentifiably *unchanged?* Can changes be effected by focusing the subject's attention on the changed input conditions? And how is this most readily accomplished?

CONCLUSION

Even partial answers to these questions would take us a distance toward open understanding of the psychoanalytic model: today, knowledge often hinges on close acquaintance with a circumscribed theoretical system; scientific assurance cannot be given to those not so acquainted. The model basic to the psychoanalytic metapsychology is, as I have here suggested, an open one—free to be tested at the neurological level by modern neurophysiological and neurobehavioral techniques, and at the psychological level by the techniques of experimental (and social) psychology, and even by computer simulation. Tests must begin by focusing on basic functions understandable to a variety of disciplines, functions such as delay, matching, and extinction; some patience will be necessary on the part of the sophisticated in every field such endeavors touch. We cannot, of course, hope to bring the entire secondary process to bay at once. However, the scientific community has devised its own form of "ego," a mechanism designed to usefully structure this necessary delay: namely, conferences and publications such as this one, since we are here dealing with a communicative network tangential to the main paths of our ingrained scientific and clinical pursuits. Do we not, as a consequence, return to these with freshly phrased expectations—perhaps a bit more appropriate to the task which confronts us? and do not these refreshments result in increasing our opportunity both for satisfaction and for gratification?

REFERENCES

1 Adey, W. R., Kado, R. T., Didio, J., and Schindler, W. J. Impedance changes in cerebral tissue accompanying learned discriminitive performance in the cat. *Exp. Neurol. 7:*259–281, 1963.

2 Bagshaw, M., and Pribram, K. H. The effect of amygdalectomy on stimulus equivalence performance in monkeys. *J. comp. physiol. Psychol.* In press.

3 Bishop, G. Natural history of the nerve impulse. *Physiol. Rev. 36:*376–399, 1956.

4 Dollard, J., and Miller, N. E. *Personality and Psychotherapy.* New York, McGraw-Hill, 1950.

5 Doty, R. W. "Conditioned Reflexes Formed and Evoked by Brain Stimulation." In *Electrical Stimulation of the Brain,* edited by D. E. Sheer. Austin, Univ. of Texas Press, 1961, pp. 397–412.

6 Eccles, J. C. *The Neurophysiological Basis of Mind.* Oxford, Clarendon Press, 1953.

7 Gill, M. M. Topography and systems in psychoanalytic theory. *Psychol. Issues 3*(2):Monograph 10, 1963.

8 Gloor, P. Electrophysiological studies on the connections of the amygdaloid nucleus in the cat. *EEG Clin. Neurophysiol. 7:*223–264, 1955.

9 Grueninger, W., Kimble, D., Grueninger, J., and Levine, S. GRS and adrenal steroid responses in frontal and normal monkeys. In preparation.

10 Koepke, J. E., and Pribram, K. H. Habituation of the GSR to repeated second stimulation. *Amer. Psychologist 19:*491, 1964.

11 Lacey, J. I., and Lacey, B. C. The relationship of resting autonomic cyclic activity to motor impulsivity. In *The Brain and Human Behavior,* edited by Solomon, Cobb, and Penfield. Baltimore, Williams and Wilkins, 1958, pp. 144–209.

12 Lawrence, D. H., and Festinger, L. *Deterrents and Reinforcement: The Psychology of Insufficient Reward.* Stanford, Stanford Univ. Press, 1962.

13 Miller, G. A., Galanter, E. H., and Pribram, K. H. *Plans and the Structure of Behavior.* New York, Henry Holt, 1960.

14 Pribram, K. H. A review of theory in physiological psychology. In *Annu. Rev. Psychol.* Palo Alto, Annual Reviews, Inc., 1960.

15 Pribram, K. H. A further experimental analysis of the behavioral deficit that follows injury to the primate frontal cortex. *Exp. Neurol. 3*:432–466, 1961.

16 Pribram, K. H. The neuropsychology of Sigmund Freud. Chapter 13 in *Experimental Foundations of Clinical Psychology,* edited by A. J. Bachrach. New York, Basic Books, 1962, pp. 442–468.

17 Pribram, K. H. Reinforcement revisited: A structural view. In *Nebraska Symposium on Motivation,* edited by M. Jones. Lincoln, Univ. of Nebraska Press, 1963, pp. 113–159.

18 Pribram, K. H. Neurological notes on the art of educating. Chapter 4 in *1964 Yearbook.* Chicago, National Society for the Study of Education, 1964, pp. 78–110.

19 Pribram, K. H., Wilson, W. A., and Connors, J. The effects of lesions of the medial forebrain on alternation behavior of rhesus monkeys. *Exp. Neurol. 6*:36–47, 1962.

20 Shakow, D., and Rapaport, D. Freud's influence on American psychology. *Psychol. Issues.* In press.

21 Sharpless, S., and Jasper, H. Habituation of the arousal reaction. *Brain 79*:655–680, 1956.

22 Sokolov, E. N. Neuronal models and the orienting reflex. In *The Central Nervous System and Behavior,* edited by M. A. B. Brazier. New York, Josiah Macy, Jr., Foundation, 1960, pp. 187–276.

SIX

A Review of Some of Freud's Biological Assumptions and Their Influence on His Theories

ROBERT R. HOLT, Ph.D.

To the contemporary student, many aspects of Freud's theories seem only partly plausible and difficult to grasp with any sense of secure understanding. Those who are predisposed to rebellion often react by rejecting psychoanalysis as a whole, or turn to a more "modern" form of it, without ever knowing just what it is they are discarding, and on the basis of some stereotyped formula like "unscientific" or "too biological." Those who are predisposed to uncritical admiration of an authentic genius, as Freud unquestionably was, accept those obscure parts of the psychoanalytic canon as the truly profound passages which are simply beyond their own capacity to follow.

To one who finds neither of these styles of reaction ego-syntonic, there remains one principal course of action: to undertake a close study of the texts themselves under light from whatever historical windows he can find open to the intellectual ambience of Freud's formative years. My own struggles for understanding have been aided first by the teaching of David Rapaport, from whom I learned how to read Freud with some structural understanding, and then by some historical readings. Of these, I would single out the brilliant series of papers by Bernfeld (in particular, *2* and *3*) and a recent doctoral

I am grateful to Dr. M. P. Amacher for a helpful reading of this paper and several valuable corrections, and also for his permission to quote from his dissertation. My friend Dr. Benjamin B. Rubinstein also earned my gratitude by a critical reading and several suggestions. This investigation was supported (in part) by a Public Health Service research career program award (number MH–K6–12,455) from the National Institute of Mental Health.

dissertation by M. Peter Amacher (*1*) entitled: "The influence of the neuroanatomy, neurophysiology and psychiatry of Freud's teachers on his psychoanalytic theories." Since the latter is as yet unpublished, I want to present a brief résumé of its main points as part of the development of my argument.

From these historical studies, the following summary formulation has forced itself on me: Many of the most puzzling and seemingly arbitrary turns of psychoanalytic theory, involving propositions that are false to the extent that they are testable at all, are either hidden biological assumptions or result directly from such assumptions, which Freud learned from his teachers in medical school. They became a basic part of his intellectual equipment, as unquestioned as the assumption of universal determinism, were probably not always recognized by him as biological, and thus were retained as necessary ingredients when he attempted to turn away from neurologizing to the construction of an abstract, psychological model.

To buttress this conclusion, I shall present, first, a summary of Amacher's findings on the doctrines of Freud's teachers, then a demonstration that their conceptions of the structure and functioning of the nervous system were incorporated into the "Project." I shall adduce evidence that, when Freud replaced the explicitly physicalistic model of the Project with a psychological one, he did so only partially and inconsistently. Next, I want to show how the same set of biological propositions were retained as fundamental assumptions in Freud's post-1900 theories, with only some terminological changes; and, finally, I shall indicate the paradoxes, inconsistencies, and other difficulties created by this set of assumptions and by Freud's ambivalence regarding the nature of the fundamental model with which he was working.

From Bernfeld's inquiries, we know that Freud received most of his education about the nervous system, its structure and functioning, during the years 1874–78 from Ernst Brücke and Theodor Meynert, who were outstanding professors at the University of Vienna medical school and were internationally known authorities; in addition, he worked in the laboratories of both men and spoke in terms of the highest admiration about each of them (*3*). He was more competitive with the younger Sigmund Exner, who was more nearly his contemporary, but who nevertheless was his instructor in physiology and his senior in Brücke's laboratory.

All three of these men wrote books between 1875 and 1894, setting forth either the actual lectures Freud attended or their essential substance. The historian Amacher has read these German tomes, informed by an acquaintance with psychoanalytic theory, and has excerpted and translated many passages that have a surprisingly familiar ring to the Freudian student. All three give an account of the structure and function of the CNS that is essentially the same and is similar to the theoretical chapter by their friend Josef

Breuer in "Studies in Hysteria" (*8*), which sketches a neuropsychology. All four of these men were members of what Bernfeld (*2*) calls "the school of Helmholtz," zealously preaching the doctrine of physicalistic physiology—an attempt to overthrow the preceding *Naturphilosophie* and vitalism by a rigorous attempt to treat the organism as a mechanical system.

Freud's teachers, Amacher demonstrates, shared "the idea that the nervous system functioned by transmitting a quantitatively variable phenomenon which was the mechanism of the nerve impulse from the afferent nerve endings to the efferent nerve endings. The entire quantity of this 'excitation' . . . originated at the afferent nerve endings"—i.e., at the sensory organs. There was no general agreement on the nature of this excitation; Brücke believed it was electrical, though he never referred to it as "energy." "They had advanced beyond the ancient idea that nervous excitation was transmitted by the movement of some sort of fluid or spirit through the [assumedly] hollow nerves, but it was still possible to think of the transmission of excitation in the nerves as analogous in many ways to the transmission of a fluid in a pipe" (*1,* Chapter 1).

Amacher makes the interesting observation that Brücke did not explicitly discuss the mind-body problem but everywhere wrote as if he assumed that all mental processes were simultaneously paralleled by physical ones. This tacit assumption "allowed him . . . to describe a process partly in physical and partly in psychological terms." "This unrestrained shifting from descriptions in terms of mind to descriptions in physical terms is characteristic of the work of Freud's teachers and of Freud," Amacher notes.

As part of his rejection of the vitalism of his own teacher, Johannes Müller, Brücke introduced the idea that there was no spontaneous central activity of the brain, but explicitly declared that the functioning of the entire brain followed the model of the reflex arc: "voluntary movements . . . too are originated by centripetal impulses; however, from them the conduction goes through parts of the cortex which serve consciousness, ideas, and will" (*9,* p. 25; translated by Amacher). The result was an implicit conception of the whole nervous system as a passive instrument which remained in a state of rest until stimulated, when it functioned so as to rid itself of the incoming exogenous energies.

One other statement of Brücke's (quoted in paraphrase not by Amacher but by Bernfeld [2]) is worthy of note: "The physical energies alone cause effects." Brücke's lectures on physiology contained a great deal about forces and energies (concepts he did not clearly differentiate), and he dwelt on the doctrine of the conservation of energy, to which his friend and colleague Helmholtz had given elegant promulgation not long before, with the "purpose of giving a sound foundation to the new physiology" (*2*). It remained an act of faith, but symbolically a very important one, to believe that the concept of energy was just what physiology needed to put it on a quantitative and thus rigorously scientific basis.

Meynert's conceptions of the nervous system were, in the respects with which we are concerned here, similar to Brücke's. Actions, the ultimate effects of consciousness, "are not the result of force innate in the brain. The brain does not, like a fixed star, radiate its own heat; it obtains all the force underlying all cerebral phenomena from outside" (*54,* p. 146; translated by Amacher). He sometimes used the term "energy" for neural impulse, but his reference to "synthetic chemical events" accompanying its passage may imply a recognition that not all the energy involved originated at the afferent nerve endings.

Exner's book is of interest largely because it contains a synthesis of the same set of ideas and appeared in 1894, when Freud was beginning to flex his own theoretical muscles and just before he wrote the Project. Exner wrote: "The excited condition of a nerve fiber appears to have no quality . . . [but] it is to the highest degree variable quantitatively" (*14,* p. 37; translated by Amacher). When this excitation reached a large enough quantity through being accumulated in a "summation center," it would be transmitted to a hypothetical "pain center." The latter could also be set in action from the activation of unpleasant memories or other cortical events. Something virtually identical with what Breuer called "tonic excitation" of a nerve center appears in Exner's discussion of sex in "every normal young man"—his cerebral "center for sexual instincts . . . has at times an increased tonus, and only a small impulse is required to establish an association between certain cortical events and this center" (*14,* p. 345; translated by Amacher). Elsewhere (*48*) I have demonstrated in considerable detail that this concept and Breuer's version of it, tonic excitation, were adopted by Freud as the original meaning of *cathexis,* and lingered on in the doctrine of "the insusceptibility to excitation of uncathected systems" (*29*). I shall therefore spend no further time on this bit of conceptual inheritance.

For convenience of exposition, I shall refer to the foregoing set of interrelated propositions about the nervous system and its functioning in relation to external inputs as "the passive reflex model."

In the preceding brief and highly selective summary I have not cited Amacher's detailed documentation of the presence of similar ideas in the works of these three of Freud's teachers, nor his presentation of certain other doctrines such as Freud's theory of learning by association (which was not very specifically psychoanalytic); nor have I brought out the qualifications and reservations with which these physiologists stated the essentials of the passive reflex model, which indicate that it was more implicit than explicit in their teachings and was probably considered a rough first approximation.

Yet it is easy to see how it was inculcated in Freud, who digested these various sources, extracted what was latent in them with brilliant clarity, and stated the implicit model with elegant economy of exposition in 1895.

II

A year after Exner's book, and only a few months after their mutual elder friend and colleague Breuer's similar neuropsychological essay, Freud turned his hand to the ambitious task of putting together the existing knowledge about the nervous system in a detailed neurological model, the psychology for neurologists that is now familiarly known as "the Project." The commitment to physicalistic physiology is obvious in its opening lines and throughout: it is an ambitious attempt to be as scientific in the nineteenth-century Helmholtzian sense as possible, which meant to be rigorously materialistic and mechanistic: ". . . to represent psychical processes as quantitatively determined states of specifiable material particles . . ." (*16*, p. 355). Indeed, so thorough-going was Freud's attempt at materialism that he adopted the Hartleyan position that the nerve impulse was a mechanical vibration of "the material particles in question . . . the neurones."

He then launches into an admirably clear formulation of "the principle of neuronic inertia, which asserts that neurones tend to divest themselves of quantity"—his shorthand term for the neural impulse conceived of as purely quantitative *à la* Exner (*16*, p. 356). Consequently, the nervous system as a whole strives to keep itself "free from stimulus. This process of discharge is the primary function of neuronic systems" (p. 357). This was the "constancy principle," which, we have seen was the prevailing, anti-vitalist neurological dogma of Freud's time.[1]

How did quantity get into the nervous system, then, if then latter did not generate any of its own? From two sources, Freud said: from external reality

[1]He had already formulated the principle of constancy in an 1893 lecture in these words: "If a person experiences a psychical impression, something in his nervous system which we will for the moment call the sum of excitation is increased. Now in every individual there exists a tendency to diminish this sum of excitation once more, in order to preserve his health" (*17*). In a published paper of the same year, he wrote: "Every occurrence, every psychic impression is supplied with a certain affective value, of which the ego rids itself either by means of a motor reaction or by a process of mental association" (*18*, p. 58). Incidentally, it is only fair to Breuer to point out that the latter did not share the view that the only energies in the nervous system are introduced from the outside: "Spontaneous awakening, which . . . can take place in complete darkness and quiet without any external stimulus, proves that the development of energy is based on the vital process of the cerebral elements themselves. A muscle remains unstimulated, quiescent, however long it has been in a state of rest . . . This is not so with the cerebral elements" (*8*, p. 196). Nevertheless, he included without question "the fact that there exists in the organism a *'tendency to keep intracerebral excitation constant'* (Freud)." (Emphasis is Breuer's; he cites no specific work of Freud's.)

via the sensory organs, and "from the somatic element itself—endogenous stimuli, which call equally for discharge. These have their origin in the cells of the body and give rise to the major needs: hunger, respiration and sexuality." In these few words are contained both a theory of reality and a theory of motivation as tension-reduction. With defiantly materialistic overtones Freud declares that "in the external world . . . there are only masses in motion and nothing else."[2] If the nerve cells, too, consisted of material particles that vibrated in accordance with the laws of motion, it is easy to see how Freud was led to the complementary assumption that external physical energies enter and traverse the nervous system almost as directly as light does a transparent body—or at least the portion (or quotient) that is not screened out by the surface of the body.

The consequence of such a conception of the nervous system as a passive conductor was that it could be disrupted or burnt out by the passage of too great a current of energy without a protective system of resistors. To take care of this problem, Freud adapted his teachers' views, which were not exactly that external energies entered the nervous system untransformed, but that the system's excitation was directly *proportional* to the amount of stimulation. in Freud's simpler model, the impinging "sums of excitation . . . from outside . . . first come up against the nerve-ending apparatus and are broken up by it into quotients . . . Here we have a first threshold. Below a certain quantity no effective quotient at all comes into being. So that the effectiveness of stimuli is restricted more or less to the *medium* quantities" (*16*, p. 374). This is what he later (*30*) called the stimulus-barrier or protective shield against stimulation.[3]

In these contexts, where Freud affirms the quantitative nature of reality, he echoes Exner's concern with the "problem of quality," which is really a major chunk of the mind-body problem: the existence of conscious phe-

[2]Note, incidentally, that in 1895 this was already an anachronistic concept of physical reality. Field theory had been implicit in Newton's laws of motion and had been made quite explicit by Maxwell in 1864; it was by no means universally believed, any more, that all energy consisted of "masses in motion." Note also the overwhelming role of energy in this concept of reality: nothing whatever is said about the static structure of the environment, the configurations of nonvibrating masses. Here is a harbinger of Freud's later persistent neglect of structural considerations and his steady preference for dynamic and economic explanations; cf. also Brücke's remark about forces as the only causes.

[3]Despite the clarity of the text, many psychoanalysts nevertheless interpret "quantity" as referring to psychic rather than to physical energy (see *57, passim*). This interpretation is attributable to the historical accident that the Project was published only in 1954, after many analysts had studied and taught the twentieth-century versions of psychoanalytic theory for many years. In those familiar works, "cathexis" does refer to psychic energy, and so it is natural to read in the later meaning when one encounters the same words, even though written at a time when Freud had a strong emotional identification with physicalistic physiology, one of the central tenets of which was the rejection of vitalistic notions like psychic energy (cf. *47, 50*).

nomena, or qualities, in a material world. "Consciousness gives us what we call 'qualities,'" he wrote; "We may ask *how* qualities originate and *where* qualities originate. . . . Not in the external world" (*16,* p. 369). He decided, after considering various possibilities, that there had to be a special system of perceptual neurones "whose states of excitation give rise to the different qualities—are, that is to say, conscious sensations." And the vehicle of quality was the frequency of the vibratory energy, which he called "period." This was an allowable hypothesis, "for the mechanics of the physicists have assigned this temporal attribute even to the motions of masses in the external world" (*16,* p. 371).

Turning back to the impingements of energy from within the organism, we should take notice of the fact that, although Freud's concept was essentially the same as that of his teachers, there is one major difference: they made no distinction as to relative odiousness between the stimuli arising from the two sources, but Freud noted one critical difference: "The organism cannot withdraw itself from them [endogenous stimuli] as it does from external stimuli" (p. 357). This fact upsets the principle of inertia "from the very first," for they cease only if "certain definite conditions are realized in the external world." Because of the "exigencies of life," to do so usually requires more energy than the endogenous quantities themselves provide, so the system "must learn to tolerate a store of quantity sufficient to meet the demands for specific actions" (p. 358). Brücke had postulated a superficially similar central summation of excitations, but of Freud's elders only Exner had what we can recognize as a central theory of motivation or a concept of drive.[4] From the beginning,[5] however, motivation was for Freud a matter of the reduction of tensions or energic inputs.

As I have pointed out elsewhere (*47*), Freud came up against an inability to furnish a satisfactory account of defense or of consciousness, because in both cases he got into a kind of regress in which he did not know when to stop. Something more like a person or a knower had to "notice" the danger signal or the indication of quality, he felt, not recognizing that the model

[4]To be sure, they spoke about "instinct," to make the point that it was a superfluous concept for human physiology; but they used the term *Instinkt,* not *Trieb.* No confusion would be entailed if it were not for the unfortunate British insistence on rendering Trieb as "instinct," despite the fact that both German words have unambiguous cognates in English. Exner, in his theory of emotions, came closest to what could pass today as a theory of drives; Amacher points out a number of resemblances between his account and Freud's in the "Three essays on the theory of sexuality" (*23*). In a personal communication, Amacher adds: "Meynert was critically concerned with drives as they determined the reaction of the *Ich.* Exner's whole book leads up to his chapter on the instincts, which involved excitation from endogenous nerve endings."

[5]An even clearer statement of the male sexual drive as originating in a somatic tension that pours drive-stimuli into the psychic apparatus until removed by appropriate action occurs in Freud (*20,* pp. 108f).

he had constructed was so well supplied with feedback loops (at least five may be distinguished) that it was as self-regulating as any cybernetic servo-mechanism of today. Though Freud was many decades ahead of his time he was too much its prisoner to see that the informational return provided by a feedback loop could obviate any hypothetical nonconscious process of attention; ironically, he concluded that he had failed to provide a "mechanical (automatic) explanation" (p. 417) and committed his first great infidelity to the anti-vitalism of his teachers: he postulated an observing ego. True, they used the same term (*"Ich"*), and Meynert had a rather elaborate and Freudian-sounding ego-theory; but they used *Ich* in the same way that Freud did at first in the Project, when it was merely "the totality of cathected neurones." In the end, however, he was forced to revive an essentially philosophical conception of the kind Johannes Müller would have felt at home with, in which the ego is a prime mover, the willer and ultimate knower, and thus a vitalistic homunculus with some degree of autonomy.

This was one respect in which the Project failed. Despite Freud's great ingenuity and inventive resourcefulness, it also failed in a number of other ways: for example, concepts underwent such changes from one section to another as to be contradictory, as he molded them to the needs of the problem under discussion at the moment. It is worth noticing, however, that Freud simply went ahead and did the best he could, letting the contradictions stand and introducing nonphysicalistic concepts when he could see no other way out. Paradoxical as it may sound, this was to be one of his saving traits as a scientist, his way of enabling his theory to grow and new ideas to emerge before he was ready to fit them smoothly into the existing corpus.

Amacher points out a number of other points made in the Project that were obviously foreshadowed by one or more of Freud's teachers, but I shall not review them here. I am deliberately focusing attention on a limited range of propositions about the nature of external reality and about the passive, reflex nature of the nervous system, because these determine the characteristics of the theoretical model and shape a great many subsequent assumptions and propositions. Moreover, these are the parts of the theory that have become testable and have been overthrown.

III

Only a few months after Freud had sent the first sections of the Project to Fliess, he became increasingly dissatisfied with it. For several years thereafter he blew hot and cold, at times rejecting the whole enterprise as "philosophical stammering," at other times making fresh efforts to rearrange its parts in a hope that it might begin to work. Finally, he turned his back on the attempt to work with an anatomical-physiological model and produced his first great work, "The Interpretation of Dreams" (*21*). As I have asserted elsewhere (*50*), this was not an isolated decision but was part of a major turn in Freud's whole life—changes in his type of professional practice, the nature of his research, his friendships, his self-understanding, his very sense of identity. It is not easy to appraise these changes accurately. In many respects Freud seems to have undergone a profound reorientation as he turned from being a neuroanatomical researcher to a clinical neurologist who experimented with psychotherapy, finally becoming the first psychoanalyst (*13*). We would be poor psychologists, however, if we imagined that there was not at least as much continuity as change in this development. Twenty years of passionate investment in the study of the nervous system were not easily tossed aside by Freud's decision to become a psychologist instead and to work with a purely abstract, hypothetical model.

Yet this is the usual assumption—that, beginning with 1900, Freud rejected all physiologizing and all attempts to localize the parts of the "psychic apparatus" within the substance of the brain.[6] I wish that there were time to give a full documentation for my contention that Freud did not succeed in making a clean break with his past theoretical position (I have cited some of the most relevant passages in another paper [*47*]; see also below). I shall have to content myself with the assertions (*a*) that he never gave up the hope to "give up explaining things psychologically and start finding a firm basis in physiology!" as he wrote to Fliess in 1896, after his first disillusionment with the Project; (*b*) that he continued to use neurological terminology and propositions from the Project in Chapter VII even after explicitly disclaiming the attempt to do so, despite the fact that the new model had no place for these elements; (*c*) that he did not attain methodological clarity about the nature and status of the non-neurological theory he ostensibly was building, particularly *vis-à-vis* the mind-body problem (cf. *68*); and (*d*) that, whenever the nature of his data demanded it, he lapsed into the silent assumption that the psychic apparatus was the brain, that the "pathways" in it were nerve tracts, and that the energy it used was physical in nature, located in and affecting the corporeal substance of the organs. I hope that some of the evidence for these points will become apparent later, as I discuss some of the theoretical difficulties occasioned by this ambivalence.

It may be appropriate also to say a few words about theoretical models[7]

---

[6]In the panel on psychic energy referred to above (cf. *57*), I found myself very much in the minority in the position I argue here.

[7]"In the last couple of decades the model has been brought out to replace the theory, which has fallen into disrepute because it has claimed to state truth without assimilating its contradictions. Truth is all-or-none. There are would-be truths but no half truths. The model does not claim truth-value. It is an aspiration for a generalization. It may be employed for a limited universe. You see how well you can get your data to fit, perhaps adjusting the model to make the fit better. If the fit is good, you have a good summary of these data and then you may use the model to predict other data and test it empirically. If the prediction is borne out, the model gains in dignity and importance" (*7*). For a discussion paralleling and supporting that in the text paragraph, see Black (*6*).

and the ways in which Freud used them. A model is a formal structure the parts of which are manipulable to generate consequences, and which in one or more important ways is isomorphic with observed reality. It may be a physical replica or mock-up in which the isomorphy is visual resemblance (a model car) ; it may be a physical system in which the emphasis is on one or more modes of functioning (the iron wire model of neural conduction or an analog computer) ; it may be a purely formal and abstract set of symbols and rules for their manipulation (mathematical models of various types of learning). In these sophisticated days, when there is so much self-conscious and explicit model-building, it is easy to overlook the fact that any extensive theory involves some kind of implicit model. In this last sense Freud always worked with some type of theoretical model, though he rarely used the term, and for all I know never heard of it in today's sense—certainly it did not become familiar to most of us until well after Freud's death. Yet a *bourgeois gentilhomme* may speak prose all his life without realizing it; and Molière's quip contains something very apposite, for naive speakers of a highly inflected language may scrupulously observe all its complicated rules—which can be extracted as a functioning formal system, a model—without ever being able to formulate one of them.

When a theory has as many difficulties as psychoanalysis does, a useful way of trying to understand and order it is to inquire into the nature of the model of man that it involves. Let us then examine some of Freud's major theoretical works from this standpoint. Our task is made easier by virtue of the fact that he spoke often about the psychic apparatus and even provided a few diagrams of this conceptual structure, indicating that he was thinking in terms of a theoretical model whatever his terminology.

Freud proposed two principal versions of the psychic apparatus: the topographic systems of Chapter VII, "Interpretation of Dreams," and the so-called structural or tripartite model of the ego, id, and superego. He began his description of the topographic model by stating: "All our psychical activity starts from stimuli (whether internal or external) and ends in innervations" (*21*, p. 537). Note, as Strachey does, the ambiguity of this last anatomical term, which is also used "to mean the transmission of energy *into a system of nerves*"—emphasis added. This is only one page after the famous statement: "I shall remain upon psychological ground." Freud then mentions in passing, as if it were almost too obvious to dwell on, "a requirement with which we have long been familiar, namely that the psychical apparatus must be constructed like a reflex apparatus. Reflex processes remain the model of every psychical function" (*21*, p. 538). So faithfully did he follow this assumed requirement that the diagrams accompanying this part of the text are one-track affairs, perfect examples of the S-(intervening variables)-R type of model, without even an input channel for drive-impulses. A little later, Freud expands on his conception of the psychic apparatus:

Hypotheses, whose justification must be looked for in other directions, tell us that at first the apparatus's efforts were directed towards keeping itself so far as possible free from stimuli; consequently its first structure followed the plan of a reflex apparatus, so that any sensory excitation impinging on it could be promptly discharged along a motor path.—(*21,* p. 565)

"The exigencies of life," he goes on, first in the form of "the major somatic needs," impel the apparatus to further development; whereupon he repeats the essence of the passage already quoted from the Project describing the development of ideation and thought, and of roundabout methods to the ultimate discharge of tension.

Recapitulating a little later (*21,* p. 598), Freud makes it virtually explicit that he is thinking in terms of a model:

We have already explored the fiction of a primitive psychical apparatus whose activities are regulated by an effort to avoid an accumulation of excitation and to maintain itself so far as possible without excitation. . . . We went on . . . to add a second hypothesis, to the effect that the accumulation of excitation (brought about in various ways that need not concern us) is felt as unpleasure and that it sets the apparatus in action with a view to repeating the experience of satisfaction, which involved a diminution of excitation and was felt as pleasure.

Here Freud adds his basic proposition about the affects of pleasure and unpleasure, closely following the formulations of Exner. It is an appealingly simple and logical assumption: if the fundamental tendency of the human being is to seek pleasure and avoid unpleasure (the pleasure principle), and if the basic property of its psychic apparatus is to rid itself of "excitation" (note the lack of specification of just what is meant by that term), why not equate them? He had done so explicitly in the Project (*16,* p. 373): "Since we have certain knowledge of a trend in psychical life towards *avoiding unpleasure,* we are tempted to identify that trend with the primary trend towards inertia."

In 1915 (*26*), Freud restated these ideas, referring to the first as "the most important" of his postulates:

This postulate is of a biological nature, and makes use of the concept of 'purpose' . . . : the nervous system [N.B.: here he slips back into neurology and does not speak about the 'psychical apparatus'] is an apparatus which has the function of getting rid of the stimuli that reach it, or of reducing them to the lowest possible level; or which, if it were feasible, would maintain itself in an altogether unstimulated condition.

After discussing the complications and developments introduced by the presence of "an incessant and unavoidable afflux of stimulation" from the drives, Freud continues:

When we further find that the activity of even the most highly developed mental apparatus is subject to the pleasure principle, i.e., is automatically regulated by feelings belonging to the pleasure-unpleasure series, we can hardly reject the further hypothesis that these feelings reflect the manner in which the process of mastering stimuli takes place . . . unpleasurable feelings are connected with an increase and pleasurable feelings with a decrease of stimulus.

He added a note of caution, indicating an awareness that this was too simple a picture, concluding: "It is certain that many very various relations of this kind, and not very simple ones, are possible" (*26,* pp. 120f).

In 1920 came the best known and perhaps most clearly formulated statement of the principle of constancy. In the first pages of "Beyond the Pleasure Principle" (*30*), he quotes Fechner (*15*) : "Every psychophysical motion rising above the threshold of consciousness is attended by pleasure in proportion as, beyond a certain limit, it approximates to complete stability, and is attended by unpleasure in proportion as . . . it deviates from complete stability." Freud continued immediately after: "The facts which have caused us to believe in the dominance of the pleasure principle in mental life also find expression in the hypothesis that the mental apparatus endeavors to keep the quantity of excitation present in it as low as possible or at least to keep it constant . . . the pleasure principle follows from the principle of constancy" (*30,* p. 9).

In 1924 (*34*), Freud returned to these same ideas:

The principle which governs all mental processes is a special case of Fechner's 'tendency toward stability,' and [I] have accordingly attributed to the mental apparatus the purpose of reducing to nothing, or at least of keeping as low as possible, the sums of excitation which flow in upon it. Barbara Low [*53,* p. 73] has suggested the name of 'Nirvana Principle' for this supposed tendency, and we have accepted the term. But we have unhesitatingly identified the pleasure-unpleasure principle with this Nirvana principle. Every unpleasure ought thus to coincide with a heightening, and every pleasure with a lowering, of mental tension due to stimulus. . . . But such a view cannot be correct. It seems that in the series of feelings of tension we have a direct sense of the increase and decrease of amounts of stimulus, and it cannot be doubted that there are pleasurable tensions and unpleasurable relaxations of tension. . . . It appears that they [pleasure and unpleasure] depend, not on this quantitative factor, but on some characteristic of it which we can only describe as a qualitative one . . . Perhaps it is the rhythm . . . We do not know.—(*34,* p. 160; cf. also *39,* pp. 15f, where the same points are repeated)

Note that, even after the introduction of the new tripartite structural model, Freud still treats it as a passive reflex apparatus, even though he provides no circuitry in his diagrams (either the one in "The Ego and the Id" [*32*] or that in the "New Introductory Lectures" [*38*] to represent a sequential course from input to output.

In his published works, Freud was never as explicit as he was in the Project about the nature of reality. Whenever he discusses it, however, the emphasis is more often on dangers than on beneficent qualities or opportunities, though of course one of the principal contexts in which he treats of reality is as a source of need-satisfying objects. In 1914, for example, he wrote, "We have recognized our mental apparatus as being first and foremost a device designed for mastering excitations which would otherwise be felt as distressing or would have pathogenic effects" (*25*, p. 85). This harsh picture of reality is repeated in "Instincts and Their Vicissitudes." "Let us imagine ourselves in the situation of an almost entirely helpless living organism . . . which is receiving stimuli in its nervous substance . . . On the one hand, it will be aware of stimuli which can be avoided by muscular action (flight) ; these it ascribes to an external world. On the other hand, it will also be aware of stimuli against which such action is of no avail . . . instinctual needs" (*26*, p. 119). In both of these works, reality is treated as primarily a source of disturbances which must be escaped or wrestled with.

This last passage foreshadows the famous introduction, in 1920, of the protective shield against stimuli:

> Let us picture a living organism in its most simplified possible form as an undifferentiated vesicle of a substance that is susceptible to stimulation. . . . It would be easy to suppose, then, that as a result of the ceaseless impact of external stimuli on the surface of the vesicle, its substance to a certain depth may have become permanently modified, so that . . . it would present the most favorable possible conditions for the reception of stimuli. . . . This little fragment of living substance is suspended in the middle of an external world charged with the most powerful energies; and it would be killed by the stimulation emanating from these if it were not provided with a protective shield against stimuli . . . its outermost surface . . . becomes to some degree inorganic and . . . resistant to stimuli. . . . *Protection against* stimuli is an almost more important function for the living organism than reception of stimuli.—(*30*, pp. 26f)

This picture of an organism as a helpless creature "threatened by the enormous energies at work in the external world" makes it amply explicit that Freud conceived of external reality as primarily a source of dangerous energies directly penetrating the organism, except for the screening effects of its protective shield.

An obvious corollary of the passive, reflex model, the conception of motivation as the reduction of tension, is perhaps too familiar to require elaborate documentation. The following passage from "Instincts and Their Vicissitudes" is typical:

> An instinctual stimulus does not arise from the external world but from within the organism itself. For this reason it operates differently upon the mind and different actions are necessary in order to remove it. . . . Since it impinges not from without but from within the organism, no flight can avail against it. A better term for an instinctual stimulus is a 'need.' What does away with a need is 'satisfaction.' This can be obtained only by an appropriate ('adequate') alteration of the internal source of stimulation.—(*26*, pp. 118f)

Thus, the assumption of endogenously arising instinctual needs ingeniously provides an explanation for the kind of behavior that the vitalists had called "spontaneous," and therefore Rapaport could write that the instinctual drives are the ultimate guarantees of the ego's autonomy from the environment (*65*). As Miller (*56*) points out, however, behavior that is dominated by instinctual drives can hardly be considered autonomous, even with respect to the environment. (He gives the example of the way the attention and efforts of starving men are captured by putatively need-satisfying objects.) Therefore, it remains exceedingly difficult to account for ego autonomy as long as the assumption of a basically passive psychic apparatus is retained.

The final basic characteristic of psychoanalytic theory in its mature form that shows an obvious continuity with and indebtedness to the doctrines of Freud's teachers is the heavy emphasis on forces and energies as explanatory concepts. Again, it is by no stretch of the imagination necessary to demonstrate by painstaking documentation that psychoanalysis is a dynamic psychology. Gill (*42*) has convincingly argued that a principal fault of psychoanalytic theory has been an overemphasis upon dynamic and economic considerations to the neglect of structural ones, a state of affairs he calls "reductionism to motivation" (cf. also *46* and *48*).[8]

IV

I have attempted to demonstrate so far that the prevailing conception of the nervous system during Freud's years as a student and budding scientist was that of a passive reflex apparatus; that Freud unhesitatingly adopted this as a set of necessary starting points in his own neuropsychological theorizing; and that the ostensibly nonphysiological models of his later years still incorporated these same assumptions.

Let us now go back briefly to the question of what I have called Freud's ambivalence about the nature of his model. Recall that the change in theoretical stance and terminology that took place between the Project and the

[8]Another possible explanation for Freud's overemphasis on the dynamic besides the influence of Brücke *et al.* may be the following: He was committed to a belief in exceptionless determinism; but he also had a fundamental concept of reality as random. Environmental influences he persistently called "accidental factors" (e.g., *23, passim*); he only dimly and occasionally admitted that there was a sociocultural patterning of the individual's surround, a nonpsychological structure that persisted without the mediation of individual heredity (instead, he tried to account for social regularity and the transmission of social forms by the genetic inheritance of acquired characteristics!). Therefore, to maintain a lawful and deterministic view, he *had* to look predominantly to internal motivation. Overdetermination usually means that there are several *motives* (some of them unconscious), rather than the sort of thing Waelder (*78*) had in mind with the principle of multiple function, or Rapaport and Gill's (*67*) metapsychological approach, which takes it for granted that every event has structural, sociocultural, and external-environmental causes as well as dynamic-economic ones.

"Interpretation of Dreams" coincided with a set of far-reaching changes in Freud's personality: his change in professional identity, his self-analysis, his withdrawal from the medical community, and other correlated changes (which I have summarized elsewhere [*50*]). It left him isolated not just personally but conceptually; before, he had been able to build on a sizable body of fact and accepted theory. In the Project, he did not create his theory from scratch, but simplified and extended what was standard doctrine. Later, with the declared intention of striking out on his own theoretically as well as professionally, he was in the exposed position of a frontiersman, forging ahead into the darkness without familiar landmarks, precedents, or findings—a prospect that would have daunted a lesser man! Small wonder, then, that he used the basic pattern of many familiar neurological concepts, with largely terminological changes.

Another less noticed change took place at the same time. The Project had been an ambitious attempt to account for normal psychological processes and also for dreams and psychopathology. He decided afterward to work with a minimum of assumptions and concepts, to explain one phenomenon at a time, and to proceed as modestly and cautiously as he could. The aim of Chapter VII is, accordingly, much smaller in scale, being primarily an attempt to provide a psychology of the dream-process. With each successive work the scope of the theory expanded so that ultimately psychoanalysis dealt with a virtually unparalleled breadth of topics. Yet even in the books like the two sets of introductory lectures (*28, 38*) and the final Outline (*39*) Freud did not go back to the attempt to write a psychology of normal thought and action. He was not confronted by the necessity to conceptualize more than he felt he could handle at any one time and thus did not have to face the inconsistencies in his theories.

When I look closely at the various passages in which Freud discussed the nature of the psychic apparatus, the realization is forced on me that it was something very much like what Hebb (*45*) calls the CNS—a conceptual nervous system or a "brain model." True, Freud at times made characteristically hyperbolic statements about its freedom from any anatomical implications; but when we see how often he lapsed into neurological terminology we may be tempted to interpret the repeated protestations in the way he taught us to do in his paper on "Negation" (*36*). It is certain, at any rate, that Freud hoped for an eventual integration of his theory with neurology (cf. *27*, p. 175) and that he always considered the biological facts to be quite relevant to his decisions about his own model.[9]

[9]For example, in 1905 (*22*, pp. 147f) he wrote: "The concepts of 'psychical energy' and 'discharge' and the treatment of psychical energy as a quantity have become habitual in my thoughts since I began to arrange the acts of psychopathology philosophically. . . . It is only when I speak of the 'cathexis of psychical paths' that I seem to

I believe, therefore, that Freud would have considered it of great significance if he had known the following five biological facts (most of which, to be sure, have become familiar to us only since his death). Taken together, they decisively refute and contraindicate the model of a passive reflex-mechanism.

1. The nervous system is perpetually *active.* Electroencephalographic data have shown that even in the deepest sleep and in coma the brain does not cease its activity; at these times of minimal input and behavioral output, hypersynchrony seems to produce the most massive discharges. The resting nerve cell periodically fires (produces a spike potential), and its nontransmitted activity waxes and wanes, all without any outside stimulation.

2. Thus, the effect of stimulation is primarily to *modulate* the activity of the nervous system. It may step up the frequency of discharge but mainly imposes an order and patterning on it; that is to say, encodes it.

---

depart from the analogies commonly used by Lipps. . . . To avoid misunderstanding, I must add that I am making no attempt to proclaim that the cells and nerve fibres, or the systems of neurones which are taking their place today, are these psychical paths, even though it would have to be possible in some manner which cannot yet be indicated to represent such paths by organic elements of the nervous system." In 1920 (*30,* p. 24): "the system *Pcpt.-Cs.* . . . must lie on the borderline between outside and inside; it must be turned towards the external world and must envelop the other psychical systems. It will be seen that there is nothing daringly new in these assumptions; we have merely adopted the views on localization held by cerebral anatomy, which locates the 'seat' of consciousness in the cerebral cortex—the outermost, enveloping layer of the central organ." At the end of the same work (*30,* p. 60): "The deficiencies in our description [of the relations between drives] would probably vanish if we were already in a position to replace the psychological terms by physiological or chemical ones. . . . Biology is truly a land of unlimited possibilities. We may expect it to give us the most surprising information and we cannot guess what answers it will return in a few dozen years to the questions we have put to it. They may be a kind which will blow away the whole of our artificial structure of hypotheses." In 1923 (*32,* p. 19): "We have said that consciousness is the *surface* of the mental apparatus; that is, we have ascribed it as a function to a system which is spatially the first one reached from the external world—and spatially not only in the functional sense but, on this occasion, also in the sense of anatomical dissection." A few pages on (p. 25): "we learn from cerebral anatomy" that "the ego wears a 'cap of hearing' "—a region marked "acoust," on the accompanying diagram—"on one side only." In 1924 (*34,* p. 164): "We are without any physiological understanding of the ways and means by which this taming of the death-instinct by the libido may be effected," in reference to fusion, indicating that he was still considering the psychic energies of drives potentially describable in physiological terms. In 1940: "The phenomena with which we have to deal [in psychoanalysis] do not belong only to psychology; they have also an organic and biological aspect" (*39,* p. 103f); "We have adopted the hypothesis of a psychical apparatus, extended in space, appropriately constructed, developed by the exigencies of life, which gives rise to the phenomena of consciousness only at one particular point and under certain conditions. This hypothesis has put us in a position to establish psychology upon foundations similar to those of any other science, such as physics" (*39,* p. 105). To the end, Freud was reluctant to give up physicalism and unwilling to create a "pure psychology" without some attempt at coordination with anatomy and physiology.

3. The nervous system does not *transmit* energy; the nervous impulse is rather propagated. An appropriate physical analogy is not current running along a wired circuit, but the traveling flame of an ignited train of gunpowder.

4. The energies of the nervous system, whether or not triggered by the sensory organs, are *different in kind* from the impinging external stimuli. The sensory surface is thus not a conductor but a transducer.

5. The tiny energies of the nerves bear encoded information and are *quantitatively negligible;* their amount bears no relation to the motivational state of the person. The electrical phenomena associated with the neuron are accessible to quantitative study today, but this work offers no basis for the economic point of view—the assumption that mental events might be meaningfully examined from the standpoint of the "volumes of excitation" involved. Rather than this kind of "power engineering," "information engineering" seems to be the relevant discipline.

Brücke, Meynert, and Exner were wrong, therefore, as Fechner had been before them: the nervous system is not passive, does not take in and conduct out again the energies of the environment, and shows no tendency to "divest itself of" its own impulses. The principle of constancy is quite without any biological basis. The notion of homeostasis, which is more a point of view than a working concept in physiology today, is only a vague analogy and cannot be used to bolster up this hoary anachronism.

If we follow Rapaport (*66*) in his attempt to order psychoanalytic theory and make it what Freud called a "pure psychology," it may be argued that these biological facts have no relevance to the fundamental assumptions of such a psychology. May one not, with Strachey, even maintain that "much of what Freud had written in the 'Project' in terms of the nervous system now turned out to be valid and far more intelligible when translated into mental terms" (*75,* p. 164)?

On the contrary, I believe that *many—perhaps most—of the obscurities, fallacies and internal contradictions of psychoanalytic theory are rather direct derivatives of its neurological inheritance.* In the space remaining, I want to sketch out these dark areas of the theory, indicating what some of their principal difficulties are and their conflicts with the facts.

Problems in the psychoanalytic theory of motivation and affect.—From preceding sections it should be obvious how the nature of the model results in a tension-reduction conception of motivation and the pleasure principle. If it is the nature of the psychic apparatus to rid itself of tension, then behavior will be driven and organized by this necessity. The pleasure principle is the conceptual link between this viewpoint and the theory of pleasure and unpleasure as falls and rises in the amount of this inherently noxious quantity. Similar theories of motivation as tension-reduction have been widespread in academic psychology.

Yet there are a number of logical difficulties with this conception. The term tension is conveniently ambiguous, to begin with; at least three types of meanings for it can be distinguished:

1. *Phenomenological*—tension is the subjective, conscious feeling of being tense. Freud espoused this definition in a passage quoted above from "The Economic Problem of Masochism": "In the series of feelings of tension we have a direct sense of the increase and decrease of amounts of stimulus," presumably meaning both exogenous and endogenous types of stimulation. This theory owes its tenacity to a number of supportive observations, which it fits neatly: if you sit on a tack, you jump up; if you get hunger pangs, you eat. Freud took these two types of motive, I believe, as paradigmatic in his conception of drives in general. Yet psychoanalysis is characteristically preoccupied with precisely the sorts of motive that operate silently, without identifiable conscious feelings of tension—which introspection does not turn up most of the time anyway, despite the assumption that *all* behavior is motivated. In general, then, conscious feelings of tension or unpleasure do not operate in the required ways often enough to serve as a satisfactory definition.

2. *Physiological*—tension is an objectively measurable disequilibrium in the body. This in turn might be of three principal types: muscular tonus or strain, a state of biochemical imbalance in the blood (glandular hyper- or hyposecretion, too little blood-sugar, too much CO_2, etc.), or an "alerted" or "activated" state of the brain as indicated by the EEG or other electrical measurement. These three do not have any simple pattern of relations, and each subtype is actually so complex that it would be a hopeless and meaningless task to try to cast up a sum of all physiological tensions at any one time and then follow its fate. This biological meaning is hardly suitable, moreover, to be a motivational concept in pure psychology.

3. The final possibility is *abstract*—tension is a hypothetical disequilibrium of purely conceptual forces. This is the way Rapaport (*66*) defined it; it is the logically implied definition if the psychic apparatus involved is itself an abstract, conceptual fiction. Tension so defined is a redundant concept, however, formally equivalent to "cathexis," "quantity," "psychic energy," or whatever else one assumes is the economic factor in psychoanalytic theory, the excitation that traverses the model's structural pathways. By this interpretation, also, it becomes so remote from any conceivable operations as to be scientifically trivial, a redundancy defined as what gets reduced when motivated behavior occurs. For a concept like tension to have scientific value, it must be measurable (at least crudely) in some way that is *independent* of the behavior it is invoked to explain.

Over fifteen years ago, Murphy (*59*) argued cogently for a group of activity drives and sensory drives ("drives manifested in a need for specific sensory experiences") and collected a good deal of evidence in their support.

Since then, empirical evidence against the theory of tension-reduction has been mounting steadily (cf. *11, 43, 45, 58, 72, 79*). Experiments with rats have shown that the sweet taste of saccharine in water will be accepted as rewarding—hungry animals will work and learn for it, despite the fact that this substance cannot reduce any known physiological tension (*69*). Male rats will similarly exert themselves considerably to get access to a receptive female, even though the experimenter removes them after they have mounted and penetrated but before ejaculation, so that the sexual tension is never allowed to be discharged (*70*). In a notable series of studies done at the University of Wisconsin, Harlow (*10, 43, 44*), has shown that monkeys will work for the stimulus-increasing reward of getting to look out of a box into the laboratory room, will work at mechanical puzzles for no reward other than the fun of doing them, and—as infants—have a strong need for the contact-stimulation provided by a mother-substitute. To revert to the human level, a number of investigators (e.g., *12, 45, 52*) working with the concept of cortical activation as a result of volleys from the reticular formations, have shown that there is optimal, mid-range level of activation (which might be taken as a physiological definition of tension) for most kinds of behavior and that people tend to seek mild to moderate levels of stimulation which maintain cortical activation.

A logical implication of the tension-reduction theory is that a state of affairs in which all stimulus inputs, both external and internal, are reduced to a minimum should be a blissful Nirvana. Experimental attempts to achieve this kind of situation for periods of time ranging from a few hours to a few days, in the wake of the pioneering experiments of Lilly (*51*) and the McGill investigators (*4*), have not been in complete agreement, but none of them has reported that Ss find the state of undistracted perceptual deprivation combined with rest and gratification of tissue needs very blissful. Many Ss grow restless and feel a positive need for stimulation, counter to the requirements of the theory. It has been assumed by a number of psychoanalytic theorists that under such conditions there would be nothing (besides the internal barriers of defense) to prevent sexual and aggressive drives from dominating the typically wandering thought-processes, since most subjects report an inability to think connectedly and purposefully for very long (cf. *71*). In point of fact, however, subjective reports reveal very little take-over by drive-fantasies (*56*), pointing to the dependence of these drives on external incitements and releasers (*49*).

The work of Olds (*61, 62*), Miller (*55*), and others on the effects of direct electrical stimulation of subcortical structures in the brain has a number of major implications for the psychoanalytic theory of motivation and affect. These studies, by now too well-known to require extensive review, have discovered septal areas which, when stimulated by appropriate pulse trains delivered by implanted electrodes, give rise to unmistakable aversive behavioral signs of intense unpleasure or distress. By itself, this finding would seem consistent with Exner's and Freud's hypotheses; but it turns out that the quantity of stimulation (above a certain threshold) is unimportant, whereas the location of the stimulated site is vital. In some instances, a shift of a few millimeters will put the electrode in a spot which, when given the same quantity of electrical stimulation, yields exactly opposite results. Rats trained to press a lever for brief pulses of stimulation will do so uninterruptedly for hours—indeed, until they drop with exhaustion—when the intracranial electrodes have been implanted in one of these rewarding or pleasure centers. Only a few studies with human Ss (*5*) have been undertaken, but the result of such stimulation is subjective reports of intense pleasure or unpleasure. Any further attempts to link pleasure with a drop in some kind of physiological tension, or other such economic theories of affect, are decisively refuted—unless a retreat is made into the untestability of the tautological concept of abstract, purely conceptual tension.

We know now from the data cited that motivation is *not* a matter of reducing either a physiological or a phenomenological tension and that pleasure is a valid and separate phenomenon in its own right, not merely the absence or reduction of pain or unpleasure. Thus, it seems clearly established that there are both positive and negative motivations, not merely negative ones. Observation surely suggests that there are adient, or approaching, as well as abient, or stimulus-reducing, motives, and we need no longer go through theoretical gymnastics to make it appear that what looks like approach and stimulus hunger is actually a way of fleeing from even stronger, internal tensions.

Aggression was always a problem for Freudian theory. For many years, Freud maintained a curious kind of blind spot concerning it; he saw and worked with it clinically, but when it came to theoretical statements tried to get rid of it as a special kind of self-preservative manifestation of ego instinct or a sadomasochistic form of sexuality (*23*). When he finally came to grips with the necessity to postulate a separate hostile or destructive motive, he produced the theory of the death instinct. Freud's shaky logic in developing his case, the questionable and speculative nature of the facts he adduced, and the general lack of evidential support for this theory are well-known. I believe, therefore, that I need not do more here than show the linkage of this concept to the reflex-arc model.

Freud introduced the argument for the death instinct by a kind of generalization of the principle of constancy into the conception of the conservative nature of instincts. It is a logical enough extension of the notion that the nervous system tends to rid itself of stimuli and restore its previous state of rest, to assume that all drives "tend towards the restoration of an earlier state of things" (*30*, pp. 37f). Then, since all living matter can be assumed to have once been lifeless, it should have a drive to return to a nonliving condition. "The attributes of life were at some time evoked in inanimate matter by the action of a force of whose nature we can have no conception. . . . The tension which then arose in what had hitherto been an inanimate substance endeavoured to cancel itself out. In this way the first instinct came into being"—the death drive. This is truly tension-reduction carried to its bitter end!

In a passage from "The Economic Problem of Masochism" which I have cited repeatedly, Freud made the linkage between the principle of constancy and the death instinct explicit by clarifying the relationship between the pleasure principle and the Nirvana principle. The Nirvana principle is the tendency to reduce stimuli to the absolute minimum and thus "expresses the trend of the death instinct" (*34,* p. 160).

In summary, the extensions and applications of his passive reflex model to problems of motivation and affect led Freud's theory into many conflicts with fact and to little of lasting value.

Problems of the energy doctrine (the economic point of view).—The propositions I have been criticizing are largely energic, despite the fact that references to a reflex-arc model may sound structural. In line with the tradition of the school of Helmholtz, however, Freud consistently followed the assumption that scientific explanation had to rely primarily on forces and energies, and devoted a great part of his theorizing to dynamic and economic propositions. At the beginning of the final section of Chapter VII of the "Interpretation of Dreams," for example, after summarizing part of his argument, which had been partly in structural terms, he said: "Let us replace these metaphors by something that seems to correspond better to the real state of affairs, and let us say instead that some particular mental grouping has had a cathexis of energy attached to it or withdrawn from it. . . . What we are doing here is once again to replace a topographical way of representing things by a dynamic one" (*21,* p. 610). It is apparent that he felt on sounder ground and closer to reality with the cathectic language than with his structural concepts, which he recognized were metaphors. What he did not see was that psychic energy was just as metaphorical a concept (*47*).

Elsewhere (*48*), I have outlined in some detail most of the vagaries of Freud's usage of the concept of binding in relation to his energy constructs. In seeking to find the core meaning, I came upon over a dozen different ways in which Freud invoked the concept, in efforts to account for a wide variety of psychological phenomena in energic terms. Even if one wishes to work with the concept of psychic energy (which no longer seems to me completely defensible [*47*]), it is difficult to see how even this hypothetical entity could exist outside of some kind of structures to accumulate, transmit, and discharge it. Once one accepts the need to work with structural concepts, it begins to seem unnecessary to try to account for the delay of inhibition in energic discharge by the postulation of qualitative changes in the energy itself, when a structural conception of defense and control can do the job with a minimum of new assumptions. In this respect, however, Freud was unable to change the habits of thought he had learned from his physicalistic mentors and seems not to have questioned the assumption that a dynamic or economic concept is always preferable to any other, even if it involves the successive postulation of a bewildering variety of types and modes of psychic energy (e.g., bound, fused, neutralized, aim-inhibited, etc.).

The classic laws of thermodynamics were taken by Helmholtz's colleagues and followers as directly and definitively applicable to all matters pertaining to energy in physiology. These laws apply to any Newtonian system within which all quantities of energy involved can be specified, thus in principle to organisms as well as solar systems; the simplest example of such a system, however, is an artificially closed system with a fixed amount of energy. Brücke understood the basic facts about the energy exchanges carried on by organisms, in nutrition, respiration, etc., which had been clearly enunciated by the 1860's, as his lectures show.[10] Nevertheless, the didactic value lent the closed system by its very oversimplification made it play an important role as a paradigm for the post-Helmholtzians, shaping their thought even when they were aware of its deficiencies. Hence, it was natural for Freud to adopt as a first approximation the assumption of a fixed amount of libido, reverberating around within a closed system so that the fate of quantities could be traced (at least in principle, for in practice no operations were ever adduced to make the measurement of psychic energy possible). Thus, if a certain amount of libido were withdrawn from objects, it had to cathect some part of the body, the ego, or another psychic structure. Within these assumptions, the economic point of view seems appealingly rigorous and scientific, apparently opening up explanatory possibilities unique to psychoanalysis. The inexorable law of entropy seems also to support the postulation of a death instinct (cf. *76*).

The work of von Bertalanffy (*77*) has brought sharply to our attention the facts that a human being or any other living organism is very far indeed from being a closed system and that there are rigorous and lawful ways of dealing with open systems. The very concept of an equilibrium of forces is inappropriate to a living system, which tends to maintain steady states in which inputs are in balance with outputs (cf. *64*). Such a system can show the characteristics of negative entropy as it grows and develops, which was inconceivable in a closed physical system.

With the advent of open-system conceptions, the main arguments for the predominance of the economic point of view (the quantitative treatment of energies, *67*) collapse, as does the entropic argument for the death drive.

[10]For the preceding facts in this paragraph, I am grateful to Dr. M. P. Amacher (personal communication).

Problems in psychoanalytic psychopathology.—For the most part, Freud's clinical theories about the nature of neurosis and its genesis stayed rather close to his clinical observation, remaining a solid and permanent contribution. Yet in a few matters, the passive reflex-model assumptions led him into clinical *culs-de-sac.* I have in mind the early theory of anxiety and the related conception of "actual neurosis," and the theory of traumatic neurosis.

In the 1890's, let us recall, much of Freud's psychopathology was built on a conception that, at some point, physical phenomena became psychic. Thus, his first account of sexuality includes the assertion that, after neural impulses generated by distending seminal vesicles in an abstinent man reached a certain threshold level, they became a psychical stimulus. This was the normal state of affairs; in hysteria, the constitutional capacity for conversion permitted the transmutation of affect-charge back into somatic excitation (*19*). At this time, the "fermentation" or "toxic" theory of anxiety appeared: "the mechanism of anxiety neurosis is to be looked for in a deflection of somatic sexual excitation from the psychical sphere, and in a consequent abnormal employment of that excitation" (*20,* p. 108). The other actual neurosis was given a similarly somatic explanation:

> Neurasthenia develops whenever the adequate unloading [of somatic sexual tension] (the adequate action) is replaced by a less adequate one—thus, when normal coition, carried out in most favorable conditions, is replaced by masturbation or spontaneous emission. Anxiety neurosis, on the other hand, is the product of all those factors which prevent the somatic sexual excitation from being worked over psychically. The manifestations of anxiety neurosis appear when the somatic excitation which has been deflected from the psyche is expended subcortically in totally inadequate reactions.—(*20,* p. 109)

In his paper on "wild" psychoanalysis, Freud (*24*) admitted that he had seen few cases of such actual neurosis, but he did not cease believing in it, and continued to classify neurasthenia and anxiety-neurosis under this heading. In an encyclopedia article (*33,* p. 243) he said that the actual neurosis "could be traced to contemporary abuses in the patients' sexual life and could be removed if these were brought to an end," adding that they occurred "by chemical agency."

Looking back on his early psychoanalytic work (*35,* pp. 25–26) Freud told about his "discovery" of the actual neurosis and confidently described the different types of abnormal sexual practice found in each. He added: "Since that time [the 1890's] I have had no opportunity of returning to the investigation of the 'actual neuroses'; nor has this part of my work been continued by anyone else." He speaks of these "early findings" slightly apologetically, maintaining however that "they seem to me still to hold good. . . . I am far from denying the existence of mental conflicts and of neurotic complexes in neurasthenia. All that I am asserting is that the symptoms of these patients are not mentally determined or removable by analysis, but that they must be regarded as direct toxic consequences of disturbed sexual chemical processes."

The connection of this theory to the biological notions we have under consideration here is directly pointed out by Strachey (*73,* p. 78):

> Following Fechner, he had taken as a fundamental postulate the "principle of constancy," according to which there was an inherent tendency in the nervous system to reduce, or at least to keep constant, the amount of excitation present in it. When, therefore, he made the clinical discovery that in cases of anxiety neurosis it was always possible to discover some interference with the discharge of sexual tension, it was natural for him to conclude that the accumulated excitation was finding its way out in the transformed shape of anxiety.

The signal theory of anxiety had existed side-by-side with the toxic theory almost from the beginning, and Freud had expressed doubts about the latter in a letter to Fliess in 1897 (as Strachey points out [*73,* p. 79]). In 1926 he gave up all but a small vestige of the toxic theory, and in the "New Introductory Lectures" (*38*) finally abandoned it even as an explanation of anxiety neurosis. Today very few clinicians indeed can be found whose experience confirms the etiological sequences Freud thought he saw in actual neuroses, so that one wonders whether the whole concept was not based on the coincidence of a few chance clinical observations with an obvious derivation from the passive reflex model.

Freud's conception of traumatic neurosis is closely linked to his "protective shield against stimuli," the relation of which to the physicalistic view of reality we have already reviewed. In "Beyond the Pleasure Principle," he wrote: "We may . . . tentatively venture to regard the common traumatic neurosis as a consequence of an extensive breach . . . in the protective shield against stimuli. . . . Because of lack of any preparedness for anxiety, including lack of hypercathexis of the systems that would be the first to receive the stimulus . . . those systems are not in a good position for binding the inflowing amounts of excitation" (*30,* p. 31). What is the effect of "this invasion" of physical energies? "Cathectic energy is summoned from all sides to provide sufficiently high cathexes of energy in the environs of the breach. An 'anticathexis' on a grand scale is set up, for whose benefit all the other psychical systems are impoverished, so that the remaining psychical functions are extensively paralysed or reduced." Freud concluded his explanation by invoking the compulsion to repeat.

This theory has a number of esthetically pleasing ingenuities, as Freud's constructions almost always do, but it also has such serious inconsistencies that it cannot be considered tenable. The central concept of the protective shield is tantalizingly elusive, an excellent example of Freud's ambivalence about mental versus physiological models. When he first introduces it, by his fanciful genetic hypothesis of a one-celled organism, the protective crust baked on by environmental energies is clearly physical in nature. Then, without warning, he switches to the realm of metaphor: the barrier is no longer physical, since "preparedness of anxiety and the hypercathexis of the receptive system constitute the last line of defense of the shield against stimuli" (*30,* p. 31). On the one hand, it sounds continually as if the protective shield is some sort of physical barrier, since it guards against the inflow of physical energies which have to be mastered lest they overwhelm the organism; yet the rupture of the barrier in traumatic neurosis does *not* mean that the skin is broken, for we are told that "a gross physical injury caused *simultaneously* by the trauma *diminishes* the chances that a neurosis will develop" (p. 33; emphasis added). If Freud had kept to an anatomical-physiological model, he would never have been able to make his concept perform such gymnastics and would not have approached an explanation in this way at all. If he had kept to a consistently "pure psychology," he would have had to eschew the attempt to explain *any* condition marked by somatic symptoms. Fortunately for the development of clinical psychoanalysis, he did not take this last course, but faced up to psychosomatic complications wherever he met them —in affects, sexuality, organ neuroses, conversion symptoms, etc.—sacrificing the internal consistency and clarity of his system rather than deny clinical reality.

Problems in the theory of object relations.—In "Instincts and Their Vicissitudes," Freud advances the rather startling doctrine of the primary hate of objects: "It cannot be denied that hating . . . originally characterized the relation of the ego to the alien external world with the stimuli it introduces. . . . At the very beginning, it seems, the external world, objects, and what is hated are identical" (*26,* p. 136). "Hate, in relation to objects, is older than love. It derives from the narcissistic ego's primordial repudiation of the external world with its outpouring of stimuli" (p. 139). This conception is sharply at variance with direct observation of infants, with their delight in new experience, their fascinated staring at freshly presented objects, their pleasure in bringing about "pleasing spectacles" (*63*). Yet it is directly consequent from the passive model: if the apparatus has as its basic principle the tendency to get rid of stimuli and if the increase in energy within it is unpleasant, then the approach of any object must be originally distressing and must arouse an emotional rejection that might as well be called hate. Only after the organism discovers from bitter experience that it is necessary to have traffic with this noxious world in order to escape the persistent and equally unpleasant tensions within does this model allow for the secondary development of any positive striving for persons, things, or experiences generally.

This basic difficulty pervades the whole Freudian theory of object-relations, which he never fully clarified. The basic paradigm of the analytic concept of objects and their interaction with drives seems to be food and food-seeking. The hunger drive arises internally, causing discomfort and restlessness; the external object, a piece of food, which formerly was indifferent, now becomes attractive, so that we can say that the percept is cathected with oral libido. This energy is discharged in the act of eating; the drive subsides, and food objects are now indifferent at best, even disgusting. This commonsense account does not completely accord with modern studies of the nature of the hunger drive, but it is appealing and easy to fit in with the Brücke-Meynert model. With only slightly more difficulty, casual sexual encounters can be conceptualized in this way too; but this kind of interaction with objects is properly a matter of discharge rather than cathexis. Major difficulty begins when one considers *enduring* object-relations. In 1921 (*31,* p. 111) Freud wrote:

> In one class of cases being in love is nothing more than object-cathexis on the part of the sexual instincts with a view to directly sexual satisfaction, a cathexis which expires, moreover, when this aim has been reached; this is what is called common, sensual love. But, as we know, the libidinal situation rarely remains so simple. It was possible to calculate with certainty upon the revival of the need which had just expired; and this must no doubt have been the first motive for directing a lasting cathexis upon the sexual object and for 'loving' it in the passionless intervals as well.

A brief digression on the concept of cathexis is in order at this point. In the basic reflex model, there is no provision for the delay of discharge; yet observation insists that there is such a phenomenon most of the time. Exner and Breuer were therefore forced to include what was a common neurophysiological assumption, that there could be a nontransmitted excitation of the nerve cell, which they called "tonic" in analogy to muscular tonus. When Freud incorporated this concept in the Project, he called it *Besetzung,* the "occupation" of a nerve cell by quantity; the conventional English rendition of this word as "cathexis" loses the static connotation of the German. As time went on, Freud began to use cathexis as a general term for the energy of the neural or psychic apparatus and referred to this energy when in a sedentary, nontransmitted state as *bound* (*48*).[11] Nevertheless, the original connotation tended to cling to the concept of cathexis, particularly in usages like object-cathexis. For example, in the just-quoted passage, note that the cathexis "expires" in the process of sexual gratification or discharge.

---

[11]Note that this is a purely dynamic-economic concept, yet one that does essentially structural service. No wonder that Freud was so fond of binding and invoked it so often in such various contexts with consequently different meanings. He had doubts about its consistency with the model at first, asking Fliess to make sure it could be squared with the laws of motion (*16,* pp. 124 and 426).

To account for lasting cathexes, which were more than temporary delays of discharge, Freud had therefore to introduce a further qualitative differentiation of energies, despite his vigorous rejection (in 1895 [*16*] and again in 1915 [*26*]) of the idea that drive-energies could have any qualitative characteristic other than "period" (frequency—itself a quantitative characteristic). This innovation was aim-inhibitedness: as a consequence of the Oedipus complex and its resolution, "the child still remains tied to his parents, but by instincts which must be described as being 'inhibited in their aim.' The emotions which he feels henceforward towards these objects of his love are characterized as 'affectionate' " (*31,* p. 111). "The depth to which anyone is in love, as contrasted with his purely sensual desire, may be measured by the size of the share taken by the aim-inhibited instincts of affection" (p. 112). This assumption nicely fits the requirement of an economic explanation for persisting attachment that does not die down after orgasm, as sexual desire proper does. The trouble is that it seems almost entirely *ad hoc;* Freud simply postulated that it takes place as a result of frustration, without explicating any mechanism or making it plausible in terms of the passive reflex model. Moreover, he does not account for the fact that as a person builds up many friendships, and consequently accumulates more aim-inhibited, undischargeable libido, there is not a general rise in the subjective sense of unpleasure. Actually, of course, the opposite tends to take place: the more affection we have for our friends, the better we feel, and surely not depleted of energy.

Freud argued just the opposite, however; and here is another respect in which his theory of object relations seems unsatisfactory and his reported observations at variance with what most of us see today. In the paper on "Narcissism," Freud declared that "it is easy to observe that libidinal object-cathexis does not raise self-regard. The effect of dependence on the loved object is to lower that feeling: a person in love is humble" (*25,* p. 98). He does allow for the possibility of "a real happy love" through the complementary assumption: "Loving in itself . . . lowers self-regard; whereas being loved, having one's love returned, and possessing the loved object, raises it once more" (p. 99). Nevertheless, it remains a puzzle that Freud should have thought that loving lowered self-esteem, until one recalls that closed-system implication of his energetics: if there is just a limited supply of libido, and if a major part of it is committed to a love-object, it must follow that less is left over for the self. This is indeed an economics of scarcity (*41*) applied to love, whereas an open-system approach allows one to observe that loving tends to be a positive feedback system: the more we give, the more we have both for ourselves and for others (cf. *40*).

There are a number of related criticisms of Freud's theory of narcissism that might be detailed if space permitted: the odd contention that schizophrenics have a great deal of self-esteem; unsolved economic problems in the relation of narcissism, identification, and sublimation; and the difficulty in comprehending how there can be "an internal draining away of excitations which are incapable of direct discharge outwards . . . by means of an internal process of working-over . . . carried out upon real or imaginary objects" (*25,* pp. 85f). But I believe that I have probably cited enough examples of theoretical difficulties that follow quite directly from Freud's basic assumptions, which as we have seen derived directly from essentially biological propositions.

V

In one of his best-known declarations of independence from neurology, Freud wrote (*27,* p. 175): "Our psychical topography has *for the present* nothing to do with anatomy; it has reference not to anatomical localities, but to regions in the mental apparatus, wherever they may be situated in the body. In this respect, then, our work is untrammelled and may proceed according to its own requirements."

He hoped, therefore, that a shift to a kind of brain model, without commitments to precise localization and even without explicit statement that it was a neuropsychology, would free him from the limitations of the biological disciplines within which he had labored so many years. Ironically, by this very shift he concealed the biological nature of his theoretical starting points and protected them from correction when at last neurophysiology and neuroanatomy began to make great strides. By taking his teachers' statements about the nature of the nervous system not as empirical propositions subject to verification or correction, but as unquestioned postulates, he put the whole theory further away from testability.

In bringing these hidden, and now clearly erroneous, biological propositions out into the open and showing their mischievous ramifications in psychoanalytic theory, Amacher and I have tried to remain true to the spirit of Freud's reiterated hopes that his science could someday be brought back into contact with biology. He wrote, for example: "we must recollect that all our provisional ideas in psychology will presumably some day be based on an organic substructure" (*25,* p. 78).

I believe that that day is fast approaching. An organic substructure can be provided today, incorporating nearly a century of research, which has greatly changed our understanding of the brain's structures—both gross and fine—and its functions since the doctrines of post-Müllerian physiology were laid down. The breathtaking rapidity of advance in neuropsychology today is in the most instructive contrast to the stately pace of change in psychoanalysis. Yet by making a relatively few basic modifications, psychoanalysis can take itself out of its dangerously encapsulated position and get back into the mainstream of scientific advance. I get an irrational glow of gratification at the poetic justice in the prospect that psychoanalysis may at last become the kind of productive science Freud wanted it to be by a return to the disciplines in which he did his first scientific and professional work. Aside from sentiment, however, we owe it not only to Freud but to ourselves to protect the many and vitally important substantive contributions of psychoanalysis from the danger of wholesale rejection to which the general theory's vulnerability to methodological criticism exposes them.[12]

REFERENCES

1 AMACHER, M. P. The influence of the neuroanatomy, neurophysiology and psychiatry of Freud's teachers on his psychoanalytic theories. Unpublished doctoral dissertation, Univ. of Washington, 1962. *Psychol. Issues,* in press.

2 BERNFELD, S. Freud's earliest theories and the school of Helmholtz. *Psychoanal. Quart. 13:*341–362, 1944.

3 BERNFELD, S. Sigmund Freud, M.D., 1882–1885. *Int. J. Psycho-Anal. 32:*204, 1951.

4 BEXTON, W. H., HERON, W., AND SCOTT, T. H. Effects of decreased variation in the sensory environment. *Canad. J. Psychol. 8:*70–76, 1954.

5 BISHOP, M. P., ELDER, S. T., AND HEATH, R. G. Intracranial self-stimulation in man. *Science 140:*394, 1963.

6 BLACK, M. *Models and Metaphors, Studies in Language and Philosophy.* Ithaca, N.Y., Cornell Univ. Press, 1962. (See especially: Models and archetypes.)

7 BORING, E. G. Science keeps on becoming. (Review of *The Structure of Scientific Revolutions,* by T. S. Kuhn.) *Contemporary Psychol. 8:*180–182, 1963.

8 BREUER, J., AND FREUD, S. "Studies in Hysteria" (first published in 1895). *Standard Edition of the Complete Psychological Works of Sigmund Freud,* edited by J. Strachey, Vol. II. London, Hogarth, 1955.

9 BRÜCKE, E. *Vorlesungen über Physiologie.* Vienna, 1876.

10 BUTLER, R. A., AND HARLOW, H. F. Discrimination learning and learning sets to visual exploration incentives. *J. gen Psychol. 57:*257, 1957.

11 COFER, C. N. Motivation. *Annu. Rev. Psychol. 10:*173, 1959.

12 DUFFY, ELIZABETH. The psychological significance of the concept of "arousal" or "activation." *Psychol. Rev. 64:*265, 1957.

13 ERIKSON, ERIK H. The first psychoanalyst: Crisis and discovery. *Yale Rev. 46:*40–62, 1956. Also in *Insight and Responsibility.* New York, Norton, 1964.

[12] After the first draft of this paper was completed, Leo Goldberger called my attention to a paper by Joseph Nuttin (*60*), which contains many of the same points. In a much briefer space, Nuttin develops the main outlines of the argument I have advanced. I have also found that, in one of his valuable appendices, James Strachey (*74*) likewise traces many of Freud's fundamental ideas to his initial neurological formulations. I cannot agree, however, with his judgment that the question "of how far these fundamental ideas were peculiar to Freud and how far they were derived from other sources . . . has been exhaustively examined by Ernest Jones in the first volume of his Freud biography" (p. 66).

14 EXNER, S. *Entwurf zu einer Erklärung der psychischen Erscheinungen.* Vienna, 1894.

15 FECHNER, G. T. *Einige Ideen zur Schöpfungs- und Entwicklungsgeschichte der Organismen.* Leipzig, Breitkopf & Härtel, 1873.

16 FREUD, S. *The Origins of Psychoanalysis: Letters to Wilhelm Fliess, Drafts and Notes, 1887–1902,* edited by M. Bonaparte, A. Freud, and E. Kris; translated by E. Mosbacher and J. Strachey. New York, Basic Books, 1954.

17 FREUD, S. "On the Psychical Mechanism of Hysterical Phenomena: A Lecture" (first presented in 1893). *Standard Edition,* Vol. III. London, Hogarth, 1962.

18 FREUD, S. "Some Points in a Comparative Study of Organic and Hysterical Paralysis" (first published in 1893). *Collected Papers,* Vol. I. London, Hogarth, 1924.

19 FREUD, S. "The Neuro-Psychoses of Defence" (first published in 1894). *Standard Edition,* Vol. III. London, Hogarth, 1962.

20 FREUD, S. "On the Grounds for Detaching a Particular Syndrome from Neurasthenia under the Description 'Anxiety Neurosis' " (first published in 1895). *Standard Edition,* Vol. III. London, Hogarth, 1962.

21 FREUD, S. "The Interpretation of Dreams" (first published in 1900). *Standard Edition,* Vols. IV & V. London, Hogarth, 1953.

22 FREUD, S. "Jokes and their Relation to the Unconscious" (first published in 1905). *Standard Edition,* Vol. VIII. London, Hogarth, 1960.

23 FREUD, S. "Three Essays in the Theory of Sexuality" (first published in 1905). *Standard Edition,* Vol. VII. London, Hogarth, 1953.

24 FREUD, S. " 'Wild' Psychoanalysis" (first published in 1910). *Standard Edition,* Vol. XI. London, Hogarth, 1957.

25 FREUD, S. "On Narcissism: An Introduction" (first published in 1914). *Standard Edition,* Vol. XIV. London, Hogarth, 1957.

26 FREUD, S. "Instincts and Their Vicissitudes" (first published in 1915). *Standard Edition,* Vol. XIV. London, Hogarth, 1957.

27 FREUD, S. "The Unconscious" (first published in 1915). *Standard Edition,* Vol. XIV. London, Hogarth, 1957.

28 FREUD, S. "Introductory Lectures on Psychoanalysis" (first published in 1916–17). *Standard Edition,* Vols. XV and XVI. London, Hogarth, 1963.

29 FREUD, S. "A Metapsychological Supplement to the Theory of Dreams" (first published in 1917). *Standard Edition,* Vol. XIV. London, Hogarth, 1957.

30 FREUD, S. "Beyond the Pleasure Principle" (first published in 1920). *Standard Edition,* Vol. XVIII. London, Hogarth, 1955.

31 FREUD, S. "Group Psychology and the Analysis of the Ego" (first published in 1921). *Standard Edition,* Vol. XVIII. London, Hogarth, 1955.

32 FREUD, S. "The Ego and the Id" (first published in 1923). *Standard Edition,* Vol. XIX. London, Hogarth, 1961.

33 FREUD, S. "Two Encyclopedia Articles" (first published in 1923). *Standard Edition,* Vol. XVIII. London, Hogarth, 1955.

34 FREUD, S. "The Economic Problem of Masochism" (first published in 1924). *Standard Edition,* Vol. XIX. London, Hogarth, 1961.

35 FREUD, S. "An Autobiographical Study" (first published in 1925). *Standard Edition,* Vol. XX. London, Hogarth, 1959.

36 Freud, S. "Negation" (first published in 1925). *Standard Edition,* Vol. XIX. London, Hogarth, 1961.
37 Freud, S. "Inhibitions, Symptoms and Anxiety" (first published in 1926). *Standard Edition,* Vol. XX. London, Hogarth, 1959.
38 Freud, S. "New Introductory Lectures on Psychoanalysis" (first published in 1933). *Standard Edition,* Vol. XXII. London, Hogarth, 1964.
39 Freud, S. *An Outline of Psychoanalysis* (first published in 1940). New York, Norton, 1949.
40 Fromm, E. Selfishness and self-love. *Psychiatry 2:*507, 1939.
41 Ghent, E. Scarcity: Governing principle in man's functioning. Paper presented to the Postdoctoral Colloquium, New York Univ., Sept. 26, 1962.
42 Gill, M. M. The present state of psychoanalytic theory. *J. abnorm. soc. Psychol. 58:*1–8, 1959.
43 Harlow, H. F. Mice, monkeys, man, and motives. *Psychol. Rev. 60:*23, 1953.
44 Harlow, H. F. The nature of love. *Amer. Psychologist 13:*673, 1958.
45 Hebb, D. O. Drives and the C.N.S. (conceptual nervous system). *Psychol. Rev. 62:*243–254, 1955.
46 Holt, R. R. Recent developments in psychoanalytic ego psychology and their implications for diagnostic testing. *J. proj. Tech. pers. Assess. 24:*254, 1960.
47 Holt, R. R. Beyond vitalism and mechanism: Freud's concept of psychic energy. Paper presented in a panel discussion, American Psychoanalytic Association, December 1962. See also ref. 57. In *Historical Roots of Contemporary Psychology,* edited by B. Wolman, in press.
48 Holt, R. R. A critical examination of Freud's concept of bound vs. free cathexis. *J. Amer. Psychoanal. Ass. 10:*475, 1962.
49 Holt, R. R. Ego-autonomy re-evaluated. Paper presented to the Postdoctoral Colloquium, New York Univ., May 1, 1963. *Int. J. Psycho-Anal.,* in press.
50 Holt, R. R. "Two Influences upon Freud's Scientific Thought, a Fragment of Intellectual Biography." In *The Study of Lives,* edited by R. W. White. New York, Atherton, 1963.
51 Lilly, J. C. Mental effects of reduction of ordinary levels of physical stimuli on intact, healthy persons. *Psychiat. res. Rep. 5:*1–9, 1956.
52 Lindsley, D. B. "Psychophysiology and Motivation." In *Nebraska Symposium on Motivation,* edited by M. R. Jones. Vol. V. Lincoln, Univ. of Nebraska Press, 1957.
53 Low, Barbara. *Psycho-Analysis, a Brief Account of Freudian Theory.* London, Allen & Unwin, 1920.
54 Meynert, T. *Psychiatrie.* Erste Hälfte. Vienna, 1884.
55 Miller, N. E. Central stimulation and other new approaches to motivation and reward. *Amer. Psychologist 13:*100, 1958.
56 Miller, S. C. Ego autonomy in sensory deprivation, isolation and stress. *Int. J. Psycho-Anal. 43:*1, 1962.
57 Modell, A. H. The concept of psychic energy. *J. Amer. Psychoanal. Ass. 11:*605, 1963.
58 Morgan, C. T. "Physiological Theory of Drive." In *Psychology, a Study of a Science,* edited by S. Koch. Vol. I. *Sensory, Perceptual and Physiological Formulations.* New York, McGraw-Hill, 1959.

59 MURPHY, G. *Personality, a Biosocial Approach to Origins and Structure.* New York, Harper, 1947.

60 NUTTIN, J. Human motivation and Freud's theory of energy discharge. *Canad. J. Psychol. 10:*167, 1956.

61 OLDS, J. Self-stimulation of the brain. *Science 127:*315–324, 1958.

62 OLDS, J., AND MILNER, P. Positive reinforcement produced by electrical stimulation of septal area and other regions of the rat brain. *J. comp. physiol. Psychol. 47:*419, 1954.

63 PIAGET, J. *The Origins of Intelligence in Children,* translated by M. Cook. New York, Int. Univ. Press, 1952.

64 PUMPIAN-MINDLIN, E. An attempt at the systematic restatement of the libido theory. III. Propositions concerning energetic-economic aspects of libido theory: Conceptual models of psychic energy and structure in psychoanalysis. *Ann. N.Y. Acad. Sci. 76:*1038, 1959.

65 RAPAPORT, D. The theory of ego autonomy: A generalization. *Bull. Menninger Clin. 22:*13–35, 1958.

66 RAPAPORT, D. "The Structure of Psychoanalytic Theory." In *Psychology, a Study of a Science,* edited by S. Koch. Vol. III. *Formulations of the Person and the Social Context.* New York, McGraw-Hill, 1959. Also in *Psychol. Issues 2*(2):Monograph 6, 1960.

67 RAPAPORT, D., AND GILL, M. M. The points of view and assumptions of metapsychology. *Int. J. Psycho-Anal. 40:*153–162, 1959.

68 RUBINSTEIN, B. B. "Psychoanalytic Theory and the Mind-Body Problem." This volume, Chapter 3.

69 SHEFFIELD, F. D., AND ROBY, T. B. Reward value of a non-nutritive sweet taste. *J. comp. physiol. Psychol. 43:*471, 1950.

70 SHEFFIELD, F. D., WULFF, J. J., AND BACKER, R. Reward value of copulation without sex drive reduction. *J. comp. physiol. Psychol. 44:*3, 1951.

71 SOLOMON, P., *et al.,* EDS. *Sensory Deprivation.* Cambridge, Mass., Harvard Univ. Press, 1961.

72 STELLAR, E. The physiology of motivation. *Psychol. Rev. 61:*5, 1954.

73 STRACHEY, J. Editor's introduction [to Freud, S., "Inhibitions, Symptoms and Anxiety"]. In *Standard Edition,* Vol. XX. London, Hogarth, 1959.

74 STRACHEY, J. "The Emergence of Freud's Fundamental Hypotheses." In *Standard Edition,* Vol. III. London, Hogarth, 1962.

75 STRACHEY, J. Editor's note [on Freud, S., "The Unconscious"]. In *Standard Edition,* Vol. XIV. London, Hogarth, 1957.

76 SZASZ, T. S. On the psychoanalytic theory of instincts. *Psychoanal. Quart. 21:*25, 1952.

77 VON BERTALANFFY, L. The theory of open systems in physics and biology. *Science 111:*23, 1950.

78 WAELDER, ROBERT. The principle of multiple function: Observations on overdetermination. *Psychoanal. Quart. 5:*45, 1936.

79 WHITE, R. W. Ego and reality in psychoanalytic theory: a proposal regarding independent ego energies. *Psychol. Issues 3*(3):Monograph 11, 1963.

SEVEN

Freud's Concept of Constitution in Psychoanalysis

SYDNEY G. MARGOLIN, M.D.

The concept of constitution in psychoanalysis is essentially that of Freud. When his followers disagree with it, in whole or in part, there is no offer of an equivalent alternative or counter-concept, and above all there is no revision of the postulates, propositions, and theories of psychoanalysis. Even the prevailing tendency among psychoanalysts to oppose a major construct in Freud's concept of constitution, namely, the Death Instinct Theory, has a quality of lameness in that its constitutional base has not been dislodged. For these reasons, I have derived what I say from Freud's statements as published in the *Standard Edition* (*23*), the *Gesammelte Werke* (*22*),[1] the *Fliess Correspondence* (*24*), and the unabridged biography by Jones (*27*). In addition, Hartmann's important book, *Ego Psychology and the Problem of Adaptation* (*25*), has been most extensively referred to. I made this possibly arbitrary decision with regard to Hartmann's book because, although it was first published in 1939, it was presented before the Vienna Psychoanalytic Society in 1937 and, therefore, conceived and written while Freud was still living and exerting his personal influence in psychoanalysis.

Freud's assumptions and analogies derived from biology went through two phases in the maturation of his psychoanalytic psychology. These differed historically and qualitatively. The first was the remarkable "Project," in which mental phenomena were described and explained in the terms of a complex of natural nonbehavioral sciences (*5*). The second phase, which was actually implicit during the first, emphasized what might be called the species characteristics of *Homo sapiens*. Here Freud dealt with broader biologic laws

[1]With respect to the biological aspects of Freud's psychological works, the indexing of the *Gesammelte Werke* is superior to that of the Standard Edition.

and principles, such as evolution, acquisition of and genetic transmission of collective experiences (e.g., certain features of symbolism and of the superego), and phylogenesis (*10, 11, 17, 19*).[2] The more specific biological content of his psychoanalytic psychology included his dualistic instinct theory, the maturation and differentiation of psychic energy (libido theory), as well as the "line of development" of object relations (*4, 19;* recently elaborated by Anna Freud [*4*]), and the developmental potential for differentiation of the constitutional ego. The biological mechanisms that were descriptively used in this psychological system were those of ontogenic, phylogenic views of embryology and of our somewhat more contemporary concepts of the genotype and phenotype (*2, 3*).

It does seem that Freud first used his biological knowledge and experience as paradigms for his theory-making. As these failed to integrate more and more of his psychoanalytic data and discoveries (and possibly because of increasing rejection by his nonpsychoanalytic colleagues in medicine), he gradually took the position that the gaps in knowledge in biochemistry, physi-

[2]In *The Acquisition and Control of Fire* (*17*), published by Freud in 1932, we are given one of the most imaginative and almost poetically creative speculations by means of which the Prometheus myth is subdued and made intelligible in terms of psychoanalysis. The essence of the myth which, incidentally, brings many dependent stories into it, is that Prometheus is chained to a rock while his ever-regenerating liver is consumed by vultures. This punishment is inflicted upon Prometheus because he had stolen fire. It is apparent that the psychoanalytic "solution" of the myth, that is to say, the bringing into conscious thinking of its hidden, latent, or unconscious meaning, is dependent upon the interpretation of the symbol fire. The conventional, or as Freud puts it, the universal meaning of the symbol fire is that of sexual excitement in its undifferentiated sense and that of the phallus which is associated to the appearance and behavior of flames.

The issue of symbolism is of the greatest importance for Freud's psychoanalytic theory and practice and, especially, for its differentiation from that of Jung. There are three properties of symbols which are pertinent to our discussion: First, the meaning of a symbol is universal regardless of time, place, culture, individuality, race, or other ethnic considerations. Second, the symbol is related to basic events in the history of every individual, that is to say, the sensations, perceptions, experiences, and values of infancy and of early childhood. Third, children, dreamers, neurotics, and primitive man all grasp the meaning of a symbol, either literally or reveal their understanding in their behavior. The adult, because of the mechanisms of infantile amnesia and repression, usually cannot independently ascertain it by free association and must be told the meaning of a symbol. Freud comments that myths about the acquisition of fire are widespread and that the themes of theft and birds are recurrent. The Indians with whom I work have two stories about fire. One bears out Freud's thesis, that is, the fire is stolen, birds participate in the theft and not in the punishment. Prometheus carried the fire hidden in a tube—a complex symbol representing the sexual and excretory functions of the penis. In the Indian myth, the fire is carried in a bundle of hair. In the second story, however, the symbol fire is the property of the mother and, in fact, represents her in the role of preparing food. The fire thus represents the basic experience of mother in her nourishing and cherishing aspects. However, if the basic event or experience involved is changed, then Freud's explanation can be brought into line with the Indians' interpretation.

ology, and pharmacology, and the absence of comprehensive field theories in biology, were problems in biology and not for his scientific work (see below). He had in mind such issues as the hypothetical tissue states whose mental representations were the instincts of psychoanalysis. His final position, similarly influenced by the environmental reaction to psychoanalysis and to its practitioners—e.g., in *The Question of Lay Analysis* (*13*) and in the *Postscript* to it (*14*)—was that psychoanalysis and medicine have similar ethical aims but different emphasis and content in education and different characterological prerequisites in its practitioners. In short, he declared psychoanalysis to be a psychological science sharing with the biological medical sciences the intensive study and treatment of the same species, namely, *Homo sapiens.*

I should like at this point to quote Freud's own statements on constitution in three aspects of his work. The first is on etiology and is taken from *A Reply to Criticisms of My Paper on Anxiety Neurosis* (1895) (*6*). The second is on the significance of constitution for therapeutic results from Lecture 34 on "Explanations, Applications and Orientations" in the *New Introductory Lectures on Psychoanalysis* (1933) (*18*). The third is from *Moses and Monotheism,* Part 3, which was written before March of 1938, and is the last detailed statement by Freud on constitution in psychoanalysis (*20*).

Freud states, "the probably very complicated etiological situation which prevails in the pathology of the neuroses" by postulating the following concepts: (*a*) precondition; (*b*) specific cause; (*c*) concurrent causes; and, as a term which is not equivalent to the foregoing ones, (*d*) precipitating or releasing cause.

> In order to meet every possibility, let us assume that the etiological factors we are concerned with are capable of a quantitative change—that is, of increase or decrease.
>
> If we accept the idea of an etiological equation of several terms which must be satisfied if the effect is to take place, then we may characterize as the *precipitating* or releasing cause the one which makes its appearance last in the equation, so that it immediately precedes the emergence of the effect.

Freud then generalizes his formulations and gives the example of pulmonary tuberculosis:

> Effect: Phthisis pulmonum
> Precondition: Disposition, for the most part laid down through heredity, by the organic constitution
> Specific cause: Bacillus Kochii
> Auxiliary causes: Anything that diminishes the power—emotions as well as suppurations or colds.
>
> The schematic picture for the etiology of anxiety neurosis seems to me to be on the same lines:
> Precondition: Heredity

Specific causes: A sexual factor in the sense of a deflection of sexual tension away from the psychical field

Auxiliary causes: Any stock noxae—emotion, fright, and also physical exhaustion through illness or over-exertion.

If I consider this etiological formula for anxiety neurosis in detail, I am able to add the following remarks: whether a special personal constitution (which need not be produced by heredity) is absolutely necessary for the production of an anxiety neurosis, or whether any normal person can be made to have an anxiety neurosis by some given quantitative increase of the specific factor—this I am not able to decide with certainty; but I incline strongly to the latter view. Hereditary disposition is the most important precondition for anxiety neurosis; but it is not an *indispensable* one, since it is absent in a class of borderline cases—the presence of a specific sexual factor can, in the majority of cases, be demonstrated with certainty. In one series of cases (congenital ones), this factor is not separated from the precondition of heredity, but it fulfilled with the help of it. That is to say, in some patients this peculiarity of the *vita sexualis*—psychical inadequacy in mastering somatic sexual tension—is innate in the form of a stigma, whereas ordinarily it is via that peculiarity that they acquire the neurosis.

When I consult my experience on this point, I cannot find that there is any antithetic relations as regards anxiety neurosis, between hereditary disposition and the specific sexual factor. On the contrary, the two etiological factors support and supplement each other. The sexual factor is usually only operative in those who have an innate hereditary taint as well; heredity alone is usually not able to produce an anxiety neurosis but waits for the occurrence of a sufficient amount of the specific sexual noxa. The discovery of the hereditary element does not therefore exempt us from searching for a specific factor. On its discovery, incidentally, all our therapeutic interest as well depends, for what can we do therapeutically about heredity as an etiological element? It has always been there in the patient and will continue to be there until the end of his life. Taken by itself, it cannot help us to understand either the episodic onset of a neurosis, or the cessation of a neurosis as a result of treatment. It is nothing but a precondition of the neurosis, an inexpressably important precondition it is true, but, nevertheless one which has been overestimated, to the detriment of therapy and theoretical comprehension.

In conclusion, I should like to repeat the few statements in which I am accustomed, as a first approximation to the truth, to express the mutual relationships between the various etiological factors:

1) Whether a neurotic illness occurs at all depends upon a quantitative factor—upon the total load on the nervous system as compared with the latter's capacity for resistance. Everything which can keep this quantitative factor below a certain threshold value, or can bring it back to that level, has a therapeutic effect. Hence by so doing it keeps the etiological equation unsatisfied.

What is to be understood by the "total load" and by the "capacity for resistance" of the nervous system could no doubt be more clearly explained on the basis of certain hypotheses regarding the function of the nerves.

2) What *dimensions* the neurosis attains depends in the first instance on the amount of the hereditary taint. Heredity acts like a multiplier, introduced into an electric circuit, which increases the deviation of the needle many times over.

3) But what *form* the neurosis assumes—what direction the deviation takes—is solely determined by the specific etiological factor arising from sexual life.—(*6*).[3]

In the *New Introductory Lectures on Psychoanalysis,* p. 210, Freud discusses the effects of constitution on what one can expect from psychoanalytic treatment:

The expectation that we shall be able to cure all neurotic symptoms is, I suspect, derived from the lay belief that neuroses are entirely superfluous things which have no right whatever to exist. As a matter of fact, they are serious, constitutionally determined affections, which are seldom restricted to a few outbreaks, but make themselves felt as a rule over long periods of life, or even throughout its entire extent. Our analytic experience that we can influence them to a far-reaching degree, if we can get hold of the historical precipitating causes and the incidental accessory factors, has made us neglect the constitutional factor in our therapeutic practice. And we are in fact powerless to deal with it; but in our theory we ought always to bear it in mind.—(*18*).

The statement on constitution in psychoanalytic theory is as follows:

The topography of the psyche . . . has in general nothing to do with cerebral anatomy; there is only one point where it impinges on it. The unsatisfactoriness of this conception—which I perceive as clearly as anyone—has its roots in our complete ignorance of the dynamic nature of mental processes. We realize that what distinguishes a conscious idea from a preconscious one, and this from an unconscious one, cannot be anything else but a modification, or perhaps also another distribution, of psychic energy. We speak of cathexes and hypercathexes, but beyond this we lack all knowledge and even a beginning for a useful working hypothesis. Of the phenomenon of consciousness we are at least able to say that it cleaves originally to perception. All perceptions which come about from painful tactile, auditory or visual stimuli are the more likely to be conscious. Thought processes, and what may be analogous to them in the Id, are unconscious per se, and obtain their entry into consciousness by their connection, via the function of speech, with memory traces of perceptions through touch and ear. In the animal, which lacks speech, these relationships must be simpler.

The impressions of the early traumata from which we started, are either not translated into the preconscious or they are soon redirected into the Id through repression. Their memory residues are then unconscious and operate from the Id. We can believe we can follow their further fate distinctly as long as they deal with personal experiences. A new complication arises, however, when we become aware that there probably exists in the mental life of the individual not only what he has experienced himself, but also what he brought with him at birth, fragments of phylogenetic origin, and archaic heritage. Then the question arises: in what does this inheritance consist, what does it contain, and what evidence of it is there?

The first and most certain answer is that it consists in certain dispositions, such as all living beings possess: that is to say, in the ability and tendency to follow a certain direction of development, and to react in a particular way to certain excita-

[3]This early discussion of etiology uses a principle that Freud retained in the subsequent developments of his concept of etiology, the "Complementary Series," "Constitution vs. accidents of experience," "Strength of Instincts vs. ego capacities," and so forth.

tion, impressions and stimuli. Since experience shows that individuals differ in this respect, our archaic inheritance includes these differences; they represent what is recognized as the constitutional element in the individual. Since all human beings go through the same experiences, at least in their earliest years, they also react to them in the same way, and this is why the doubt arose whether these reactions with all their individual differences should not be reckoned as part of that archaic heritage. This doubt must be rejected; the fact of this similarity does not enrich our knowledge of the archaic heritage.

Meanwhile analytic research has yielded several results which give us food for thought. First of all, there is the universality of speech symbolism. Symbolic substitution of one object through another—the same applies to actions—our children are conversant with, and it seems quite natural to them. We cannot trace the way in which they learned it and must admit that in many cases to learn it would be impossible. It is original knowledge, which the adult later on forgets. He employs, it is true, the same symbolism in his dreams, but he does not understand them unless the analyst interprets them for him and even then he is loathe to believe the translation. When he has used one of the common phrases of speech in which this symbolism is crystallized, he has to admit that its true meaning had quite escaped him, symbolism even ignores the difference in languages; investigation would probably show that it is ubiquitous, the same with all peoples. Here there seems to be an assured case of archaic inheritance from the time when speech was developing, although one might attempt another explanation: one might say that these are thought connections between ideas which are formed during the historical development of speech and which have to be repeated every time the individual passes through such a development. This then would be a case of inheriting a thought disposition as elsewhere one inherits an instinctual disposition; so it again would contribute nothing new to our problem.

Analytic research, however, has also brought to light other things which exceed in significance anything we have so far discussed. In studying reactions to early traumata we often find to our surprise that they do not keep strictly to what the individual himself has experienced, but deviate from this in a way that would accord much better with there being reactions to genetic events and in general can be explained only through the influence of such. The behavior of a neurotic child to his parents when under the influence of an Oedipus and castration complex is very rich in such reactions which seem unreasonable in the individual and can only be understood phylogenetically, in relation to the experiences of earlier generations. It would be amply worthwhile to collect and publish the material on which my remarks are based. In fact, it seems to me convincing enough to allow me to venture further and assert that the archaic heritage of mankind includes not only dispositions, but also ideational contents, memory traces of the experiences of former generations. In this way, the extent as well as the significance of the archaic heritage would be enhanced in a remarkable degree.

On second thought I must admit that I have argued as if there were no question that there exists an inheritance of memory traces of what our forefathers experienced, quite independently of direct communication and of the influence of education by example. When I speak of an old tradition still alive in a people, of the formation of a national character, it is such an inherited tradition—and not one carried on by word of mouth—that I have in mind or at least I did not distinguish between the two, and was not quite clear about what a bold step I took by neglecting this difference. This state of affairs is made more difficult, it is true, by the present attitude of biological science which rejects the idea of acquired qualities being transmitted to descendants. I admit, in all modesty, that in spite of this I cannot picture biological development proceeding without taking this factor into account. The two cases, it is true, are not quite similar; with the former it is a question of acquired qualities that are hard to conceive, with the latter memory traces of external expressions, something almost concrete. Probably, however, we cannot *au fond* imagine one without the other. If we accept the continued existence of such memory traces in our archaic inheritance, then we have bridged the gap between individual and mass psychology, and can treat peoples as we do the individual neurotic. Though we may admit that for the memory traces in our archaic inheritance we have so far no stronger proof than those remnants of memory evoked by analytic work, which call for a derivation from phylogenesis, yet this proof seems to me convincing enough to postulate such a state of affairs. If things are different, then we are unable to advance one step on our way either in psychoanalysis or in mass psychology. It is bold, but inevitable.

In making this postulate we also do something else. We diminish the over-wide gap human arrogance in former times created between man and beast. If the so-called instincts of animals—which from the very beginning allow them to behave in their new conditions of living as if they were old and long established ones—if this instinctual life of animals permits of any explanation at all, it can only be this: that they carry over into their new existence the experience of their kind, that is to say, that they have preserved in their minds memories of what their ancestors experienced. In the human animal things should not be fundamentally different. His own archaic heritage—though different in extent and character—corresponds to the instincts of animals.—(*20*)[4]

II

For obvious reasons, an examination of psychoanalysis in relation to biology should be rigorous and specific as to the principles, laws, theories, propositions, operations, and evidence that are to be evaluated, compared, analogized, and homologized. Because psychoanalytic theory and the strategy of its development were powerfully determined by Freud's professional background in morphogenetic biology and by his well-known nonprofessional preoccupation with highly selected aspects of the history of man, it is important to know somewhat of the states of knowledge in these fields throughout Freud's lifetime.

It seems that Freud's use of biology, anthropology, ethnology, and archaeology did not tend to vary with the advances in these sciences but remained rooted in the "pre-psychoanalytic" phase of his scientific life. As far as can be determined, he never referred to the paleontological and to the fossil evidence of prehistoric man or to other highly significant relevant information

[4]This passage is controversial because of its neo-Lamarckian thesis. It should be recognized, however, that Freud implicitly uses the postulate of the psychological unity of man, at least for the hypothetical prehistory of the human species of which he writes. The problem, of course, is: how did this homogeneity come about? Is it true for all ethnic groups today?

that emerged in his lifetime (*1, 31*).[5] Neither did he avail himself of or contribute to the mounting controversy over the "species problem" (*32, 33*) or take account of the far-reaching consequences of the extraordinary advances in Mendelian genetics (*2, 3, 34*). He did, however, cite some "cultural" anthropologists. Robertson Smith (*37*) and James Frazer (cited in Freud [*9*]) were among the most appreciated by Freud.

Lest I be misunderstood, I wish emphatically to assert at this point that Freud was in no way obliged to consider these developments and advances in science. Indeed, it is apparent that the "hard" and enduring core of psychoanalysis was and could be constructed without reference to these contributions to the science of man. Freud's attitude toward his own data was one of conviction. He was ready, but not in a hurry, to change his conclusions when *his own data* did not support them. He seemed least responsive to the psychological findings and interpretations which he did not personally verify. Despite such historic facts, many psychoanalysts in their speculative discussions about their own work or their commentaries on Freud and his psychoanalytic contributions make extensive and sometimes extended excursions into nonpsychoanalytic disciplines (*38*). This has led to "soft" and vulnerable spots in the otherwise vital and vigorous system of psychoanalysis. Parenthetically, Freud would not approve of my association of the meaning of "system" to psychoanalysis. (*13*). To the extent that psychoanalysis is a "system," generalization to nonpsychoanalytic disciplines would be limited. He was of the opinion that psychoanalysis was a general science or at least a general psychology—that is to say, its own internally cohesive laws and principles were of explanatory and descriptive value to other sciences and to psychology in particular (*14*). Jones (*28*), Hartmann (*26*), and Schilder (*36*)[6] strongly and declaratively support this point of view in the form of

[5]The books by Dobzhansky (*3*) and Coon (*1*) contain excellent bibliographies. These list many publications by the early "cultural anthropologists." In addition, the second volume of the *Evolution of Man* (*32*) provides a picture of cultural anthropology as it was known during Freud's lifetime. Of some significance is that the early writers on the evolution of culture were almost contemporary with Freud and were read by him. To quote from Kroeber, see Reference (*32*), some of them are: Bachofen, "The Matriarchate" (1861) ; Tylor, "Primitive Culture" (1871) ; Morgan, "Ancient Society" (1877). It becomes apparent that Freud, who cites these writers, shared their hypothesis of a unilineal cultural development of man, that is, that culture went through a well-defined series of stages. The contemporary availability of data not known to these 19th-century writers, makes it abundantly clear that multilineal lines of cultural development had occurred and that geographical factors were a major consideration (see *2, 3*).

[6]Schilder (*36*) provides an extensive review of all of Freud's biological concepts and illustrates these with biological examples and analogies. He apparently subscribed to Freud's view that psychoanalytic biological generalizations which are not supportable by biology are due to "gaps" in biology. In commenting on biology's rejection of Freud's insistence on the genetic transmission of acquired characteristics, he declares that biology has not solved the problem of genotype variation. Schilder's mode of argument is completely unnecessary since, 30 years later, biology now perceives "the outlines of a genetic code that conveys the message for the evolution and survival of all living creatures" (*30*).

general allusions without, in my opinion, furnishing adequate supporting documentation.

A detailed examination of Freud's use of biology in its widest sense in relation to psychoanalysis makes possible a number of statements which, however, do not readily lead to easy generalizations:

1. Freud was trained in biology and used this frame of reference for analogies, homologies, and as a source of laws and principles and other categorizing generalizations. The latter were used most extensively in his speculations about the behavior of prehistoric man and the instinctual life of animals.

From among the laws and principles of biology, Freud applied the following to his growing conceptualizations of psychoanalysis: First and foremost, Lamarckian and Darwinian evolution; second, Haeckel's generalization that ontogeny recapitulates phylogeny; third, the cell theory and its relationship to embryological development, especially the principles of differentiation and dedifferentiation; fourth, metabolism as a shifting homeostatic balance between anabolic processes (libido) and catabolic processes (death); fifth, the thermodynamic concept of physical and biological energy transformations; sixth, hypotheses based upon the neuron and its connections and ramifications in the central nervous system; seventh, the psychosensory physiology based on the work of Fechner and of Helmholtz; eighth, anthropology, especially, the forerunners of what we now call "cultural anthropology."[7]

2. In psychoanalysis, Freud studied one species, Man. Hence, in his inferences about that species, he used biological generalizations such as the above. In addition, however, from his data he developed generalizing hypotheses about other biological species. His theories led him to make speculative contributions to fields such as anthropology, archaeology, sociology, and linguistics. He was concerned not only with the anatomy and physiology of man and his ontogenetic development but also with man's development in both historical and prehistorical times.

3. It is understandable that Freud's mode of work would receive the closest scrutiny from the point of view of scientific logic. Basically, Freud studied the behavior of individuals and thereby raised the first of methodological storms that have come and gone around psychoanalysis. For example, from the point of view of the quantity and quality of data required for a scientific statement, the number of patients studied by Freud and, indeed, probably by

[7]It should be pointed out that Freud's competence as a biologist is unquestioned. His contributions to biology, however, were those of a morphologist who concentrated on morphogenesis in relation to morphostasis. The physicalist principles of procedure in this work contrast vividly with the psychoanalytic scientific method. Of the greatest significance for the latter, namely, introspection, free association, and, above all, verbalization of self-observations, was the fact that Freud was reared in the midst of the romantic era with its permissive emphasis on self-expression and on vivid uninhibited dramatized individuality.

all psychoanalysts, was small in relation to populations of cities or states and therefore, from a statistical point of view, trivial; the number of observations, however, made on a single subject was very large, and therefore significant, at least for that individual. To make generalizations about past and present man from a large quantity of "significant" observations made on a "trivial" number of contemporary subjects requires a crucial prerequisite, namely, the postulate of the psychological and biological unity of man at all times and in all places. That Freud used this premise in his declaration that psychoanalysis was a general psychology is amply illustrated in *Totem and Taboo* (*9*), *Future of an Illusion* (*15*), *Civilization and Its Discontents* (*16*), *Moses and Monotheism* (*20*), *Biography of Leonardo da Vinci* (*7*), and in many of his clinical papers such as his discussion of the Schreber Case (*8*).

III

Freud began his reports of his investigations and findings in psychoanalysis in terms of the biological principles of phylogenesis, ontogenesis, heredity, and of psychosensory physiology as these were understood at that time. The term "constitution" was used synonymously with "innate," "congenital," a "biological fact," "archaic heritage," "hereditary," and the like. All these expressions were usually in contrast to that which was experienced or accidental or acquired by an individual in his lifetime.

It is of great interest that, as Freud's work in psychoanalysis deepened and extended into many areas, his concern whether his discoveries and formulations were compatible with biological information and terminology progressively decreased, until he was able to defend the independent development of psychoanalysis by pointing out "that it is left for the science of the future to bring together these isolated data into a new understanding. It is not psychology but biology that is responsible for this gap." This quotation comes from the last general considered statement of psychoanalysis which Freud wrote—namely, the *Outline of Psychoanalysis* (*21*). The context for this comment was his observation of the significance of the diphasic history of sexuality in man. He had in mind the characteristics of infantile and post-pubertal sexuality and the immense psychic elaboration that was consequent on this.

It is easy to document the declarative statement that psychoanalysts had not objected to the generalizations and extrapolations from psychoanalysis into the nonclinical sciences of man. For example, despite the fact that a substantial part of Freud's total written output consisted of such speculations, very few psychoanalysts have performed basic research in these areas. This omission is all the more notable because of the increasing tendency to assert that psychoanalysis has the characteristics of a general science.

The extension of the clinical discoveries of psychoanalysis into such areas is a remarkable phenomenon. It is not a simple question of applied analysis, such as use of psychoanalytic psychology to classify the data of rituals, magic, and the like. It is a matter of theory-making on a scale that has not caused psychoanalysts to follow through with the required validating studies. This is all the more striking in view of the fact that so much remains to be done in the area where psychoanalysis is so firmly rooted—namely, in clinical work.

It cannot be strongly enough asserted that almost everything on which psychoanalysis is solidly based comes from the psychoanalytic couplet of a psychoanalyst and the patient in analysis. Out of this situation have emerged the theories, propositions, and constructs that organize the psychoanalytic data —organizations that are still undergoing the process of systematic verification and validation. As a result, there have been fundamental changes in psychoanalytic theory. In the new circumstances, what happens to the extrapolations based on the prior states of theory? Conscious, preconscious, and unconscious are no longer "systems," but are "qualities" of the ego. That is to say, the functions of the ego can have more or less of these qualities. The properties of the "preconscious," therefore, may be redistributed to the functions of the ego. Thus, what had been previously classified as the "preconscious" may be more logically structured as the dynamic interaction of defenses and affect, and as a "storage" depository at the service of conflict-free and autonomous ego activity.

It is probably fair to say that a general theory for psychoanalysis in biological terms does not exist, and as far as I know the possibility for such a formulation has not been seriously asserted. The contrary is true, namely, that there are innumerable efforts, hypotheses, and some theories to describe biological processes in psychoanalytic terms, thus giving rise to the widespread view that psychoanalysis has the promise of being a general science for biology as well. For this to be the case, it would be necessary to reject any psychobiological dualism, as Hartmann has done (*25*). He does not seek correlations between psychology and biology. His questions follow from the fact that the two disciplines have two differing methodologies, each capable of investigating mental and bodily events and thereby giving meaningful scientific order to the data. This does not compel the data of biology and psychoanalysis to be epiphenomenal co-variants of each other; neither does it exclude the possibility that they may indeed have causal relationships. The difficulty, of course, is that such statements are but one of many possible opinions. None are as yet authoritatively weighted by the strategic scientific knowledge. For example, the biological basis of instincts is both constitutionally a species characteristic of man and a complex physio-chemical process and state which achieve mental representation in forms such as percepts and urges. That these bodily events are hypothetical (Freud thought of them in terms of endocrine substances and drugs) or even speculative is not a defect in psychoanalytic proposition and theory-making. If neither discipline can go any farther at this time, there need not be any controversy. It does seem, therefore, that in our present state of knowledge it would be premature to declare that psychoanalysis is a general science because it can speculate about biology, or that, whereas dualism is operationally a fact, it is philosophically improbable.

All of this means, of course, that biological phenomena as yet are only speculatively linked to psychoanalysis and that the solidifying of our notions is still remote. For example, the statement that instincts are biopsychic in that they originate in the borderland between the mind and the body raises many difficulties in that it does not indicate what to investigate in this borderland or how to investigate it. Moreover, if one attempts to set up a circumscribed experiment there is always the legitimate criticism that the psychoanalytic method, e.g., free association, cannot operate under the restrictions of controlled manipulation. So simple an example as requiring a patient in analysis not to eat for several days should create precisely the hypothetical tissue state (and I emphasize *hypothetical*) out of which an instinctual need should arise, along with its psychic representation and affective elaborations. The arguments based on transference and counter-transference that would be provoked by this suggestion prove my point. Even those arguments have not been systematically tested in psychoanalytic practice. The area of child psychoanalysis, however, seems unaffected by such assertions as to what is or is not psychoanalytically legitimate. The problems in psychoanalysis and the unresolved discrepancies between its theories and practices cannot be ignored. Judgments about potentially relevant research are too often made despite the many serious gaps in psychoanalytic theory. The tradition for some of this can be traced back to Freud, who recognized that the wounds caused by his rejecting colleagues led him to reappraise his relation to medicine and its value for psychoanalysis (*13*).

In areas outside of biology and the instrumented laboratory, Freud had an unsurpassed genius for bringing together into a framework of provocative and exciting plausibility the most diverse and unexpected elements. For example, to the formulations of the rigorously studied, psychoanalytically observed individual who was also ontogenetically viewed, Freud added, by speculation, the study of the human species in terms of anthropology and phylogenesis. Similarly, the thinking and affects revealed in dreams and neuroses were genetically related to early childhood. Again, by plausible speculation, the thinking and affective life of the adult savage, and I might add parenthetically that we do not hear of the thinking and the affect of the savage as a child, were classified as an early phylogenetic phase in the development of civilized man. Finally, the anthropological, phylogenetic counterparts of the individual and of his ontogenesis are extrapolated to the reconstruction of the mental states and processes of primitive man.

To illustrate the way in which Freud fused nonpsychoanalytically derived biological principles with those of psychoanalysis in order to develop the above generalization, I shall quote a pertinent passage in his postscript in the Schreber Case (*8*):

> . . . I am of the opinion that the time will soon be ripe for us to make an extension of a thesis which has long been asserted by psychoanalysts, and to complete what has hitherto had only an individual and ontogenetic application, by the addition of its anthropological and phylogenetically conceived counterpart. "In dreams and in neuroses," so our principle has run, "we come once more upon the *child* and the peculiarities which characterize his modes of thought and his emotional life." "And we come upon the *savage,* too." We may now complete our proposition by adding "upon the *primitive* man, as he stands revealed to us in the light of the researches of archeology and of ethnology."

It is apparent that Freud operated with a basic credo, based on his conviction of the psychological and biological unity of man; that is to say, man (past and present) was a species whose psychological characteristics he had defined. Consequently, it would then be possible for psychoanalysis to be a comprehensive psychology of man. Moreover, the credo of unity made it possible for Freud to extrapolate from the adult to the child, from the individual to the group, from the immediate present to the historical past, from civilized man to uncivilized man, from historical man to prehistoric man, and, in addition, from the primal horde to civilization, from the Stone Age to the metallurgical age, from the nomadic state to the sessile community, from food-gathering to food-producing. Throughout all these runs the thesis of the common psychobiological identity of man. Thus, the psychobiological ontogeny of the individual recapitulates his psychobiological phylogeny.

Grand, sweeping, brilliant, and breathtaking is this comprehensive panorama of unified man. The fact still remains, however, that it is only in the psychoanalytic couplet of analysand and analyst that the empirical data and observations and the scientific categories of psychoanalysis are demonstrable. Outside of this situation, we plunge quickly into a vast sea of unlimited and mercurial variables that cannot be controlled by the essential psychoanalytic principle of procedure, namely, free association.

Examples of these extra-analytic fields are human biology, in the narrow sense used by Freud in the origin of instincts, and ethnology. As I have pointed out, the psychoanalytic method is not easy to apply in these instances except by speculation. For example, it is technically possible by remote control to observe, record, and measure fluctuating organ functions in the human being undergoing psychoanalysis. Two problems are at once apparent. The first is that the physiological modes of observation may be an intrusion upon what might otherwise be free association, thus constricting the uniquely psychoanalytic mentation in the patient and the psychoanalyst. It has been proposed that this problem should be handled by "analyzing" and thereby identifying the transference reactions and other disturbances in the psychoanalytic couplet. That this can be done is denied by "conservative" psychoanalysts who wonder whether the design and designer of such experiments may be antipathetic toward psychoanalysis. Freud warned psychoanalysts against flirting with endocrinology and the autonomic nervous system (*14*). I suspect, however, that the conditions which motivated this dictum by Freud do not exist to the same degree at the present time. Certainly, the gaps in biology are narrowing as, hopefully, they are in psychoanalysis, and the highly charged criticisms of Freud and his theories no longer prevail in the form that Freud encountered. It is not at all clear why the study of archeology, linguistics, rituals, biography, philology, works of art, and certain traits of birds are legitimate libidinal investments of service to psychoanalysis, whereas the direct and intimate study of biological man is not. But then, the scholars trained in these fields were closely associated with Freud, whereas the biologists were not (*29*). Moreover, just as man has recovered from, and then integrated into his adaptive behavior, the discoveries of Copernicus and Darwin, so will he sooner or later repeat the same process with the analogous contribution of Freud.

IV

It will prove useful if at this point I were to illustrate by reference to current research some of the issues raised by the enigmatic and in my opinion premature need to promote psychoanalysis as a general science. To begin with my selection of the topic, "Constitution in Psychoanalysis," this biological concept is basic to the ongoing psychophysiological research in our Human Behavior Laboratory[8] and to the ethno-psychiatric studies of the Ute Indian Project[9] both within the University of Colorado School of Medicine.

In both areas of research the study of human biology as a potent determinant of immediate behavior is a dominant feature. Conversely, the effect of behavior on human biology, if narrowly defined, can be described. It is probably more correct to view behavior from a broad point of view as a factor in the principle of natural selection and, therefore, as a determinant of human biology in the sense of evolution.

The behavioral data in these investigations were not and could not be

---

[8]Financed by National Institutes of Mental Health, Grant No. 5 T2 6380–08.

[9]Financed by University of Colorado School of Medicine, Continuing Research Fund, and by Ute Mountain Ute Indian Tribal Council.

obtained by the clinical psychoanalytic methods used by the patient and psychoanalyst in the psychoanalytic situation. These conditions and the method of free association are possible only to a very limited degree in the laboratory where nonverbal behavior is monitored and in the field of ethno-psychiatric research. Despite such restrictions, psychoanalytic psychology played a major part in the design of our studies and in the strategy of data analysis.

It is not fair to psychoanalysis to say that its heuristic qualities are being used in an operational way. As a rule, training and experience in the theory and practice of psychoanalysis tend to determine what to study in an undifferentiated field of inquiry and how to study it. What to study is easy to decide, because of the unique elements of psychoanalytic propositions, theories, and hypotheses. How to study is another matter, in view of the fact that the psychoanalytic method in its most legitimate sense cannot be applied, either in laboratory research or in field research in ethno-psychiatry. Consequently, we are obliged to *apply* the constructions and theories of psychoanalysis in the form of hypotheses based on the data obtained through nonpsychoanalytic methods. If the data support the hypothesis, we usually would say that the hypothesis has a right to stand as is. To go even further, if our hunches hold out we might ultimately propose a law or a principle. Because, however, the hypothesis seeks to apply psychoanalysis to the nonanalytic data, there is a sense of obligation to the parent theories and principles. All too often, questionable logic is used in discharging this obligation. The data which support the hypothesis that had been "borrowed" from a psychoanalytic theory or principle repay by serving to validate the theory or proving the principle. Perhaps this accounts for the often commented upon fact that the application of psychoanalysis outside of the clinical analytic situation has not led to refutation, revision, or even to a significant challenge of the psychoanalytic system or its parts.

It might be argued that hypotheses based on psychoanalysis are primarily developed within the nonpsychoanalytic field and that is where the revisions, if any, should occur. It is a remarkable fact that in clinical medicine, where psychoanalysis has exerted its major influence in the form of "psychosomatic medicine," significant revisions of medical science have not been effected. The same may be stated for ethnology, despite Freud's early and persistent interest in culture and personality, or "National Character."

I should like to cite an example from our Psychophysiological Laboratory. Because psychoanalysis has not specifically considered such research methods, except negatively, I shall be brief. One of the current research activities of the Human Behavior Laboratory is the study of the bodily epiphenomena of affects and moods. There are several reasons for this. One is that a satisfactory theory of affects is lacking, not only for psychoanalysis (*35*) but for general psychology and human biology as well. Another is that the basic phenomenology of affects is far from fully described. Finally, of great importance, is the role of affects for consciousness and for the ego functions of perception, association, and defense. For example, it is apparent that a patient's report of his perceptions of his body is highly selective for both psychological and psychophysiological reasons. We have observed that the eating habits of pathologically obese individuals cannot be verbally described by these patients in such a way as to elucidate the motivations and preconditions for the maladaptive eating. Direct observation and psychophysiological monitoring have yielded this information.

The problems of the psychoanalyst making observations in so-called non-psychoanalytical situations are remarkably clear in the principles of practice in child psychoanalysis. The use of play therapy and the principle of "forced fantasy" are forms of direct activity on the part of the child psychoanalyst. Perhaps the psychophysiological monitoring and the direct observation of obese patients when they are offered food are consistent with the theory and practice of child analysis if not with adult analysis.

Let me illustrate further from our ethno-psychiatric studies. I shall spend more time on this example because of its direct pertinence to Freud's own writing. You may recall my quotation from Freud which asserts the interrelation between neuroses, dreams, early childhood, the thinking of primitive and, possibly, of prehistoric man. If we take the principle as stated by Freud we would predict, i.e., hypothesize, that the thinking of members of the tribe of Indians in the Southwest, whom I have been studying very intensively, is like the mental activity in a dream, a neurosis, or in a child. In the thinking and language of the contemporary Ute Indian, one can observe the properties of animism, magic, and concretism. Our psycholinguistic studies indicate that these traits of thinking, language structure, and of communication are equivalent to generalizations and abstractions. This is strikingly apparent in the elaboration and dramatization of reported dreams. It is understandable that an individual whose waking thinking is essentially animistic and concretistic would deal with his dreams not as thoughts of varying remoteness from reality but as representations of reality. Therefore, the content of the manifest dream is regarded as a part of his waking thinking. He might use the dream as an indication that he should or should not be a medicine man, that he is or is not in danger in relation to a particular ghost, and that he should make negative or affirmative decisions about a variety of enterprises, such as traveling, tending to cattle, or seeking a woman. Similarly, when an Indian uses his own language to tell a story or narrate a folk tale or myth, the features of animism and concretism persist.

The story might be about an Indian hunter who is tracking game. He looks for the trail which is marked by hoof prints, signs of cropping, and feces of the game. The Indian comes to a decision as to which part of the trail is freshest and therefore closest to the game. Let us compare the thinking of the Indian with that of a hunter whose mental processes are those of abstraction and generalization. He estimates the degree of desiccation of the hoof prints and of the feces. Such judgments would be correlated with his knowledge of the antecedent and present climatic conditions. He would infer from the cropping marks whether re-growth had begun. From the point of view of the Indian whose thinking is animistic and concretistic, however, the mental process goes as follows: a question is asked of the feces—how long ago were you put there? and the grass is asked—when were you eaten, when were you stepped upon? The remarkable fact is that in the Indian's story, the feces and the grass are represented as giving the same answers as to the time and behavior of the game that are finally deducted by the hunter with the capacity for generalizing, correlating, and abstracting. As a result, the two hunters, each with very different mental processes, take precisely the same realistic course of action in pursuing the prey.

V

At one level, a hypothesis based on Freud's principle of the communality of a kind of mental activity in dreaming, children, neurotics, and primitive men has been supported. Does the fact that the data support the hypothesis prove the principle that Freud had in mind? I doubt it! The dreamer, the child, and the neurotic all have particular inadequacies of the ego which affect perception, reality-testing, and problem-solving. However, the Indian in his behavior does not show an ego impairment in his perception, reality-testing, or problem-solving. It would take me too far afield at this time to discuss the significance and difference between endogenously and exogenously experienced ideation, or what is "internal and external" and what is introjection or projection, for psychoanalysis in general and ego theory in particular. This discussion will appear in another publication.

This example of psycholinguistics, incidentally, parallels the animistic and concretistic content of many fairy tales. The difference, however, is that reality-testing as a basis for gratification cannot occur if the fairy tale is to persist.

How justifiable is Freud's basic premise of the psychobiological unity of man? As a credo, it receives intense doctrinary support both from Christian theology and ethics, as well as from our political culture with its emphasis on democracy and constitutional rights of individual man. As a scientific postulate, however, it must be supported by knowledge of a different order. In all probability, the psychobiological unity of man can be more or less demonstrated in the populations of the countries that communicate, collaborate, or compete with one another in terms of the same value systems. There are several questions, however. How did this relative homogeneity come about? When and under what circumstances? What influence have the theological and ideological forces in our lives had on our ability to investigate this credo in our own time?

The Ute Indians and possibly other Indian tribes have not fulfilled the destiny of a surviving, conquered people, namely, identification with their conquerors. Other ethnic groups, notably the African Negroes who made up the slave populations in North Africa and in the United States, have successfully identified with their conquerors or masters. The American Indians have at times come close to the destiny of the nonidentifying vanquished of the historical past, namely, extermination.

It is obvious that this "join them if you can't beat them" outlook tends to operate as a massive homogenizer of peoples and their ways. The rise and fall of empires, for example, tend to provide one of the ecological settings in which the biological and psychological unity of man can develop. In several centers of the Western Hemisphere, notably Central and South America, this process had been proceeding independently of the same course in the Eastern Hemisphere. It should be emphasized, however, that, whatever biological and psychological homogeneities come to be established in the two hemispheres, they need not necessarily be the same. When it is considered that the two geographical groups have had more or less independent development over thousands of years, such a hypothesis gains some support. This isolation, incidentally, is relative, since there is no reason to suppose that only one migration of Indians had occurred or that prehistoric contact with the Eastern Hemisphere had not taken place from time to time. There is evidence that the blood group characteristics of Indians is significantly and statistically different from those of other peoples.

The American Indians have not identified with their conquerors. The American people, depending on regional and national conditions, have had markedly ambivalent and inconsistent attitudes toward the American aborigines. These have consisted of attempts at ruthless extermination, reactive and overdetermined benevolence and idealization with playful imitation of Indian ways in nature, concerted efforts to transform the Indian into a middle-class American Christian while urging him to retain his Indian culture.

VI

It seems to me that psychoanalysts have created a paradoxical situation. On the one hand, psychoanalysis is declared to be a general psychology without, however, providing the basic scientific work outside of psychopathology to justify this assertion. The conviction that psychoanalysis is a general science of man is similarly unsupported by the necessary biological and ethnological research performed by psychoanalysts. The paradox further lies in the fact that psychoanalysts encourage one another to work with patients and to investigate psychopathology. The education and accreditation of psychoanalysts are based exclusively on psychoanalytic psychopathology.

This circumstance makes the authentic psychoanalyst a therapist of selected mental illnesses with all the ethical commitments of a physician. Moreover, if he is not trained to work outside of this specialized area of applied psychology, he is hardly justified in believing that he is disciplined in the theories and methods of a general psychology, let alone a general science.

Perhaps these dilemmas are not inherent in psychoanalysis, with its wide range of definitions as to what it is, but in psychoanalysts and the history of the values that activate and direct their judgments. Because of this, I believe it entirely justifiable and not an irrelevant digression to discuss a corollary of Psychoanalysis and Biology—namely, Biology and the Psychoanalyst. I propose to consider this in terms of psychoanalytic education.

It seems to me possible to defend the position that systematic training in psychoanalysis should not include, and realistically should not require, education in biology. An examination of the available curricula of psychoanalytic training institutes does not reveal courses, seminars, or even special lectures on biology. There is one small exception, namely, the vague area of psychosomatic medicine, which tends to be regarded as a special and limited case of applied psychoanalysis. Perhaps in the United States a background in biology is assumed, because candidates in a training institute are required to be physicians trained in an accredited medical school. This, in turn, also means premedical training in at least elementary biology, chemistry, and physics.

As is happening more and more, the decision of an individual to become a psychiatrist and a psychoanalyst may crystallize in college or earlier. In most instances that I have observed over the past ten years, there is an associated tendency to limit education in the basic sciences and mathematics in favor of the humanities and social sciences. Though I would like to do so, I should not use this place to discuss the significance of these observations for the "image" of psychiatry and of psychoanalysis and the determining effect of these images on the choice of these careers. It is consistent with this statement that several psychoanalytic institutes admit for training in psychoanalysis highly qualified nonmedical candidates who wish to master psychoanalysis as a research method to be applied in so-called nonpsychoanalytic disciplines, or to problems within psychoanalysis itself. As far as I can learn, such nonmedical candidates appear to come from the academic settings of the social sciences, the nonbiological behavioral sciences, and the humanities.

VII

To return to biology in the education of the contemporary physician, I believe that it is fair to say that there is much controversy over the biological subdivisions and depth that should be required. No one would or could argue today that medical education makes the student an expert in any one of the subjects which he studies so intensively and devotedly in medical school, or that he is expected to be competent to do research, teach, or apply his knowledge to the understanding of new problems, or even new principles. It is generally agreed that several years of postgraduate education are required in order for the graduate physician to be suitably equipped for these tasks. In short, premedical and medical education consists of compacted (sometimes desiccated) introductions to a selected number of areas of science that are deemed necessary for the comprehension of the theory and practice of medicine. This state of medical education and indeed of the contemporary theory and practice of medicine is widely recognized by responsible educators and administrators in medical schools. The solutions that are offered and some of the experiments that are attempted lend themselves to being classified in the following ways:

1. De-emphasis of what seem to be the scientific pretensions in medical education and training of the physician to be a skilled craftsman and technician. The impact of such a development in medical education upon the group from which future psychoanalysts are to be selected is self-evident.

2. Transformation of medical education from a dilettante exposure to basic sciences to a serious study of behavioral and social science, on the grounds that at the present time etiology, pathogenesis, preventive medicine, therapy are as influenced by behavioral and social factors as by biological ones. This point of view (to which I shall return later) is consistent with Freud's position as expressed in the *Problem of Lay Analysis* (*13*), in a supplement he wrote to it (*14*) and in his *Autobiography* (*12*).

3. In any case, development of a science of biological medicine in which professionals would be trained who would be generally expert in human biology in the narrow sense, such as, for example, in molecular biology, immunology, psychophysiology, organ culture, neurochemistry, and in the branches of clinical medicine at the highest levels of available knowledge and experience, such as surgery of organ transplants, rehabilitation, developmental medicine, and geriatrics, to mention a few.

It would not take much reflection to come to the realization that in practice (but not in principle) these three classes of physicians already exist, both because of and in spite of medical education.

In the light of considerations such as: the discrepancy between the content of medical education and vast scope of contemporary human biology and culture; the understandably limited training obligations of a psychoanalytic institute, its emphasis on psychopathology and clinical practice, and its concept of the field of psychoanalysis as expressed in its admission policies; the changing social and scientific "images" of psychoanalysis in different places, from its beginnings to the present; and finally, the improbability that applicants for psychoanalytic training would be expert in biology, it is unlikely that the gap between psychoanalysis and biology will be appreciably narrowed by psychoanalysts. It might be argued that this is as it should be. In that case, traditional psychoanalytic organizational policy will compel psychoanalysis to carry the unnecessary burden of a largely inert medical education, a view unequivocally expressed by Freud (see below).

The American Psychoanalytic Association and its policy-making bodies should examine the "ecology" of psychoanalysis and of psychoanalysts, from the point of view of prerequisite education. As matters stand now, psychoanalysis selects its candidates from a group of physicians previously culled by premedical advisors, a medical aptitute test, and an admissions committee of a medical school. The Association and its component Institutes can only influence or stimulate a small part of the research that should be done because of the very real lack of appropriately trained individuals capable of becoming "medical" research psychoanalysts. This problem should be solved if psychoanalysis is to live up to its belief that it is or can become a "general science."

Because medical education is in the process of being extensively reviewed, major changes in its guiding philosophy are very probable. These can be predicted, and psychoanalysis should have available prepared or at least considered positions on the various possibilities.

It will be useful to quote Freud on this problem. In *Postscript to a Discussion on Lay Analysis,* published in 1927 (*14*), Freud clearly states an opinion on medical education which he held to the end of his life:

> What is known as medical education appears to me to be an arduous and circuitous way of approaching the profession of analysis. No doubt it offers an analyst much that is indispensable to him, but it burdens him with too much else of which he can never make use, and there is a danger of its diverting his interest and his whole mode of thought from the understanding of mental phenomena. A scheme of training for analysts has still to be created. It must include elements from the mental sciences, from psychology, the history of civilization and sociology, as well as from anatomy, biology, and the study of evolution. There is so much to be taught in all this that it is justifiable to omit from the curriculum anything which has no direct bearing upon the practice of analysis, and only serves indirectly (like any other study) as a training for the intellect and for the powers of observation.
>
> It will not have escaped my readers that in what I have said I have assumed as axiomatic something that is so violently disputed in discussion. I have assumed, that is to say, that psychoanalysis is not a specialized branch of medicine. I cannot see how it is possible to dispute this. Psychoanalysis falls under the head of psychology; not of medical psychology in the old sense, nor of the psychology of morbid processes, but simply of psychology. It is certainly not the whole of psychology, but its substructure, and perhaps even its entire foundation. The possibility of its

application to medical purposes must not lead us astray. Electricity and radiology also have their medical application, but the science to which they belong is nonetheless physics. Nor can their situation be affected by historical arguments. The whole theory of electricity had its origin in an observation of a nerve-muscle preparation, yet no one would dream today of regarding it as a part of physiology. It is argued that psychoanalysis was, after all, discovered by a physician in the course of his efforts to assist his patients, but that is clearly neither here nor there. On the other hand, the historical argument is double-edged. We might pursue the story and recall the unfriendliness and, indeed, the animosity with which the medical profession treated analysis from the very first. That would seem to imply that it can have no claims over analysis today, and though I do not accept that implication, I still feel some doubts as to whether the present wooing of psychoanalysis by the doctors is based, from the point of view of the libido theory, upon the first or upon the second of Abraham's sub-stages—whether they wish to take possession of their object for the purpose of destroying or of preserving it.

I might make my true opinion on this question clear by echoing a cynical remark about women. One man was complaining to another about the weaknesses and troublesome nature of the fair sex. "All the same," replied his companion, "women are the best thing we have in that line." I am bound to admit that so long as schools such as we desire for the training of analysts are not yet in existence, persons who have had a preliminary education in medicine are the best material for future analysts. We have a right to demand, however, that they should not mistake their preliminary education for a complete training; that they should overcome the one-sidedness that is fostered by instruction in medical schools, and that they should resist the temptation to flirt with endocrinology and the autonomic nervous system, when what is needed is an apprehension of psychological facts with the help of a framework of psychological concepts. I also share the view that all those problems which relate to the connection between psychical phenomena and their organic, anatomical and chemical foundations can be approached only by those who have studied both—that is, by medical analysts. It should not be forgotten, however, that this is not the whole of psychoanalysis, and that for its other aspect we can never do without the co-operation of persons who have had a preliminary education in the mental sciences. For practical reasons we have been in the habit—and this is true, incidentally, of our publications as well—of distinguishing between medical and applied analysis. But, that is not a correct distinction. The true line of division is between *scientific* analysis and its *applications* alike in medical and in non-medical fields.

The context and timing of Freud's publication of these statements were related to the public controversy over the practice of psychoanalysis by those of his followers who were not physicians. In addition, however, the fundamental revision of the psychoanalytic theory of the systems unconscious, preconscious, and conscious associated with the new topography (Id, Ego, and Super-Ego) in the metapsychology were primarily developments in *psychology*. Ego psychology, at least in its initial stages, imposed a methodological shift away from what was professionally biological in Freud's experience (i.e., morphogenesis), as opposed to what was biological in his general knowledge. The latter was the source of his views on heredity, constitution, evolution, anthropology, ethnology, and archaeology. In this connection it is not fully appreciated that Darwinian evolution was far from proved during most of Freud's life and that only in recent years can it be stated that evolution is no longer a hypothesis.

It would seem that the selection, education, training, supervision, and accreditation of a psychoanalyst have come to be organized around the aims of clinical psychoanalysis, that is, the special application of an assumed general psychology of psychoanalysis. This assumption appears to rest on speculative extrapolations of clinical generalizations into the biological and behavioral sciences of man.

It is a curious paradox that psychoanalysts have come to view, as examples of applied analysis, basic research into the biological and ethnological foundations of its theories toward a general psychology. In contrast, psychoanalysts regard the special area of psychoanalytic psychopathology as the main source of information for a general science of man. The significance of this paradox lies in its probable effect on admission policies and curriculum designs of psychoanalytic training institutes.

REFERENCES

1 Coon, C. S. *The Origin of Races.* New York, Knopf, 1962.

2 Dobzhansky, T. *Evolution, Genetics and Man.* New York, Wiley & Sons, 1955.

3 Dobzhansky, T. *Mankind Evolving; The Evolution of the Human Species.* New Haven, Yale Univ. Press, 1962.

4 Freud, Anna. The concept of developmental lines. *Psychoanal. Stud. Child 18*:245–265, 1963.

5 Freud, S. "Project for a Scientific Psychology" (first published in 1895). *The Origins of Psychoanalysis: Letters to Wilhelm Fliess, Drafts and Notes, 1887–1902,* edited by M. Bonaparte, A. Freud, and E. Kris. New York, Basic Books, 1954.

6 Freud, S. "A Reply to Criticisms of my Paper on Anxiety Neurosis" (first published in 1895). *Standard Edition of the Complete Psychological Works of Sigmund Freud,* edited by J. Strachey. Vol. III. London, Hogarth, 1962.

7 Freud, S. "Biography of Leonardo da Vinci" (first published in 1910). *Standard Edition,* Vol. XI. London, Hogarth, 1957, p. 59.

8 Freud, S. "Psychoanalytic Notes on an Autobiographical Account of a Case of Paranoia" (first published in 1911). *Standard Edition,* Vol. XII. London, Hogarth, 1958. pp. 9–82.

9 Freud, S. "Totem and Taboo" (first published in 1913). *Standard Edition,* Vol. XIII. London, Hogarth, 1955, pp. 1–162.

10 Freud, S. "Psychoanalysis and Religious Origins" (first published in 1919). *Collected Papers,* Vol. V. London, Hogarth, 1950.

11 Freud, S. "The Libido Theory" (first published in 1922). *Collected Papers,* Vol. V. London, Hogarth, 1950, pp. 131–135.

12 FREUD, S. "An Autobiographical Study" (first published in 1925). *Standard Edition,* Vol. XX. London, Hogarth, 1959.
13 FREUD, S. "The Question of Lay Analysis" (first published in 1927). *Standard Edition,* Vol. XX. London, Hogarth, 1959, p. 179.
14 FREUD, S. "Postscript to Discussion on Lay Analysis." *Standard Edition,* Vol. XX. London, Hogarth, 1959, p. 251.
15 FREUD, S. *The Future of an Illusion.* London, Hogarth, 1928.
16 FREUD, S. *Civilization and Its Discontents.* New York, Norton, 1930.
17 FREUD, S. "Acquisition and Control of Fire" (first published in 1932). *Collected Papers,* Vol. V. London, Hogarth, pp. 288–294.
18 FREUD, S. "New Introductory Lectures on Psychoanalysis" (first published in 1933). *Standard Edition,* Vol. XXII. London, Hogarth, 1964.
19 FREUD, S. "Analysis—Terminable and Interminable" (first published in 1937). *Collected Papers,* Vol. V. London, Hogarth, 1950, pp. 316–357.
20 FREUD, S. "Moses and Monotheism," Part III (first published in 1939). *Standard Edition,* Vol. XXIII. London, Hogarth. In press.
21 FREUD, S. *An Outline of Psychoanalysis* (first published in 1940), translated by J. Strachey. New York, Norton, 1949.
22 FREUD, S. *Gesammelte Werke.* 17 Vols. London, Imago, 1940–52. (*Aus den Anfangen der Psychoanalyse* [1950] including *Entwurf einer Psychologie* can be considered Volume 18 of this set.)
23 FREUD, S. *The Standard Edition of the Complete Psychological Works of Sigmund Freud,* edited by J. Strachey. London, Hogarth, 1953—.
24 FREUD, S. *The Origins of Psychoanalysis.* New York, Basic Books, 1954.
25 HARTMANN, H. *Ego Psychology and the Problem of Adaptation,* translated by D. Rapaport. New York, Int. Univ. Press, 1958, p. 121.
26 HARTMANN, H. *Ibid.,* pp. 28ff.
27 JONES, E. *The Life and Work of Sigmund Freud.* 3 Vols. New York, Basic Books, 1953.
28 JONES, E. "Historical Reviews of Certain Topics." *The Life and Work of Sigmund Freud,* Vol. III. New York, Basic Books, 1953, pp. 302–333.
29 JONES, E. *Ibid.,* Vol. II.
30 JUKES, T. H. The genetic code. *Amer. Scientist 51:*227–245, 1963.
31 KEITH, A. *The Antiquity of Man,* Vol. I. London, Williams and Norgate, 1925.
32 KROEBER, A. L. "Evolution, History and Culture." In *The Evolution of Man,* edited by S. Tax. Vol. II. *Mind, Culture and Society.* Chicago, Univ. of Chicago Press, 1960.
33 MAYR, E. "Species, Concepts and Definitions." In *The Species Problem.* Washington, D.C., American Association for the Advancement of Science, Publication No. 50, 1957, pp. 1–22.
34 MORGAN, T. H. *The Physical Basis of Heredity.* Philadelphia, Lippincott, 1919.
35 RAPAPORT, D. On the psychoanalytic theory of affects. *Int. J. Psycho-Anal. 34:*177–198, 1953.
36 SCHILDER, P. Psychoanalyse und biologie. *Imago 19:*168–197, 1933.

37 SMITH, R. *Kinship and Marriage* (1885). Cited by Freud in "Group Psychology and the Analysis of the Ego" (first published in 1921). *Standard Edition,* Vol. XVIII. London, Hogarth, 1955.

38 WITTELS, F. *Freud and His Time.* New York, Liveright, 1931.

EIGHT

Structural Aspects of the Psychoanalytic Theory of Instinctual Drives, Affects, and Time

WILLIAM C. LEWIS, M.D.

A PARADOX

There is an apparent contradiction embedded in psychoanalytic theory, which can be called a paradox. This paradox results from the fact that psychoanalysis has roots in biology. It has confused psychoanalytic theory and its terms, has preserved a gap betwen psychic and biologic views, and has hampered the full use of knowledge in both areas. This contradiction seems to have troubled Freud recurrently and still gives rise to intricate theoretical debate. The paradox is that the two opposing propositions about structure in the human psyche are true. By *structure* we mean an ordered arrangement of elements, which may be perceptions, events, thoughts, reactions, et cetera of sufficient stability to give some predictability. It is important to note that structure may refer to sequential, as well as to simultaneous, relations among elements.

One proposition is the more familiar and enjoys current acceptance among psychoanalysts. It states that the most unstructured types of psychic function are those associated with unconscious drives—the id. The other proposition is that the most highly structured types of psychic function are these same instinctual id processes. This second proposition was stated by biologists but is tacitly assumed by psychoanalysts. It is obvious that both propositions cannot be true if all their terms are taken to have the same meaning, since both

The author wishes to thank a number of friends for helpful suggestions, especially Robert R. Holt, Paul Bergman, and Benjamin Rubinstein.

refer to the same organism. We must therefore examine the meanings of the terms of the propositions in order to show how a reconciliation of the propositions is in fact possible.

THE PROPOSITIONS

The first proposition.—The first proposition is so common in the literature that it hardly requires expanded discussion or documentation. It is contained explicitly in many of Freud's formulations from the beginning, but one example will suffice for our purposes. In 1933 (*26*) he said:

> We can come nearer to the id with images and call it a chaos, a cauldron of seething excitement. We suppose that it is somewhere in direct contact with somatic processes, and takes over from them instinctual needs and gives them mental expression, but we cannot say in what substratum this contact has been made. These instincts fill it with energy, but it has no organization and no unified will, only an impulsion to obtain satisfaction for the instinctual needs in accordance with the pleasure principle.

We may let this formulation stand for a whole family of correlated and derivative ideas—primary process fluidity, freely mobile energy, lack of structure, lack of logic and of a concern for contradiction, lack of a sense of time and of a regard for the limitations of space, lack of moral values and so on—all of which are familiarly attributed to the deeper layers of psychic functioning.

This is only one of many statements about the id, and about its organization or disorganization, to be found in Freud's writings. In other contexts (*20, 21, 23, 24*) he attributed many types of structure to the id: repressed memory traces, inherited ideas, the differentiation into perceiving and perceived, the repetition compulsion, and fixations. Yet the "seething cauldron" metaphor expresses a view anyone is apt to find sympathetic who listens for a while to analytic material in the consulting room; it has the ring of truth in it. Since one is using a most orderly type of human psychic function to examine psychic function itself, one understandably tends toward the bias that, when this type of order begins to melt before one's eyes and ears, one is falling into chaos. When precise speech is replaced by turgid, vague, elliptical, or arbitrary gibberish, alarm is almost automatic: things seem to be getting out of hand.

The consulting room emphasizes in other ways the view of psychic structure as that associated with conscious, rational processes. We try to dissolve old rigid patterns, to promote a state of "fluid" emotion, and to assist the verbal expression of freed-up affects, fantasies, wishes, etc., in new forms. Direct action, direct yielding to instinct or its derivatives, is discouraged in the treatment setting. We request only verbal reports about instinctual matters. True, the transference neurosis sometimes mobilizes our own responses as well as those of our patients, giving us a direct experience of instinctual drives. Outside the consulting room, in our less disciplined daily life, we are caught up in instinctual processes which have a different type of directly perceptible structure from that of rational thought. Just how these instinctual processes are perceived will be considered later, but we are certainly more in contact with whatever instincts we have when we are engaged in passionate activity than when we are practicing psychoanalysis.

The second proposition.—The second proposition, assigning precise structure to primitive layers of the mind, can best be clarified by reference to primitive organisms. The very creatures most dominated by instinct have the least choice, the least confusion, the least ambiguity in their responses to the world. In this view, the type of psychic function characteristic of man, particularly his thinking power, permits the greatest range of disorder—of violation of fixed function, of confusion, doubt, uncertainty, and choice: in short, of freedom from "given" structured patterns—ever attained in the universe known to us. Man, and, to some degree, higher animals can transcend rigid patterns, can respond to distant possibilities and dangers, and can "long-circuit" the automaticity of instinct. They can hesitate, doubt, and make mistakes of judgment not possible for an ant.

STRUCTURE AND PSYCHIC FUNCTION

Two views of structure.—'Structure' in the mode of patterned instinctual response must then differ from 'structure' in the mode of controlled rational processes. One view of structure in mental events, that of the psychoanalysts, begins at the structured pole with the manner in which we observe people using language in accordance with grammar and logic, in strict accord with clearly perceived reality. At the unstructured pole it seems to dissolve in an amorphous cloud, hardly to be labeled either thought or feeling, but something perhaps in between. Another view of structure, that of the ethologists, starts with the intricate but fixed patterns of insects and lower animals. As one observes higher animals one sees mixures of learned and instinctual patterns including structured rage and sexual behavior. This latter type of structure appears to blur when one views the animal, man, who is said to possess no true 'instincts,' or at least only rudimentary ones (*38, 39, 79, 87*). This is the type of structure underlying the "drive organization of memory" of Rapaport (*72*), the theory of impulse, zone, and mode of Erikson (*12*), and the regular cycles of drives and affects of Benedek (*2*). Thus there appear to be two modes of organization which overlap and interpenetrate in the evolutionary scheme and in the individual.

The overlapping of the two types of structure.—In individual ego development, learning and maturation take time, and the mode of organization characteristic of conscious adult reasoning is rudimentary for a considerable period. Thus, the human infant begins life with blurred, imprecise structuring in both modes of organization, as we are told by both psychoanalysts and ethologists. As a good example, the ethologist Schneirla (*79*), says, "In the higher animals, developmental processes are progressively more labile in relation to capacity for profiting by experience and for behavioral plasticity. In the higher mammals, earlier behavior, although not formless, is most generalized of all, and the individual is most radically influenced by experience in the course of later development." For a statement of the similar psychoanalytic position, see Hartmann (*38*). These views of structure in psychic life, to which we will raise objection, seem to leave the infant, or the adult who has regressed for whatever reason, in a no-man's-land in which there is only disorganization—"the seething cauldron"—with neither sure instinct, nor right reason, to guide him.

We are left with a puzzle about the relations of modes of organization. What evidence have we relevant to the problem of their relationship to one another? Logical thought is familiar enough to us; but what of perception of instinct? On purely subjective grounds we recognize that a part of our direct experience intertwines with thinking and sense perception yet is separable from these pale and shallow distillations. All of us have felt a persistent, incessant pull in some periods of passion—whether it be hunger, or love, or the desire to run away from danger. In recognizing subjectively a type of organization pertaining to our emotions and instinct derivatives, however, we discover that *time* is the dimension in which these processes reveal their structure. The starving man first wants food, later has vivid dreams of banquets, still later may have vivid, waking visions of feasts, and may come to the point of finding repulsive organic material tolerable (*65*). Structured thought is invaded by a "drive" to embark on an ordered course of action. Thus we have, however vaguely, some hint of subjective structure coming from our depths. We can also see this in our dreams. This direct awareness of something we are impelled to do, some other place we must seek, some pattern we must follow *now,* for peace to be achieved later, gives a hint of form and structure. We are caught up in a process. The usual formulation of instinct as having source, aim, and object, and our use of 'drive' as a synonym for instinct also hint at a type of structure. All these suggest a primitive awareness of the continuity of a 'given' program on which we are embarked, and of particular things in the world which are acting upon us. This is not really chaos.

Structure in time as related to instinctual drives.—In psychoanalytic theory an instinctual drive is usually looked upon as something pressing for discharge, and the major theoretical study has been devoted to delay and control structures. What is apt to be overlooked is that instincts have complex structure, as shown in the orderly sequence of behavior which results from their release. They are complex coordinations, like computer programs, organized not only in space but in time. Structure may be revealed sequentially, as in a Morse code telegram, as well as immediately, as in a diagram. Migrations, courting and mating, nesting and giving birth do not occur in a moment, like the burst of a balloon. The discharge of instinct takes time and has its syntactic structure which is as complex as that of language—which latter is also organized in time (*6, 7*). Instincts also have their own cycles and critical periods in time.

Furthermore, the "learned" kind of structure involves time in several ways. Control apparatuses imply *delay* of discharge in time. David Rapaport comments, "The general development of psychic structure begins with innate discharge-regulating thresholds, is fostered by delays of discharge enforced by reality conditions, and progresses by internalization of the delay of discharge caused by reality, establishing an ability to *delay*" (*76*). In a series of papers (*73–75*) Rapaport has used this basic model for the psychoanalytic theory both of thought and of affect. Thought, in this hypothetical model, arises in the presence of drive tension when the drive object is absent, and affect at this stage is a safety valve discharge of tension into the interior of the body. The subsequent development of thought and affect involves the erection of a hierarchy of taming, detouring, and controlling structures. These give rise to drive-derivatives of great complexity and accomplish an active, long-range mastery of the self in relation to the world. Rapaport was able to trace such familiar concepts as the reality principle, neutralization of cathexis, signal affects in place of affect as discharge, memory, and secondary-process thinking, et cetera, to various aspects of this basic model and its modification via progressive structure formation.

Since this is, then, a basic psychoanalytic model we may use it to simplify the complexity alluded to . Time is involved in the model and in all the derivatives of the model. 'Delay of discharge' is too easily thought of as a dam or a road block of a static nature, which is misleading. First, the word *delay* itself needs to be understood as a relative alteration of what was flowing—in other words, a relative change in a *continuity*. Second, since drives have a syntactic programed structure, delaying structures must take this into account and reflect this temporal structure also. There must be memory of a sequence of related events, and not just a file case of static photographs, in order for memory to serve the function of control. There must be a capacity to extrapolate and to anticipate where a drive is leading to in space-time in order for the reality principle to operate. Anyone who has struggled with temptation can easily verify this. No static system of memory traces will serve unless aided by some continuous causally oriented system of memory. The temporal organization of memory is immediately obvious when we observe our own recollections. Every memory has space-time continuity attached to it, which is less obvious in visual memories than in memories of occurrences, conversations, musical themes, et cetera; but even in memories of visual scenes we are aware of ourselves, observing in the continuity of space-time.

Thus on grounds of logic and subjective observation, we must take account of temporal structuring when we consider drives, drive regulatory structures, and their various derivatives. However, there are other grounds for doing so. Lashley, in 1948, said (*57*):

> Attempts to express cerebral functions in terms of the concepts of reflex arc or of associated chains of neurons, seem to me doomed to failure because they start with the assumption of a static nervous system. Every bit of evidence available indicates a dynamic, constantly active system, or rather, a composite of many interacting systems. . . . Only when methods of analysis of such systems have been devised will there be progress toward understanding of the physiology of the cerebral cortex.

He examined speech and the motor behavior of men and animals, attempting to analyze the mechanisms which control the serial ordering of these activities. He showed that memories must have space-time coordinates and sequential order to account for such phenomena as musical recall, rhythmic behaviors like walking, language syntax, etc. An example is an attempt to play backward a tune like "Yankee Doodle." This can be done, but a preliminary translation to a spatial image of the tune, which is then scanned backward, is necessary, at least for most of us. In connection with this example Lashley says:

> First, the assumption is that the memory traces are associated, not only with other traces, but also with the system of space coordinates. By this I do not mean that the engram has a definite location in the brain; our experiments show conclusively that such is not the case. Rather, when the memory trace is formed it is integrated with the directional characters of the space system, which give it position in reference to other associated traces. Second, the assumption is that these space characters of the memory trace can be scanned by some other level of the coordinating system and so transformed into succession.

The relation of elements in the remembered patterns does not inhere in the elements themselves. The motor movements which produce the word 'tire' can be reversed to produce 'rite' and have no intrinsic order of association in themselves. "The order must therefore be imposed upon the motor elements by some organization other than direct associative connection between them." Lashley asserted that the essence of the problem of serial order lies in the existence of generalized schemata of action which determine the sequence of specific acts, which acts in themselves seem to have no temporal valence.

These schemata of organization have been directly demonstrated by Wilder Penfield (*70*) in the case of memory. Stimulation of the cerebral cortex in appropriate areas produces a temporally organized stream of memories rather like a video-tape. The development of communication and computer theory in the last decade has sharpened interest in the schemata of organization called programs, and research in these and many other related areas is beautifully brought together and applied to psychological problems in a book entitled *Plans and the Structure of Behavior,* by Miller, Galanter, and Pribram (*64*). These authors reject as inadequate any concept of a 'passive' brain, as in the reflex-arc theory of behavior, and develop a concept of continuously operating schmata of sequential order involving feed-back mechanisms, which supply the building units of behavior. The reader is referred to this work for a discussion of possible mechanisms underlying the ordering of such diverse phenomena as motor skills and habits, memory, speech, problem-solving, and 'givens' of behavior—the 'plans' involved in instincts.

Concern with schemata of temporal order and their relation to instinctual drives has increased among psychoanalytic theorists. In the 1959 symposium on psychoanalysis and ethology (*88*) at Copenhagen, both Kaufman and Bowlby questioned the adequacy of the earlier hydrodynamic models of instinct and instinct discharge, as had Colby (*9*) earlier, characteristic of psychoanalytic theory and of some ethological theory, particularly that of Lorenz (*59*). In both theories, instinct had been compared to a reservoir of stored up specific energy, which is released, as if there were a valve in the base of the reservoir, by some appropriate stimulus. This concept includes the idea that discharge of the accumulated energy is what brings instinctual behavior to an end. This hydrodynamic model had the power to explain the gradual rises and falls in responsiveness, unusual levels of responsiveness, and of long sequences of behavior apparently guided by some motivational "pressure."

Kaufman (*46*) points out, however, that recent ethologic research has conclusively demonstrated that most instinctual behaviors are interrupted by certain *stimulus* situations: "The crying of a baby and the distress calls of a chick end when mother appears. Lest you think this is true only of disturbance behavior, let me point out that a bird stops building a nest when there is a nest, and resumes building if it is taken away. A bird which normally lays a clutch of four eggs and then stops, will go on laying eggs to a total of more than 60, if the eggs are continually removed from the nest so that there are less than four present." Kaufman concludes that such observations cannot be explained by the hydrodynamic model or by the reflex-stimulus-response model (because of the prevalence of terminating stimuli) but *are* consistent with the cybernetic model of instinct, such as we have just mentioned.

In brief, the "bursting balloon" metaphor for instinct discharge will not serve to explain all aspects of instincts. It appears that instinct should be thought of as a continuous rhythmic activity, perhaps like breathing, in which each phase is followed by another phase, integrated into the total ongoing behavior of the organism with respect to changing environmental conditions. This is, after all, implicit in the genetic viewpoint of psychoanalysis.

The central point of this discussion is that any of the conceptualizations of the organization of behavior thus far advanced imply temporal scanning of a plan, process, or program. Even if our psychic apparatus contains some static "maps" to guide either learned or instinctive behavior, these maps must be scanned in *time,* just as one reads a set of instructions or follows a road map or the diagram of a football play. The impression that the guiding structures for activity of any sort are spatially organized in the brain and present themselves all at one instant, like a diagram of a reflex-arc, is misleading. As in a computer, memory is dynamic and depends upon a continuous activity of the apparatus into which are fed instructions in temporal sequence.

Temporal structure and instinctual drives in Freudian theory.—We have seen the pervasive importance of temporal structure in all behavior and the relation of temporally programed patterns to the instinctive behavior of animals. When we turn to the application of these ideas to man's nature we encounter difficulties and must watch our usage of terms. Since we will aim for some change in the common usage of terms like 'instinct,' an example of the terminological problem is apropos. Thus, Schur (*80*) says:

> The great variety of "inherited releasing mechanisms" of the appetitive behaviors, but especially the importance of learning in man, makes it difficult to unravel the instinctive links even in such chains of reaction as the "consummatory act" of the sexual drive. It is by now a truism that our wishes (instinctual drives, their derivatives and representations) are traceable in some way in all our functions, even in perception. However to call any single "behavior" which is *influenced* by instinctual drives "instinctive behavior" is a distortion of both ethological and psychoanalytic concepts. Ethologists will rightly object to the inclusion under this heading of learned responses and psychoanalysts to that of ego functions.

(See, for instance, Ostow: *66, 67.*)

What is crucial are the points of contact between instinct and controlling structure, and the relation of these points to perception. Freud seems, as Strachey (*85*) has pointed out, to have moved in his theorizing consistently away from an early theoretical position in which little or no distinction was made between an instinct and its 'psychical representative' to a later one in which instinct is conceived of as incapable of entering consciousness directly, but only via the idea representing it. In the "Project for a Scientific Psychology" (*27*) he hypothesized certain 'nuclear systems' (psi neurons) which received contributions both from the receptors (phi neurons) and from drives, and, even further, that these nuclear systems were connected in a feed-back loop with secretory neurons (key neurons) which by their secretions influence the contributions of drives to the nuclear systems. The nuclear systems were supposed to be in reciprocal connection with the cortical systems (*W* systems) and consciousness. Thus, in this early view rational processes and consciousness were in contact with a mixed product coming from both drives and the receptor systems, and the continuous, standing, cathexis of the psi system provided continuity of activity in time. Pribram (*71*) has pointed out the sophistication of this early model in terms of present-day neurophysiologic knowledge and, especially for our purposes, the concept of cathexis, which he believes can include the idea of continuous graded activity in time, such as that of dendritic networks (*62*). This continuous neural activity contrasts with the discontinuous activity associated with transmitted nerve impulses in the reflex-arc model.

In Freud's model, Pribram says:

> Propagated neural activity has two aspects, a quantitative (number of impulses) and a qualitative (pattern of impulses). The propagation of quantity of excitation results in changes in cathexis; the transmission of quality does not. Perceptions result when patterns of excitation developed in the nuclear systems and those developed in the receptors are matched, i.e., when thought and perception are compared. An incongruity may exist. Thinking is considered productive or cognitive when the incongruity is met by actions that either change the environment directly and thus the percepts, or the experience of the individual in the environment, and thus the traces in the nuclear systems from which the thoughts take origin. . . . There must therefore be in the cortex a mechanism which allows the input from projection (of receptor inputs) and from nuclear systems to be distinguished. In fact, evidence is beginning to accumulate that such a mechanism does exist and that it serves as a comparator that matches the inputs for congruity.

I present this quotation at such length because included in it are important elements relevant to the problem of structural modes in psychic function. In this model, continuity, drive contribution to cognitive processes, and active referential processes between modes of perception are all well accounted for. After Freud gave up the "Project" and attempted to devise pure psychologic formulations there seems to be evidence that he felt subtle theoretical difficulties in accounting for the interplay of temporally organized instinctual drive structure and rational structure.

In "Instincts and Their Vicissitudes" (*20*) he wrote: "An instinct can never become an object of consciousness—only the idea that represents the instinct can. Even in the unconscious, moreover, an instinct cannot be represented otherwise than by an idea. If the instinct did not attach itself to an idea or manifest itself as an affective state, we should know nothing about it." In the paper entitled "Repression" (*21*) he put it thus: "Clinical observation now obliges us to divide up what we have hitherto regarded as a single entity: for it shows thus that besides the idea, some other element representing the instinct has to be taken into account, and that this other element undergoes vicissitudes of repression which may be quite different from those undergone for the idea. For this other element of the psychical representation *quota of affect* has been generally adopted" (emphasis Freud's).

Thus, in these views Freud seems to conceive of instinctual drive as some thrust of energy, not structured in itself. Further evidence of his dissatisfaction seems clear from a passage Kaywin (*47*) has already pointed out.

> Are we to suppose that the different instincts which originate in the body and operate on the mind are also distinguished by different qualities and that is why they behave in qualitatively different ways in mental life? This supposition does not seem to be justified; we are much more likely to find the simpler assumption sufficient—

that the instincts are all qualitatively alike and owe the effect they make only to the amount of excitation they carry, or perhaps, in addition, to certain functions of that quantity. What distinguishes from one another of the mental effects produced by the various instincts may be traced to the differences in their sources. In any event, it is only in a later connection that we should be able to make plain what the problem of the quality of instinct signifies.

As the editor comments, "It is not clear what later connection Freud had in mind" (*85*). Here he seems to be reverting to the formulations of the "Project," and to be hinting at a concept of temporally structured patterns of frequency changes in the inputs from instinctual drive sources, analogous to FM (frequency modulation) rather than to AM (amplitude modulation) in radio transmission.

The term 'drive,' with its connotation of the pressure of a persistent force, experienced passively, conveys the quantitative aspect to which Freud referred. We say we are 'driven' by lust, rage, or hunger. Yet, it appears from these passages that Freud must have felt a twinge of doubt about qualitative aspects of perception of the drives (that is, their directional, patterned aspects). He does not in the quoted passage explicitly concern himself with temporally structured aspects of drives or with the nature of time itself. In innumerable other places, from the earliest of his writings, however, it is clear that he did not think of instinctual drives as having temporal structure: he stated that unconscious processes were marked by a lack of sense of time; that the id was timeless (in later terminology) ; that a sense of time was a part of ego functioning and had to be laboriously learned. Freud's theories were based on the physics of Helmholtz[1] (that is to say, essentially Newtonian), a point of view that works relatively well when one is dealing with large elements of experience like a neurosis (comparable to the macrostructures of Newtonian mechanics) but a view that gives trouble when one attempts to deal with the basic units of experience (comparable to the microstructures of atomic physics). For Freud, until very late in his life, time referred to mere succession. Before the learned, clock-type of time, he postulated that there is 'timelessness.' These views concerning the nature of time have persisted to the present day in psychoanalytic theory with little change.[2]

These traditional theoretical formulations concerning time perception and temporal structuring have certain obvious theoretical consequences. To assign psychic structure and time-sense exclusively to the ego is to conceive of the

[1]Holt (*43*) makes clear the problems Freud had to deal with because of the prevailing scientific views given him by his teachers.

[2]Considerations of space prevent extensive discussion of varying views of time in psychoanalytic theory. For the most recent statement of psychoanalytic views of time and time-sense, see Gifford (*29*). Freud himself, according to remarks he made in conversation with Princess Bonaparte (*4*) had begun in his last years to view time in more relativistic terms, and especially to recognize continuity of process as being the essence of time.

deeper layers of the psyche—those most dominated by instinct—as timeless, structureless, and essentially lacking in different qualities of function. It is true that to say that the id is lacking in 'time-sense' is not equivalent to saying that the id has no temporal relevance or organization, but I submit that these statements are so equated in common usage among psychoanalysts. Thus, Bonaparte: "Life can only visualize itself in terms of living; in the unconscious of every individual it is depicted as outside time, which does not exist for the unconscious, and without limitations of any kind" (*4*). Also Bergler and Roheim: "Infantile omnipotence and time perception are mutual contradictions. Omnipotence is in unalloyed accord with the pleasure principle" (*3*).

Yet, the need to account for clinical facts by postulating some qualitative and structural aspects of drives came back gradually. It is perfectly obvious, for example, that intrusive murderous thoughts and impulses are qualitatively different from intrusive impulses of a loving sexual nature. Both may seem to come unbidden from the depths of the psyche and approach irresistible strength. This type of observation led to the postulation of qualitatively different *kinds of psychic energy*. By now, this has developed into something of a theoretical nightmare—with various kinds of energy proliferating exuberantly in the literature (pure aggression, pure libido, de-aggressivized, de-libidinized, or neutral energies).

REVISIONS IN THE MEANINGS OF THE TERMS OF THE PROPOSITIONS

The terms 'time' and 'instinct.'—The assumption that time sense depends upon learning, and that it is connected with pure succession, has hidden defects. The basic units of subjective experience seem not to be discrete points, ticks of the clock, or quanta, as Freud once suggested (*25*), but to be spans, as a number of philosophers have concluded (William James [*44*]; A. N. Whitehead [*37, 90*]; Heidegger [*40*], and others). Mere succession is an abstraction applicable to all sorts of other sequences. The raw material of experience is *continuity* in space-time and the derivation of the present state from the state immediately preceding it. This continuity of experience and the inevitable derivation of one moment from its precursors is the basis of all natural law, and of the special case of natural law exemplified in the rigid patterns of instinctive behavior. We are accustomed to thinking of instincts in terms of the higher animals, in which complex coordinations of behavior unfold in relation to their environment. Even in such animals, in which interplay of genetically "given" patterns with learned patterns of behavior and with primitive forms of thinking make definition of what instinct means difficult, the temporal factor is obvious. However, if we consider the more primitive organisms, we see that their behavior is fixed in space-time and is guided by continuous relationships of a physical nature with the surrounding world.

As long ago as 1729 a French astronomer, DeMairan, showed that plants which had been moved into caves, into total darkness, continued to orient their leaves to the position of the sun outside, in a diurnal rhythm (*5*). Flatworms show rhythmic behavior, moving in and out of their burrows to correspond with the timing of tides even if removed to the laboratory. A crustacean called the beachflea has an innate migratory pattern related specifically to the geographic contour of the shoreline home of its ancestors, whereas its cousins will show a *different* direction of migration appropriate to a *different* ancestral beach, even when both these families of beachfleas are raised in the laboratory. The lowly oyster has the capacity to open and close with the tide and to adjust its periodic movements, if it is moved some distance from home, to correspond with the movements of the moon (*14, 78*). The evidence thus far available concerning the mechanism underlying such time-sense points to a physical mechanism (which is relatively insensitive to temperature) rather than to a chemical one, but the essential point is that rhythmicity and temporal organization can be demonstrated in the behavior of organisms from those of the one-celled level up to the circadian and other periodic rhythms of man's biological behavior. As a concrete instance of the latter, consider the disorganization of one's biological rhythms which occur during travel in this day of the jet airplane! Not merely is this a passive response to forces in the environment, however, but it involves in addition some internal regulator which sets rhythms in partial independence of the surrounding world. When, as in the case of the oysters cited, primitive or higher organisms are moved far from their native surroundings, their periodicity ('instinctual behavior') remains for a time attuned to their old homes, and they require an adjustment period to 'reset' their internal clocks.

The epitome of the human element is doubt and delay. Hamlet's familiar "and thus the native hue of resolution is sicklied o'er by the pale cast of thought" expressed one extreme of human experience, but we may easily forget that in moments of greatest dominance by our instinctual drives we never doubt the continuous existence of a real person who will be present in the next moment as the causal object of our continued intentions. The more instinct takes part in our experience, the more absorbed in this continuity we become. The long search for a love-object, with the elaborate rituals and maneuvers of dating, courting, and winning, leading through preparatory acts and mounting arousal, has a continuity, persistence, and a basic certainty of the derivation of this moment's world from that of the moment before. Only in the consummatory orgasm does the word "discharge" seem an appropriate term to apply to the sexual instinctual drive, and even during orgasm there is cyclic continuity of activity. Since we tend professionally to concentrate on the human doubting, rather than on the continuity of the love relationship, we forget the instinct is there, with its quiet program. The menstrual cycle with its mood changes, studied so well by Therese Benedek (*2*), and the long sequence of the process of giving birth are other examples. The time structure of instinct is obscured in humans by the operation of thought, but it can be seen at birth in the basic rhythms of sleep-wakefulness, hunger and satisfaction, and in all the larval periodicities of our later lives.

The concept of the id.—We have already quoted one of Freud's statements about the id. There were a great many, and the concept has become very unclear. Merton Gill has recently reviewed these varying views, and a clear exposition of the problem involved in this concept is to be found in his monograph (*30*). He asks "whether we must continue to conceptualize the id as without structure, despite the evidence it is hypothesized as including memories, symbols, mechanisms, or if we can admit that the discrepancy between Freud's conceptions of the id which clearly involves some degree of structure and his conception of it as 'chaos, a cauldron of seething excitement' presumably without structure demands an explicit resolution." He proposed three alternatives: (*a*) that all motives be called id and all counterforces and discharge structures ego; (*b*) that the id is a chaos and all of the mental apparatus is ego; (*c*) that the id is the most primitive level of a continuum but a level at which there is some secondary process organization and structure. Gill favors the third view, with emphasis on the functional inseparability of drive and drive restraint. We can adopt this hierarchic view unchanged for our present discussion.

The terms 'rational processes' and 'psychic structure and function.'—Once we grasp the temporal structure of instinctual drives and adopt a hierarchic concept of the id we can conceive of a progressive interplay between two types of structure in the development of rational processes and of psychic structure and function. I have already quoted Rapaport's model of the psychoanalytic theory of thought and commented that the development of both delay and control structures must involve time in the strucutre of the controlling apparatuses themselves. Now, what exactly is involved in these processes and apparatuses? The essential mechanism of man's intellect appears to be the capacity to create and to manipulate symbols. The Freudian theory of thought and affects depends upon this symbolic capacity. Thus, in this theory, thought begins in infantile life when instinctual drive tension mounts, in the absence of the object of that drive. Memory traces of the object are pushed into consciousness as an hallucinatory image—in other words, as a symbolization of the object. At first, the hypothesis states, the image is diffuse and global but gradually differentiates into other associated images (symbolizations) or 'instinct representations' (*76*) which are mutually interchangeable. This is the 'drive organization of memory' (*72*). These hypothetical events are linked together in psychoanalytic theory and serve to explain many observations about our early and primitive modes of thought.

The subsequent development of thought involves further hierarchic symbolizations. An example is the loss, via symbolic representation, of certain of the original elements of the psychic content symbolized. The second order symbol then stands for only part of the raw data; this is the relation of simple abstraction, which I suggest lends itself to the type of defensive function involved in 'primal repression' (also described as 'withdrawal of cathexis'), the defense called *isolation* (and intellectualization), and also to the defense *displacement*. More complex types of symbolic function are involved in the types of thinking described as secondary process. This type of thought organization involves active countermaneuvers against instinctual drive representations, over and above the rather passive ones thus far mentioned. These countermaneuvers are, of course, called 'countercathexes' and operate continuously in time. They depend upon an aspect of the symbolic process which must be left for another occasion for full discussion. For the moment, it suffices to say not only that instinctual drives probably enter the symbolic process as *objects* of symbolization, but also, via their temporal structure, that they have a part in guiding the symbolizing process itself. In this way, a continuity of motivation in thought can skew the direction of thought and can be expressed in such defenses as reaction formations and other continuously operating defenses. We speak, for example, of "killing with kindness." The concept *repetition compulsion* simply derives from the repetitive intrusion of instinctual drive structure in skewing adaptive thinking along 'given' lines.[3]

What is the nature of symbolism? Though prominent in psychoanalytic theory, this process has received relatively little attention until recent years. Symbol-formation has been traditionally viewed in a restricted sense as a defensive ego function (*11, 13, 45*), but there are signs of a gradual recognition that the symbolic function goes to the roots of all psychic functioning (*69*). The most extensive and systematic analysis of the symbolic process in psychoanalytic literature is that of Kubie, who has traced, in a series of penetrating papers (*49–56*), the role of symbolism in health and disease. He has advanced lines of evidence supporting the idea that there is a continuity of the symbolic process through all strata of mental life and all periods of development. He asserts that in its formative process every concept and its symbolic representatives develop from *two* points of reference, one internal, with respect to the boundaries of the body, and one external. The internal reference is rooted in the instinctual tension and deprivations of infancy, to which are related various external events as experience continues.

[3]For a different interpretation of the relation of instinct to repetition compulsion, see Schur (*80*).

> Consequently, every evolving conceptualization of the outer world comes into relationship with evolving conceptualizations of the body world, creating new conceptual gestalts, in which the bodily world and the outer world establish specific symbolic relationships, such that each can be and is used to represent the other. At first this relationship is conscious and we encounter it in the language of the games and songs of early childhood (e.g., "This little pig goes to market." Legs are "dogs." The female genital is a "pussy." The male genital is a "bunny" or "cock." The whole body is a "horse," etc.). Later in life, however, the dual relationship becomes unconscious and is found chiefly in the manifest symbolism of dreams, in hypnagogic reveries, in delirious states, in art and literature, and in the symptom formations of the neuroses and psychoses. (*52*)

In his later papers Kubie makes clearer the connection of the internal reference pole of symbolism to instinctual processes (*53–56*). He recognizes that continuous relations with the environment and external objects are implicit at least in certain phases of our instincts, and that the organism plays an active role in implementing these interchanges and the transformations and synchronizations of them which result in integrated behavior. Kubie supplies many vivid examples of the modification of instinctual behaviors by symbolic processes in subhuman species as well as in humans. He recognizes the temporal structure of instincts and their rhythmic fluctuations, but he stresses time mainly in respect to the importance of the time *gap* between need and satisfaction in all of psychological development. Kubie goes deep into the problem of how instinctual processes and their symbolic representation in psychic functioning arise from biochemical processes in the body. He uses Adrian's concept that an afferent impulse can influence the brain by synchronizing in some measure the asynchronous discharge of individual brain cells and cell masses, thus imposing an orderly pattern on that previously chaotic movement. The afferent impulses involved in instinct patterning come, Kubie proposes, fom bodily organs whose biochemical processes have become synchronized under the influence of deprivations, accumulations, or distentions.

At this point, we may have established, with Kubie's guidance, an adequate underpinning to explain the temporal structuring of instinctual drives and their role in the symbolic process. We could leave these matters, perhaps, and return to the main thesis, which is the relation of this type of structuring to other psychic structures and functions. Yet, one further speculative step is very tempting, since it allows us to make certain potentially testable predictions which can then be verified or refuted. This step also allows us to include matters usually considered unconnected with one another into a coherent pattern of relation. The further step is to examine more closely the nature of the perception of instinctual drive, and since the spirit of these papers is one of free-ranging thought I may be forgiven if I advance too far into the realm of epistemology.

The main gap in Kubie's theory is that it focuses on various afferent inputs to the brain in explaining the symbolic process, to the neglect of considering brain activity itself. Various philosophers and theorists have pointed out that the body is part of the external world, as far as our inner awareness is concerned. Sense impressions, whether of body pain or of distant landscape, are all of a piece. Freud and especially Tausk (*86*) pointed this out in terms of infantile psychic development, and philosophers of the solipsist school (Descartes, Berkeley, Hume) have noted this long before (*91*). Yet, we are aware of some other type of perception which centers in the continuity of a process in time, and of causal chains of events between ourselves and external objects. Hume granted the practical necessity of behaving as if there were a real world, but his philosophy could not dispel an unconquerable doubt that anything beyond mirage existed. But what of the activity of the brain itself? What of Lashley's observations about the continuity of brain function? Is there any reason to limit "perception" to the perception of sensory inputs from *outside* the brain? We know that there are complex, spatially organized reverberating circuits within the brain. We know that there are hierarchies of scanning, storing, and recall apparatuses, and activating systems, and that functions such as memory, affect states, and thought involve many simultaneously interlocking apparatuses, rather than simple reflex-arcs. These complex interrelated structures presuppose some *active* internal organization in the brain in order for integration and substitution among these apparatuses to be possible. Can we perceive our own brain *function* directly? Descartes thought so: his classic *Cogito, ergo sum* expressed an awareness of his own thinking activity. Neither Descartes nor philosophers thereafter were able to escape the trap of the solipsist position, however, in which all that can really be known is a series of sense impressions (and impressions of operations upon those sense impressions). In this view, all else is illusion. Any other awareness of the existence of outside objects via a perceptual mode differing qualitatively from that of sense impressions escaped detection, as far as I know, until it was discovered by Alfred North Whitehead (*61, 90, 91*). Since Whitehead's theory of a different mode of perception is relevant to the perception of the instinctual drive structure, it is only an apparent digression to consider his proposal briefly.

Whitehead starts by making a distinction between the kind of sensory experience possessed by only a few of the higher animals, namely, sense impressions, and another mode of perception common to all organisms. This perceptive mode he called "perception in the mode of causal efficacy." He pointed out that, first, continuous time; second, the conviction of real objects acting causally upon us to attract or to repel; and, third, the operations of instinct, are welded together to comprise a primary perceptive mode of experience which is distinguishable from the bright but shallow world of sense impression. This mode of perception is the primitive element in our experience, linking us with the lower animals, which do not possess brain sensory projection areas but which, nevertheless (as the oyster) are blindly attracted or repelled in instinctual cycles in relation to real shorelines and tides. This type of experience—poorly localized and vague beyond our bodies—is inherent in our physical relations with the surrounding world, including all temperature, gravitational, and other physical participations implied in the theory of relativity. This concept of 'instinct,' expressing relatedness and lawful fixity at a physical level, is far away from the 'instinct' of the ethologists, who study animals possessing sense impressions and symbolic functions. Yet there is no discontinuity in nature, and it is not hard to see the continuity between the lawfulness of a rock's behavior on a shoreline, through the more elaborate lawfulness of the oysters on the same shoreline, and of the continuation of this lawful fixity of relationship into some of the behavior of a fish or a porpoise or a man on that same shore.

Higher animals can respond to distant possibilities via their sensory receptors. They can choose and doubt and, hence, are in part free. But man's perceptive experience is not merely that mediated by sense impressions. We are directly aware of the continuity of our existence, and of vague presences acting powerfully upon us in this continuity. In fact, 'sense impression' implies something forcing itself on something already existing. I suggest that the continuous reverberating circuits of brain activity supply the perception of continuity, upon which are impressed various "messages from a distance" via afferents of many kinds. However, these sensory afferents can affect only the continuous brain activity via propagated causally efficacious changes in nerve tracts. Hence, 'sense impressions' can never be separated from the 'instinctive' operation of nerve tissue with its continuous physical lawfulness. Ultimately, the brain functions in relation to its sensory inputs as does the oyster to the physical influences from the shoreline. In sense impressions there is both information and "press" (*65*).

Rather than merely possessing proprioception of our body images in space-time, I submit that we are aware of some 'proprioception' of our brains as structures in space-time: in other words, that we have a 'brain image.' I might as well go all the way and suggest that this is what we call the ego, and that it has vague shape, form, and familiar boundaries. This 'brain image' or 'ego image' must be constituted in earliest life through perceptions of its own activity in integrating the types of sensory and instinctual drive activity permitted to an embryo. From birth on, its development proceeds by complex interactions, symbolizations, rational conceptual analyses, etc., of the most bewildering complexity. Throughout all of this there is the directly perceptible 'carrier wave' activity of normal processes, awake or asleep. This 'carrier wave' is, I suggest, the instinctual activity of the brain itself. This is perhaps the 'asynchronous' activity of Adrian and Kubie, upon which may be impressed by afferents the instinctive activity of other parts of the body. When I hereafter speak of 'awareness of instinctual drive' it is meant to refer to the combination of both these intrinsic and extrinsic activities or various symbolic representations of these.

For Whitehead (*90*), the fundamental symbolic reference is this reference between the two modes of perception of the surrounding world (the modes of 'causal efficacy' and 'presentational immediacy') which we have sketched above. All subsequent thought has, as its roots, the comparison of experience of the world and of ourselves in these two cross-referential modes. In this way, and by subsequent symbolization and conceptual analysis, human psychic life develops. We cannot discuss Whitehead's theories further here except to say that from these basic concepts and relations he builds a philosophy of symbolism in language, mathematics, social relations, religion; in short, of all of man's highest attainments. However, his discovery of an unfamiliar (yet familiar) mode of perception helps us recognize what is easy to overlook: our brain is always active in time and, I propose, can perceive its own activity as well as the relation of that activity with the world surrounding.

What is striking is that Freud's early model in the "Project" (*27*) contains a structural scheme which could express graphically the relationships which are involved in Kubie's and Whitehead's theories. Thus, the continuous activity of psi neurons receives contributions from receptors, from drives directly, and from other psi neurons, and there are feed-back loops with each of these. In other words, our psychic experience is based on our own activity (the cathexis of nets of the psi neurons) in integrating instinctual drive perception with sensory perception, whereby the totality of experience is achieved. Consciousness of this process (the relation of the *W* system to the nuclear system) is a variable element not essential to the basic process.

To return to our main thesis, in conscious logical reasoning we are relatively unaware of any contribution of structured drive to the process of the manipulation of symbols, as in language and mathematics. Yet, language itself is a discursive symbolic form and depends on structure in time; that is, one word is organized after another rather than in presentational form, as in a map. If we examine less clearly structured forms of thought, logical relations *seem* to loosen in fantasies, dreams, and other altered states of psychic functions (hypnosis, LSD, etc.). The 'primary process' *has* order, though drive elements and temporal patterning are more prominent and insistent than in waking thought. It is very difficult to detect any discontinuity between the various levels of thought, as many writers have shown (*17, 42, 48, 76*). Thus it seems parsimonious to conclude that there is only one 'thought' and that we can maintain the term 'primary process,' as a valuable way of expressing a type of symbolic process dominated by drive. It is a 'drive organization of thought' along the model of Rapaport's (*72*) 'drive organization of memory,' but it is not a different kind of thought. If there is only one thought it is based on the interaction of three factors, and one can attempt a formulation of the following nature:

$$T = f\ (d, s, c),$$

where T equals thought, and the terms d, s, c refer, respectively, to instinctual drive, sense impressions, and conceptual analysis.

The two propositions about structure only appear to stand in opposition. There are two types of structure in psychic events. One is associated with instinctual drives and is structured in space-time. It has continuity. It is perceived in the psychic depths and extends into conscious awareness, though dimly appreciated for the most part. The other form of structure is associated with high levels of the symbolic process, but this type of structuring extends deep into the earliest forms of thinking. The question is not one of more or less structure but of the relative contribution of the two varieties.

SOME PREDICTIONS FROM THEORY AND EVIDENCE RELEVANT TO THESE PREDICTIONS

The concepts we have been considering are so abstract that it is not easy to reduce them to testable predictions, especially since we are dealing with two continuously overlapping and interpenetrating types of organization. Nevertheless, some rough predictions are possible.

Classical psychoanalytic views hold the following to be learned functions: cause-and-effect reasoning; time sense; awareness of external objects as different from the self.

Infancy and ego regression from any cause should *reduce* the vividness and accuracy of perception in these dimensions. Dreams, fantasies, psychosomatic states, sensory isolation, and powerful emotional states should be associated with loss of structure in psychic functioning, relative to the structure observed in conscious rational processes. Alertness, wakefulness, and vivid sense impressions should foster these learned functions.

The proposed modified view links together: perception of causality (causal efficacy), awareness of *continuity* in time, the influence of external objects on the self, temporal structuring of psychic function in accord with instinctual drive patterns. These are all considered aspects of a single perceptual mode separable at least in theory from sense impressions and conceptual analysis. Fantasies, dreams, regressed states of any type, infancy, sensory deprivation, etc., should supply evidence of the operation of this perceptual mode at an increased level as compared with conscious rational thinking.

Subjective waking experience.—We first mentioned subjective experience as supplying evidence of the temporal structuring of psychic function. Conscious fantasy is easy to evoke as proof. Consider, for a moment, seduction. As you do so you will note a sequence, not a photographic "still" picture. Or arrange for yourself a banquet. Take revenge on your worst enemy in fantasy. Temporal pattern is inescapable. Some conscious fantasy is so ordered by instinctual drive as to result in raw discharge. As an example, it is not at all infrequent for adolescents to engage in sexual fantasy in examination situations, resulting in mounting sexual excitement which culminates in orgasm. One such student was strictly limited to this pattern of sexual experience, though he had had no heterosexual, homosexual, or masturbatory experience. He had a number of orgastic discharges on occasions when, following a long sequence of preparatory fantasy, he heard the teacher call for the papers.

Another aspect of subjective conscious experience relevant to the predictions from theory was pointed out by Whitehead. He cited the relative indifference to causal consequences we have in moments of the greatest heightening of pure sensory experience (music, art, beauty intensely experienced in any form). On the other hand,

> anger, hatred, fear, terror, attraction, love, hunger, eagerness, massive enjoyment are feelings and emotions closely entwined with the primitive functioning of "retreat form" and of "expansion towards" . . . these primitive emotions are accompanied by the clearest recognition of other actual things reacting upon ourselves. The vulgar obviousness of such recognition is equal to the vulgar obviousness produced by the functioning of any one of our five senses. When we hate, it is a man that we hate and not a collection of sense-data . . . a causal, efficacious man. (*90*)

Affect states and psychosomatic regression.—We take for granted certain aspects of the perception of instinct such as our reflexes and responses to gravitation, Newtonian conceptions of force, mass, and acceleration in all our motor activities such as driving a car, playing tennis, etc. We do not take for granted as part of our immediate perception that certain other reactions of our bodies conform in a structured way to the 'givens' of instincts. David Graham and his co-workers (*31–36*) have discovered that there are a great many more such regular relationships between our bodily reactions to the world surrounding us and our symbolizations, in language, of these relationships than was previously suspected. In Graham's view, the probability is that there is a specific physiologic (instinctual) ground for every affect state. These formulations were based on observation of patients in certain psychosomatic states, which we are accustomed to class as 'illnesses.' In these illnesses a regular association of exacerbations of symptoms (the results of intensified specific physiologic processes) was observed to be specifically connected with particular types of life stress. The 'psychological' expressions of response to these life stresses takes the form of specific verbalizations.

The physiological processes involved are automatic, not subject to ego control, and are of considerable duration, like moods. They are more primitive than the structured discharge processes which are subject to some ego control, like laughter or weeping. When it comes to affect expression, what is considered illness is of course purely conventional. So is the 'sense' made between the thought processes involved and the accompanying somatic expression. We regard it perfectly sensible that someone should lacrimate when speaking of a sad event; but these other physiological changes involved in psychosomatic illnesses make much less "sense" than laughter or tears, when one tries to understand their relation to the specific verbal statements.

Let us look at several examples. Patients suffering either the onset or the relapse of the following illnesses will make, regularly, the following typical statements:

Hives: Patient felt he was taking a beating, and felt helpless to do anything about it.
Asthma: Felt left out in the cold, wanted to shut the person or situation out.
Hypertension: Felt threatened with harm and had to be on guard.

It seems impossible to explain such linkages in the terms with which we started the discussion in this paper. Either of the original statements expressing the two views of 'structure' would obviate specific linkage, since two kinds of structure are here clearly welded; and if the most precise invariant structure is that of instinct, one would expect to observe blurring and vagueness, as instinct structure is supplanted by thought and verbalization. If the most precise structure is that of rational thought, its connection with instinct should be fluid. One wouldn't expect regularity and specificity in the area of intersection of two vaguenesses. However, as we have reviewed the concept of structure there seems no conflict: We are aware of some haunting, vague pull or push directly in the sense of instinctual drive, and of some localization to an object or situation in the mode of perception of sense impressions; and we refer symbolically and conceptually to the relation between these perceptions. These 'attitude statements,' therefore, elegantly demonstrate a number of precise points of contact between highly structured instinctual drive processes and highly structured symbolic rational processes, and they document the continuity of interpenetrating structures.

In another publication (*58*) I have discussed the defensive aspects of these 'attitudes' and have suggested that such linkages are the bases of certain primitive defenses. These can be understood as the somatic beginning of what, in later psychic development, are the more familiar psychic defenses. Freud (*22*) pointed out that the psychic defense called projection, for example, begins in infancy with the spitting out of what is unpleasant. Here I have stressed more the instinctual drive aspects of these attitudes. This is no real contradiction if we adopt the view which Merton Gill (*30*) has expressed with regard to all psychic processes: every psychic content or structure has both discharge *and* defensive aspects.

Infantile omnipotence.—Some direct knowledge of the primitive mode of perception of instinctual drive (causal efficacy) must have colored the various formulations given us by those who studied the mental life of infants. Perhaps the earliest efforts in this direction were those of Freud and particularly of Ferenczi (*13*). Both of them hypothesized various stages of magical thinking in infancy. Offhand, there is no reason to assign to the infant any convictions about causation and, hence, to assign omnipotence to the thinking of the oral stage. Why should a baby attach to his magic gesture or magic thought any particular relevance to what happened thereafter? Association alone will not serve—this would only serve arbitrary *association,* not causation. *Post hoc* does *not* necessarily imply *propter hoc* unless there is an essential perception of the connection and derivation of this moment from the last, and of the effect of the one upon the other. 'Association in time' contains that elusive hidden reference which it took a man of Whitehead's stature to identify—association in time involves direct perception of causal efficacy, which is another name for perception of instinctual drive structure. The self-conscious search for cause-and-effect relationships develops slowly; so does the formation of perceptual object constancy and some knowledge of the laws of the external world as relating to inner events. Yet, all who have grappled with the earlier stages of mental life have concluded that there is perception of causal efficacy at these times, although it is not thus stated, but expressed in other terms—usually involving magic or omnipotence. The studies of Piaget (see *93*), Werner (*89*), and Spitz (*83, 84*) all confirm this; in fact, no matter how observers approach the problem—whether from direct contact with children, reconstruction from the clinical material of adult cases, or comparisons of organisms at various levels of evolution—all studies support the conclusion that the sense of causality begins very early and hinges on conformity and derivation in time, and upon lawful, instinctual relationships rather than upon learning. The Belgian psychologist Michotte (*63*) has attempted to demonstrate by various ingenious methods that causality is directly perceptible. His reports might not, however, be as convincing to one who holds the classical analytic view about the developments of causal reasoning, which was also Hume's view (*91*)—namely, that ideas of causality develop from a learned association between elements, a matter of 'habit of thought'—as would the other lines of evidence mentioned above.

I suggest that all conditioning experiments depend upon perception of instinctual drive structure as the *glue* between the separate elements of the stimuli, actively organized by the perceiving animal through symbolic reference with sense perception. The hungry dog responds to a *real* bell, with salivation for *real* food, in his world—he does not respond like a canine Descartes, puzzling as to whether anything at all exists. This appears to be the stumbling block of behaviorist theories—most recently, those of Skinner (*82*). In these theories, memories and the control of behavior are based on the idea that pure association and replication of an experience can explain subsequent behavior. They cannot, as has been argued at great length in many places, account for abstraction and generalization, symbolization in all forms, and, in short, the operation of human intelligence. There has to be some type of organizing, symbolizing, referential process which must include, beside immediate sense presentation, perception of instinct in order for the operation of human intelligence to be understandable.

Perception of instinctual drives gives a sense of 'vague presences'—of magically efficacious powers, independent of immediate sense perception. This quality is what makes sensory isolation, darkness, infancy, and febrile delirium all so poignantly terrifying. Numerous observers have reported a tendency to near-delusional paranoid thinking in certain subjects exposed to sensory deprivation experiments. These subjects develop vivid ideas of influence by unseen sources, by the experimenters, or by some unknown machines. Heron (*41*) has reported a significantly increased tendency in subjects under such conditions to accept propaganda arguing for the belief in psychical phenomena like telepathy, ghosts, poltergeists, etc. This is of course in the direction of the predictions I made earlier. The effects of sensory deprivation on time sense are harder to evaluate. Some subjects are less and some are more aware of time passage, though there seems to be some indication that a sense of the continuity and flowingness of time is enhanced by sensory deprivation.

Deikman (*10*), who was interested in the unfamiliar types of perception reported by mystics over the centuries throughout the world, has studied contemplative meditation experimentally and reports changes in subjective time-sense and the awareness of external objects. Some subjects felt less time had passed during the experiment than was actually the case, though a few had the reverse impression. It is hard to evaluate whether the reported results are in the direction predicted not only because it is difficult to define the difference between 'continuity in time' and sequential time, but also because the subjective difference was not stressed in questioning experimental subjects. However, Deikman's subjects, who fixed their gaze on an object, a blue vase, in the experimenter's room, report considerable changes in their 'personal involvement' with the vase. When it was removed in later stages of the experiment all subjects reacted as if they had lost something they were very attached to. Some subjects felt a sense of merging with the vase, and another described a peculiar impression of radiation from the vase.

Melanie Klein's formulations about elaborate fantasies concerning internal objects in the earliest years of life may stem from her attempts to account for the predominance of this type of perception in the infant's mental life, just as the primitives tend to anthropomorphize their sense of instinct in inventing rain gods and other angry presences to account for the misunderstood phenomena of nature.

Evidence of the penetration of rational structure into the deeper psychic processes.—Robert Holt (*42*), using a variety of sources, has pointed out many evidences of structure in the 'primary process.' These are, first, that myths, religions, and magic use materials which are usually attributed to primary process, but which in these phenomena exist in stable, synthetically integrated form; second, that disguise, displacement, and condensation require stability in order for there to be any possible defensive use of them, because otherwise offensive content could flood back; third, that a drive organization of memories is involved in the primary process but the memories themselves are highly stable and structured; fourth, that dream symbolism requires structure; fifth, that there are repetitive dreams and dream figures; sixth, that symptoms involve structuralized products of primary processes; seventh, that composite images in dreams require structures; and eighth, that not just any images can be condensed—they must have some structural similarity.

Fisher (*15–19, 68*) has demonstrated that subliminal stimulation is followed by complex organizing processes leading to distorted or selective reappearance of the registered stimuli in dreams and in waking drawings. Rational "causal" inferences must take place outside of awareness, without dependence of conscious schoolroom logic. This is consistent with the idea that perception of instinctual drive (causal efficacy) is a basic mode of perception and not the result of logical deduction, and adds the thought that at any moment only a part of our basic perceptions in either mode, drive, or sense impression are focused in consciousness. George Klein and his associates (*48*) have shown that subliminal presentation of sexual pictures and symbols, and even words like 'happy' or 'angry,' can influence conscious impressions of supraliminal stimuli. They propose that meanings must be known at subliminal levels. Again, these results weigh against assigning 'reasoning' to conscious rational processes exclusively, and they support the idea that causality is part of our basic perception independent of conscious conceptual analysis.

Whitman and his associates (*92*) have demonstrated that evaluations of dreams take place out of conscious awareness, which of course has been a tenet of Freudian theory for a long time. These workers were able to show that, of all the dreams of a given night, only a small fraction are remembered and told in therapy during the subsequent day. By awakening subjects whenever they showed signs of dreaming in a dream laboratory and by comparing notes the subsequent day with the therapist of their subjects, perfectly sensible 'reasons' for the unconscious editing process became obvious. Rechtschaffen and his associates (77) have also demonstrated the pattern of penetration of conscious types of organization into the depths of dreams by recording the kinds of speech observed during periods of rapid eye movement. It is the opinion of these observers that these (presumably) dreaming utterances were more associated with feelings and affect expression than were fragments of sleep-talking in periods in which there were no rapid eye movements.

As mentioned earlier, Freud was initially interested in contrasting dream thinking with logically structured thinking; but this should not obscure what he demonstrated so clearly—there is a kind of structure in dreams. Examples of the exquisite sophistication of condensation and symbolization in dreams are so commonplace as to require no documentation. I offer one gratuitously: One of my physician patients, in a time of annoyance at me for the frustrations of his analysis, dreamed of a friend. This friend, in reality, was thinking of entering analysis. In the dream, the friend was suffering some obscure type of fatal illness which my patient immediately understood, diagnosed, and prescribed medicine for. The disease was caused by arsenic poisoning, and the medicine prescribed was "B.A.L." ointment. As he related the dream, memory dawned, and my patient burst into a guffaw as he recalled what he had forgotten: the initials of this well-known remedy for mustard gas poisoning stand for "British-Anti-Lewisite."

SUMMARY

A paradoxical contradiction in psychoanalytic theory assigns both the least and the greatest structure to those psychic proceses closest to instinctual drives. The reasons for the seeming contradiction were examined, and a resolution was attempted. This required the demonstration and clarification of: (*a*) the continuous activity of the brain, organized in structured temporal patterns, (*b*) temporal organization of instinctual drives, their derivatives, and the defenses against them, (*c*) the fundamental nature of the symbolic process, and (*d*) the interplay between the type of structure associated with conscious rational processes, on the one hand, and this temporal drive structure, on the other, at various levels of the symbolic process. We took account of Whitehead's insights concerning an unfamiliar form of perception, that of direct perception of causality and temporal continuity, and explored the relation of this type of perception to instinctual drive structure. Predictions were made about the conditions most likely to maximize this perceptive mode, both on the basis of the more usual psychoanalytic models and also on the basis of the modified views proposed. Some evidence suggesting the worth of these modifications was presented.

REFERENCES

1 Arlow, D. A. In report of panel on "The psychoanalytic theory of thinking." Reported by Jacob Arlow in *J. Amer. Psychoanal. Ass. 6:*143, 1958.

2 Benedek, Therese. An investigation of the sexual cycle in women. *Arch. gen. Psychiat. 8:*311–322, 1963.

3 Bergler, E., and Roheim, G. Psychology of time perception. *Psychoanal. Quart. 15:*190–206, 1946.

4 Bonaparte, M. Time and the unconscious. *Int. J. Psycho-Anal. 21:*427–468, 1940.

5 Bünning, E. "Biological Clocks." In *Cold Spring Harbor Symposia on Quantitative Biology,* Vol. XXV. Long Island, N.Y., Biological Laboratory, 1960, p. 1.

6 Carnap, R. *The Logical Syntax of Language.* London, Kegan, Paul, 1937.

7 Chomsky, N. *Syntactic Structures.* The Hague, Netherlands, Morton, 1957.

8 Cohen, S. I., Silverman, A. J., Bressler, B., and Shmavonian, B. "Problems in Isolation Studies." In *Sensory Deprivation,* edited by Philip Solomon *et al.* Cambridge, Harvard Univ. Press, 1961, p. 120.

9 Colby, K. M. *Energy and Structure in Psychoanalysis.* New York, Ronald Press, 1955.

10 Deikman, A. J. Experimnetal meditation. *J. nerv ment. Dis. 136:*329, 1963.

11 Donadeo, J. In report of panel on "The psychoanalytic theory of the symbolic process." *J. Amer. Psychoanal. Ass. 9:*146, 1961.

12 Erikson, E. H. *Childhood and Society.* New York, Norton, 1950.

13 Ferenczi, S. "Stages in the Development of the Sense of Reality." In *Sex in Psychoanalysis: Contributions to Psychoanalysis.* New York, Basic Books, 1950.

14 Fingerman, M. "Tidal Rhythmicity in Marine Organisms." In *Cold Spring Harbor Symposia on Quantitative Biology,* Vol. XXV. Long Island, N.Y., Biological Laboratory, 1960, p. 481.

15 Fisher, C. Dreams and perception: The role of preconscious and primary modes of perception in dream formation. *J. Amer. Psychoanal. Ass. 2:*389–444, 1954.

16 Fisher, C. A study of the preliminary stages of the construction of dreams and images. *J. Amer. Psychoanal. Ass. 5:*5–60, 1957.

17 Fisher, C. In report of panel on "The psychoanalytic theory of thinking." Reported by Jacob Arlow in *J. Amer. Psychoanal. Ass. 6:*143, 1958.

18 Fisher, C. Subliminal and supraliminal influences on dreams. *Amer. J. Psychiat. 116:*1009, 1960.

19 Fisher, C., and Paul, I. H. The effect of sublinimal visual stimulation on images and dreams: A validation study. *J. Amer. Psychoanal. Ass. 7:*35, 1959.

20 Freud, S. "Instincts and Their Vicissitudes" (first published in 1915). *Standard Edition of the Complete Psychological Works of Sigmund Freud,* edited by J. Strachey, Vol. XIV. London, Hogarth, p. 120.

21 Freud, S. "Repression" (first published in 1915). *Standard Edition,* Vol. XIV. London, Hogarth, p. 152.

22 Freud, S. "The Unconscious" (first published in 1915). *Standard Edition,* Vol. XIV. London, Hogarth.

23 FREUD, S. *Reflections on War and Death.* New York, Moffat, 1918.
24 FREUD, S. "The Ego and the Id" (first published in 1923). *Standard Edition,* Vol. XIX. London, Hogarth, p. 13.
25 FREUD, S. "A Note upon the 'Mystic Writing Pad' " (first published in 1925). *Standard Edition,* Vol. XIX. London, Hogarth, p. 227.
26 FREUD, S. *New Introductory Lectures on Psychoanalysis.* New York, Norton, 1933, p. 104.
27 FREUD, S. "Project for a Scientific Psychology." *The Origins of Psychoanalysis; Letters to Wilhelm Fliess, Drafts and Notes, 1887–1902,* edited by M. Bonaparte, A. Freud, and E. Kris. New York, Basic Books, 1954, p. 347.
28 FRIEDMAN, S. M., AND FISHER, C. Further observations on primary modes of perception. *J. Amer. Psychoanal. Ass. 8:*100, 1960.
29 GIFFORD, S. Sleep, time and the early ego: Comments on the development of the 24-hour sleep-wakefulness pattern as a precursor of ego functioning. *J. Amer. Psychoanal. Ass. 8:*5–42, 1960.
30 GILL, M. M. Topography and systems in psychoanalytic theory. In *Psychol. Issues 3*(2):Monograph 10, p. 144, 1963.
31 GRACE, W., AND GRAHAM, D. T. Relationship of specific attitudes and emotions to certain bodily diseases. *Psychosom. Med. 14:*243, 1952.
32 GRAHAM, D. T. The pathogenesis of hives: Experimental study of life situations, emotions, and cutaneous vascular reactions. *Res. Publ. Ass. Res. Nerv. Ment. Dis. 29:*987, 1950.
33 GRAHAM, D. T., KABLER, J. D., AND GRAHAM, F. K. Physiological responses to the experimental suggestion of hives and hypertension atitudes. *Psychosom. Med. 22:*321, 1960. (Abstract.)
34 GRAHAM, D. T., KABLER, J. D., AND GRAHAM, F. K. Physiological responses to the suggestion of attitudes specific for hives and hypertension. *Psychosom. Med. 24:*159, 1962.
35 GRAHAM, D. T., LUNDY, R. M., BENJAMIN, L. S., KABLER, J. D., LEWIS, W. C., KUNISH, N. O., AND GRAHAM, F. K. Specific attitudes in initial interviews with patients having different "psychosomatic" diseases. *Psychosom. Med. 24:*257, 1962.
36 GRAHAM, D. T., STERN, J. A., AND WINOKUR, G. Experimental investigation of the specificity of attitude hypothesis in psychosomatic disease. *Psychosom. Med. 20:*446–457, 1958.
37 HAMMERSCHMIDT, W. W. *Whitehead's Philosophy of Time.* New York, King's Crown Press, 1947.
38 HARTMANN, H. Comments on the psychoanalytic theory of instinctual drives. *Psychoanal. Quart. 17:*368–388, 1948.
39 HARTMANN, H. *Ego Psychology and the Problem of Adaptation.* New York, Int. Univ. Press, 1958.
40 HEIDEGGER, M. *Being and Time.* New York and Evanston, Harper and Row, 1962.
41 HERON, W. "Cognitive and Physiological Effects of Perceptual Isolation." In *Sensory Deprivation,* edited by Philip Solomon *et al.* Cambridge, Harvard Univ. Press, 1961, p. 6.

42 Holt, R. Some reflections on the development of the primary and secondary processes. Unpublished manuscript.
43 Holt, R. "A Review of Some of Freud's Biological Assumptions and Their Influence on His Theories." This volume, pp. 93–124.
44 James, W. *Principles of Psychology.* New York, Am. Sci. Series, 1890.
45 Jones, E. "The Theory of Symbolism." In *Papers on Psychoanalysis.* London, Balliere, Tindall and Cox, 1948.
46 Kaufman, I. C. Some theoretical implications from animal behavior studies for the psychoanalytic concepts of instinct, energy and drive. *Int. J. Psycho-Anal. 41:*321, 1960.
47 Kaywin, L. An epigenetic approach to the psychoanalytic theory of instincts and affects. *J. Amer. Psychoanal. Ass. 8:*613, 1960.
48 Klein, G. S. Consciousness in psychoanalytic theory: Some implications for current research in perception. *J. Amer. Psychoanal. Ass. 7:*5, 1959.
49 Kubie, L. S. Body symbolism and the development of language. *Psychoanal. Quart. 3:*430, 1934.
50 Kubie, L. S. Instincts and homeostasis. *Psychosom. Med. 10:*15, 1948.
51 Kubie, L. S. The central representation of the symbolic process in psychosomatic disorders. *Psychosom. Med. 15:*1, 1953.
52 Kubie, L. S. The distortion of the symbolic process in neurosis and psychosis. *J. Amer. Psychoanal. Ass. 1:*59, 1953.
53 Kubie, L. S. Some implications for psychoanalysis of modern concepts of the organization of the brain. *Psychoanal. Quart. 22:*21–68, 1953.
54 Kubie, L. S. The fundamental nature of the distinction between normality and neurosis. *Psychoanal. Quart. 23:*167, 1954.
55 Kubie, L. S. Influence of symbolic processes on the role of instincts in human behavior. *Psychosom. Med. 18:*189, 1956.
56 Kubie, L. S. The neurotic process as the focus of physiological and psychoanalytic research. *Brit. J. Psychiat. 104:*518, 1958.
57 Lashley, K. S. "The Problem of Serial Order in Behavior." In *Cerebral Mechanisms in Behavior: The Hixon Symposium,* edited by Lloyd A. Jeffress. New York, Wiley, 1951 (paper read in 1948).
58 Lewis, W. C. Some observations relevant to early defenses and precursors. *Int. J. Psycho-Anal. 44:*132, 1963.
59 Lorenz, K. *King Solomon's Ring.* London, Methuen, 1952.
60 Lorenz, K. *The Nature of Instincts in Instinctive Behavior,* edited by C. Schuller. New York, Int. Univ. Press, 1957.
61 Lowe, V. *Understanding Whitehead.* Baltimore, Johns Hopkins Press, 1962.
62 McCulloch, W. S. "Why the Mind Is in the Head." In *Cerebral Mechanisms in Behavior: The Hixon Symposium,* edited by Lloyd A. Jeffress. New York, Wiley, 1951, p. 42.
63 Michotte, A. *The Perception of Causality.* New York, Basic Books, 1963.
64 Miller, G. A., Galanter, E., and Pribram, K. H. *Plans and the Structure of Behavior.* New York, Holt, 1960.
65 Miller, S. C. Ego autonomy in sensory deprivation, isolation and stress. *Int. J. Psycho-Anal. 43:*1, 1962.

66 OSTOW, M. The erotic instincts, a contribution to the study of instincts. *Int. J. Psycho-Anal. 38*:5, 1957.
67 OSTOW, M. The death instinct, a contribution to the study of instincts. *Int. J. Psycho-Anal. 39*:5, 1958.
68 PAUL, I. H., AND FISHER, C. Subliminal visual stimulation: A study of its influence on subsequent images and dreams. *J. nerv. ment. Dis. 129*:315, 1959.
69 PELLER, L. In report of panel on "The psychoanalytic theory of the symbolic process." *J. Amer. Psychoanal. Ass. 9*:46, 1961.
70 PENFIELD, W., AND ROBERTS, L. *Speech and Brain Mechanisms.* Princeton, New Jersey, Princeton Univ. Press, 1959, pp. 50–55.
71 PRIBRAM, K. H. "The Neuropsychology of Sigmund Freud." In *Experimental Foundations of Clinical Psychology,* edited by Arthur Bachrach. New York, Basic Books, 1962, p.442.
72 RAPAPORT, D. *Emotions and Memory.* New York, Int. Univ. Press, 1950.
73 RAPAPORT, D. "The Autonomy of the Ego." In *Psychoanalytic Psychiatry and Psychology.* New York, Int. Univ. Press, 1954, p. 248.
74 RAPAPORT, D. "The Conceptual Model of Psychoanalysis." In *Psychoanalytic Psychiatry and Psychology.* New York, Int. Univ. Press, 1954, p. 221.
75 RAPAPORT, D. "On the Psychoanalytic Theory of Affects." In *Psychoanalytic Psychiatry and Psychology.* New York, Int. Univ. Press, 1954, p. 305.
76 RAPAPORT, D. "On the Psychoanalytic Theory of Thinking." In *Psychoanalytic Psychiatry and Psychology.* New York, Int. Univ. Press, 1954, p. 259.
77 RECHTSCHAFFEN, A., GOODENOUGH, D. R., AND SHAPIRO, A. Patterns of sleep talking. *Arch. gen. Psychiat. 7*:418, 1962.
78 RENNER, M. "Time Sense and Orientation in Bees." *Cold Spring Harbor Symposia on Quantitative Biology,* Vol. XXV. Long Island, N.Y., Biological Laboratory, 1960, p. 361.
79 SCHNEIRLA, T. C. "The Concept of Development in Comparative Psychology." In *The Concept of Development.* Minneapolis, Univ. of Minnesota Press, 1957, p. 95.
80 SCHUR, M. Phylogenesis and ontogenesis of affect- and structure-formation and the phenomenon of repetition compulsion. *Int. J. Psycho-Anal. 41*:275, 1960.
81 SEGEL, N. S. In report of panel on "The psychoanalytic theory of the symbolic process." *J. Amer. Psychoanal. Ass. 9*:146, 1961.
82 SKINNER, B. F. *The Behavior of Organisms.* New York, Appleton-Century-Crofts, 1938.
83 SPITZ, R. A. *No and Yes.* New York, Int. Univ. Press, 1937.
84 SPITZ, R. A. Some early prototypes of defenses. *J. Amer. Psychoanal. Ass. 9*:626–651, 1961.
85 STRACHEY, J. Editor's note [on Freud, S., "Instincts and their Vicissitudes"]. In *Standard Edition,* Vol. XIV. London, Hogarth, 1957, pp. 111–116.
86 TAUSK, V. On the origin of the "influencing machine" in schizophrenia. *Psychoanal. Quart. 2*:519, 1933.
87 THORPE, W. H. *Learning and Instinct in Animals.* Cambridge, Harvard Univ. Press, 1956.

88 TIDD, C. W., BOWLBY, J., AND KAUFMAN, C. Symposium on "Psychoanalysis and ethology." *Int. J. Psychol-Anal. 41:*318, 1960.
89 WERNER, H. *Comparative Psychology of Mental Development.* New York, Science Editions, 1961.
90 WHITEHEAD, A. N. *Symbolism, Its Meaning and Effects.* New York, Macmillan, 1927, p. 45.
91 WHITEHEAD, A. N. *Process and Reality.* New York, Harper, 1957.
92 WHITMAN, R. M., KRAMER, M., AND BALDRIDGE, W. Which dream does the patient tell? *Arch. gen. Psychiat. 8:*277, 1963.
93 WOLFF, P. H. The developmental psychologies of Jean Piaget and psychoanalysis. *Psychol. Issues 2*(1):Monograph 5, 1960.

NINE

Operational Research Concepts and Psychoanalytic Theory

DONALD OKEN, M.D.

In recent years there has been an encouraging upsurge of concern with research in psychiatry and psychoanalysis. More important, there has been a growth of research activity characterized by its soundness in adhering to basic principles of scientific methodology. The self-conscious need to make such a statement, however, indicates how recently we have begun, and how far we have to go. Many crucial areas remain *terra incognita,* ripe for exploration.

In this situation it is heartening to note the increasing numbers with which young psychiatrists are turning to research careers. The veritable vacuum which these investigators will help to fill is a consequence not merely of the vast compass of our field and its relative youth, or of the immense social need which has placed a priority on turning out therapists. Many special difficulties confront those who do research because of the complex and intensely personal nature of our subject matter. There is no need to review these, since they have been well covered elsewhere, particularly in two recent reports of the Group for the Advancement of Psychiatry (*35, 36*) ; but it is germane to indicate that there has been an added impediment in the form of certain antiscientific attitudes promulgated by some psychiatrists. The most destructive of these is the presumption that psychoanalytic and psychiatric[1] research is unnecessary, owing to the self-evident truth of our theoretical "knowledge." Closely related and particularly pertinent to the present discussion is the

[1]It should be noted that, throughout, my discussion refers to both psychiatric and psychoanalytic research ; and that I shall move loosely back and forth between psychiatry and psychoanalysis, making little distinction between the two. I do so because the issues I will cover apply to both ; and because my major concern and interest in psychiatric and psychosomatic research are with theory derived from psychoanalysis, to which the term psychodynamic is often applied.

view that systematic research based on sound methodological principles is impossible.

The unsoundness of such anti-scientific attitudes has been exposed many times. Those who have done so and who have pointed out our current theoretical and methodological shortcomings include many distinguished psychoanalysts: Among them Kubie (*47, 48*), Grinker (*32*), Alexander (*1*), Gill (*7, 29*), Pumpian-Mindlin (*55*), Masserman (*50*), Ernst Kris (*7*), Escalona (*17, 18*) and also John Benjamin (*4, 5*), whom we are fortunate to have as a participant in this conference. I make a special point of singling out analysts who have taken on the role of responsible critics—for some of the worst offenders in espousing anti-research attitudes have been members of the self-styled analytic "orthodoxy."

As a result of these destructive attitudes, progress in developing a sound research methodology has been seriously impeded. A variety of shortcomings might be cited. Of these, perhaps the most culpable is the persistent reliance on the single case study. With discouraging consistency our literature is dominated by such reports, in which complex generalizations are extrapolated from one case or a very few. No one can deny the great value of using inferences drawn from a single patient as a source of fresh insight. An astute clinician may perceive new relationships which stand out in bold relief in a particular patient. Such observations are the very essence of research at the primary level of hypothesis-finding. They constitute the usual first step in opening up new areas.[2] Yet the repetition-compulsion of some modern psychiatrists who continue to work as if there were nothing beyond the single case approach has little to commend it. Only occasionally do they go on to the important next step of validation by more systematic, intensive observation of a group of similar patients; and further methodological refinements are almost uniformly ignored. A wealth of excellent clinical observation has been acquired. Meanwhile, theoretical speculation has "growed like Topsy," neither validated nor integrated. As a result, theory has changed from a luxuriant growth to a thicket and then to a tangled jungle of ideas, whose validity and interrelationship have become remarkably obscured.

Responses to this kind of criticism commonly take the form of accusations that the central validity of psychoanalytic thought is being undermined. What such a view fails to consider are the dividends which accrue from progressive refinements of research. Erroneously it is assumed that the advantages of systematic research are restricted to the mere *confirmation* of hypotheses. Yet scientific theories do not spring whole from the forehead, even of a Freud.

---

[2]The brilliant studies of Freud and the other psychoanalytic pioneers exemplify this approach in its very best sense. As a matter of fact, however, Freud went considerably beyond this level. Frenkel-Brunswik (*27*) has pointed to neglected evidence of a rather considerable sophistication about scientific methodology in Freud's work.

They mature by the elaborations, modifications, and extensions which refine and amplify the original hypothetical constructs. To establish the existence of a phenomenon or relationship is merely the *first* step. What must follow is a knowledge of the *when,* the *in what sequence,* the *how,* the *under what circumstances,* the *modifiable by what?* etc., which constitute real understanding. This can occur only by a sequential process in which appropriate methods of experimental control play an ever important role. Obviously, there is no need to "prove" the existence of the unconscious, of defense mechanisms, of transference, and the like; but we still have a great deal to learn about how these and similar processes function and how they are interrelated. Self-appointed defenders of the faith do more than miss the point. Their protest blocks the development of the very theory it presumes to protect As Gill says, "Any discipline has its share of those who clutch to it as to a religion, and these are not always its strongest members" (*29*).

II

Inextricably tied to the disordered state of our theoretical development are the semantic confusions with which our conceptualizations abound. Meaning is taken for cause, description for explanation, and construct for fact. Metaphors imperceptibly begin to acquire existential reality. Most of our concepts have multiple significances, conforming to different levels of meaning. These may include observed behavior as such; the symbolic meanings of behavior; hypothetical constructs referring to underlying motive states; and broad explanatory propositions which may encompass complex developmental sequences. Unwittingly, we condense two or more meanings or slide imperceptibly from one to another. When the particular denotation is evident, usually by its anchoring to the clinical situation, clear communication is possible. Case discussions with colleagues may be both rich and definite in meaning. In general, however, the further we get from observation, the more fuzzy we become.

When it comes to research, the understanding which derives from multiple implicit personal 'agreements' does not suffice. Scientific knowledge cannot depend upon covert messages derived from shared personal knowledge about a specific patient or upon nuances of understanding which stem from common residency or psychoanalytic institute training. If we are to make a valid study of a given phenomenon, we must be able to define it more clearly than that. We must define it so that any qualified scientist in our field knows what is meant—no more and no less; that is, we must be able to identify it in reproducible communicable terms which have some ties to direct experience. This, then, is the "operational" to which my title makes reference.

If, for example, we are studying 'castration anxiety,' we might use a definition which refers to a series of observable behaviors: anxiety, which can be specified and which occurs in consequence of overt threats to bodily harm, which can also be specified; or, we can refer to anxiety consequent upon exposure to symbolically significant instruments which have a cutting capability. If, however, we use the term to mean both of these and, simultaneously, the reaction to implied and direct threats made for sexual behavior, wishes, or fantasies which can occur in children or adults; for the fearful reaction of a boy in a specified age range to harsh punitive attitudes in his father; or for projections which make benign authority interpreted as dangerous—plus a number of further unlisted definitions which you can fill in for yourself—then the concept becomes useless for research. Each of these definitions is a satisfactory specific phenomenon which is accessable to study. When the various definitions are merged, however, so that the particular referents are lost, this is true no longer. This is not to say that the series of phenomena are not meaningfully related; nor does it deny the great value of using the term 'castration anxiety' as a generic construct encompassing all these meanings. However, the relationships among the components, by which the generic usage acquires intelligibility and meaning, become evident only as the individual components acquire distinctness.[3]

I choose castration anxiety as an illustration (though it represents far from the most glaring example of the problem), because it is relatively easy to indicate its multiple meanings. Even in its generic sense it is a construct at a moderate level of abstraction. Were I to try to examine an even higher-order construct, the vagueness of meaning would make my expository task impossible.

Benjamin (*5*) has stated that our greatest conceptual clarity exists in the area of theories of psychopathology.[4] This is precisely because this theory is constantly reinforced by observational referents in our daily work. Contrast, for example, the relative definiteness of the concept of anal erotism and its associated character traits with the indeterminate notion of psychic energy.

This is not to imply that every concept in our theoretical system must have direct observational referents or be discarded. Even some concepts of a relatively low order of abstraction may not now be fully definable in this way. This means rather that we must be energetic in seeking methods to remedy this deficiency. Some may be close at hand, if we forgo our complacency and search for them. Meanwhile, we can take care constantly, as

[3]There is nothing intrinsically erroneous in research based on the generic concept in its broadest sense or in the use of a part of it which encompasses several of the more discrete definitions. The problem is a practical one. Use of a broad definition requires the specification of so many observational referents as to make research exceedingly complex. Thus, it usually becomes necessary to settle for somewhat less rigor if the research requires that such broad concepts be used.

[4]In a similar vein, Benjamin has also indicated that our dynamic propositions are more subject to validation than those which are genetic, using the distinction clarified by Hartmann and Kris (*37*).

we use such concepts, to avoid misuse based on falsely assumed validity. Of course, too, higher-order constructs will never satisfy the criterion directly; but we can insist that they do so indirectly, in the sense that the lower-order constructs to which they are logically related can themselves be specified and defined in terms of observed phenomena.

It would be a mistake to get hung-up in an attempt to delineate what constitutes an ideal operational definition. In fact, I would stress the need to remain within practical limits of current knowledge and to settle for approximations of meaning which can be specified to the point of reasonable common sense. Further, I want to state emphatically that observable evidence of the most subjective data constitute entirely appropriate referents. Free associations to a dream or the verbal report of consciously experienced anxiety are no less real empirical data than the number of bar presses made by a hapless rat. Subjectivity refers only to the position of the observer *vis à vis* the observed. As long as a phenomenon has observable manifestations, it can be objectified. But objectification will be established to the degree that the phenomenon is definable in operational terms.

III

Operationism is concerned with measurement. What we have been discussing so far concerning operational definitions similarly has to do with quantity. In one sense, the essential attribute of all science is quantification. I mean here something more than a compulsive concern with counting. Although full knowledge may eventually depend upon knowing precise magnitudes, current research progress does not require this. I use the term quantification in a much broader sense. Our primary decisions have to do with the presence or absence of a given phenomenon: Is it there or is it not? This is merely another way of stating what I referred to earlier as the necessity to specify or identify the object of study. But considered in terms of modern number theory, this is also no more than the yes-no binary quantity which constitutes the element of digital computer function.

Similarly, the assignment of phenomena into a series of categories can also be viewed as quantification, in this instance founded on tertiary, quaternary, or whatever number base system corresponds to the total number of categories. It may seem artificial to classify even simple categorical judgments as quantities, but this view serves the useful purpose of indicating the essential continuity of definition and quantification and illuminates the fact that the basic element of operationism is definition. It emphasizes the centrality of operational definitions for science, and it points to the ultimate goal of using quantification to the maximum extent appropriate to the research question. *Appropriate,* of course, is the crucial word here. Premature attempts to force data into speciously precise quantities is more than wasteful—it is stultifying to research and leads to the exclusion of crucial variables, which at present cannot be represented in magnitude terms.

At this point it may be helpful to turn from generalities to a concrete example. Over the past several years considerable attention has been focused on the work of Dr. Charles Fisher. His studies of the effects of subliminal perceptions upon imagery and dreams are often cited as a particularly fine example of psychoanalytic research. It in no way underestimates the excellence of Fisher's work to indicate that much of his success can be explained by his ability to translate psychoanalytic concepts into operational terms. The content and formal properties of his subjects' drawings constitute his empirical referents. Reviewing his published experiments as a series (*22–25*) is impressive in revealing the steady sequential progress toward explicating these referents. His later studies included the use of multiple judges, differing stimuli, a scoring checklist, before and after measures, and 'blind' judgments. Customarily, such devices are thought of as controls designed to eliminate sources of error. Equally well, they can be viewed as devices which increased the precision with which the phenomena in question were *defined*. In other words, Fisher's methods moved progressively toward an operational ideal. By removing possible cues or interpretations derived from sources other than the data itself, he more sharply delineated the definition of his criteria.[5]

IV

It is not within the scope of this paper to attempt any philosophical discussion of the doctrine of operationism. Nevertheless, my advocacy of the use of operational research variables makes it incumbent upon me to consider certain points. As defined by the physicist Bridgman (*9–11*), operationism is concerned with the assignment of meaning to terms or concepts. Meaning is defined only by specifying the particular set of operations performed to determine the quantity or establish the identity for which the term or concept stands.

In the 1930's and early 40's operationism was in vogue among psychologists. Much of this occurred under the impact of Stevens, who saw operationism as basic to psychology: which thus established this discipline as "the science of sciences" (*63, 64*). During this phase there was a tendency to consider all theorizing as suspect and inconsistent with operationism. Psychodynamic

[5]It is appropriate here to raise a question about the intense stir which gripped the psychoanalytic community following the original reports by Fisher. The exaggerated response would seem to offer some insight into the critics of research. It is as if they breathed a sigh of intense relief and a paean of self-congratulation that certain psychoanalytic views had been 'proved' correct. What did they expect?—that it would be possible somehow to disprove the existence of the unconscious? One wonders if that is precisely what they feared; and whether their denigration of research does not represent the rigidity of self-doubts rather than confident, mature conviction.

theory in particular came in for a lion's share of criticism. Skinner (*6, 61, 62*) can be mentioned as one who still holds to this radical position, with his rejection of everything which goes on inside the 'black box' of mental function. More careful logical analysis by modern philosohers of science (*26, 38, 39*) has revealed the errors in this point of view. Feigl (*6, 19–21*) particularly (though himself a positivist) has indicated the fallaciousness and sterility of the outmoded, extreme positivistic stand which this type of thinking represents. There is nothing inherent in operationism incompatible with theory which contains highly abstract theoretical constructs.

The inherent falsity of the view which unfavorably compares psychoanalysis with the supposedly more exact physical sciences has also been pointed out. No clearer statement of this can be offered than that made by Frenkel-Brunswik (*27*) :

> An appraisal of the scientific legitimacy and operational status of psychoanalytic concepts must first consider certain fundamental changes in the views concerning theoretical structure which have taken place within physics itself as the model discipline for the unity of science and for operationism. Both Philipp Frank and Einstein have pointed to the ever-widening gap between observation and theory; there is increasing realization of the fact that the basic concepts and principles of science must be formulated in an abstract, "non-pictorial" language which seems to belie its origin in the world of direct perceptual experience. Much of the seeming absurdity of psychoanalytic assumptions is resolved by setting them side by side with established physical constructs which in many cases are as much in opposition to the perceptually given as are those of psychoanalysis to the data of manifest "phenotypical" introspection.[6]

Harold Israel (*6, 40*) stands out among the opponents of the operationist position within psychology. Especially valuable is his point that the operationist viewpoint of many psychologists differs significantly from that of Bridgman himself. Israel emphasizes that their usage involves the specification of the operations necessary to *produce* or elicit phenomena rather than the operations used to measure (or define) the phenomenon itself. His analysis, moreover, highlights the preferences of many such psychologists for physicalistic definitions—e.g., those which specify neural events.

There *is* a tendency to equate the operationist position with emphasis upon purely physical data such as can be derived from neurophysiology and biochemistry. This is an erroneous interpretation. Although it is true that concepts specifying neural events can be translated more easily into operational terms, there is nothing intrinsically more operational about such concepts than intrapsychic phenomena.

Similarly, operationism may be mistakenly associated with a focus upon the literally or figuratively microscopic—on 'molecular' as opposed to 'molar'

[6]Along this line, it is interesting to note that theoretical physicists seem far more disposed to view psychoanalytic theory as congenial than do biologists or experimental psychologists.

phenomena. This molar versus molecular controversy has characterized much of the disagreement between psychiatrists and academic psychologists for years. Like the great majority of psychiatrists, I am convinced that most human behavior cannot be dissected into neat little bundles without losing its meaning. Therefore, it is essential to stress that there is nothing in the operational approach which necessitates fragmentation. If a concept can be broken down into simpler components, well and good. Simpler concepts can be translated more readily into terms which have greater operational precision. Yet this does not mean that such a breakdown is to be attempted when it renders a concept void of meaning. Moreover, our increasing awareness that simple linear cause-effect relationships have little meaning for psychiatry does not negate an operational approach. It is entirely feasible (albeit more difficult) to utilize operationally defined variables in research within a field theoretical system (see, for example, Grinker's analysis of anxiety [*33*]).

My purpose in reviewing these aspects of operationism is to preserve the baby while discarding the bath water. Perhaps it will be helpful to summarize our position. Transformation of concepts into operational terms reduces their obscurity, ambiguity, and vagueness, and establishes their logical context. It is superfluous where common sense and clarity provide an already specific referent. The degree of precision to be demanded of a definition will depend on the nature of the concept and its place within the broader theoretical system to which it belongs. As knowledge is expanded by research, this precision will increase. Within such limits operational definitions provide an essential device for establishing the empirical meaningfulness of any concept, and thus its utility for research. This view in no way limits consideration of 'subjective' or complex molar phenomena, nor does it put any brake on theorizing. Theory is often useful because it explains events not yet even specifiable; but constructs at lower levels of explanation within the theoretical system *are* subject to operational analysis and thus to test which provides the essential observational underpinning for the theory as a whole.

V

Let me now return to a consideration of some areas which have a more direct relation to psychiatric research. One such area is that of interpretation. Much has been made of the usefulness of this process as a bit of research in miniature. Each interpretation is to be considered as a hypothesis arising from preceding data whose validity can be confirmed or denied by the patient's response. I cannot agree with such a view. My basic objection is that interpretations are made in terms of commitments to theoretical formulations made long before the patient's communications. To this extent they are unrelated to empirical data at hand. Further, the patient's responses cannot be considered a valid test.[7] Transference may play a more important role than the actual content of the message, as may the more general tendency for man to live by those "propositions whose validity is a factor of belief" (*3*).[8] Finally, there is inadequate basis for establishing the reliability of the therapist-observer, since no one else is present. A recent study (*59*) conducted by a group at the Chicago Institute for Psychoanalysis indicated the great difficulty in obtaining reliable consensus in identifying various parts of the focal conflict, from protocols of therapeutic sessions. Part of the explanation for this may rest in the use of a second-hand material rather than the primary data. One is reminded here of the great potential value of recordings and films of the original therapeutic session, a suggestion made by Kubie a number of years back (*7*). Moreover, when material can be replayed as often as desired there is sufficient time for judicious observation, and it becomes possible to delineate the precise indicants in the material from which the interpretation can be derived.

There is another aspect of interpretations which is instructive to consider. An interpretation is essentially a translation. Body language and the symbolic derivatives of primary process 'thought' are put into rational secondary-process language by the therapist for the patient's use. This can be said another way by stating that there has been a translation into more operational terms. Keeping this in mind may offer a clue on how to construct operational variables for productive research. If we can translate our concepts into terms which could be communicated intelligibly to a patient, they will probably be expressed in terms of specific referents which constitute satisfactory operational definitions. Thus they will be accessible to test.

Whereas *post*-dictive interpretations are open to grave question regarding their suitability as research instruments, *pre*dictions can be very satisfactory. This is an area in which John Benjamin has provided strong leadership. His 1959 essay (*5*) which analyzes this approach and supplies a number of helpful illustrations, stands out particularly. I refer especially to Benjamin's clarification of the necessity for making explicit both the nature of a given prediction (e.g., intuitive, deductive, correlational, etc.) and its precise observational

---

[7]I am not, of course, simple-mindedly referring to explicit verbal affirmations or denials by the patient. Included are changes in behavior or the path of associations, recovery of repressed memories, etc. Although such indirect responses are more dependable than what the patient says, even these can represent highly sophisticated resistance phenomena in a sensitive patient; nor is the interpretive proposition validated even when an interpretation is confirmed as 'correct.' Such an interpretation may represent an approximation containing a (perhaps dangerously misleading) part-truth. The problem of the confirmation of interpretations has been considered at length by Kubie (*47*), among others.

[8]Although I am convinced of the truth of this statement, it is preferable to note that it is, at present, unproved. However, it is testable—provided that the concepts of transference and self-fulfilling prophesies are translated into operational terms.

bases. There is no necessity to review this, since the original paper covers these issues far better than I can. The important point is Benjamin's lucid demonstration that the correctness of a prediction does not validate its theoretical underpinning unless it can be shown that hidden contaminating cues can be eliminated as alternative explanations. The specification of the source which he demands is a very good example of maximizing the operational quality of research data, because it explicates the process by which phenomena are defined. Although formidable difficulties are involved, prediction has a very real utility for application to psychoanalytic data. Janis (*41*), for example, has made a notable beginning in this area.

I do have some disagreement with those who suggest that prediction has a greater usefulness than experimentation. Kubie (*7*) and, especially, Escalona (*17*) have taken this position. Yet Escalona (*17*) herself has recognized the weakness of prediction as a method for subjecting a hypothesis to proof or disproof.[9]

Any segment of behavior has a very large number of determinants. Some of these fall outside the psychological realm (belonging to the biological domain at one end and the social at the other). The determinants of any bit of behavior are accessible to discovery in retrospect. Since so many are outside the field of practical observation, however, and especially since most of them are parts of causal nets which themselves cannot be predicted, knowledge of these determinants is not available in advance. There is an analogy here to the theory of evolution. This is one basic scientific theory which was established entirely on a post-dictive basis. Looking into the future, it is impossible to anticipate what mutations will arise. And the subsequent unpredictable role of ecological variables (long- and short-term climate conditions and the like) makes it impossible to ascertain whether a mutant species variant which does appear will survive. Only hindsight gives a clear view of the process of natural selection, making understandable the survival of what evidently has turned out to be the fittest under the conditions subsequently known to have occurred.

A certain degree of prediction is possible in psychiatry. Short-term predictions, especially, are feasible because of the more limited opportunity for extraneous interference. One special type of prediction is of particular interest to us: *contingency predictions*. These are the 'if–then' propositions which specify a predicted outcome in terms of a given conditional antecedent which cannot itself be predicted. Such statements occupy a special place in psychodynamics because of the fact that so many of our theoretical concepts (e.g., unconscious hostility) refer to action tendencies which become overt only under particular stimulus conditions (what have been referred to by

[9]I use the terms *proof* and *disproof* in their loose, general sense. There is, of course, no such thing as absolute validation, only confirmation (*12*).

Carnap (*12*) as 'dispositional concepts'). The usefulness of such predictions is based on their operational quality. The 'under such-and-such conditions,' which they include, is an elaborated specification for identifying the phenomenon. The psychotherapy research project of the Menninger Foundation is one instance in which good use is made of this type of prediction (*57, 65*). Differing specific outcomes of therapy are predicted for a patient contigent upon the intercurrence of different types of life events which have relevance for that patient.

VI

I have already stated my belief that it is a mistake to underestimate the usefulness of experimentation in our science. Perhaps the fact that the major part of my own research has been in the field of 'psychosomatics' is responsible for my bias. The few toes which I keep planted in physiology serve as a constant reminder of the virtues of the experimental method; and it is possible that such techniques are more feasible in the psychosomatic area.

There is somewhat of a paradox here. The least satisfactory (i.e., least operational, most reified, and most nebulous) of psychoanalytic theories are those which touch upon the biological sphere. Consider the source of instincts; or the energy concept of libido theory.[10] Our current perspective makes clear that much of the reason for this lies in the influence of the nineteenth-century ultra-mechanistic biology and general scientific climate which had its impress upon Freud's development.[11] Biology has come a long way since then. Unfortunately, evidence of this type of thinking can be found persisting in the more recent psychosomatic literature. Consider such views as: that energies, dammed-up by conflict "spill over" into somatic channels to produce "vegetative neuroses" (Dunbar [*13*]) ; or, even more extreme, the oral incorporative fantasies of Garma [*28*]). On the other hand, some of the best research utilizing operational principles has been done in the psychosomatic area. Witness the pioneering studies of gastric psychophysiology carried out by Margolin, in which he obtained gastric juice specimens from a patient in analysis who had a gastrostomy (*49*) ; or consider the elegant

[10]In this connection, I feel constrained to mention my disagreement with the conclusions reached by still another of the distinguished contributors to the present symposium, Dr. Ostow. (See this volume, Paper 16, and Ostow's book [*54*].) I refer to the notion that psychopharmacologic agents operate by altering the quantity of psychic energy. As creative, and heuristically useful is this view, I do not believe it will prove of value in the long run. My difference from Ostow stems partly from the very dubious nature of the concept of psychic energy (which Kubie criticized at length a few years ago [*46*]). Additionally, I am concerned about the direct translation of a physiologic event into psychological terms which mistakes analogy for relationship.

[11]See the excellent paper by Holt (Paper 6) in this volume for a scholarly exposition of this point.

research carried out by Kepecs and Robin on the psychophysiology of the skin (*42–45*).

Two additional examples of fine psychosomatic research are the work of groups led by David Graham (continuing at the University of Wisconsin) and Franz Alexander. Both groups have worked in the same general area: elucidating personality correlates which may be linked etiologically to psychosomatic diseases. Although there are differences between their approaches, important methodological parallels can be indicated. Both groups developed their ideas out of informal clinical observations and clarified these with systematic scrutiny of clinical data. Subsequent controlled studies were conducted, with judges who were kept 'blind' as to the nature of the patient's disease. At each step the formulations were corrected and tightened-up as indicated by the data. Finally, both groups have carried out laboratory experiments to put their hypotheses to test. Graham used hypnosis to induce the specific attitudes he found associated with psychosomatic disorders (*31*). When a Raynauds Disease attitude was suggested, vasoconstriction was found; with a hives attitude, there were signs of vasodilitation. Alexander has used films to stimulate his proposed "specific dynamic constellation." His initial experiment included measures of thyroid function in patients with thyrotoxicosis, with patients with other disorders used as controls (*2*). These preliminary results have been confirmatory of his theoretical hypothesis.

Still another example comes from the studies of the infant Monica by Engel and Reichsman in Rochester (*15, 16*). This was a neglected child in whom a gastrostomy was performed because of congenital esophogeal atresia. Through this opening it was possible to obtain samples of gastric juice directly from the stomach. Levels of hydrochloric acid were measured and correlated with a number of behavioral variables. Several aspects of this work are worth our attention. Many of the early studies capitalized on spontaneous fluctuations in the child's behavior. Soon these became predictable. Monica developed a warm attachment to Dr. Reichsman; but when approached by strangers she responded by distress and withdrawal. Thus it became possible to manipulate the situation deliberately to obtain samples during a variety of contrasting affect states. The fact that this represents experimentation in the best sense should not be lost in the ideal simplicity of such a procedure. As a matter of fact, the spontaneous situations comprised experiments too—experiments in nature. Capitalization upon a natural situation is a time-honored research method, useful precisely because of its realism. If a situation can be anticipated, adequate controls can be planned just as in conventional research designs.

The behavioral categories in this study did not arise *de novo*. Leads were suggested by theory. Hence, the variables included the intensity of object relationships, non-nutritive oral behavior, and affective states. Nevertheless, the specific categories and the criteria used to specify these grew directly from Monica's behavior. The affect categories, for example, did not slavishly correspond to conventional stereotypes, but included such states as joy, contentment, and depression-unpleasure. The use of a second, nonparticipant experimenter, who made independent observations and ratings, and the subsequent review of filmed records of experimental sessions permitted considerable refinement of these operational measures. Conclusions drawn from this study provide useful insight into early psychological development and the concept of orality, as well as considerations concerning the role of depression as a primary stress response. We have here a classic illustration of the role of operational variables growing out of theory, feeding-back to provide valuable modification of that theory.

Despite the risk of making what seems an invidious comparison, I will mention some contrasting research also coming from the Rochester group. This is the study of the relationship of separation and depression to disease, carried out by Arthur Schmale (*58*). You will recall that he has reported finding, as an antecedent condition for the development of disease of all forms, a situation of real, fantasied, or threatened object loss, with attendant feelings of hopelessness and helplessness. The central problem in evaluating this conclusion is the almost totally nonoperational nature of the object-loss categories. Before one can begin to explore this hypothesis it will become necessary to establish some degree of reliable specificity for the referents by which fantasied and threatened object loss can be identified. This is a formidable task. Until it is carried out, however, Schmale's concept remains in the class of an interesting speculation. As it stands, it can be neither established nor disproved.

VII

The program in our own psychosomatic laboratories at Michael Reese has been in different areas. Our major efforts have been a series of studies of basic psychophysiological relationships concentrating on anxiety and stress (*34*). Throughout this work we have maintained the view that psychological stress can be defined only as a response—more specifically, as a condition in which anxiety develops. To use a stimulus definition, i.e., to equate stress with the stimulus condition, is to ignore the fact that human responses are unpredictable. We would be left with a situation in which there were no dependable external referents. By focusing on the anxiety response and categorizing it in terms of empirically evident phenomena (as I will describe in a moment), our approach remains operational. Over the course of our studies we have learned increasingly more about what constitutes the stress response and several of its variants. Another way of putting this is to state that we have progressively developed an operational definition of stress.

All of our experiments have been characterized by the use of rating scales for quantifying psychological variables, whose anchor points were defined in a series of explicit criterion statements about observable behavior. In this connection, I am reminded of a scale designed for one of the earliest studies. Aspiring paratroopers were asked to make self-ratings of the intensity of their anxiety during focal experiences in their training regimen. Each rating point was defined in a brief meaningful phrase. At the extremes were the statements: "completely calm" and "scared shitless." Surely the latter is the very acme of an operational definition!

Several points of interest are illustrated by the scale used to estimate anxiety, referred to above. We have stated consistently that what we are measuring is a conscious reportable state, in which overt verbal behavior provides the observational criteria. 'Unconscious anxiety' cannot be measured. It is no less true, however, that the rationale which influenced our choice of anxiety as a significant variable and the general design of our studies stem directly from theoretical concepts, including that of unconscious anxiety. We would never have studied anxiety had we not a biased assumption of its central role in psychosomatic functioning. Our view of anxiety includes its signal functions and thus a whole series of theoretical assumptions about properties called the 'ego.' Moreover, we assume a meaningful relationship between what we study and unconscious anxiety. The link includes notions of defense mechanisms which, when rendered ineffective, lead to anxiety 'becoming' conscious. Yet in our experiments it is essential to act as if there were no such thing as unconscious anxiety, because we are restricted to a consideration of what can be defined operationally.

This restriction to phenomenal data does not preclude making contributions which extend theoretical understanding. If, for instance, we can specify psychological and physiological events which occur during conscious anxiety, we can look for the presence of these under differing conditions. We might then infer unconscious anxiety (although for a time we might preferably restrict ourselves to a term like latent or nascent anxiety, which is free from implicit theoretical assumptions).

An alternative approach can be based on the quantification of defenses. Again, it is possible to develop a scale based on appropriate overt behavioral criteria. At a symposium held at the University of Wisconsin two years ago, I had the privilege of describing such a scale which we had devised (*52*). Using this measure might provide another method for defining a state which we could call unconscious anxiety. It happens that our work has proceeded in a somewhat different direction. We have become concerned with exploring the psychosomatic attributes of states of defense in their own right. Thus, we have described the characteristic over-homeostatic control exhibited by a certain type of chronically ill psychiatric patients in their psychological as well as their physiological function. More recently we have begun to turn our attention to the relation of muscle tension to states of defense and control (*53, 60*).

The question always exists whether our anxiety scale represents that affect in the same sense with which those in Wisconsin, or other groups, would use the term. Perhaps a better name for the scale would be "Michael Reese Anxiety." The answer depends on the degree to which we have validly explicated the actual referents of our rating judgments in the scale criteria. How much are contaminant cues involved, of which we are unaware? Evidence concerning this can be obtained by testing the reliability of the scale in the hands of others who have a different background of implicit assumptions. We have obtained satisfactory results using a laboratory assistant and, in another study, a newly arrived staff member, trained elsewhere.

A tougher test would involve replication of our work, using our scales, by a completely separate group. Such repetition occurs all too infrequently in psychiatric research. Its value extends far beyond the narrow issue of the validation of given experimental results. The area in which results do overlap provides an improved set of referents for defining stress or whatever is being studied; and the places of disagreement become avenues for discovering surplus meanings and sub-categories hidden in the loose original concept. These possibilities are afforded also by studies using both our scale and a new instrument designed to measure the same phenomenon or one closely related. Recently, we have had the good fortune to have Louis Gottschalk carry out some research (*30*) using several measures of verbal hostility designed by him, together with our anger scales (*51*). The fruits of this research will be a more precise definition and, hence, a better understanding of 'anger.' This is tedious, difficult work, but its value in developing our theoretical understanding is considerable.

VIII

Theory-building is an integral part of all science. Empiricism which denies this can lead only to sterility. We have no lack of theory, however; instead, many of our problems stem from the fact that the overgrowth of theory has far outstripped the data which it attempts to explain. Research serves no end in itself, nor does preoccupation with methodology. Understanding, however, depends upon research carried out in such a fashion that it can be a dependable guide to the maturation of theory.

If I have seemed to place too much emphasis upon the necessity for an operational approach to research, it is not because of any glamor which this doctrine holds.[12] It is because there is a great need to supply a corrective for

[12]In fact, its application requires hard, even dirty work. Perhaps this is why there is a preference for nice, clean (often indeed, sterile) abstract theorizing.

the opposite tendency which has been the dominant one in our field. Operationism has no mystical properties. Not all methodological problems can be solved by a healthy dose of operationism. There is a great deal more to scientific method than that. To mention the obvious, for example, a trivial idea defined in magnificently operational terms remains trivial. The selection of meaningful problems occurs only from a solid foundation of theory. Clarification of the problem then leads back to better theory. Probably the best antidote for the over-emphasis and inadequacies of my exposition comes from the words of Bridgman himself (*11*) :

> . . . I myself never have talked of "operationalism" or "operationism" but I have a distaste for these grandiloquent words which imply something more philosophical and esoteric than the simple thing which I see. What we are here concerned with is an observation and description of method which at least some physicists had already, perhaps unconsciously, adopted and found useful. . . . We have here no esoteric theory of the ultimate nature of concept, nor a philosophical championing of the primacy of the "operation." . . . So far as it is anything definite at all, it is a technique of analysis which endeavors to attain the greatest possible awareness of everything involved in a situation by bringing out into the light of day all of our activity or operations when confronted with the situation whether the operations are manual in the laboratory or verbal or "mental." . . . Operational analysis is valueless without a background of experience and the inclusion from such an analysis can have no validity which is not already conditioned by the experience.

Our need is not for some grand system of scientific philosophy. Certainly is it not the abolition of theory. Indeed, our goal must be to develop theory as much as we can. To do so requires a body of solid data and, equally important, a set of concepts whose links to such data are clear. My purpose in this essay is merely to emphasize how best this can be done and to provide an impetus to carry on this vital job. In the long run, down-to-earth research does more for theory-building than does anything else.

REFERENCES

1 Alexander, F. "A Review of Two Decades." In *Twenty Years of Psychoanalysis,* edited by F. Alexander and H. Ross. New York, Norton, 1953.

2 Alexander, F., Flagg, G. W., Foster, S., Clemens, T., and Blahd, W. Experimental studies of emotional stress. I. Hyperthyroidism. *Psychosom. Med. 23:*104–114, 1961.

3 Bateson, G. "Conventions of Communication." Chapt. 8 in J. Ruesch and G. Bateson, *Communication, the Social Matrix of Society.* New York, Norton, 1951.

4 Benjamin, J. D. Methodological considerations in the validation and elaboration of psychoanalytical personality theory. *Amer. J. Orthopsychiat. 20:*139–156, 1950.

5 Benjamin, J. D. "Prediction and Psychopathological Theory." In *Dynamic Pathology in Childhood,* edited by L. Jessner and E. Pavenstedt. New York, Grune & Stratton, 1959.

6 Boring, E. G., Bridgman, P. W., Feigl, H., Israel, H. E., Pratt, C. C., and Skinner, B. F. Symposium on "Operationism." *Psychol. Rev. 52:*241–294, 1945.

7 Brenman, M. (Chairman), Kubie, L. S., Murray, H. A., Kris, E., Gill, M., *et al.* Problems in clinical research. Round Table 1946. *Amer. J. Orthopsychiat. 17:*196–230, 1947.

8 Brenman, M. (Chairman), Kubie, L. S., Rogers, C. R., Gill, M. M., *et al.* Research in psychotherapy. Round Table 1947. *Amer. J. Orthopsychiat. 18:*92–118, 1948.

9 Bridgman, P. W. *The Logic of Modern Physics.* New York, Macmillan, 1927.

10 Bridgman, P. W. *The Nature of Physical Theory.* Princeton, Princeton Univ. Press, 1936.

11 Bridgman, P. W. Operational analysis. *Phil. Sci. 5:*114–131, 1938.

12 Carnap, R. "Testability and Meaning." Reprinted in *Readings in the Philosophy of Science,* edited by H. Feigl and M. Brodbeck. New York, Appleton-Century-Crofts, 1953.

13 Dunbar, F. *Emotions and Bodily Changes.* 4th edition. New York, Columbia Univ. Press, 1954.

14 Ellis, A. "An Operational Reformulation of Some of the Basic Principles of Psychoanalysis." In *The Foundations of Science and the Concepts of Psychology and Psychoanalysis,* edited by H. Feigl and M. Scriven. Minneapolis, Univ. of Minnesota Press, 1956.

15 Engel, G. L., and Reichsman, F. Spontaneous and experimentally induced depressions in an infant with a gastric fistula. *J. Amer. Psychoanal. Ass. 4:*428–452, 1956.

16 Engel, G. L., Reichsman, F., and Segal, H. A study of an infant with a gastric fistula. I. Behavior and the rate of hydrochloric acid secretion. *Psychosom. Med. 18:*374–398, 1956.

17 Escalona, S. Problems in psychoanalytic research. *Int. J. Psycho-Anal. 33:*11–21, 1952.

18 Escalona, S. (Chairman), *et al.* Approaches to a dynamic theory of development. Round Table 1949. III. Discussion. *Amer. J. Orthopsychiat. 20:*157–160, 1950.

19 Feigl, H. Existential hypotheses. *Phil. Sci. 17:*35–62, 1950.

20 Feigl, H. "The Mind-Body Problem in the Development of Logical Empiricism." Reprinted in *Readings in the Philosophy of Science,* edited by H. Feigl and M. Brodbeck. New York, Appleton-Century-Crofts, 1953.

21 Feigl, H. "Some Major Issues and Developments in the Philosophy of Science of Logical Empiricism." In *The Foundations of Science and Concepts of Psychology and Psychoanalysis,* edited by H. Feigl and M. Scriven. Minneapolis, Univ. of Minnesota Press, 1956.

22 Fisher, C. Dreams and perception: The role of preconscious and primary modes of perception in dream formation. *J. Amer. Psychoanal. Ass. 2:*389–444, 1954.

23 Fisher, C. Dreams images and perception: A study of unconscious-preconscious relationships. *J. Amer. Psychoanal. Ass. 4*:5–48, 1956.

24 Fisher, C. A study of the preliminary stages of the construction of dreams and images. *J. Amer. Psychoanal. Ass. 5*:5–60, 1957.

25 Fisher, C., and Paul, I. H. The effect of subliminal visual stimulation on images and dreams: A validation study. *J. Amer. Psychoanal. Ass. 7*:35–83, 1959.

26 Frank, P. G. Modern Science and Its Philosophy. Cambridge, Harvard Univ. Press, 1941.

27 Frenkel-Brunswik, E. Psychoanalysis of the unity of science. *Daedalus 80*:271–350, 1954.

28 Garma, A. On the pathogenesis of peptic ulcer. *Int. J. Psycho-Anal. 31*:53–72, 1950.

29 Gill, M. The present state of psychoanalytic theory. *J. abnorm. soc. Psychol. 58*:1–8, 1959.

30 Gottschalk, L. A., Winget, C. M., Gleser, G. C., and Springer, K. J. "The Measurement of Emotional Changes During a Psychiatric Interview: A Working Model Toward Quantifying the Psychoanalytic Concept of Affect." In *Methods of Research in Psychotherapy,* edited by L. A. Gottschalk and A. H. Ayerbach. New York, Hoeber, 1964. In press.

31 Graham, D. T., Stern, J. A., and Winokur, G. Experimental investigation of the specificity of attitude hypothesis in psychosomatic disease. *Psychosom. Med. 20*:446–457, 1958.

32 Grinker, R. R., Sr. "A Philosophical Appraisal of Psychoanalysis." In *Science and Psychoanalysis,* edited by J. H. Masserman. Vol. I. *Integrative Studies.* New York, Grune & Stratton, 1958.

33 Grinker, R. R., Sr. Anxiety as a significant variable for a unified theory of human behavior. *Arch. gen. Psychiat. 1*:537–546, 1959.

34 Grinker, R. R., Sr., Korchin, S. J., Basowitz, H., Hamburg, D., Sabshin, M., Persky, H., Chevalier, J., and Board, F. A theoretical and experimental approach to problems of anxiety. *Arch. Neurol., Chicago 76*:420–431, 1956.

35 Group for the Advancement of Psychiatry. *Collaborative Research in Psychopathology.* Report No. 25, January 1954.

36 Group for the Advancement of Psychiatry. *Some Observations on Controls in Psychiatric Research.* Report No. 42, May 1959.

37 Hartmann, H., and Kris, E. The genetic approach in psychoanalysis. *Psychoanal. Stud. Child 1*:11–30, 1945.

38 Hempel, C. G. "Fundamentals of Concept Formation in Empirical Science." *International Encyclopedia of Unified Science,* Vol. II, No. 7. Chicago, Univ. of Chicago Press, 1952.

39 Hempel, C. G. "A Logical Appraisal of Operationism." In *The Validation of Scientific Theories,* edited by P. G. Frank. New York, Collier Books, 1961.

40 Israel, H., and Goldstein, B. Operationism in psychology. *Psychol. Rev. 51*:177–188, 1944.

41 Janis, I. *Psychological Stress.* New York, Wiley, 1958.

42 Kepecs, J., and Rabin, A. Personality structure in atopic dermatitis: A Rorschach study. *J. gen. Psychol. 50:*171–180, 1954.

43 Kepecs, J., and Robin, M. Studies on itching. I. Contributions toward an understanding of the physiology of masochism. *Psychosom. Med. 17:*87–95, 1955.

44 Kepecs, J., Robin, M., and Brunner, M. Relationship between certain emotional states and exudation into the skin. *Psychosom. Med. 13:*10–17, 1951.

45 Kepecs, J., Robin, M., and Munro, C. Responses to sensory stimulation in certain psychosomatic disorders. *Psychosom. Med. 20:*351–365, 1958.

46 Kubie, L. S. The fallacious use of quantitative concepts in dynamic psychology. *Psychoanal. Quart. 16:*507–518, 1947.

47 Kubie, L. S. "Problems and Techniques of Psychoanalytic Validation and Progress." In *Psychoanalysis as a Science,* edited by E. Pumpian-Mindlin. Stanford, Stanford Univ. Press, 1952.

48 Kubie, L. S. "Psychoanalysis as a Basic Science." In *Twenty Years of Psychoanalysis,* edited by F. Alexander and H. Ross. New York, Norton, 1953.

49 Margolin, S. The behavior on the stomach during psychoanalysis: A clinical study. *Psychoanal. Quart. 20:*349–369, 1951.

50 Masserman, J. H. "Comparative Research in Ethology, Biodynamics and Psychoanalysis." In *Science and Psychoanalysis,* edited by J. H. Masserman. Vol. III. *Psychoanalysis and Human Values.* New York, Grune & Stratton, 1960.

51 Oken, D. An experimental study of suppressed anger and blood pressure. *Arch. gen. Psychiat. 2:*441–456, 1960.

52 Oken, D. "The Role of Defense in Psychological Stress." In *Physiological Correlates of Psychological Disorder,* edited by R. Roessler and N. S. Greenfield. Madison, Univ. of Wisconsin Press, 1962.

53 Oken, D. "Tension," stress and self control. *Psychosomatics.* In press, 1964.

54 Ostow, M. *Drugs in Psychoanalysis and Psychotherapy.* New York, Basic Books, 1962.

55 Pumpian-Mindlin, E. "The Position of Psychoanalysis in Relation to the Biological and Social Sciences." In *Psychoanalysis as a Science,* edited by E. Pumpian-Mindlin. Stanford, Stanford Univ. Press, 1952.

56 Rapaport, D. "The Structure of Psychoanalytic Theory: A Systematizing Attempt." In *Psychology: A Study of a Science,* edited by S. Koch. Vol. III. *Sensory, Perceptual, and Physiological Formulations.* New York, McGraw-Hill, 1959.

57 Robbins, L., and Wallerstein, R. S. "The Research Strategy and Tactics of the Psychotherapy Research Project of the Menninger Foundation and the Problem of Controls." In *Research in Psychotherapy,* Vol. I, edited by E. A. Rubenstein and M. B. Parloff, Washington, D.C., The American Psychological Ass., 1959.

58 Schmale, A. The relation of separation and depression to disease. I. A report on a hospitalized medical population. *Psychosom. Med. 20:*259–277, 1958.

59 Seitz, P. F. D. "The Consensus Problem in Psychoanalytic Research." In

Methods of Research in Psychotherapy, edited by L. A. Gottschalk and A. H. Auerbach. New York, Hoeber, in press.

60 Shipman, W., Oken, D., Grinker, R. R., Sr., Goldstein, I., and Heath, H. A. A study of the psychophysiology of muscle tension. *Arch. gen. Psychiat.* In press, 1964.

61 Skinner, B. F. *Science and Human Behavior.* New York, Macmillan, 1953.

62 Skinner, B. F. "Critique of Psychoanalytic Concepts and Theories." In *The Validation of Scientific Theories,* edited by P. G. Frank. New York, Collier Books, 1961.

63 Stevens, S. S. The operational basis of psychology. *Amer. J. Psychol. 47:*323–330, 1935.

64 Stevens, S. S. Psychology and the science of sciences. *Psychol. Bull. 36:*221–263, 1939.

65 Wallerstein, R. S., Robbins, L. L., Sargent, H. D., and Luborsky, L. The psychotherapy research project of the Menninger Foundation: Rationale, method and sample use. *Bull. Menninger Clin. 20:*221–278, 1956.

TEN

The Ego and Bodily Responses

NORMAN S. GREENFIELD, PH.D.
AND A. A. ALEXANDER, PH.D.

The psychosomatic concept in human behavior has a long past but a short history, as does psychoanalysis itself. It is a likely assumption that ever since man began to experience himself as an object of his own awareness he has had some intuitive notion that bodily changes were, in some measure, related to his moods, his sentiments, his frustrations, his elations.

Zilboorg and Henry (*67*) and, most recently and more succinctly, Franz Alexander (*3*) have ably chronicled the conceptual seesaw which has keynoted attempts to comprehend the relationships between emotion and somatic phenomena. This history of ideas has witnessed these cycles of action and reaction: physical and mental, material and human, organic and dynamic, and, more recently, specific and nonspecific.

Alexander has also pointed out that one of the most common characteristics of the human mind—the tendency toward dichotomous thinking and the related need for monocausal explanations implicit in the either/or approach—has tended to stifle the development of a truly sophisticated and heuristic psychosomatic approach.

In one sense the almost dramatic insight into organic disease which was revealed when viewed from psychoanalytic perspectives paradoxically resulted in a narrowing of the field of this exciting new area. During the first half of the present century the discipline of psychosomatic medicine, riding on the shoulders of psychoanalytic insight, demonstrated in a far more rigorous fashion than ever before the integral relationship between psyche and soma. As Wolff has pointed out (*66*) however, the early emphasis was placed on those disorders in which the 'psychosomatic' relationship was most demonstrable, and this had the inadvertent and undesirable effect of introducing a class of diseases which came to be known as 'psychosomatic.' By undisciplined and somewhat distorted inference this class of psychosomatic diseases came to stand in opposition to the remainder of disease processes—the 'real' diseases. Indeed, there is probably not one among us who does not have an instant chain of associations to the terms hypertension, ulcer, ulcerative colitis, neurodermatitis, and so forth. It has become increasingly clear, however, that this is yet another spurious dichotomy, another surrender to the intolerance for the ambiguities of multicausal phenomena.

Gradually this ideological pendulum is also beginning to swing into accord with the facts of everyday observation. Recognition grows that the stresses to which man is exposed in his daily atempts to come to terms with his environment, and with his fellow man, have the most far-reaching implications relative to his over-all somatic integrity. We have stressed elsewhere (*31, 56*) some of our own views that all diseases, so-called psychic and so-called somatic, are essentially disturbances in the adaptive functions of the organism. We have suggested that the distinction between the dependent and the independent variables in psychosomatic research is a function of observer perspective and bias rather than a true reflection of dichotomous events within the organism.

It is unlikely that the laws governing adaptive behavior will eventually rest on a dichotomous foundation based on oftentimes arbitrary designations regarding 'psychological' and 'somatic' function. In order to reduce the distance between these two sets of constructs let us suggest that, just as some of the constructs of biological theory have enriched psychoanalysis, so too can some of the constructs of psychoanalytic theory serve a heuristic purpose in elucidating somatic events. We think we are doing more than simply analogizing or dealing with a congenial community of ideas. We believe we are dealing with an essential and basic unity, and this implies a more fundamental position than would be achieved simply by resorting to Pavlov's assertion that psychology is really only physiology (*48*). This position states that all somatic phenomena in the service of adaptation may, in a very real sense, be viewed in the context of ego psychological theory. The rationale for this emphasis rests on the facts that not only is there a relevant established set of concepts and intervening variables, but it is also a reflection of the thesis that man is a multi-dimensional organism.

The Protestant theologian Paul Tillich captures a similar sentiment most eloquently when he refers to man as a "multi-dimensional unity" (*61*). Tillich stresses the facts that in each dimension every dimension is present and that man's life qualities are present within one another rather than existing side by side.

Though this concept of a "multi-dimensional unity" has powerful intuitive appeal to the more holistically oriented observer, it is often regarded as little more than the tender-minded, wishful thinking of the philosophically inclined by that brand of tough-minded laboratory scientist who looks upon reductionism as the only proper brand of ultra-science and who likes to think that, the more infinitesimal is the unit under study, the more valuable will be the insights derived. This has too often left the study of human behavior in the position of the elephant being explored by the blind men. A kind of intellectual chauvinism emerges with the naive belief in the one 'real' solution. Indeed, we must look to the molecular scientist for crucial insights, but we must continually retain our awareness that the answers for which we search must be viewed in terms of the conceptual level of the question which is asked. How often are we told that the problems of mental life will be solved by the chemist, for example; this is rarely the position of the chemist, who has learned enough to ask what the questions are. It is, however, often the position of the chemist, or neurophysiologist, or computer expert who has experienced success in some more parochial endeavor and who wishes to present us with the gifts which have been revealed to him. Fortunately, the enthusiastic notion is waning that we may chart a path through the forest only by studying the molecular constitution of the trees. There is a growing awareness that hierarchical levels of conceptual organization need be looked upon not as of greater value, but rather as value judgments. As Kline has pointed out (*40*), one universe of discourse need not necessarily be reduceable to another. It is perhaps indisputable that vital phenomena rest upon physical-chemical activities, but it does not follow that knowledge of behavior will rest upon these facts alone. The limitations of space do not permit a fruitful elaboration of the logical aspects of this issue, but it has been well represented by Colby (*15*), Kline (*40*), Engel (*24*), and most charmingly by Seymour Kety (*39*).

Even in the more traditional aspects of investigative medicine the trend is away from reductionism toward an increasing concern with the dynamic activity and coordinating principles within the organisms. Enzyme chemistry has brought into focus the integral relationship between the five biological theories—germ, hormone, nutrition, genetics, and cells—which form the foundation of much modern medicine (*4*). As Wolf (*65*) has pointed out, oncology, virology, allergy, and genetics, fields which were believed widely divergent two decades ago, have been joined together by the discovery of DNA and RNA, offering a new unifying concept which has accelerated scientific progress. Increasing emphasis on the understanding of disease in terms of metabolic vicissitudes is yet another guidepost in this direction (*21*).

Indeed, in the study of all human behavior common threads in the fabric of coherence are emerging. Scientific medicine has transcended the monocausal bacterial era to a more enlightened view of the very complex array of host factors in disease. Psychoanalytic psychology has evolved from the study of drives and instincts and repressed traumatic events, through an elaboration and refined comprehension of defense activities, to a concern with those adaptive behaviors which we subsume under the heading 'ego functions.'

The field of psychosomatic medicine is both a product of and a contributor to this *Zeitgeist*. Indeed, it is of minor historical note that the journal *Psychosomatic Medicine* was conceived in the same year that Heinz Hartmann presented his paper *Ego Psychology and the Problem of Adaptation* (*32*) before the Vienna Psychoanalytic Society.

The primary thesis which is advanced in this paper and which underlies most of the work being carried out in our Psychophysiological Laboratory has neither the intellectual novelty of a truly new concepetual approach nor the elegance of a scientific discovery. We hope only to achieve some degree of success in making more explicit to medical and psychological practitioners and scientists a point of view which has threaded its way throughout the history of psychoanalytic thinking since some of Freud's earliest formulations (*26*) and which we believe has been increasingly implicit in the thinking of many of us who are actively and intimately engaged in psychophysiological and psychosomatic research.

In our advancing the thesis that constructs of ego psychology are directly applicable to problems of biological adaptation it may be readily apparent that we are simply casting into a new mold the teachings of Claude Bernard (*10*) and Walter Cannon (*14*). Paul Schilder, three decades ago (*58*), pointed out the potential contribution of psychoanalysis to biological thought, and Hartmann (*32*) has noted the ". . . heuristic potential of psychological analysis in regard to the biological realm of adaptive functions and regulative principles. . . ." As the editors of Hartmann's book point out, "The idea that ego defenses may simultaneously serve the control of instinctual drives and the adaptation to the external world finds its expression in this essay. Hartmann's concept of adaptation is in no way restricted to the 'cultural' sense of the term. It is a truly inclusive conception, and he views it as an ongoing process, reflecting constant attempts of the ego to balance intrasystemic and intersystemic tensions." In pointing out the essential continuity between biologic, physiologic, and social evolution, Engel (*24*) reminds us that the concepts and methodology developed by Freud provide for a truly unitary concept of disease.

In attempting to map out in our laboratory some of the relationships between the ego and somatic responses we have thus far concentrated on the general state of the ego's adaptive potential and capacity for integration which has become known as 'ego strength.' Ego strength may be defined in many ways; our point of view has been somewhat global, emphasizing the degree to which the ego can perform functions which are primarily in the service of adaptation and survival. These include the synthetic functions which mediate the demands of the internal and external environments, the ego's defensive role, and the perceptual, conceptual, and motor substructures which the newer ego psychological point of view has emphasized.

Much of our work was designed primarily to test the general hypothesis that there is indeed a reciprocal relationship between ego strength and somatic adaptive response. We wished to avoid the pitfalls of clinical evaluations of ego strength and thus employed as an operational measure the Ego Strength Scale of the Minnesota Multiphasic Personality Inventory, which was designed by Frank Barron (*6*). This inventory was originally developed from items of the MMPI which distinguished patients who improved in psychotherapy from patients who failed to improve. The scale successfully distinguishes psychiatric from nonpsychiatric patients (*51, 60*) and has been related to the ability to resolve discrimination conflicts (*42*). Although the Ego Strength Scale has a significant negative correlation with several of the psychopathological scales of the MMPI, as might be expected, the correlations are of a magnitude suggesting some independence from these scales (*16*). Dahlstrom and Welsh (*16*) suggest that the capacities which this scale appears to have are "the ability to deal with the environmental pressures facing one, the motivational pressures prompting one to various conflicting actions, and the emotional pressures acting to disorganize and disrupt usual patterns of behavior. It means sufficient control to deal with others, to gain their acceptance and create favorable impressions upon them. It means using available skills and abilities to full advantage."

In one of our earlier studies (*31*) we tested the hypothesis that there would be a positive relationship between ego strength and rapidity of recovery from infectious mononucleosis, as determined by objective hematological criteria. We chose infections mononucleosis because of its fairly predictable course, which may be observed through hematological examinations, and because it runs its natural course free of significant therapeutic amelioration. Additionally and importantly, the frequency of occurrence of the disease in a university population permitted the gathering of an adequate sample with a safe likelihood of availability for follow-up study. This factor was especially important, because we waited until six months after recovery from the illness before the psychological test was administered. Our hypothesis was confirmed; according to hematological criteria independent of subjective patient report the Ego Strength Scale differentiated fast recoverers from slow recoverers.

There are many studies in the recent literature which add further credence to this line of argument. Some of them have been reviewed by Roessler in a recent report (*54*). For example, relationships have been established between psychological health and length of symptomatic recovery from acute brucellosis infection (*38*), influenza (*37*), and other respiratory diseases (*12*).

Holmes and his colleagues (*34, 35*), studying tuberculosis, have demonstrated a relationship between psychological adaptive capacity and severity and duration of the illness. Reviews of this literature on tuberculosis have been offered by Berle (*9*), Daniels and Davidoff (*17*), and by Day (*18*). Sir William Osler has been quoted as saying, "It is just as important to know what is in a man's head as what is in his chest if you want to predict the outcome of pulmonary tuberculosis" (*62*). Although the evidence is far from conclusive, a similar relationship has been reported with regard to longevity and neoplastic disease (*5, 28, 41, 45, 49, 59*).

Having established a relationship between ego strength and somatic processes in the mononucleosis study plus the confirmatory findings of other investigators, we then tested the hypothesis that psychiatric patients would demonstrate a greater incidence of somatic disease than would a controlled group (*56*). Doust had demonstrated such a relationship using the questionnaire method with a comparatively sick psychiatric group (20). We attempted to refine the hypothesis by comparing the medical records of 500 University of Wisconsin students who were seen in our Psychiatry Out-Patient Clinic with the medical records of 500 students who were of the same sex in the medical clinic files.

Again the hypothesis was confirmed: it was found that the incidence of physical disease was greater in the psychiatric group; and within each category of disease psychiatric patients demonstrated a greater frequency of occurrence. These findings are also supported by the results of other research. One of the earliest studies was performed by Lewis (*46*), who noted that the frequency of occurrence of cancer was greater in paranoid patients in a mental hospital population than in the general population, a finding which was later confirmed by Scheflen (*57*). More recently, Ostfeld demonstrated this relationship in men who developed myocardial infarction (*47*).

These findings, plus a wealth of data in the literature which cannot be reviewed here because of space limitations, appear to establish at least a very strong presumptive case that the hypothesized relationship does, indeed, exist. Psychological adaptive capacity, or ego strength, does appear to be related to the incidence and course of a wide spectrum of disease processes.

From an ego psychological point of view it may be reasoned that the ability to resist disease or to master it in a relatively uncomplicated fashion reflects the enhanced performance of certain organismic adaptive capacities—such as the ability to make appropriate discriminations and the adequacy of response to the stimuli which have threatened the somatic integrity. Thus a new series of experiments was designed to test the general hypothesis that there is a relationship between ego strength and physiological responsivity (*30, 55*). Every worker in this field recognizes that physiological responsivity is an investigative area fraught with myriad complexities. Problems of recording, measurement, and the rationale of data analysis are usually only preliminary pitfalls. Even when these problems are satisfactorily mastered one is never really certain of the meaning of his results. Weiner has presented a very enlightening discussion of the problems of evaluating physiological response in which he emphasized the critical significance of psycho-social and interpersonal factors in the experimental situation (*64*). Thus, though we were not unmindful of the problems which could be encountered, much of our pilot work, as well as the work reported by activation theorists such as Elizabeth Duffy (*22–24*), supported our theoretical bias, and we tested the hypothesis that there would be a relationship between physiological responsivity and ego strength. Specifically, it was predicted that a high ego strength group would show a greater magnitude of response to various intensities of sound on skin resistance, heart rate, finger blood volume, and muscle potential measures than would a middle and low ego strength group. The results were encouraging; when each physiological variable was considered separately the differences in the predicted direction were significant for skin resistance and finger blood volume and closely approximated significance for muscle potential. The heart rate measure was in a predicted direction but did not approach significance. When all measures were considered together, by computing the probability that the ego strength groups' physiological responses would rank in the predicted direction, it was found that the probability was very small that the rank obtained could have occurred by chance. We are currently in the process of attempting to relate other parameters of physiological responsivity to ego strength.

A closely related and extremely provocative dimension of our research activity has dealt with physiological periodicity and its possible adaptive psychodynamic implications. In the present context periodicity has been defined as the cyclic, rhythmic, oscillatory nature of much of the seemingly random activity in the levels of various peripheral physiological systems.

Relatively high-frequency spontaneous rhythms in both cortical and subcortical structures have been well documented (*8, 27, 29, 50, 53*), as have neuroanatomical pathways and functional relationships between central and peripheral systems (*19, 44*). Such considerations led A. A. Alexander and his co-workers (*2*) to hypothesize and demonstrate the existence of concomitant or comparable periodicities in measures mediated by peripheral physiological systems. The methodology involved the sampling of skin resistance, heart rate, muscle potential, and finger blood volume activity at every second of the last six minutes of a 21-minute resting period; 360 data points for each of these four measures were recorded from each of 40 subjects. Electronic computer techniques made it possible to subject the data to a variance (or power) spectrum analysis (*11*) to determine whether a statistically significant proportion of the total variance of the six-minute series was at any one of 60 different frequency intervals. The technique involves correlation of a given record of electrical activity with itself displaced in time. If such a correlation is obtained at each of a series of regularly increasing temporal displacements, periodic changes and the degree of correlation will indicate the presence of a periodic wave from within the record under analysis. Such an analysis is capable of detecting the periodicity, even when masking activity prevents it from being seen in the original record. The technique permitted the quantification of frequency and amplitude of periodicity in the measures under study.

There has been a marked paucity of experimental studies attempting to relate spontaneous autonomic activity—rhythmic or otherwise—to aspects of personality. Burch and his co-workers investigated this subject in 1942 (*13*), and the Laceys revived interest in this question in a monograph published in 1958 (*44*).

In keeping with our interest in the heuristic application of psycho-dynamic principles to somatic phenomena we were, of course, motivated to study the relationship betwen physiological periodicity and ego strength. The concept of periodicity is certainly not new to psychoanalytic theory. Indeed, the phenomena of responsivity and periodicity are integral if not often explicit in the structural-dynamic-economic model which defines psychoanalytic theory. Hartmann, in his classic work *Ego Psychology and the Problem of Adaptation* (*32*) notes that ". . . apparently every organism has mechanisms for maintaining or re-establishing equilibrium . . . we can picture the process as an oscillation around the equilibrium . . . But psychoanalytic experience has also taught us that because of the complex structure of the mental apparatus, internal disturbances readily cause disturbances in the relation to reality." More recently, Benedek (*7*) underscored the regulatory nature of ego functions in the maintenance of psycho-physiological equilibrium toward the aim of survival. Rapaport (*52*), in stressing the organismic view in psychoanalytic psychology, notes the potentiality for internalized regulation of behavior which develops as a function of the growth of the ego.

It occurred to us, during what was perhaps a burst of speculative excess, that physiological periodicity might be conceived of as a somatic correlate of the hypothetical constructs of bound and free energy which were cornerstones of Freud's theories from his very earliest through his final efforts. It is beyond the purview of this paper to discuss this aspect of psychoanalytic theory in detail, and the reader is referred to the very exhaustive and scholarly exposition and critique of Freud's views which have been offered by Dr.

Robert Holt (*36*). Couched in terms of a psychoanalytic conceptual model we may note, however, that ego strength is a function of ego differentiation or, more precisely, structure formation within the ego. Rapaport has pointed out (*52*) that these structures serve to raise the threshold of drive energy discharge and are, in effect, "dams" which obstruct the tendency toward direct discharge of energy. This makes possible the production of adaptive functions such as ordered thought, controlled affect, and goal-directed behavior—behavior associated with secondary process. Rapaport further notes that, "Compared with the great expenditure of energy in primary processes, the structures formed by binding can function (autonomously) with a minimal expenditure of psychological energy, and by controlling the discharge of mobile (great intensity) energies they create high potentials for action."

Therefore, a premise central to our thinking follows the economic point of view in psychoanalytic psychology which assumes the existence of some form of energy model. Although we are painfully aware of the conceptual confusion and the logical boobytraps which have littered the wake of the energy theorist, we share Engel's view (*25*) and ". . . adhere to the strict determinism of Bernard and Freud and hold that energy sources are physiochemical in nature." It would be unprofitable to enter into polemics at this point. The reader interested in scholarly discussions of the energy problem is referred to the works of Colby (*15*), Engel (*25*), and Hinde (*33*). Our fundamental position relative to the unity of psyche and soma, as well as our bias in favor of measurement (with due respect to Kubie's [*43*] admonitions regarding the "seductive fallacy" inherent in measurement), would seem to make any other position untenable, at least at this time. The test of viewing organismic phenomena—including the stuff of psychoanalysis—as fitting into the paradigm of the dynamics of open biological systems as defined by von Bertalanffy (*63*) will of course stand or fall on the kinds of research it supports.

Our hypothesis translated into operational physiological terms the sequence which Rapaport had outlined: Binding facilitates the creation of structure which is essential for secondary process functioning—a requirement of the adaptive behavior which maintains energy excitation in a more or less steady state. The reverse sequence occurs in the pathological process of regression in which structure dissolves, controls and defenses weaken, free energy is liberated, and primary process maladaptive behavior assumes ascendency with the resultant disturbance of homeostasis. In this sense our hypothesis states that low ego strength subjects would demonstrate physiological periodicities paralleling primary process activity—i.e., less ordered, less controlled, more mobile. In other words, the prediction was made that the greater the departure from a physiological steady state the poorer would be the individual's psychological adaptive capacity or ego strength. The details of this experiment have been reported elsewhere (*1*) but will be summarized briefly here. Subjects could be easily divided into two groups on the basis of the frequency of periodic activity in one or more of the four physiological measures recorded. Those subjects termed 'high frequency' demonstrated periodicities in a range of from .01 cps to .25 cps. Those subjects termed 'low frequency individuals' evidenced cyclic autonomic activity in a range of from .25 to .50 cps. (These ranges represented the fastest and slowest 30 frequencies of the 60 frequencies examined.) Subjects who are periodic at high frequencies had significantly lower ego strength scores than did subjects who were periodic at low frequencies. Furthermore, within this group of high frequency subjects, those with periodicity evident on more than one physiological variable had significantly lower ego strength scores than did those with high frequency periodicity on only one variable. It is noteworthy that predictions derived solely from the power spectra based on frequency alone would have allowed a 75 per cent accurate classification of individuals as to whether they were in upper or lower half of the ego strength range of the entire sample. Prediction from the spectra on the basis of both frequency and number of periodic variables would have discriminated those individuals whose ego strength scores fell in the lower quartile of the entire range with better than 90 per cent accuracy. In comparing the physiological periodicities of a patient and nonpatient group, post-diction based on the low frequency of the periodic activity and number of periodic variables would also have permitted 90 per cent accuracy. Discrimination between patients and nonpatients at this level of accuracy is probably better than that achieved by most psychological methods. The hypothesis was rather impressively confirmed.

Thus we are suggesting the possibility of a relationship between lowered ego strength, the amount of free energy, and physiological periodicity. Since responsivity has been posited as a correlate of adaptive capacity or higher ego strength, logical consistency insists upon the prediction that there should be an inverse relationship between physiological responsivity and physiological periodicity. Indeed, this turns out to be the case. And, indeed, this turns out to be the prediction to be drawn from the work of Rapaport previously cited.

Much of the work now being carried out in our laboratory, as well as a crowded schedule of future projects, will serve as the final adjudicator of the validity of these premises. For the present purpose the final verdict is relatively unimportant. We will be quick to concede that the application of psychoanalytic constructs to physiological phenomena may, in the final analysis, prove to be little more than a bold metaphorical exercise. We believe that we have demonstrated, however, that for us this approach has served a very real and useful purpose.

REFERENCES

1 Alexander, A. A., Roessler, R., and Greenfield, N. S. Ego strength and physiological responsivity. III. The relationship of the Barron Ego Strength Scale to spontaneous periodic activity in skin resistance, finger blood volume, heart rate and muscle potential. *Arch. gen. Psychiat. 9:*142–145, 1963.

2 Alexander, A. A., Roessler, R., and Greenfield, N. S. Periodic nature of spontaneous peripheral nervous system activity. *Nature, London 197:*1169–1170, 1963.

3 Alexander, F. The development of psychosomatic medicine. *Psychosom. Med. 24:*13, 1962.

4 The American Foundation. *Medical Research: A Midcentury Survey.* Boston, Little, Brown & Co., 1955.

5 Bacon, C. L., Renneker, R., and Cutler, M. Psychosomatic survey of cancer of the breast. *Psychosom. Med. 14:*453, 1952.

6 Barron, F. An ego strength scale which predicts response to psychotherapy. *J. consult. Psychol. 17:*327, 1953.

7 Benedek, T. "On the Organization of Psychic Energy: Instincts, Drives, and Affects." In *Mid-Century Psychiatry,* edited by R. R. Grinker. Springfield, Charles C Thomas, 1951.

8 Benitez, H. H., Murray, M. R., and Wooley, D. W. Effects of serotonin and certain of its antagonists upon oligodendroglia cells in vitro. *Proc. Second Int. Cong. Neuropath.,* London, 1955. Excerpta Medica, Amsterdam, Vol. 2, pp. 423–428, 1958.

9 Berle, B. Emotional factors and tuberculosis: A critical review of the literature. *Psychosom. Med. 10:*366, 1948.

10 Bernard, C. *An Introduction to the Study of Experimental Medicine* (1865), translated by H. G. Greene. New York, Macmillan, 1927.

11 Blackman, R. B., and Tukey, J. W. The measurement of power spectra. Reprinted by Dover Publications, N.Y., from *Bell Sys. tech. J. 37:*Nos. 1 and 2, 1958.

12 Brodman, K., Mittelmann, B., Wechsler, D., Weider, A., and Wolff, H. G. The relation of personality disturbances to duration of convalescence from acute respiratory infections. *Psychosom. Med. 9:*37, 1947.

13 Burch, G. E., Cohn, A. E., and Neuman, C. A study by quantitative methods of spontaneous variations in volume of the finger tip, toe tip, and postero-superior portion of the pinna of resting normal white adults. *Amer. J. Physiol. 136:*433, 1942.

14 Cannon, W. B. *The Wisdom of the Body.* New York, Norton, 1932.

15 Colby, K. M. *Energy and Structure in Psychoanalysis.* New York, Ronald Press, 1955.

16 Dahlstrom, W. G., and Welsh, G. S. *An MMPI Handbook.* Minneapolis, Univ. of Minnesota Press, 1960.

17 Daniels, G. E., and Davidoff, E. The mental aspects of tuberculosis. *Amer. Rev. Tuberc. 62:*532, 1950.

18 Day, G. The psychosomatic approach to pulmonary turebculosis. *Lancet 260:*1025, 1951.

19 Dell, P., and Bonvallet, M. Somatic functions of the nervous system. *Annu. Rev. Physiol. 18:*309, 1956.

20 Doust, J. W. L. Psychiatric aspects of somatic immunity: Differential incidence of physical disease in histories of psychiatric patients. *Brit. J. prev. soc. Med. 6:*49, 1952.

21 Drabkin, D. L. Kinetic basis of life processes: Pathways and mechanism of hepatic protein synthesis. In "Some aspects of metabolic diseases in man and animals," edited by W. D. Malherbe. *Ann. N.Y. Acad. Sci. 104:*469, 1963.

22 Duffy, Elizabeth. The concept of energy mobilization. *Psychol. Rev. 58:*30, 1951.

23 Duffy, Elizabeth. The psychological significance of the concept of "arousal" or "activation." *Psychol. Rev. 64:*265, 1957.

24 Duffy, Elizabeth. *Activation and Behavior.* New York, Wiley, 1962.

25 Engel, G. L. "Homeostasis, Behavioral Adjustment and the Concept of Health and Disease." In *Mid-Century Psychiatry,* edited by R. R. Grinker. Springfield, Charles C Thomas, 1951.

26 Freud, S. "Project for a Scientific Psychology." In *The Origins of Psychoanalysis: Letters to Wilhelm Fliess, Drafts and Notes, 1887–1902,* edited by M. Bonaparte, A. Freud, and E. Kris. New York, Basic Books, 1954.

27 Geiger, R. S. Subcultures of adult mammalian brain cortex in vitro. *Exp. Cell Res. 14:*541, 1958.

28 Gengerelli, J. A., and Kirkner, F. J. *The Psychological Variables in Human Cancer.* Berkeley and Los Angeles, Univ. California Press, 1954.

29 Granit, R. *Receptors and Sensory Perception.* New Haven, Yale Univ. Press, 1955, pp. 81–112.

30 Greenfield, N. S., Alexander, A. A., and Roessler, R. Ego strength and physiological responsivity. II. The relationship of the Barron Ego Strength Scale to the temporal and recovery characteristics of skin resistance, finger blood volume, heart rate and muscle potential to sound. *Arch. gen. Psychiat. 9:*129–141, 1963.

31 Greenfield, N. S., Roessler, R., and Crosley, A. P. Ego strength and length of recovery from infectious mononucleosis. *J. nerv. ment. Dis. 128:*125, 1959.

32 Hartmann, H. *Ego Psychology and the Problem of Adaptation.* New York, Int. Univ. Press, 1958.

33 Hinde, R. A. "Energy Models of Motivation." *Symposia of the Society for Experimental Biology,* No. 14. Cambridge, Cambridge Univ. Press, 1960.

34 Holmes, T. H. "Multidiscipline Studies of Tuberculosis." In *Personality, Stress and Tuberculosis,* edited by P. J. Sparer. New York, Int. Univ. Press, 1956.

35 Holmes, T. H., Joffe, J. R., Ketcham, J. W., and Sheehy, T. F. Experimental study of prognosis. *J. psychosom. Res. 5:*235, 1961.

36 Holt, R. R. A critical examination of Freud's concept of bound vs. free cathexis. *J. Amer. Psychoanal. Ass. 10:*475, 1962.

37 Imboden, J. B., Canter, A., and Cluff, L. E. Convalescence from influenza. *Arch. int. Med. 108:*393, 1961.

38 Imboden, J. B., Canter, A., and Cluff, L. E. Symptomatic recovery from medical disorders. *J. Amer. Med. Ass. 178:*1182, 1961.

39 Kety, S. S. A biologist examines the mind and behavior. *Science 132:*1861, 1960.

40 Kline, N. S. On the relationship between neurophysiology, psychophysiology, psychopharmacology, and other disciplines. In "Pavlovian conference on higher nervous activity," edited by N. S. Kline. *Ann. N.Y. Acad. Sci. 92:*1004, 1961.

41 Kowal, S. J. Emotions as a cause of cancer. *Psychoanal. Rev. 42:*217, 1955.

42 Kroman, M. Ego strength and conflict discrimination. *J. consult. Psychol. 24:*294, 1960.

43 Kubie, L. S. The fallacious use of quantitative concepts in dynamic psychology. *Psychoanal. Quart. 16:*507, 1947.

44 Lacey, J. I., and Lacey, B. C. The relationship of resting autonomic activity to motor impulsivity. *Res. Publ. Ass. Res. Nerv. Ment. Dis. 36:*144, 1958.

45 LeShan, L. Psychological states as factors in the development of malignant disease. *J. nat. Cancer Inst. 22:*1, 1959.

46 Lewis, N. D. C. *Research in Dementia Praecox.* New York, National Committee for Mental Hygiene, 1936.

47 Ostfeld, A. M., Oglesby, P., and Lepper, M. H. An anterospective study of coronary heart disease. (Abstract.) *Psychosom. Med. 23:*448, 1961.

48 Pavlov, I. P. *Experimental Psychology and Other Essays.* New York, Philosophical Library, 1957.

49 Perrin, G. M., and Pierce, I. R. Psychosomatic aspects of cancer: A review. *Psychosom. Med. 21:*397, 1959.

50 Pomerant, C. M. Pulsatile activity of cells from the human brain in tissue culture. *J. nerv. ment. Dis. 114:*430, 1951.

51 Quay, H. The performance of hospitalized patients on the ego-strength scale of the MMPI. *J. clin. Psychol. 11:*403, 1955.

52 Rapaport, D. The structure of psychoanalytic theory. *Psychological Issues 2*(2):Monograph 6, 1960.

53 Roeder, K. D. Spontaneous activity and behavior. *Scient. Monthly 80:*362, 1951.

54 Roessler, R. Relation of psychologic health to disease resistance. *Geriatrics 18:*93, 1963.

55 Roessler, R., Alexander, A. A., and Greenfield, N. S. Ego strength and physiological responsivity. I. The relationship of the Barron ES Scale to skin resistance, finger blood volume, heart rate, and muscle potential responses to sound. *Arch. gen. Psychiat. 8:*142–154, 1963.

56 Roessler, R., and Greenfield, N. S. Incidence of somatic disease in psychiatric patients. *Psychosom. Med. 23:*413, 1961.

57 Scheflen, A. E. Malignant tumors in the institutionalized psychotic population. *Arch. Neurol., Chicago 66:*145, 1951.

58 Schilder, P. Psychoanalyse und biologie. *Imago, Lpz. 19:*168, 1933.

59 Shrifte, M. L. Toward identification of a psychological variable in host resistance to cancer. *Psychosom. Med. 24:*390, 1962.

60 TAFT, R. The validity of the Barron ego-strength scale and the Welsh anxiety index. *J. consult. Psychol. 21:*247, 1957.

61 TILLICH, P. The meaning of health. *Midway 10:*50, 1962.

62 VITALE, J. H. An investigation of some personality correlates during the clinical course of tuberculosis. Unpublished doctoral dissertation, Stanford Univ., 1953.

63 VON BERTALANFFY, L. The theory of open systems in physics and biology. *Science 111:*23, 1950.

64 WEINER, H. "Some Psychological Factors Related to Cardiovascular Responses: A Logical and Empirical Analysis." In *Physiological Correlates of Psychological Disorder,* edited by R. Roessler and N. S. Greenfield. Madison, Univ. of Wisconsin Press, 1962.

65 WOLF, S. Asking the question. Psychosom. *Med. 24:*4, 1962.

66 WOLFF, H. G. A concept of disease in man. *Psychosom. Med. 24:*25, 1962.

67 ZILBOORG, G., AND HENRY, G. W. *A History of Medical Psychology.* New York, Norton, 1941.

ELEVEN

Autonomic Responsivity and the Concept of Sets

RICHARD A. STERNBACH, PH.D.

THE PROBLEM OF AUTONOMIC VARIABILITY

In psychophysiological research, as in other research with humans, the variability of the data constitutes a real problem. Not only are there the well known differences among individuals and among certain groups of individuals, but there are remarkable fluctuations within individuals over periods of time. If an experiment is being conducted in which a patient appears in the laboratory for *one* day to receive one of several treatments, several techniques are typically employed to minimize his physiological response variability:

1. He is made to rest quietly before proceeding with the experiment.
2. The impingement of nontreatment or extraneous variables is greatly reduced, by placing the subject in a sound-, light-, temperature-, and humidity-controlled room.
3. The assumption is made, in handling the data which the patient produces, that they are samples from his possible responses which are normally distributed about some hypothetical average and that the odds are in favor of the samples' having come from the hypothetical average value.
4. The data from a number of patients are pooled, and the assumption is made that a possible atypical response from one will be countered by an atypical response in the opposite direction from another, and thus the distribution of data from the sample group will approximate the hypothetical distribution of the population from which the group is drawn.

These technical and statistical procedures have permitted the collection of considerable information and a number of important concepts have emerged, such as the principles of autonomic balance, of activation, and of individual- and stimulus-response specificities.

This work was supported by Public Health Service Fellowship MSP–15,670 from the National Institute of Mental Health.

If, however, our subject comes to the laboratory over a long period of time, we can observe fluctuations both in his levels of ongoing physiological activity and in his physiological responsiveness to our experimental treatments. At least one aspect of these fluctuations casts some doubt on the assumption of sampling made in one-session experiments, as will be discussed later.

This type of variability deserves further consideration. We know that it is not entirely to be accounted for by uncontrolled atmospheric variables (*11*), and intuitively we suspect that social and psychological variables may be important. It is precisely at this point, where social and psychological and physiological factors interact, that psychoanalysis has contributed to our understanding, at one level, of how these factors may interact.

What will be explored here is a concept which may explain some of the variability we encounter and which involves physiological and nonphysiological factors at different levels of discourse.

THE CONCEPT OF SETS

The concept of sets is as old as experimental psychology; it was early invoked to account for differences in simple and disjunctive reaction times (*2, 12*). A *'set'* has been variously defined by a number of synonymous phrases, such as a *readiness to respond,* a *predisposition* or *tendency* or *propensity to respond,* or, from another view, an *expectancy* or *anticipation* of an event. The first group of phrases is primarily oriented to the production of responses; the second group primarily to the reception of stimuli. The important point, however, is that in any case *'set'* is accorded the status of an intervening variable, a process which either mediates between input and output or modulates input and output, and which is not itself directly observable.

The existence of such an intervening variable is reasonably inferred from a number of considerations. First, it is a common and classic observation that not every input has a corresponding output. Second, it is similarly known that an input at Time 1 may result in an output different from that elicited by an identical input at Time 2. Third, we observe outputs whose corresponding inputs are not specifiable. For these reasons we find it necessary to postulate processes "in there" which effectively give the conceptualized organism some "slack" in its operations. The word 'set' is being chosen to represent these postulated processes because it has some surplus connotations which, as will be seen, are easily related to physiological mechanisms.

In addition to the above reasons for employing the concept, there must be considered a number of indirect measures which may be used to give the concept an operational definition. When all specifiable input is held constant, a set to respond may be said to exist when there is an increase in the amount, rate, or strength of response; or, if we are emphasizing the receptive rather than the productive aspect of the process, we may say that a perceptual set exists when the threshold is lowered. Conversely, a set *not* to respond or perceive may be defined as a decrease in the amount, rate, or strength of response, or as an increase in threshold.

However preferable such operational definitions may be as compared with synonymous phrases, they are direct measures of the output only, and it must not be forgotten that it is the very complex relationship between observable input and output that justifies our inference about the existence of sets.

We have tried to indicate in what sense *set* has been used in psychology, as an inside-the-black-box concept. We would propose that in psychophysiology we may be reductionistic and consider what may be the mechanisms underlying sets.

Neurophysiological considerations.—Most physiological responses, as we measure them (and sets, as we infer them), do not either occur or not occur. As the spike potential is a digital-like process and the response systems look more like analog, or graded, processes, it has been necessary to assume that *rate* of neural discharge is the gradually varying activity and that both input and output are pulse-coded in terms of rate. As we have learned more about recruitment and multi-synapsing neurons, we have come to speak of the 'spatiotemporal patterning of impulses' as being the basis for particular sensations or responses (or, monistically, as *being* the sensations or responses). However, what could be said to be the neurophysiological equivalent of the intervening variable—set—which seems to modulate spatiotemporal patterns?

An impressive amount of evidence is accumulating for graded local processes within the central nervous system. This refers to the single-cell decremental activity, or electrotonic conduction, which occurs along the membrane of the neuron cell body and in its dendrites and axons (*3*). This activity is continuous and continuously fluctuating and is related to the movements of ions through the membrane. Recently, we have had the privilege of seeing records from cortical and subcortical cells, recorded with ultramicroelectrodes less than 1 μ in diameter—for example, records of membrane potential changes in Betz cells of cat motor cortex, following midbrain and thalamic reticular stimulation (Y. Saito, personal communication). A conspicuous feature of all such cells is the continuous fluctuations in their resting membrane potentials, and thus in their excitability. We propose that these graded changes in membrane potentials are the neural equivalents of sets.

Some structural considerations.—Few psychologists are familiar with the work of the neuroanatomist Paul I. Yakovlev. Because his conceptualizations of the nervous system are particularly useful to the psychophysiologist and directly relevant to our present discussion, we will briefly summarize his views. Yakovlev is concerned with the functional organization of the brain, on anatomical grounds, in what he calls the three spheres of motility (*13, 14*).

The sphere of effectuation concerns the ability to make use of the distal effectors to manipulate the environment. The functions involved derive from the outer of three anatomically discrete concentric areas of the brain, the homocortex, or ectopallium. This system has strati-laminated, crossed motor fibers which are organized in parallel, and lesions in the system result in distal immobility—the pyramidal syndrome.

The sphere of expression concerns the outer display of internal states, or emotions. It derives from the isocortex, or mesopallium, a concentric ring around the entopallium. The nucleated, extrapyramidal fibers in this system are organized in series—i.e., multisynaptically. Lesions in the system result in disturbances of emotional expression (Huntington's chorea), in posture, and in axial and proximal limb immobility (Parkinsonism)—what Ross Adey has aptly termed "a loathness to move."

As psychophysiologists concerned with visceral motility or, more properly, with peripheral measures of autonomically innervated activity, we are particularly interested in the sphere of visceration. It derives from the allocortex, or entopallium, which comprises the rhinic lobe forming a closed ring around the foramen of Monro—the pyriform lobe, hippocampus, and supra- and infra-callosal rudiments, with the hypothalamus as the head of the system. The diffuse, unmyelinated, reticulated fibers project from the rhinencephalon to the hypothalamus, central gray, and the autonomic system. Lesions in this system typically are incompatible with survival, in that it involves respiration, circulation, and metabolism.

It will be assumed here that the central representation of peripheral autonomic variability *is* the fluctuation in membrane permeability of the cells of the rhinic lobe. More specifically, we would say that changes in set, measured in terms of thresholds or response variability, *are* the changes in membrane potentials of assemblies of cells in the rhinic lobe. A major difficulty with this proposal is that the shifts in potentials which have been observed in experimental preparations are of the order of milliseconds, whereas the aspects of set we will be considering, behavioral as well as physiological, are of the order of minutes. We can only assume that in the intact organism such shifts may be maintained over the requisite period of time.

Thus far we have attempted to define the concept of sets and to postulate a basis for the concept in neurophysiological processes and loci. Although this neurologizing is not necessary for much of what follows, it helps to illustrate how the function, *set,* must be considered on several different levels. We will turn now to preliminary considerations of subjective, clinical, and experimental aspects of sets.

SETS AND PHENOMENOLOGICAL EXPERIENCE

Since ancient times men have speculated about "free will," whether it is real or an illusion. The *subjective* reality of our having control over our actions gave rise, in the older psychologies, to concepts of intention, or volition, or will. These concepts, as part of a mentalistic or of a faculty psychology, were of little explanatory value and seem to have seen their day. We hope that the postivistic rejection of the problem as "metaphysical" has also seen its day, because the subjective reality of self-determination persists and must be accounted for.

When Dr. Johnson kicked the rock in the road and thus refuted Berkeley, he was affirming the *reality* of subjective experience, not its illusoriness. If the squiggles coming from my polygraph are real to me, so too are my feelings and intentions. And, it might be added, both "kinds" of reality derive their empirical validity from a comparable consensus. Although the materialistic monist may prefer to think of feelings and intentions as epiphenomenal, it would seem that the more useful approach is to consider in what sorts of conceptual schema the 'subjective' and 'objective' realities may be articulated.

We are not competent to deal with more than a fraction of this problem. Elsewhere in this volume are highly sophisticated attempts at its resolution. The aspect with which we are concerned is the experience of *intending*. Intending represents both motivational and perceptual-cognitive functions, in that both a generalized level of activation and a specific goal are implied. I *intend* to drive a car from here to there; the intention is a representation of both internal drive and external stimulus. The intention, in short, is the subjective counterpart of what we have called 'set.'

Two major problems confront us here. One is that the performance of what was intended need not be accompanied by any conscious awareness of the behavior. The other is that the reasons for the formation of the intention (set) may also be imperfectly realized in awareness. We will examine these problems in order.

When we decide to drive our car over a familiar route, we are aware of making the decision and, perhaps, have a peripheral image of the route we will traverse. However, in the process of driving over the route we may be completely unaware of what we are doing. We can maneuver through traffic, display the most complex behavior involving multiple contingencies and feedbacks, but all the while be preoccupied with some problem or other so that we arrive at our destination totally unable to recall any of the events of the journey.

This type of problem is not new. The notion of "imageless thought" developed by the Wurzburg school was that, given a set established by instructions, a response would run off automatically at the appearance of the appropriate signal. Introspection revealed awareness of a process, but not the content, of thought immediately preceding the act (*2*). Awareness of content accompanies the intention to respond in a given way—i.e., the formation of the set but not the response itself.

It is perhaps for this reason that we have the experience of self-determination. In intending to act in a certain way, we affirm for ourselves our uniqueness in having the fewest possible constraints on our behavior: we have the apparent freedom to choose this action or some other. With our choices, real or apparent, we are convinced of our freedom; our action does not come from others "out there," but from ourselves "in here," because we willed it. Our uniqueness is confirmed not through awareness of automatic behavior, but through awareness of decision-making, which proclaims our choices. Automatic behavior, we should add, is disrupted in its efficiency by awareness, as is nicely illustrated in the verse about the centipede which fell in the ditch while trying to think how it maneuvered its legs.

Thus we can understand Sartre (*8*) when he says that every man is a free choice, and that every act, big and small, expresses this choice. It cannot be the act itself, we would say, that is the existential display of freedom, but the choice, the intention, the set which precedes the act.

Sartre also observes that we can deceive ourselves as to the reasons for our choices, that we may act in bad faith. This is the other major problem we have mentioned, our imperfect awareness of the factors involved in the formation of our intentions. It is one thing when a simple experimental set is formed by instructions which can be used to operationalize the set; it is quite another when complex behavior appears in a natural setting—the set(s) may be inferred, but only haphazardly specified.

It is in this context that Freudian dynamics have added a great deal to the limited insights available to the introspectionists of Wurzburg. We are now able to understand somewhat more clearly not only the kinds of factors which influence apparently free decisions (set-formation) but also some of the unconscious content accompanying acts which previously seemed to have no conscious accompaniment. The theoretical basis for this understanding comprises Freudian metapsychology; the factors determining specific set-formations in a given individual must be clinically determined.

SETS AND CLINICAL PHENOMENA

Two kinds of clinical events are instructive with respect to the understanding of sets: psychosomatic disorders and pain.

In psychosomatic disorders we may see clearly the associations between sets and clearly specifiable responses (symptoms). The work of Graham (*5, 6*) is an example of this. He has found, in a variety of disorders such as eczema, asthma, ulcers, etc., that patients with a given disease share certain attitudes—i.e., a common response among multiple persons is shown to be associated with a common attitude among these persons. Attitudes refer to preferred modes of dealing with feelings, particularly with respect to interpersonal situations. As Graham has defined it, an attitude is a specific instance of what we have called set. Thus, in a variety of patients with a common symptom, there is a common (verbal) set associated with their common (physiological) response specificity.

The verbal attitude associated with any symptom represents a set for the physiological response for the particular person. What the factors influencing the set may be, i.e., the person's dynamics, will vary as a function of his unique genetic determinants and his unique exposure history. For such a person there is little awarenes of 'choice' in the phenomenological sense we have discussed. Typically, the 'choice' consists of responding or failing to respond to interpersonal situations in a certain way (asthma, ulcers), or of perceiving them in certain ways (demanding, threatening). The pathology, in fact, although the end-product of a series of contingent events, really consists of the very lack of choice of responses available to the person. Improvement is usually dependent upon the bringing into awareness ('with affect') this stereotypy, and in increasing the number of alternatives available so that 'choice' becomes a meaningful process.

In responses to pain, also, we can see the pervasive effects of sets. Buytendijk (*4*, footnote 52) cites Larrey, in a dramatic example, to demonstrate the stoicism possible:

> . . . The famous surgeon in Napoleon's army . . . amputated legs and arms in the field and the wounded men simply sat and watched. In his memoirs he tells of an officer whose arm was amputated at the shoulder joint. He mounted his horse with the bandage on and took part in the normal cavalry expeditions right across Europe. Finally he arrived back in Paris fully well. . . .

The shock and incomprehensibility to us of such behavior are eloquent evidence of differences in sets.

Zborowski (*15*) has shown how responses to pain are in large part influenced by cultural factors associated with the meaning of (set toward) the stimulus, what Beecher (*1*) has called the "reaction component" in pain. The significance of the stimulus, whether perceived as one of impending deterioration or just another of life's unpleasantnesses, seems to be of critical importance in determining an individual's behavioral responses. Although Beecher uses this concept to argue that experimental pain lacks any significant meaning to subjects and can shed little light on 'real' pain, the same concept suggests that experimental manipulation of the *meaning* (set) may be a promising approach (see next section).

'Attitudes' in psychosomatic disorders, and 'meaning' in pain, are both instances of sets as we have defined them. In each instance the set represents a subjective intention to respond or perceive in a certain way: a decision is made—a choice taken, a set formed—although often without awareness of the factors influencing the decision. In each instance, too, the amelioration of the condition consists of making alternative choices available to the individual—i.e., changing the set.

SETS AND THEIR EXPERIMENTAL MANIPULATION

We have already suggested that two aspects of sets may be differentiated: that emphasizing the receptive or sensory phase of the process and that emphasizing the productive or motor phase. Let us consider these in order. (Portions of this work were reported earlier [*9*].)

Changes in reported perceptions.—Our first attempt to study modifications of responses to electric shocks was in a study of 'audioanalgesia.' In this experiment three groups of eight patients each received different instructions: that shocks accompanied by noise would hurt more than shocks presented alone; that shocks accompanied by noise would hurt less than shocks presented alone; and that shocks accompanied by noise would feel the same as shocks presented alone. For convenience, these were called the hyperalgesic, analgesic, and neutral groups, respectively. Each subject received a total of 40 shocks on each of two experimental days. At the end of each session the subject was asked to compare the strength of the shocks in the two conditions. The hyperalgesic group gave 56 per cent of their verbal responses as acknowledging hyperalgesia; 69 per cent of the analgesic group's responses, and 75 per cent of the neutral group's responses, also conformed to instructions.

To better quantify the subjective report, another study (with Greenblatt and Tursky) is in progress, a portion of which may be described. In this experiment twelve subjects, male college students, were asked to estimate the strength of a series of shocks under two different conditions. In one "60 cps" condition the instructions were to give numerical values to a series of shocks of different current strengths, following verbatim the instructions used by Stevens (*10*), although our electrodes and milliamperage differed from his. In the other "75 cps" condition the same subjects had the same task and received the same stimuli, but were told we were now using "75 cps" which might produce some unpleasant sensations and, perhaps, some slight damage. The results are shown in Figure 11.1. It is clear that, in estimation of electric shock intensity (as in many other situations), responses are easily modifiable by instructions which, presumably, alter subjects' sets.

Changes in autonomic responsivity.—The most dramatic evidence for alteration of autonomic activity with changes in set is that which is often considered a contaminant of psychophysiological research. We are referring to the common "first-day phenomenon," in which subjects display levels of resting autonomic activity which are markedly different in their first session as compared with subsequent sessions. Typically, blood pressure, heart rate, skin conductance, etc., are at considerably higher values than they will be later. Often experimenters will have one or more practice sessions with their subjects before beginning the experiment proper, for purposes of "adapting the subjects." What is the nature of this set in the first session? Anxiousness about the situation certainly seems to be involved: subjects make feeble jokes about being "wired for sound," or "sitting in the electric chair," or, lately, being "shot to the moon." In our eagerness to proceed with other studies we often ignore or eliminate this phenomenon, which clearly points to the importance of sets in physiological activity and which contributes to the variability of our data.

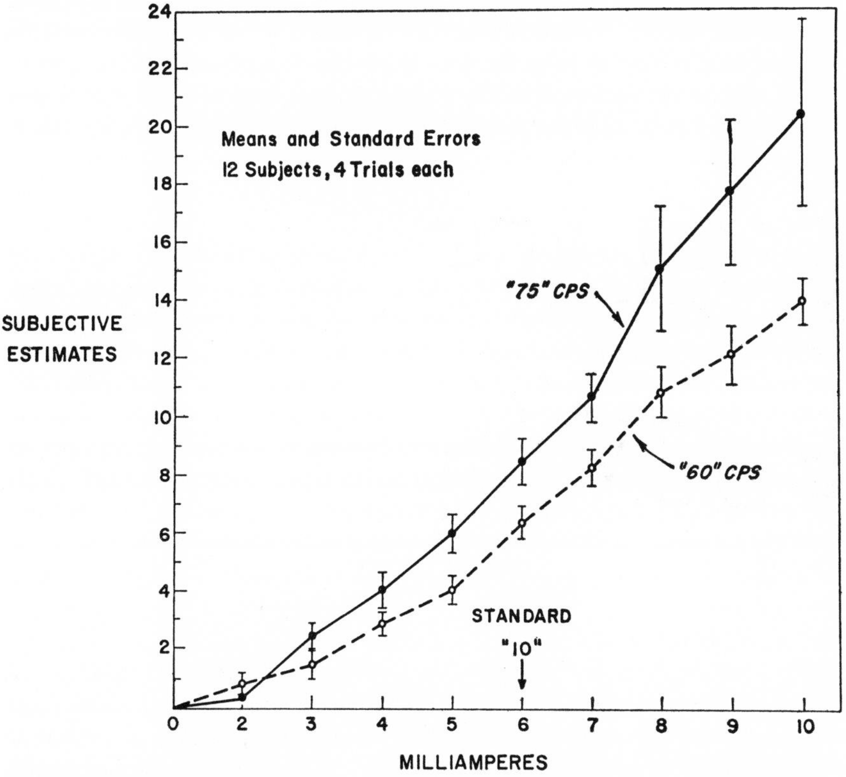

Fig. 11.1.—Changes in subjective estimates of shock magnitude with different instructions. The same subjects received identical stimuli and had the same task in each of the two conditions, but "75 cps" was more threatening, resulting in greater magnitude estimates and greater variability.

In our first study on shock and noise, mentioned above, measures of heart rate, finger pulse volume, and palmar skin resistance were obtained for each of the groups. Difference scores, between pre-shock levels and maximum responses to shock, under noise and non-noise conditions, permitted intra-group evaluation of the effectiveness of the instructions. Although there was little consistency among the groups with respect to which variable was most responsive, it was found that some of the responses were modified in the predicted directions.

A more direct attempt to modify physiological responses was made in another study, also previously reported (*9*). Six subjects each swallowed a small magnet on three different occasions, permitting the recording of their gastric peristaltic rate. On one occasion they were told that this was a drug which slowed the stomach; on another occasion they were told it was a drug which increased the rate of stomach movement; on a third occasion they were told it was a placebo, a control condition. The results demonstrated that, for four of the six subjects, there were clearly significant differences in gastric motility in the predicted directions. Instructions sufficiently modified the subjects' sets to alter the rate of functioning of this autonomically innervated organ.

DISCUSSION

Since any given set can be specified in terms of the observed output, the "readiness to respond" is, by definition, a change in a given response. Thus, any measurable behavior becomes, in this scheme, a response; and every response is, presumably, a function of a set to respond. Thus, for each behavioral act there exists a set, but for every set there may be multiple responses.

As we conceive it there must be classes of sets, each of which subsumes a variety of behavior patterns which are consonant with it. For example, as therapists are aware, an individual with a strong dependency need will manifest this set in a wide variety of behavior patterns, all of which have in common the message "Take care of me." From another approach, a person may respond to a certain class of situations with a characterisic gastritis. Thus, there are conceptual savings in determining the single set which is associated with multiple responses.

We have not specified what are the factors which produce sets. Our discussion of fluctuations of membrane potentials of assemblies of rhinic cells was not an attempt to specify cause, but rather to postulate a physiological definition. 'Cause,' in this context, refers to some process occurring earlier in time and thus implies either a genetic determination, a given exposure history, or both, for an individual. Without specifying the content of a set, it may not be possible to specify the cause.

From the initial results we have presented here, the implication is clear that instructions may 'cause' sets under certain conditions. The nature of these conditions may be implicit, as has been suggested by Orne (*7*), and may involve subjects' pre-existing sets toward helping Science in general and The Experimenter in particular. Obviously these parameters need further specification. The subject-experimenter relationship seems to be crucial to the outcome of instructionally induced sets, and this implies the need for investigation of the experimenter's own sets toward the experiment.

Our own research in this area has only begun, and our studies are preliminary. What we have attempted here is to focus on some of the possible factors contributing to intra-individual response variability and to suggest ways of investigating them. If our preliminary results are substantiated by future research, we may understand better the factors contributing to the variability of our data.

REFERENCES

1 Beecher, H. K. *Measurement of Subjective Responses: Quantitative Effects of Drugs.* New York, Oxford Univ. Press, 1959.

2 Boring, E. G. *A History of Experimental Psychology.* 2nd edition. New York, Appleton-Century-Crofts, 1950, pp. 401–410.

3 Bullock, T. H. Neuron doctrine and electrophysiology. *Science 129:*997, 1959.

4 Buytendijk, F. J. J. *Pain: Its Modes and Functions.* Chicago, Univ. of Chicago Press, 1962.

5 Graham, D. T. "Some Research on Psychophysiologic Specificity and Its Relation to Psychosomatic Disease." In *Physiological Correlates of Psychological Disorder,* edited by R. Roessler and N. S. Greenfield. Madison, Univ. of Wisconsin Press, 1962, pp. 221–238.

6 Graham, D. T., Lundy, R. M., Benjamin, L. S., Kabler, J. D., Lewis, W. C., Kunish, N. O., and Graham, F. K. Specific attitudes in initial interviews with patients having different "psychosomatic" diseases. *Psychosom. Med. 24:*257, 1962.

7 Orne, M. T. On the social psychology of the psychological experiment: With particular reference to demand characteristics and their implications. *Amer. Psychologist 17:*776, 1962.

8 Sartre, J.-P. *Existential Psychoanalysis.* Chicago, Henry Regnery, 1962 (paperback).

9 Sternbach, R. A. The effects of instructional sets on autonomic responsivity. *Psychophysiol. 1:*67, 1964.

10 Stevens, S. S., Carton, A. S., and Shickman, G. M. A scale of apparent intensity of electric shock. *J. exp. Psychol. 56:*328, 1958.

11 Wenger, M. A., and Cullen, T. D. "Some Problems in Psychophysiological Research: The Effects of Uncontrolled Variables." In *Physiological Correlates of Psychological Disorder,* edited by R. Roessler and N. S. Greenfield. Madison, Univ. of Wisconsin Press, 1962, pp. 106–114.

12 Woodworth, R. S., and Schlosberg, H. *Experimental Psychology.* New York, Henry Holt, 1954, pp. 10–11.

13 Yakovlev, P. I. Motility, behavior and the brain: Stereodynamic organization and neural co-ordinates of behavior. *J. nerv. ment. Dis. 107:*313, 1948.

14 YAKOVLEV, P. I. Patterns of neuronal assemblies and the anatomical substratum of seizures. *Epilepsia* (Third Series) *1*:51, 1952.

15 ZBOROWSKI, M. Cultural components in responses to pain. *J. soc. Issues* *8*:16, 1952.

TWELVE

Autonomic Monitoring of Ego Defense Process

JOSEPH C. SPEISMAN, Ph.D.

This paper is a report primarily of two studies which were undertaken as part of a research program on psychological stress. The relationship between these studies and the theme of this conference on biology and psychoanalysis is somewhat tenuous. In fact, one might say that the only relationship is a rather fragmentary use of the measurement of biological activity (the autonomic nervous system) and a somewhat opportunistic use of psychoanalytic theory (a derivation from ego defense process). In another sense these studies may be viewed as a demonstration of the operation of one aspect of psychoanalytic theory in an experimental setting. Although it may be true that the operation of ego defense processes needs no further demonstration within the context of the psychoanalytic consulting room or within the context of psychoanalytic theory, nevertheless all other scientific approaches to these data require some translation of psychoanalytic process, and systematic experimental approaches are one means of such translation. A demonstration in this sense thus has value primarily as an additional exploration of these concepts in a setting which is different from the original.

The first study is presented to provide an experimental demonstration of the occurrence of psychological stress within a laboratory setting which makes use of rather naturalistic stimuli. The second study is presented as a demonstration of efforts to cope with the stressor stimulus, and in this instance the coping mechanisms are derived from ego defense processes.

Before a brief review of the experiments themselves is presented, a statement of the frame of reference of this experimental program is necessary. It is assumed that psychological stress is most conveniently represented as an internal and personal event. Of course, one can only tap into such events on the basis of overt behavior; but the assumption is made because of the particular combination of variables and dimensions which appear to be necessary in order to represent a theoretical statement of stress. To clarify this point a brief diversion from the main theme may be worth while. Stress is often discussed as though it were a state of the organism when, in fact, for purposes of investigation, it is much more appropriately conceptualized as a reaction or series of responses on the part of the individual. A state such as is discussed by Selye (*14*), for example, implies an end-point and a pervasiveness of one attribute of the individual's existence in time which does not actually permit sufficient exploration. A state implies a suspension of other activities and other attributes of the person, both physiological and psychological, which, by definition, must be an extremely rare occasion in human life; whereas a sequence of responses defines the events as an ongoing, developing situation which feeds into the life process and permits of exploration both in time and space.

In the long run when it becomes possible to provide a definitive theory of psychological stress it may be most efficient and parsimonious to reserve the term stress for just such an end-point or resultant. Given the current nature of our theories and research information, however, it is premature to categorize stress as a state, since we are confounded by a multiplicity of constructs such as anxiety, arousal, conflict, etc., all of which have some bearing on the issue. As a working theoretical statement only, psychological stress is conceived of as the process whereby a combination (perhaps in an additive fashion) of arousal and anxiety arises and is reduced.

For purposes of experimentation we conceptualize stress rather crudely, it is to be admitted, as a sequence of events with a beginning, a middle, and an end (*9, 15*). The substance of this sequence is the simple statement that stress results from a transaction between the environment and the personal internal situation so that a stimulus complex becomes an individual psychological event. The sequence may be thought of as starting with a motive condition. Given the current state of this theoretical position it is actually irrelevant whether one conceives of the motive in terms of need, drive, instinct, or even a sequence of learned behaviors dependent only on reinforcement schedules. The second stage of the sequence is seen as an appraisal of the interaction of the given motive with the particular stimulus complex then available. This appraisal concept is similar to that proposed by Magda Arnold (*2*), and, briefly stated, it is thought to contain the elements of the perceptual event and cognitive assessment.

Four outcomes may be considered possible at this stage: (*a*) that the situation may be seen as an appropriate need-satisfier, (*b*) that the situation may be seen as appropriate for a sequence of instrumental acts which will lead to delayed gratification, (*c*) that the world in view may be seen as momentarily inappropriate for the motives and thus either partially or wholly ignored, and (*d*) that the situation may be seen as threatening in some aspects. If the events as they transpire follow any of the first three outcomes, then it is assumed that no stress is occasioned; but if the fourth or appraisal of threat is made, then this is considered to be the first step of the stress sequence. The notion of threat is critical in order to be able to distinguish the process of arousal from that of stress. One may become aroused in a competitive situation to a point where it would be difficult if not impossible to distinguish the physiological reaction from that resulting from a dangerous situation. This first stage also demonstrates the need to conceptualize stress as an internal and personal event—i.e., this step implies that the appraisal of the stimulus complex is seen as having adaptive consequences for the individual, and it is only when these adaptive consequences are perceived as immediately or potentially threatening that the stimulus becomes a noxious one. Such appraisal may occur in at least two ways: First, the individual may assign negative qualities to the stimulus on the basis of a cognitive interpretation of the probable outcome of danger, and this would receive consensual validation. Second, the transaction may occur within an idiosyncratic framework, and the threat perceived by the individual may be puzzling to another participant. The latter situation is, of course, descriptive of a neurotic repetition, and in this instance the entire stress sequence may be much more dependent upon the personal dynamic than on the process of cognitive, judgmental decision.

Given an appraisal of threat, it is assumed that the immediate response is one of finding a means of coping with threat. This coping may be in terms of physical, cognitive, or emotional activity or combinations of these. However, since stress is seen as a response to threat which in turn is seen as a highly personal reaction, an appropriate and perhaps inevitable reaction would therefore be an ego defensive operation so as to maintain, insofar as possible, the stability and integrity of the ego or self system. To the extent that the defense process is successful then to that extent the stress reaction will be reduced.

This brief excursion into a theoretical statement is meant primarily as an illustration of the derivation of the experimental work rather than as a statement of definitive theory. The two studies to be reported enter into this sequence of events essentially at two points—the first as an effort to discern the threat quality of a motion picture, and the second study as an effort to provide a defensive orientation for the subject viewing the film.

THE FIRST STUDY

An interpretation of this initial study has been completely presented in a prior publication (*10*). Although not all the elements of the study are directly pertinent, certain aspects must be provided in order to make the discussion meaningful. The stimuli for this study were two films. The stressor film is entitled "Subincision," and previous work (*1, 13, 18*) had indicated that the film was highly disturbing on both a physiological and a psychological level. The movie depicts a ceremonial of an Australian aboriginal tribe, the Arunta, and very clearly portrays a sequence of crude operations performed on the genitalia of adolescent boys. The control film entitled "Corn Farming in Iowa" was intended to provide minimal emotional content, while at the same time it was not without some intrinsic interest.

Several attributes of personality were measured by means of standard psychological tests including some scales from the Minnesota Multiphasic Personality Inventory (MMPI) and the California Psychological Inventory (CPI). A very brief, structured interview occurred subsequent to the administration of the films, and an effort was made to assess change in mood by the administration of the adjective checklist of mood development by Nowlis (*11*). Autonomic nervous system activity was assessed by peripheral measures of skin resistance and heart rate, and these were continuously recorded during the experimental sessions.

The subjects were recruited from among the undergraduate population of a large university and were essentially a homogeneous group. The actual experimental work was conducted in a small laboratory, which contained the motion picture projector, a screen, and, behind some partitions, the dermohmmeter and the cardiotachometer. After the electrodes for this equipment were in place the subject was asked to find a comfortable position in a reclining chair. He was instructed to maintain physical movements at a minimum and was literally asked to do nothing further except to relax and watch the film. Data from all the dependent measures were, of course, analyzed (see *10*), but our purposes will be most efficiently served by concentrating on the reactions as assessed by the skin resistance measures of autonomic nervous system activity. The use of a single indicator of autonomic nervous system activity is admittedly a treacherous procedure. The reader may convince himself, by reference to the prior publications (*10, 17, 18*), that sufficient attention has been paid to experimental, statistical, and interpretive problems so that the use of the measures of skin resistance as the only dependent variable for this demonstration is justifiable.

There are some findings from this experiment which are of central interest: the first, a simple comparison of reaction to the stress film is compared with that to the control film. Figure 12.1 presents this comparison graphically. It is perhaps unnecessary to state that the magnitude of difference in response to the two films is statistically reliable. These data are presented in standard score form derived from the combined distributions of means of subject responses to both films. It is worth noting that in this form one may perceive several patterns of response. The first is that nowhere do the two curves representing the two films overlap. The stress film provides a consistently elevated reaction as compared with the pattern for the control film, and, further, the

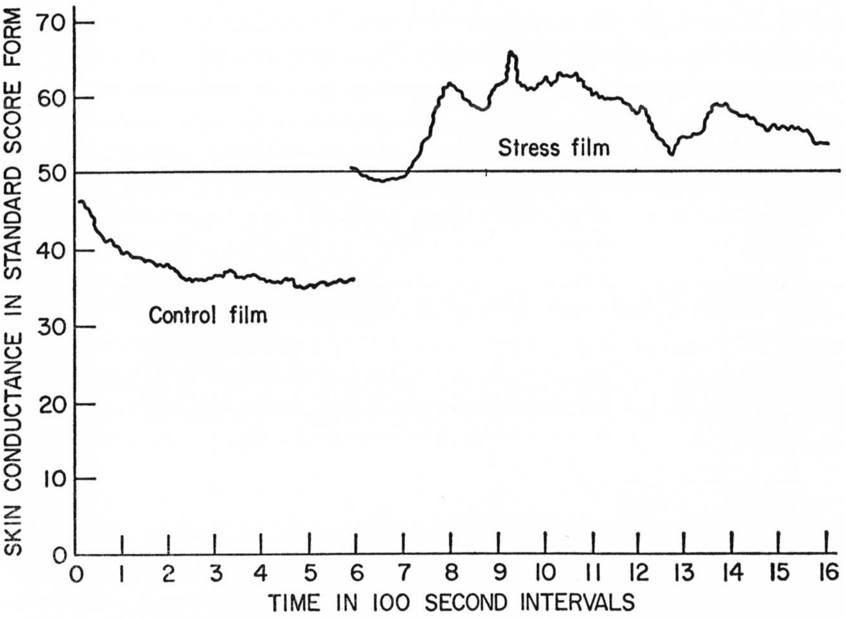

12.1.—**Comparative response to stress and control films.**

response to the stress film is apparently much more variable than that to the control film.

In Figure 12.2 the curve representing response to the stress film is reproduced, and overlaid upon this curve are several of the incidents which occur in the film itself.

It is clear that the variation of the curve is by no means random but rather follows quite faithfully the content of the film. The peaks of response occur at those points in the film where one views the actual operations and incisions upon the genitalia; and the lowest points occur at the beginning of the film, before the first operation, and during the middle of the film, where a relatively innocuous hair-dressing ceremony occurs. Thus, it is clear that the subjects are not responding to any general sense of shock or outrage at the events portrayed but rather the autonomic response, as measured by skin resistance at least, ebbs and flows in rather neat correlation with the content being presented. This point is worth some elaboration. First, as a comment on methodology, it is clear that this kind of finding can occur only when one has a continuous recording of response taken during the incidence of the stimulus. Second, this finding of variation which is correlated with the content of the stimulus argues very clearly for a conceptual separation between findings generated by a single stimulus, or a very brief stimulus such as electric shock,

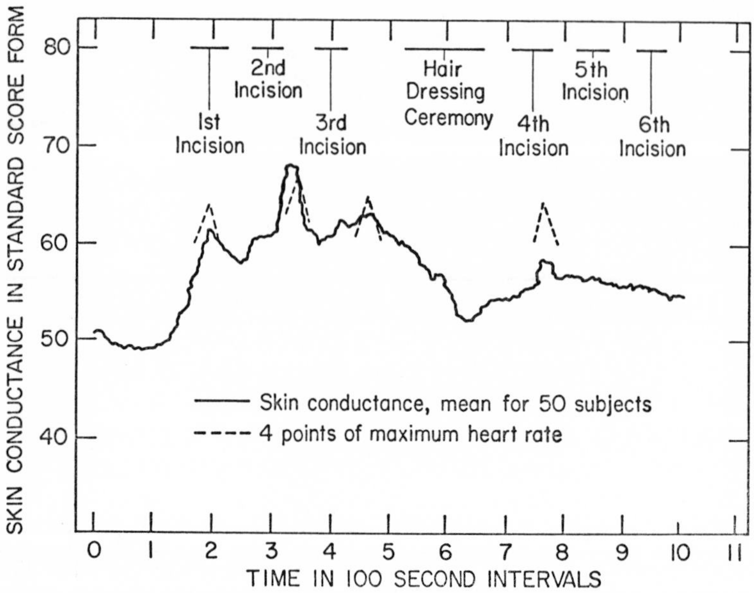

12.2.—Skin conductance and heart rate response compared with major events in the stress film.

and those findings generated by a more elaborate and longer stimulus which provides for a coherent, cognitive message. It is also worth noting that, whereas it is probably true that the most effective means of studying human response to various stimulus situations is an individual approach allowing for all the unique variations of the individual personality, it is still entirely possible to obtain a sensible and meaningful set of data when the individual responses are grouped together.

THE SECOND STUDY

Despite the fact that the principal interest in the first study was centered on the response of the autonomic nervous system, the second study to be presented actually derives to some extent from an informal analysis of the interview with the individual students and from the analysis of the adjective checklist of mood. In the analysis of the mood responses it was noted that those elements which may be termed affective apparently provided for most of the response to the film—that is, among the various categories assessed by this instrument are anxiety, social affection, pleasantness, concentration, and egotism. It is not necessary for present purposes to describe fully the implications of these categories, but it is worth noting that the effective categories such as anxiety and affection were much more clearly and much more intensively utilized by the subjects to describe their mood states than were the more cognitive elements of the instrument. Added to this finding was the fact that a perusal of the interview materials, which had been in each case recorded, provided in many instances a clear demonstration of the operation of psychological defenses. Some subjects attempted to deal with the obviously stressful stimulus provided by the film by obtaining psychological distance from the content. Such individuals would describe their reactions as if they were engaged in an intellectual exercise and would make comments such as, "This is an interesting depiction of a primitive culture," or "This is the kind of material which an anthropologist might find of utmost interest in discussing unusual societies." Still other subjects might be characterized by efforts to displace or project their own feelings so that blame was ascribed to either the photographer or, even in some instances, the experimenter for permitting such crude and unsanitary operations to be carried out. A third category, somewhat less noticeable but nonetheless in evidence, included efforts to deny the occurrence of the subincision operation in a manner reminiscent of the subject reported by Basowitz *et al.* (*4*). All these elements led almost inevitably to a decision to attempt to achieve some experimental control over the defensive activities of the subject.

A full account of this study will appear shortly (*17*). The design of the experiment was essentially similar to that of the first study, but two critical differences were introduced—first, the nature of the subject population and, second, additions to the stimulus value of the film. The study was conducted in the same laboratory setting, subjects were seen individually, the same assessment procedures were administered, and the film was viewed from the reclining chair in the semi-darkened laboratory. In the previous study the entire subject population was composed of college students. In this instance, however, one group consisted of college students, and a second group consisted of somewhat older men from a large business concern who were attending a summer course at the university. These groups were selected primarily because of some assumptions concerning their possible preferences as to defensive mode. Since this is a critical aspect of the study, a description of the groups and the rationale for their use are provided. An ideal circumstance to discern the ego defensive operations would perhaps be to assess the utilization of defensive modes for each individual and then to attempt to provide for the operation of this defense during exposure to the stressor stimulus. Aside from the practical problems of such assessment for a group of any size, enormous problems are faced if an effort is made to be at all precise in such an effort.

Verbal descriptions of ego defense process, to be found in such standard sources as Fenichel (*6*), A. Freud (*7*) and others, are remarkably difficult to put into operational terms even when there is agreement as to the conceptual status of such descriptions among the sources. Thus, for both practical and conceptual reasons it was decided to take the first exploratory step represented by this experiment by utilizing groups of subjects rather than individuals. Although the relationship between the operation of a defensive mode for a group is somewhat more tenuous and provides more opportunity for error, our previous finding of the relationship between content and autonomic response convinced us that one could use group data and obtain a reasonable approximation of the individual response. In addition, there was no compelling reason to specify the defensive operations except in general terms.

Our first approach was to distinguish between more primitive and more sophisticated defensive operations, and we decided upon a primary distinction between denial and intellectualization. Following this notion we proceeded upon the assumption that college students, and especially those at higher levels of education, would be more oriented toward ideation and conceptual activity and thus, given such a life style, would be more apt to find compatible an intellectually oriented defensive opportunity. On the other hand, the business group was composed primarily of individuals who were largely oriented toward practical engineering and mechanical solutions to problems. These were largely a group of self-made men whose career orientation was toward a motoric expression rather than an ideational one and, in fact, whose play activities and social orientation was toward the sensory motor rather than the cognitive. This group would presumably find more amenable to defensive necessity the more primitive denial orientation.

The central notion of the study was to provide sound tracks for the previously silent subincision film which would carry a defensive message to the subjects while they were viewing this stimulus. As has been described, the defensive themes for these sound tracks were, on the one hand, denial and, as it turned out, some elements of reaction formation and, for a second sound track, an intellectualization theme. The denial-reaction formation sound track provides essentially a straightforward denial of some of the more emotional elements of the film. For example, where it appears on the screen that some of the boys are suffering considerable pain, the sound track comments to the effect that these boys are not feeling pain. The reaction formation conception is carried by an emphasis on the positive attributes of these puberty rites in a manner reminiscent of a Pollyanna aproach to painful stimuli. In this sense the emphasis was placed upon the happiness and joy that the boys would feel upon completion of the rites and their positive motivation in undergoing these manifestations of their culture.

The sound track which was oriented toward intellectualization is stated in rather cold, detached, scientific terms. The effort here was to obtain, insofar as possible, psychological distance from the simuli without in any sense negating their occurrence. The sound track is characterized by efforts to provide a frame of reference such as a scientific observer might take to these events specifying a detached air of data-collection rather than any involvement in the actual activities of the people. Emphasis was placed on the instrumental activity of the persons involved rather than their feelings or emotions.

There is the possibility that if these sound tracks were to be found useful in reducing the impact of the film upon the subjects this might be due to the mere presence of the additional stimulus of a sound presentation rather than the silent version. In order to provide a control for this possibility a third sound track called the trauma track was devised. The aim of this presentation was to specify the actual events occurring and to make clear statements about the operations and the procedures involved. This was not done in an effort to overemphasize the crudeness and painful aspects of the film but in no sense were these attributes underplayed. Instead, there was a clear description in each case of the activities being portrayed. As a means of describing somewhat more specifically the actual contents of the sound tracks the following are excerpts from each track at a specific point in the film.

In this particular scene a young adolescent of about 14 years of age is seated on the backs of three members of the tribe; the background is the dry, dusty plain in which these people live. Holding him rather firmly are three older men. The scene provides a rather clear view of the dirt embedded in the older men's beards, the filth of their hands, and flies and other insects. The boy is exhibiting what is obviously distress and pain as the entire ventral surface of the penis is incised with a piece of sharpened flint. As this scene appears the intellectualization sound track comments as follows: "As you can see, the operation is formal, and the surgical technique, while crude, is very carefully followed." The denial-reaction formation sound track comments, "You will soon see that the words of encouragement offered by the two older men have their effect, and the boy begins to look forward to the happy conclusion of the ceremony." The trauma track states at this point, "Several men hold the boy, the penis is grasped, stretched taut, and cut on the under side from the tip to the scrotum."

It might be well to emphasize at this point that the design of the experiment did not indicate to the subjects that the effort was to provide them with a means of coping with the stressor material being presented. In each case the only rationale provided was that we were assessing their reactions to an emotionally powerful film and that this was justifiable by a description of the physiological measures being utilized. Also, the sequence within which the experimental sound tracks were provided were counterbalanced across both groups. The individuals from each of the groups were selected for participation in only one of the tracks according to a prearranged schedule, so that half of each group participated with each stimulus.

The results of this study as presented in Figure 12.3 indicate conclusively that the sound tracks do, in fact, accomplish the task of reducing the impact

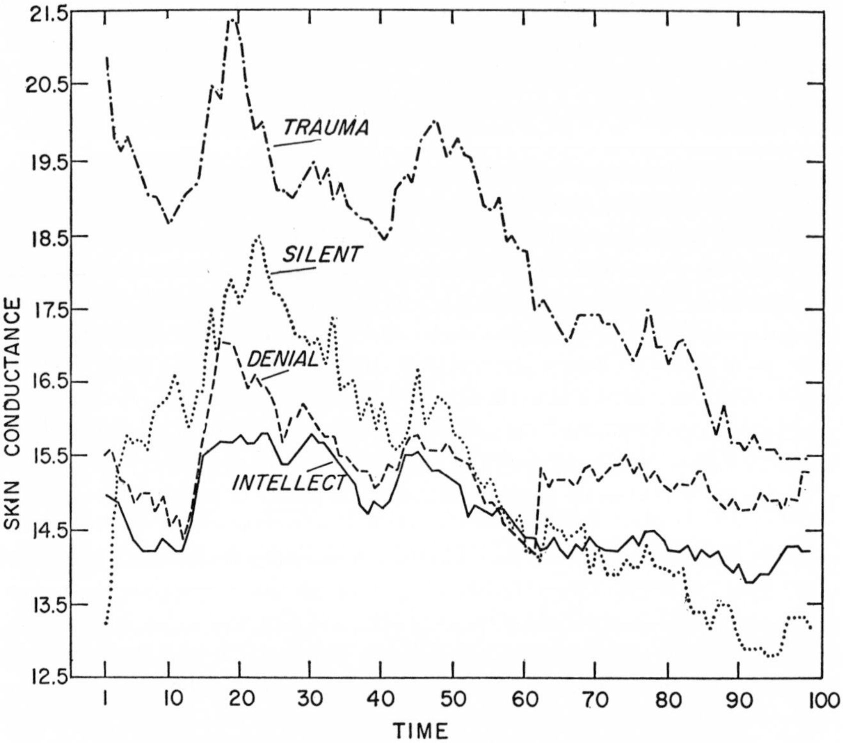

12.3.—**Response to the stress film under four experimental conditions.**

of the stressor film upon the autonomic response as measured by skin resistance.

Both the denial and the intellectualization sound tracks reduce the level of autonomic activity substantially compared with the level of activity encountered during the trauma track. The defensively oriented sound tracks also provide for a significant reduction below that of the silent film, although this latter result is not as dramatic as is the comparison with the trauma track. This finding is of considerable interest. It should be emphasized that what has been controlled by means of verbal descriptions and comments added to a silent film is the activity of the autonomic nervous system. It would be a sufficiently interesting finding if the reaction of the subject had been measured, by some verbal means, as an indication of the activity of ego defense process in the psychological realm; but it is perhaps of greater interest that control of a physiological response appears to be possible by indirect verbal activity.

One element of the presentation in Figure 12.3 should be specified. For the total group the intellectualization sound track appears to be somewhat more effective that the denial sound track. However, there is an artifact involved in these data which is perhaps best exemplified by pointing out that the silent film, where the subjects are left entirely to their own devices, actually reaches the lowest point on the graph toward the latter portion of the film. What is encountered here is a compounding of the two elements of the defensive orientation of the sound track and the two populations which, for purposes of presentation in this instance, have been grouped together. One sees here only the combined reaction of both the student and the business groups for each of the sound tracks; and, since the two groups react in opposite ways, the curves in Figure 12.3 do not accurately represent the effects of the sound tracks for each group. In order to assess the reaction of each of the groups individually these same data are presented in Figure 12.4, where

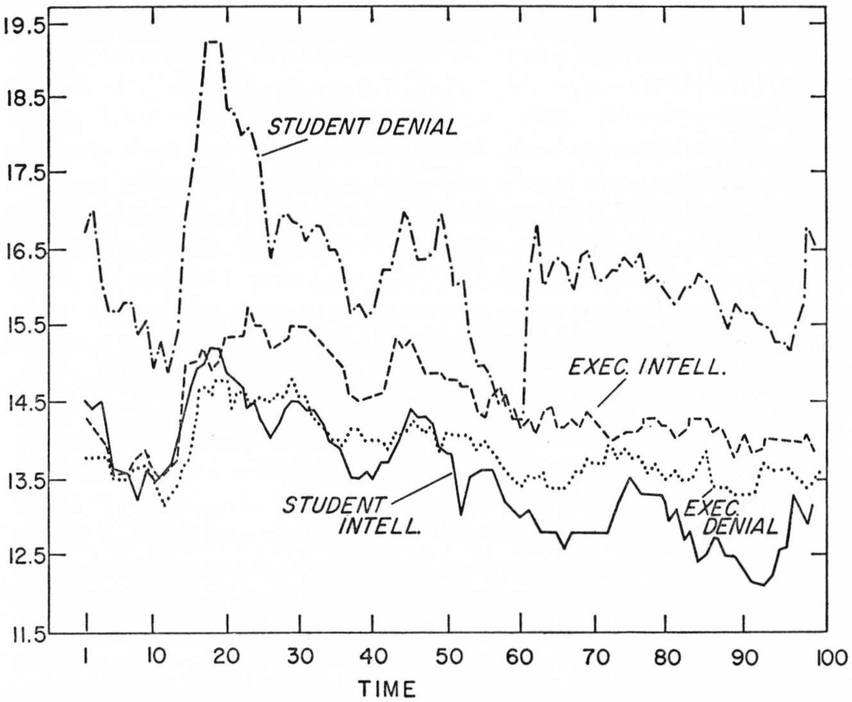

12.4.—Response to the stress film by student and executive groups under intellectualization and denial conditions.

the response of the four groups are separately presented. These groups are: those students who viewed the denial track, those students who viewed the film during the intellectualization track, and the comparable groups for the business executives.

Several facts are immediately apparent upon inspection of the graph presented in Figure 12.4. First, it should be noted that the students who viewed the film under the denial sound track apparently were benefited least, whereas those students who viewed the film during the intellectualization track were benefited most—with both of the executive groups falling somewhere in between. Thus, the student group provides the greater variation in response. Apparently, the students viewing under the denial condition not only were not benefited but in some instances were actually hampered in their efforts to cope with the stimulus material. This point is seen most clearly if one contrasts the curve presented in Figure 12.3 for the silent film, which is also a student group, with that of the student denial curve presented in Figure 12.4. It will be seen that the student denial curve closely approximates the silent curve up to the point where the benign portion of the film is shown (the hair-tying ceremony). Subsequent to that presentation the student denial curve returns to an extremely high level of reaction, whereas the curve of the silent film and of the other conditions continue to reduce in magnitude.

The curves representing the executive groups lend credence to the hypothesis that this group finds more compatible the more primitive denial-defensive orientation, since the denial curve is consistently lower than the intellectualization curve for this particular group. The executives' response, as portrayed by the curve, appears to be flatter—that is, less variable than the student denial curve, and compares favorably with the response of the student group under the intellectualization condition. The response of the executive group is less dramatic than that of the students. Both the denial and the intellectualization sound tracks appear to have been of use in reducing the impact of the film, although denial does appear to be a more compatible mechanism for this group.

A number of alternate explanations are possible. Among these are, for example, that the executive group may be less homogeneous than the students, and different members were aided by the different sound tracks. It is also possible that the group represents what Blum (*5*) has called general defenders and can make somewhat more opportunistic use of available defensive orientations. It is clear that the executives were not aided under either sound track as much as the students were under intellectualization.

REVIEW OF FINDINGS AND DISCUSSION

It might be useful at this point to review the findings and their implications for a theoretical position on the concepts of coping and defense. Instead of attempting to qualify each statement as it is made, it should suffice to note that the findings are tentative; and, although some of the results have been replicated through repeated experimentation (*9, 10, 16*), in other instances it is obvious that further work is necessary.

The findings may be categorized in four ways:

1. The simple fact of physiological indications of arousal under conditions

where the primary stimulus is essentially a psychological one (that is, a film) and where no physical involvement of the subject occurs.

2. The demonstration, as is presented in Figure 12.2, that the response to the film is not a random one or a general response to shock but rather is directly tied to the contents of the film itself.

3. The manipulation by verbal means of the reactions of the autonomic nervous system as assessed by skin resistance. This finding may be elaborated somewhat: (*a*) The fact that three of the four sound tracks caused a definite reduction in autonomic response compared with the silent condition. This provides a comparison of the reactions of individuals, when left to their own devices, to the stimulus and to conditions where a defensive orientation is provided. (*b*) The comparison between the defensive sound tracks of denial and intellectualization and the nondefensive or trauma tracks. These comparisons indicate that it is not simply the addition of sound to the stimulus value of the film that provides for a reduction in response but rather the content of the verbal material which is important. The trauma track indicates a further kind of manipulation of the response by verbal means, since the trauma track increases the response above that of the silent version.

4. Finally, the relationship between the sound tracks with specific defensive orientation and the groups selected because of presumed differences in life style, which is indicated at least in the limited sense of a contrast between an ideational approach and a motoric approach to work and play. It is clear that the influence of the particular sound tracks is again not a random occurrence, nor is it simply reflective of a general effect of reduction of the autonomic response to the film. Rather, we find that there is specificity between the type of defensive orientation represented within the track and the particular group, so that the cognitively oriented student group is dramatically aided by the intellectualization sound track, and, although to a lesser extent, the motoric executive group is aided by the denial sound track.

Of particular interest is the finding that the magnitude of response of three of the groups—the students under intellectualization conditions, the executives under intellectualization, and the executives under the denial condition—all were significantly reduced as compared with that either to the nondefensive sound track or the silent condition. On the other hand, the student group under the denial condition apparently encountered serious difficulty, since their autonomic response maintained a level approximately at the same degree of magnitude as under the trauma track. This particular finding demonstrates most clearly the crude but very specific selectivity and interaction of the two dimensions, life style and defensive orientation.

If both groups of individuals had been equally aided by both sound tracks, one might justifiably ascribe this occurrence to the impact of the set provided by the sound tracks themselves, and one could attempt to explain the data quite simply on the basis of set. Under such a circumstance nothing more could be said beyond the fact that the stimulus and, consequently, the response had been changed. Given the differential response of the students under the denial sound track, however, it is evident that there are consistent personal variables which are introduced in addition to the quality of the objective stimulus itself. These differential reactions cannot be ascribed to the stimulus condition alone, since all subjects operated under the same conditions and we do have a demonstrably different reaction within the student group.

Actually, there is little to be specified on the basis of these data as to individual or even group patterned personality differences occurring between the two groups. It can be stated relatively clearly that the findings support the notion that important albeit general elements of personal description such as career choice, work activity, and recreational preference are predictive of dynamic personality attributes such as defensive preference and defense orientation. Beyond this we must be content for the moment to reiterate the fact that systematic experimentation in this area must take cognizance of the interaction between the personal characteristics and the properties of the situation and stimulus complex. To this end and it would be useful to attempt to describe more fully the particular situation and the conditions under which these data were collected. This then, should provide a clearer notion as to the situations and the set provided for the subjects.

Both executives and students were seen in the same laboratory. This room is located in a large experimental and classroom building on the campus of the university. Since there are biological as well as psychological laboratories in the building, there are many visual and olfactory cues as to the nature of the experimentation occurring. Animal cages and food are usually in evidence, and the results of digestion are also represented in the form of odors. The laboratory itself is relatively free of the foregoing cues, but as the subject proceeds through the corridors he is met by these facts. Each subject was seen individually and was met at the door by the experimenter in a lab coat. He was immediately seated in a reclining chair, but even a casual and cursory inspection by the subject would reveal the nature and purpose of his presence in the room—that is, he was clearly a subject in an experiment, with very little option or voluntary control over what was to occur. He was given explicit and clear direction as to how to move and what to do. As has been indicated, the laboratory itself contained a motion picture projector, two laboratory sinks, a motion picture screen, and a partition behind which was located the apparatus for obtaining skin resistance and heart rate records. These latter pieces of equipment were shown to the subjects briefly when their function was described to them.

The physical characteristics of the experimental procedure differed in only one respect for the two groups. The students were asked to come to the laboratory, since they knew the building and the campus and needed no guidance, and thus up until the time when they actually walked into the room they were more or less on their own. In contrast however, the executives were in class on another part of campus while the data were collected, and they were picked up and personally delivered by an assistant to the door of the laboratory.

All these attributes of the situation may, of course, have provided cues to the subjects before the actual beginning of the experiment itself. Among these perhaps is the fact that the individual was expected to react to some form of stimulus. He was an unnamed subject who was to be observed objectively and scientifically, and presumably he was keyed to the fact that all his movements, thoughts, and comments were open to interpretation by the experimenter. In addition, there was in all likelihood an element of test and challenge involved in the setting, both in the nature of the building as housing the instruments of scientific inspection and to some extent in the psychological testing which occurred during the first session.

In addition to the physical characteristics with which the subject was confronted were the instructions provided him as to his movements in the laboratory and to the disposition of the results of his participation. First, actual verbal instruction indicated to the subject that there was to be some continuity—he would be returning to the laboratory for several long sessions. Second, it was implied all his responses, many of which would be highly personal, would be treated in confidence. The restrictions on his physical movements were quite severe, although benign in that he was requested to achieve the most comfortable, relaxed position he could in the reclining chair; but, once this position had been achieved, he was not to move any more than was minimally necessary for comfort. The majority of his time in the laboratory was of course, spent in a semi-darkened room while the film was being shown. Again, although there are many possibilities as to the subject's interpretation of the requests and instructions, it is probable that these latter conditions provided for the same kind of opportunity for regression and passive acceptance of the situation that the couch and other physical attributes of the psychoanalytic consulting room provide. Thus, we may obtain a picture of the individual in a situation which permits interpretation of challenge and of being scrutinized and at the same time where comfort, relaxation, and passiveness are encouraged and the use of motoric responses discouraged.

The rather surprising finding that mature and effective individuals, such as the executives, would respond as clearly as they did to the denial sound track may be clarified by these conditions. The scientific atmosphere may have encouraged a passive, perhaps even resigned, response to scientific authority; the relaxation on the chair in the darkened room presumably also would effect a regressive orientation. Further, the specific stricture against the use of motoric expressions—a modality which was presumably preferred by these people—conceivably was additive and permitted a compatible instance for them to use this rather primitive mechanism. The students, on the other hand, who apparently found the intellectualization condition well suited to their needs, were not nearly so restricted by the loss of the motoric option and presumably were responding much more critically to the testing and challenging attributes of the situation. The fact that the denial condition interfered with the students' defensive efforts might be related to their efforts to maintain cognitive control and a reaction against the passive-regressive aspects of the situation.

In any event, the situational context within which any tendency or predisposition for defense preference is elicited becomes a critical factor, and hypotheses within ego defense theory which emphasize the interaction between the social context and the availability of dynamic defensive choice receive support from these findings.

In addition to those concepts of defense preference and defense heirarchy which are implicit in the preceding discussion, we might propose at least one intervening variable for further exploration of the ego defense process. This might be best expressed as a continuum, with the end-points defined as compatibility and incompatibility. Incompatibility refers specifically to a conflict between the attributes of a social context which pull for particular kinds of defense and the defense preference of the individual. This notion is stated in active terms, because it implies more than simple inhibition. Compatibility, of course, refers to a positive match between dynamic preference and situational pull for defense. Even though the general sense of this concept has been stated, at least implicitly, many times (*3, 8, 12*), it should be emphasized that compatibility in this instance refers to specific relationships between defensive preference and heirarchy and the immediate situation. In other words, the reference is not only to the general interaction between environment and person, which is often enough ignored, but also to the immediate and specific attributes of the moment. For example, the attributes of the analytic hour or of the analyst often lend themselves on both conscious and unconscious levels to manipulation of opportunities for, or interference with, the use of a preferred defensive mode.

If the findings presented are reliable, then some concept such as compatibility becomes essential for theoretical coverage. The inclusion of this concept would provide at least for further systematic exploration of the dynamic interaction between immediate situational variables and consistant attributes of personality.

This paper was introduced with a brief statement of a theoretical position on psychological stress, but no effort will be made to return to any of the specifics of this position, since it is not critical for the moment whether the statement is "correct" in any detail. What is critical is the postulation of a microgenetic sequence of events, especially the inclusion of the defensive or coping concept as an integral part of the total stress response and not simply as a reaction to a stress stimulus. The research reported here may be seen as an initial step in this direction.

REFERENCES

1 Aas, A. *Mutilation Fantasies and Autonomic Response.* Oslo, Norway, Oslo Univ. Press, 1958.

2 Arnold, Magda B. *Emotions and Personality.* New York, Columbia Univ. Press, 1960.

3 Basowitz, H. Experimental studies on affects. *Psychiat. res. Rep. 8:*89, 1958.

4 Basowitz, H., Korchin, S., Oken, D., Goldstein, M., and Gussack, H. Anxiety and performance changes with a minimal dose of epinephrine. *Arch. Neurol., Chicago 76:*98, 1956.

5 Blum, G. An experimental reunion of psychoanalytic theory with perceptual vigilance and defense. *J. abnorm. soc. Psychol. 49:*94, 1954.

6 Fenichel, O. *The Psychoanalytic Theory of Neurosis.* New York, Norton, 1945.

7 Freud, Anna. *The Ego and the Mechanisms of Defence,* translated by C. Baines. New York, Int. Univ. Press, 1946.

8 Janis, I. *Psychological Stress.* New York, Wiley, 1958.

9 Lazarus, R. S., and Speisman, J. C. A research case history dealing with psychological stress. *J. psychol. Stud. 11:*167, 1960.

10 Lazarus, R. S., Speisman, J. C., Mordkoff, A. M., and Davison, L. A. A laboratory study of psychological stress produced by a motion picture film. *Psychol. Monogr. 76:*Whole No. 553, 1962.

11 Nowlis, V., and Nowlis, Helen H. The description and analysis of mood. *Ann. N.Y. Acad. Sci. 65:*345, 1956.

12 Oken, D. "The Role of Defense in Psychological Stress." In *Psychological Correlates of Psychological Disorder,* edited by R. Roessler and N. S. Greenfield. Madison, Univ. of Wisconsin Press, 1962, pp. 193–210.

13 Schwartz, B. J. An empirical test of the two Freudian hypotheses concerning castration anxiety. *J. Pers. 24:*318, 1956.

14 Selye, H. *The Stress of Life.* New York, McGraw-Hill, 1956.

15 Speisman, J. C., and Lazarus, R. S. Outline for a theory of psychological stress. Paper presented at the Annual Meeting of the American Psychological Association, Chicago, Illinois, 1961.

16 Speisman, J. C., Lazarus, R. S., Davison, L., and Mordkoff, A. Experimental analysis of a film used as a threatening stimulus. *J. consult. Psychol. 28:*23–33, 1964.

17 Speisman, J. C., Lazarus, R. S., Mordkoff, A., and Davison, L. A. The

experimental reduction of stress based on ego defense theory. *J. abnorm. soc. Psychol. 68:*367–380, 1964.

18 SPEISMAN, J. C., OSBORN, J., AND LAZARUS, R. S. Cluster analysis of skin resistance and heart rate at rest and under stress. *Psychosom. Med. 23:*323, 1961.

THIRTEEN

On Hearing One's Own Voice: An Aspect of Cognitive Control in Spoken Thought

GEORGE S. KLEIN, PH.D.

A grievance once commonly heard about psychoanalysis was that it seeks to base a psychology of normal behavior exclusively upon the events of abnormality. Developments in contemporary ego psychology, with its emphases upon ego autonomy, conflict-free functions, adaptedness, and the like, have made this criticism look a bit anachronistic. Indeed, the focus on normal development in contemporary ego psychology is having an interesting by-product in the other direction—of carrying implications for a concept of abnormality. Hartmann's view (*16*) that the development of primary autonomous functions proceeds from coordinations, present from birth, with an "average expectable environment" offers guidelines for understanding pathological impairments of reality-testing when this environment is disrupted. These implications do not supplant psychoanalytic theory's earlier and still central emphasis upon conflict, but do supplement it in significant and useful ways.

An important feature of the "average expectable environment" is that response to organized change and to recurrent regularities of the environ-

Research Career Professor, Grant No. K–6–MH–19,782, National Institutes of Health.
I am grateful to Drs. Harry Fiss and David Wolitzky for their helpful comments on earlier drafts of this paper. The collaborative studies with Dr. Wolitzky, described in later sections of the paper, are being carried out under a grant from the National Institutes of Health, Research Program: Psychoanalytic Studies in Cognition, MH–06733–01.

ment goes on against a background of persisting, nonchanging arrays of stimulation—what Ivo Kohler has called the "stimulus milieu" (*27, 28*) and Harry Helson, "contextual and background" stimulation (*22*). There is a difference, as Helson puts it, "between saying that a certain perception is more or less independent of immediately present stimuli and saying that a given perception is independent of the stimulus milieu in which the individual lives and develops. The first statement may be true; the second is not" (*22*, p. 573).

Undoubtedly one reason such supportive stimulus conditions have been overlooked is that they are not themselves perceived. Persistent conditions of the environment, as Gibson (*11*) and Helson (*22*) have shown, tend to become stimulus zones of phenomenal neutrality. It would be wrong to speak of these backgrounds of stimulation as "expectancy" levels or to say that the organism is "prepared" for them. They are not *psychological* stimuli as such, since they are not perceived as such. Though themselves unperceived, such background levels are critical for what is perceived and for perceptual stability. They provide supportive adaptational levels in relation to which the functions that serve reality contact can signify facts of the environment. Perception specifies the environment, but it can do so only because the arrays of constant stimulus levels in the average expectable environment make possible, in Gibson's words (*11*), stable, psychologically "neutral" zones in relation to which variations in the array can be distinguished. For instance, the gravitational field provides a pervasive background of unperceived stimulation that is nonetheless a critical context of spatial orientation. Such a supportive, nonchanging stimulus array contributes not only to the stability of object perception but to constancy of the self as a perceivable object in space and over time. Continued availability and constancy of nonchanging stimulus arrays is presumed to be a critical condition of normal perceptual development. In Kohler's view (*27*) the gestalt tendencies of perception, often believed to be nativistic in origin, arise from and depend upon such constant stimulus levels of the environment.

The adaptive importance of nonspecific constants in the sensory environment are now coming more clearly into focus through experiments in which drastic changes are produced in the "average expectable environment." Wholesale, persistent shifts in the usual optimal background levels of stimulation have behavioral and phenomenological consequences. In these studies the unusual, the unfamiliar environment now becomes the "average expectable" one. New sensory backgrounds are created in the context of which the functions governing reality contact must operate—as, for example, in stimulus isolation and disarrangement studies (*13, 14, 20, 21, 27, 28*), studies of zero-gravity effects (*3, 10, 15*), of immobilization (*51*), and of disrupted feedback (*4, 45, 46*). All these involve profound disruptions of usually optimal background stimulation. A persistent change or inhomogeneity in such constant values of the external stimulus array challenges the organism to develop new zero or neutral zones of psychological correspondence. Ivo Kohler's work (*28*), for example, on the effects of optical inverting lenses shows that a persistent abnormality of optical stimulation levels leads in the end to a reduction of this phenomenal abnormality; and that a reversion to what was before the optimal level yields a new phenomenal abnormality.

By thus isolating an organism from its usual sources of stimulation, we can attempt to gauge its relative autonomy—the degree of independence of the organism's functional repertory from particular levels and varieties of inputs. By studying behavior defects in such circumstances we can try to observe how disturbance of a part affects the rest of the living system—how much of normal performance continues in the presence of the gap. From a psychoanalytic viewpoint, a particularly important feature of these studies is that they involve disruptions of supportive stimulus conditions upon which secondary-process thinking ordinarily depends; for instance, the altered conditions may make it more difficult to maintain effectively the inhibitions that are so fundamental to reality-oriented behavior and secondary-process thinking. Through its traditional concern with deviant behaviors, psychoanalysis is favorably supplied with descriptive concepts for assessing the quality and directions of behavior in the face of such disruptions. Assumptions about the behavioral consequences of a loss of function-autonomy are aided on a descriptive level by such concepts as the balance of drive, defense, and control, generally, and by the complementary conceptions of primary- and secondary-process modes of thinking.

Among the taken-for-granted constant conditions of the average expectable environment it is likely that few surpass in importance the stimulations that arise from self-produced movements or the consequences of one's own actions—a property now popularly known as 'feedback.' An uninterrupted supply of unperceived, movement-produced stimulation appears to be essential to insure effective accommodation to changing conditions in the environment. The guidance provided by feedback is most of the time neither obvious nor in one's awareness, becoming so only when the appropriate feedback is no longer available. For instance, walking and standing produce sensations that are indispensable to normal gait and posture. Impair this feedback and the walk becomes uncertain and abnormal. Or consider the consequences of having people wear lenses that turn the visual field upside down, as in Ivo Kohler's studies (*28*). These circumstances set off an anxious battle to obtain adequate feedback, suggesting that a primary source of anxiety, in addition to drive eruptions and drive conflict, are states which threaten the adequacy of integrative efforts that ordinarily depend upon informational returns from self-produced movements, states in which conception and perception do not fit the environment in a manner that makes action possible or effective.[1]

In the present paper, I will be concerned with one of the major avenues of informational feedback—the auditory return of one's own speech: the importance of *hearing* what one is saying in the course of saying it. Specifically, I will be concerned with the content and form of *spoken* thought when such monitoring is not possible. I will propose that the return afferentation of one's own speech is a critical supportive factor in maintaining reality-oriented, *communicated* thought—that is, of thought conveyed through speech. If we accept the general principle that *motor* behavior seems always to require a monitoring process, then it is likely that some degree of auditory monitoring helps keep communicated, spoken thinking on track. If vocalization is informative stimulation, it should, like all movement-produced stimulation, depend for its success upon an appropriate feedback to the speaker himself. The auditory return of speech may be a critical source of this informative return, perhaps even a vital condition of maintaining sequential order in *spoken* thought. I will draw upon some observations from an experimental situation of vocal isolation which produces a substantial reduction in the auditory feedback from one's own voice. Since I am interested in conditions that promote regressive thinking, I will approach the subject with an eye toward the implications of such a situation for promoting a regressive momentum or primary process in thinking.

A clinical example.—I start with a phenomenon that is I believe fairly common. A patient often falls into one of those all-too-familiar silences which, like speech itself, convey information. I am able by now to distinguish when her silences are hostile or are of the "my-mind-is-blank" type. But this particular kind of silence is neither of these. Our dialogue usually goes as follows: "Why are you silent?" "I'm having unpleasant thoughts." "And you are reluctant to tell them to me." "No, it's that I don't want to hear them myself." The patient is alluding to the echo of her spoken thoughts and its importance. On the face of it we seem to be encountering a paradox. If she is *aware* of her "unpleasant thoughts," she is

[1]Norbert Weiner writes: ". . . for effective action on the outside world, it is not only essential that we possess good effectors, but that the performance of these effectors be properly monitored back to the central nervous system, and that the readings of these monitors be properly combined with the other information coming in from the sense organs to produce a proportioned output to the effectors" (*49,* p. 114). Rapaport's comment is pertinent: "On the way towards the discovery and conquest of the need gratifying object, detours are made, and these detours are governed both by the need (and its derivatives) and the realities encountered. While the goal is sustained in the course of the detour, the momentary direction, the preferred path is determined by 'feedback' of information. . . . The thought disorder of the schizophrenic . . . is amenable to description in terms of such disturbed feedback processes" (*43*). One is reminded here, too, of the dereistic directions of thought that occur when the attention function, so critical for effective feedback, falters during drowsiness.

already "listening" to them and in that sense saying them. What could she mean that she doesn't want to *hear herself* say them? The crux of the matter is that by vocalizing a thought she makes it an external stimulus—giving the thought a perceptual, and therefore a tangible, quality; she makes it more real for herself as well as for me. The reality and impact of thought seem to be aided by its vocalization. This example suggests, then, that whether speech is covert or overt is a critical factor in thinking. One is tempted to ask: Would her thoughts be more easily stated to me if she did not hear herself say them? But I am getting ahead of myself, for this question is actually the subject of a program of investigation which it is my aim to tell you a bit more about in the course of this paper.

There are, however, a few bridges to cross before we can appreciate the full significance of the auditory feedback in spoken thought. These have to do with the *functions of voice in primary- and secondary-process thinking,* the *collaboration of voice and word in spoken thought,* the *distinction between silent and communicated secondary-process thought,* and the importance of *self as audience* to one's speech.

THE FUNCTIONS OF VOCALIZATION

Vocalization, like spoken words and language generally, is first and foremost a motoric instrument whose importance, in psychoanalytic terms, is defined by the aims of drive and affect discharge, the representational and expressive requirements of reality-oriented thought, the strictures of defenses, and of other forms of control. Spoken thought involves qualities of voice, quite apart from the qualities of words themselves, that are responsive as well as expressive to the audience as well as to one's intended thoughts and subjective states. This calls for a distinction between the vocal and the verbal aspects of speech. The untrained voice, as Gordon Allport points out, is a highly expressive instrument that can produce wide variations in pitch, timbre, and mannerism, including such fugitive and hard-to-analyze features as "intonation, rhythm, brokeness or continuity, accent, richness, roughness, musical handling" (*1,* p. 483). Moreover, as a *motor* instrument, voice not only conveys thought; it is capable of directly discharging emotional states and drives without the intervention of words. The varied characteristics of voice are often overlooked by psychologists because usually speech is taken to mean simply verbalization. The distinction between voice and verbalization can also be appreciated by noting that while, on the one hand, most words are objectively oriented—to things and events—voice qualities are uniquely capable of representing bodily or subjective states, and in a fashion that is sometimes impossible to accomplish with words (*40*). A "trembling" voice and an "ecstatic moan" communicate what words often cannot express.

Glover gives an interesting account of how orality may shape speech (*12,* p. 34):

> . . . as with all other stages of development we see reflected in speech characteristics and in the play with words the influence of the oral stage. Output may vary from extreme verbosity to extreme taciturnity; words are poured out in a constant flow or on the other hand there is a tendency to dwell on special phrases which are treated like choice morsels and rolled around the tongue. Ambivalent selection and use of words is also a striking characteristic and there is an obvious preference for the use of terms descriptive of mouth activities, particularly of biting activities, the effect being commonly described as "incisive speech."

To be sure, words, and words via speech, are the principal medium or carrier of thought. Whether one is engaged in silent thought, in speech, or in written communication, words are omnipresent. Psychoanalysts of course need not be reminded of the important functions of words in speech and verbalization generally (see Loewenstein [*36*]; Stone [*47*]). It is words that give existence or reality to thought. In a tachistoscopic experiment impressions are the more fleeting if they elude words; as soon as one finds the apt word, the impression itself crystallizes and the experience changes. So strong is the reality-giving power of words that, whenever we have coined a word to denote a phenomenon, we are disposed to infer actuality—some hard fact. Conversely, difficulty in naming can lead to an opposite impression and cause us to ignore phenomena. "Words," said William James, "lend reality, a source of comfort and delusion. . . . It is hard to focus our attention on the nameless" (*25,* Vol. I, p. 194).

It does not minimize the importance of words to emphasize the relatively independent role of vocal qualities as carriers of thoughts. Words themselves acquire their sound component through their close functional proximity to the vocal apparatus; we *say* words in learning words. In directly involving a *motor* apparatus for the emission of sounds, speech goes beyond words by enlarging the means of coding thoughts and of conveying the affect and motive organizers of behavior. This is a factor that sometimes lends a touch of artificiality to voiced expression, as when a patient says he is not able to 'express' his thoughts precisely. The manner of putting a thought into words on the psychoanalytic couch may often be off the mark of the thought itself. Who has not noticed that saying a thought aloud often makes a difference, the sound of one's voice often affecting the tone of subsequent associations.

Voice and word in discharge and control.—Freud had much to say about the role of voice and language in relation to the discharge and delay functions of behavior. A most instructive source of Freud's views on this subject is his "Project for a Scientific Psychology" (*9*), in which his conception of the secondary process and of reality-testing, and the relations of both to speech, are spelled out with a degree of specificity which he never again matched in his later writings. His views are particularly interesting, because, without using the word, Freud attributed great importance to feedback and the informative significance of the motoric aspect of language generally in the disciplining and regulating of thinking.

Freud ascribes the functions of mental structures to two fundamental sources of behavior. The primary function of practical behavior is to *discharge* nonoptimal levels of tension arising from within the organism—those of endogenous origin which he was later to call "drives." Among the methods of discharge those are preferred and retained which involve the cessation of the stimulus. The first attempts in development to bring this about follow, Freud says, "paths of internal change," either through perception via hallucination or through diffuse motor activation—as, for example, in the vocal activations of screening. For the discharge aim, the primary function of psychical functioning, the musculature is all important; and all pathways leading to motor innervation are *ipso facto* potential pathways and channels of discharge. Here, then, is one important function of voice. Independently of the *verbal* links it acquires, the vocal apparatus, because it is a motor structure, is from the beginning in the category of a discharge channel. We must expect that the sound-emitting properties of the vocal apparatus will retain this capacity of being direct discharge channels of drive states and of organismic states associated with them such as affects, and that this function is originally independent of the word-making function with which this apparatus comes in time to be most intimately associated.

However, survival—"the exigencies of life"—says Freud in the Project, dictates that discharge not be indiscriminate, that it be oriented to "indicators of reality" such that the discharge produce an *effective* change in nonoptimal levels of tension. It is under the aegis of this requirement that the "secondary function" of regulating the "flow of quantity" and of apparatuses pertaining to it come to develop. The identifying characteristics of secondary-process thinking are inhibition, selective responsiveness to reality, reality-guided action even when behavior is drive-impelled, and a capacity for testing the appropriateness of a perception or of a response against standards defined by intention. Effective carrying out of these functions delays discharge. The autonomy of secondary-process thinking, to use the terminology of contemporary ego psychology in stating this early idea of Freud's, derives from ideational activity rather than from afferent input; this autonomy is made possible by the person's ability to hold on to the effects of stimulation for some time before acting upon it. At the same time, the motor apparatus must be capable of being *readied* for discharge; it must be capable of *partial* innervations, such that small quantities of energy will serve as signals of the presence of the "appropriate reality" which will be quickly responded to with correspondingly appropriate and complete motor release. A crucial requirement of reality-oriented thinking and behavior then, in Freud's view, is that the apparatuses of discharge must be capable of acquiring responsiveness to *signals of contact* with reality. Affective response and the musculature, including, of course, the vocal apparatus, must develop links with a signaling system through which the full discharge potentialities of these structures are brought under control.

Here is where *words* in relation to utterance become crucial. Eventually, through what Freud called the 'reports'—or what contemporary usage would call 'feedback'—of action or of discharge (among which one must certainly include *auditory* reports as well as kinesthetic and proprioceptive ones), words through their association with vocal movements acquire the *secondary* function of signaling the appropriateness of a "passage of quantity." In Freud's view the importance of vocal associations of words lies in the fact that vocal links convert words into motor *surrogates* of action. When sounds emitted by the vocal apparatus become associated with the word-representations of objects, sound-making becomes speech; speech acquires a *signal* function as "an indicator of action-reality." Vocalization in words thereby adds a secondary function to the primary function of vocal activity. It is when vocalization becomes linked with words that speech becomes critically important in implementing reality-testing. This is perhaps simply another way of saying that words in the form of speech make thoughts *real.* As one reflection of this view, Freud asserts that speech associations make it possible to establish traces of the outcomes of thoughts; linkages of thoughts with the *motor* components of words enables one to remember one's thoughts.

The importance of vocalization consists, then, partly in its potential discharge function—i.e., in implementing the discharge of affects and bodily tensions—and partly in its secondary-process function. From the direct motoric expression of affect and drive states, vocalization advances to speech when sounds are coded into lingual forms that represent objective experiences with recurrent events of the environment. It is to be expected that the nonverbal aspects of vocalization retain their value as primary discharge valves through which drive and affect states are directly conveyed by vocal properties.

Silent and spoken thought.—It will add to our appreciation of the functions of vocalization in uttered thought to consider briefly the differences between silent and spoken thought. It makes a difference whether secondary-process thinking occurs in the context of overt speech or not. It is surely important that sound and the voice apparatus are involved in *communicated* secondary-process thinking, whereas they need not be in silent secondary-process thinking.

When thought is silent and guided by the secondary process, the accomplishments of secondary-process aims need not involve the vocal apparatus and speech. In silent thinking, the syntactical forms of thought need not be the same as those involved when thought is communicated in conversation or in writing (*32*). In silent thought the tolerances of awareness are very broad; effective or 'correct' *outcome* is all-important. Efficiency requires the rejecting of irrelevant lines of association as these spring into awareness en route to a desired terminal point, but the gamut of consciously apprehended, if fleeting, ideas and associations can be very extensive.

In *communicated* thinking another order of events is involved, that of speech, and another requirement, that of being understood and of reacting to the audience. Since most of the time the speaker is seen as well as heard, additional functions must be carried by the speech apparatus—reactiveness to the audience and respect for rules of being understood. The succession of words consummated in sound must conform to a system that is appropriate to the thought and to the audience. The number of options for reversing the direction of thought are still considerable, but the rules and conventions for making oneself understood are now also implicated. Of course, the discrepancies that may develop between our thoughts and the meanings and sounds of the actual words *said* can often be poignant, as psychoanalytic experience often illustrates.

In silent thinking, then, reversibility and range of awareness are very much less restricted than in spoken thought; it is the end-result only that gives the mark to secondary process to the events that lead up to it. In silent secondary-process thinking the grammar of thought need not respect the syntactical rules that are essential to vocal communication. You can take back a thought or a word more quickly in silent thinking than you can in spoken thinking. (And, of course you can do so more easily in spoken thinking than in written thinking.) It is when the assistance of the voice is no longer present, when writing alone is required, that reversibility is most severely restricted. Because of the irreversibility of the written word, the goal of writing has to be that of achieving unequivocal meaning in order to control one's audience. One must like to write to make up for the loss of vocalization, and the comfort one feels either in speaking or in writing reflects one's ease or unease with these distinctions. If vocalization is less restrictive than writing, however, so it is more so than silent thought.

A function that distinguishes spoken thought to a greater degree than silent thinking is the necessity of controlling *peripheral lines of thinking*—that is, irrelevant, preconscious trains of thought that have verbal representation. Preconscious thought may be said to consist of a series of parallel and intersecting centers of activated ideas only one of which, however, is accessible to the final motor path of vocalization. One of the important tasks of spoken thought is that of maintaining the dominance of a central focus of thought —to give verbal coherence to a train of thought without impediment from conflicting lines of thought. The voice helps in this respect. In communicated thought, control is accomplished not only by pauses but through forms of vocalization itself, as well as through the forms and content of language. Talleyrand is said to have remarked that the function of language is to conceal as well as to communicate, and this can be as true of the qualities of voice as it is of words. Inhibition and concealment are served by properties of voice as well as by the forms and content of words in communicated secondary-process thought. Of course, there are also the more primitive or peremptory concealments determined by defense, and these too are assisted by vocal qualities. Fenichel (*6*) describes instances of complete muting when vocalization is completely eliminated under the necessity of dealing with conflictful ideas. Usually, however, more benign forms of defensive *editing* occur, producing changes both in vocalization and in the forms of language in speech. It is possible that the control or inhibition of potentially intrusive ideas is as important an accomplishment of speech as its directly communicative function; it may indeed be a precondition of the latter.

One more function served by vocalization deserves mention—the maintenance of a sense of self. Man is both an acoustical generator and receiver; in vocalization he hears himself in the act of producing sounds. The auditory component of vocalization makes it possible to distinguish one's covert from overt speech, one's own speech from that of others, distinctions that are surely important in providing a continuing reinforcement of the distinctions between oneself and others in the environment. Thus, eliminating the sound of one's own voice can be experienced by some as a profoundly isolating experience (*30; 31,* p. 454). On the other hand, vocalization can be a useful antidote to social isolation; men are prone to talk to themselves—aloud— when they have been alone for long stretches of time.

Self as audience for one's own speech.—That speech is an *auditory* as well as a motor and language affair is a fact often overlooked in speech analysis. To appreciate this auditory component and, specifically, the importance of auditory feedback it is well to be reminded that in speaking one has two audiences—himself and others. George Miller remarks: "Speech has the interesting characteristic that it affects the talker acoustically in much the same way it affects the listener. Since every talker is his own listener, it is as natural for a person to respond to himself as to respond to others" (*39,* p. 172). The auditory return from one's speech is one of the constant, taken-for-granted components of our sensory environment. Just as most of the time we take gravity for granted, so do we ignore the fact that we also hear ourselves when we speak aloud. The act of vocalization is always accompanied by corresponding auditory stimulation except, of course, in those cases of deafness where bone-conduction of sound is no longer intact. The sound of one's own voice is not a fact perceived from moment to moment but is rather a constant background feature of the optimal stimulus environment characteristic of spoken communicated thought.

This fact has enormous significance for the development and control of behavior and for the effective control of vocalization. A child must hear others before he can begin to listen to himself. He quickly learns, too, that there is a range of optimal speech intensities that are tolerable to others. The child must learn "not to speak loudly," to speak "properly," to give commands to himself. Control of speech volume continues to be a critical function; upon it depends the capacity to distinguish between making one's thoughts public and keeping them private. The child must also learn, however, to distinguish his own talk from the speech of others. In distinguishing between himself and others as audience, the child learns to separate his *thoughts* from those of others, an important basis of developing and maintaining a sense of intact and independent self.

Effective control in these respects depends upon the child's being able to reinforce or edit himself in his verbal behavior; to do this he must learn to appreciate that he is also part of the audience to his own speech. Zangwill (*50*) points out that, in the acquisition of speech, the infant's perception of his own speech sounds plays a most important part in the development of orderly speech. A neat demonstration of the developmental importance of self-hearing of spoken words is shown in experiments with children which have been carried out in the Soviet Union by Luria and his colleagues (*37*). They show that for the child to hear himself utter "stop" and "go" instructions plays an important role in the development of controlled behavior. If a child is told to press a rubber balloon only when a colored light flashes, this instruction alone is ineffective until the child has been additionally instructed to call out the signal "stop" or "go" himself. Children of three to four succeed in controlling their reaction quite efficiently if they accompany it with a loud vocal response appropriate to the action; to give the command to oneself *silently* is not enough. In time the child does become capable of actively modifying the environment that influences him by using silent speech signals, but this must be preceded by a phase of administering the signals *aloud* to himself.

The capacity of being aware of oneself as audience to one's speech is especially important in converting other people's commands to commands given to oneself. Thereby it also helps to establish a basis for the prohibitions of the adult becoming "the voice of conscience." Isakower (*24*) has amplified the superego function that Freud assigned to the "auditory lobe." It is when such listened-to words also become words that we say *aloud* and *hear* that they become more meaningful to us. "Thus," as Isakower puts it, "the auditory mechanism keeps us oriented in the world of conduct, as the adjacent and embryologically similar vestibular apparatus does in the world of space" (*24*). This is not to say that audition is the sole architect of the superego; only that the capacity to distinguish oneself from others as audience to one's speech furnishes an important reinforcement of the distinction between oneself and the environment upon which the development of a firm superego depends.

Loss of the capacity to distinguish self from others as audience is reflected in pathological disturbances, when the lines between covertness and overtness of speech are variable or weakened, or where, for example, the inner promptings of superego are externalized as projected voices in auditory hallucinations. One of Freud's obsessional patients remarked: ". . . at that time I used to have a morbid idea that my parents knew my thoughts; I explained this to myself by supposing that I had spoken them out loud, without having heard myself do it. I look on this as the beginning of my illness" (*8*, p. 164). Freud comments: "We shall not go far astray if we suppose that this attempt at an explanation 'I speak my thoughts out loud without hearing them' sounds like a projection into the external world of our own hypothesis that he had thoughts without knowing anything about them; it sounds like an endopsychic perception of what has been repressed" (*8*, p. 164).

Such a failure in distinguishing thought and speech took the form of a delusion of reference in one of our subjects in a study on the effects of mescalin. He reported that his thoughts had been so "loud" that surely everyone else in the room could hear them. He began to look quietly and sharply into the eyes and faces of those around him for clues that they were hearing what he was thinking and for evidence of silent condemnation. When later he was questioned about how his thoughts had "sounded," he said they were best likened to a record coming through a secretary's earphones while typing; the head is filled with sound, and one can easily get the idea that since what one is hearing is so loud, surely others in the room must be hearing it too.

An interesting pathological *converse* of losing the self-other distinction is illustrated in the speech of a patient. Here there appeared an exaggerated defensive *emphasis* upon this distinction, with a corresponding intensification of the controlling and concealing properties of speech. Speech in this patient was dedicated almost exclusively to control rather than to communication or expression. It is as if, in a depersonalized way, she watchfully let words and sentences go by only after screening before, and censoring during, vocal release. The vocal and formal linguistic structure of her speech during therapeutic hours was like an elaborate veil designed simultaneously both to reveal and conceal, creating for the therapist continually intriguing problems of decoding their message. Ornateness, ambiguity, double meanings were typical. Take these examples: "There is something about wanting to be seduced on my part which in turn is linked to its opposite" (i.e., to act *as* seducer). "One of us is no longer missing links" (referring, among other things, to an idea expressed long before that she felt "ape-like"); "I touched his penis but not his unclothed penis"; "I anticipated a chocolate hunger" (referring to what she could eat as well as the "black" mood it would create); "I would assume that the thread of sanctions sits behind all this" (i.e., referring also to the analyst seated behind). The ornateness was not without charm: thus, "To have a name is to be defined in oneself and I was never at one with my name." "This fantasy came out of a sea of amorphous thoughts." And a summary weblike thought: "We're both kind of grim here. I am and you are too. There's not the least bit of lightening so that some perspective could be gained by the distance which humour allows. There is a too literal adherence to the surface meaning of language so that I am always trapped by what I say which is something I don't always mean."

A ruthlessly exacting editing process is at work here, more appropriate perhaps to writing than to speaking; she leans heavily upon it for protection, and it produces qualities that would seem stilted even in writing. In the give-and-take context of speech, they are bizarre. Far from losing a sense of herself as audience for her speech, this patient relies upon vocalization as a defensive reinforcement of it.

AUDITORY FEEDBACK IN THE MONITORING OF COMMUNICATED THOUGHT

Now we may turn to the specific importance of *auditory feedback* for vocal communication and for the maintenance of the secondary process in spoken thought. How significant is it to *hear* oneself speak in carrying out the functions of discharge, control, inhibition of preconscious trains of thought, and of maintaining the self-other distinction? One can be deaf to others and think effectively, but whether one can think effectively in speaking *aloud* without being able to hear one's own voice is an open question.

Reliance on auditory feedback is not only important developmentally: it appears to remain a crucial factor in the control of speech. One can demonstrate in a simple way the importance of heard speech both to the continuity of spoken speech and to the regulation of its pitch and flow. Marked disorders of speech result when the speaker's hearing of his own voice is delayed by a fraction of a second, so that he hears himself say one syllable while producing the next (*4, 45*). Some subjects are completely blocked, whereas others can speak only very slowly. Responsiveness to distraction may be involved here, but as Hebb points out: "This can hardly be simple interference, or distraction, because there are no such effects when the speaker hears other material, or in fact his own speech if the sounds are delayed by more than a second or so" (*18,* p. 62). The fact that experimentally deafened subjects tend to shout also suggests that under normal conditions the sound of one's own voice plays an important part in integrating and controlling the quality of speech production.

All this has to do with demonstrating the importance of the auditory return from one's own voice in maintaining serial *order* in speech. What has auditory feedback to do with the regulation of *thinking?* If thought directs speech, then on what premise can we assume that vocalization, and the auditory self-monitoring of it, affect thought itself?

It is sometimes forgotten that most speakers are seen in the act of speaking. The speaker must be able to adjust his voice as well as the form and content of his spoken language, according to the indications of interest, lack of interest, boredom, query, etc., that he is getting from the vocal and facial responses of his audience. It is within this context that the importance of an informational feedback return from the environment impresses itself on our attention as a functional support of the reality orientation in behavior. By means of it thought keeps on track with a secondary process orientation. As with all behavior, the ultimate effectiveness of verbal behavior too depends upon the action the listener takes with respect to it. But this action includes that of the speaker as well, since he is part of his audience. The metaphor "to play it by ear" implies the importance of an informational return from action—the perceived consequences of action—for keeping oneself reality-oriented. When *spoken* thought is the behavior, then the pertinent feedback of this 'action' comes from the auditory return to the speaker; this becomes an important adjunct of the speaker's knowing whether he has correctly conveyed the intended thought in speech. Hearing oneself makes it possible to change vocalization; what one will say next depends upon some kind of implicit "OK" reaction to one's uttered words. This is the basic idea of an action-correcting feedback, which itself remains in the background of awareness.

A reasonable proposition is that the auditory feedback from one's speech derives its importance from what Skinner (*44,* p. 370) has aptly termed the *editing* process in spoken thought.

A response which has been emitted in overt form may be recalled or revoked by an additional response. The conspicuous external record of written verbal behavior may affect the "speaker" before it reaches any "listener" and may be crossed out, erased, struck over, or torn up. The writer has reacted to, and rejected, his own behavior. . . . Comparable "editing" of vocal behavior is more ephemeral and hence

> harder to describe. Withholding audible speech may seem to be nothing more than emitting it. Some restraining behavior may, however, be detectable, such as biting the tongue or lips or holding the hand over the mouth. . . . Subvocal behavior can of course be revoked before it has been emitted audibly. . . . Inadequate withholding, when there are strong reasons for emitting a response, may lead to whispered or mumbled or hesitant behavior of low energy and speed.

The editing of speech is to be seen in the *formal structure* of spoken speech, as for example in qualifying statements, pretended slips, and in the formal qualities of vocalization, in nervous laughs, colorless intonations, and low unmodulated energy, in excessive talking itself, in not speaking at all, or in stuttering.

Loewenstein (*36*) has described the importance of the auditory self-perception of speech, and of what we would call editing, in the analytic situation. In general, how the patient sounds to himself will determine whether he talks or not, as well as what he thinks the analyst will hear. By hearing himself vocalize the patient controls his own reactions to his thoughts and attempts to control the reactions of the analyst. It seems safe to assume that hearing one's own speech provides at least an important support to the process of monitoring the efficiency of speech through editing and in this way assists in safeguarding the discipline of thought.

Editing of speech is, therefore, a crucial activity of the speaker that may depend in part upon the auditory return of vocalization. When we take away this feedback we may expect changes in the flow of speech and in the quality of thinking. In sleep-deprived people, for example, conversation may appear to observers as listless, shallow in quality, and the speech lacking in normal variations of loudness and inflection (*31, 41*). It has been noted that, as sleep deprivation increases, subjects seem less concerned with how well an interviewer understands what they are saying, and, indicative of their impaired discrimination, they show less evidence of self-correction of errors in their speech, becoming unaware of the changes in their own speech and in that of others. Auditory hallucination is also encouraged under such conditions when the sound of one's vocal output is poorly monitored.

The editing function may be rendered inefficient because inadequate feedback stimulation prevents editing from occurring. Deaf persons are likely to talk slowly, in part because it is more difficult for them to make the distinction between covert and overt behavior. The consequences to speech when the feedback and editing functions are impaired are strikingly illustrated by the characteristics of speech when it actually occurs *during* sleep. Speech in sleep does not affect the speaker as *listener;* its organization, therefore, does not follow the usual syntactical rules. Editing may also be disrupted when the pressure of an idea is too great to be handled by available editing strategies. In any case, in editing, the speaker reacts as audience to his own speech. If he cannot listen it is more difficult for him to edit.

In this respect, a wholesale reduction of the auditory feedback from one's voice is somewhat in the same category as the couch in the analytic situation. The upright position is important in sustaining the integrity of certain thought functions and certain thought operations. Undoubtedly, a great deal of disciplined thinking can go on while one is on one's back—indeed, some seem to prefer it; but there is no doubt that by-and-large the upright posture and associated tonic patterns of the organism are part of an orientative structure that is helpful to concentrated disciplined thought. Hence, when one is on one's back the potentiality at least for alterations in the course of associations is increased, though the reactions may vary, as we know indeed they do (cf. Kubie's important comment [*30,* p. 42]). Similarly, we may expect changes in thought, but differing in form, when the ordinarily relied upon auditory return from one's own voice is taken away. As with reactions to the couch in the psychoanalytic situation it is to be expected that vocal isolation may inspire opposite reactions. For some, *not* hearing one's own speech may facilitate the intrusion of peripheral lines of thought into the speech sequence, perhaps encouraging a condition of automatic talking analogous to that of automatic writing; removal of auditory feedback may promote detachment and unconcern with reality constraints and an introspective involvement in the flow of one's thinking. In others, the loss of auditory feedback may produce doubt, indecision, anxiety, and blocking. It may exacerbate sensitivity and control, and intensify in a compensatory way certain modes of reality-testing, rather than reduce the effectiveness of reality-testing altogether. It is known that people differ in how easily they can suspend a reality-testing orientation in circumstances that put a strain upon reality-testing and in the ease with which they can give themselves up to fantasy without anxiety (*5*). Effects may depend, then, on the state of consciousness induced and the manner in which the disrupted feedback affects one's sense of ego integrity and of reality generally.

It is necessary to add a qualifying consideration to this emphasis on the importance of auditory feedback for the editing and controlling processes of speech. I am far from suggesting that the sensory feedback of one's own voice is the whole story of the monitoring of spoken thought. The reason I say this is that thinking is not to be identified with vocalization (*18, 32–34*). Organization of thought is prior to expression; vocal accompaniments are additional not inevitable accompaniments of thinking. To the extent that vocalization is centrally mediated, point-for-point monitoring of vocalization may to some extent not be required. As Hebb remarks (*18,* p. 60) :

No one, for example, has succeeded in explaining a speaker's sentence construction during the course of ordinary speech as a series of CR's linked together by feedback alone, and there are strong indications that his thought processes run well ahead of his actual articulations. . . . Also, in some cases of aphasia . . . thought is not impaired in the way or to the degree that one would expect if it consisted solely of muscular reaction plus feedback.

It must be admitted that not much is known about the extent to which automatization of vocalization preserves or insures continuity in speaking and thinking without auditory reception, nor is it known what qualities of vocalization are not so automatically emitted and therefore specifically require such aural monitoring. Moreover, it must be stressed that *listening* to one's speech is to be distinguished from *hearing* one's speech. The former is presumed *not* to be essential for monitoring any more than awareness of one's locomotor movements is essential for the feedback processes upon which walking depends. A reasonable possibility is that the monitoring process of speech served by auditory feedback does not consist of specific word-for-word policing or of actual *listening;* the essence of speech monitoring may be mainly the detection of asynchronies between a train of thought and its vocalization, in the manner in which we correct a Spoonerism—e.g., we utter a Spoonerism, *hear* it, and follow it wtih corrective "excuse me, I really meant. . . ."

It seems safe to say, too, that aural monitoring is a less important aspect of vocalizations which are serving primarily a *discharge* rather than communicative function. To the extent that vocalized thought is drive-determined or affect-organized, it is presumably less reliant on such feedback, since this is partly what one would assume to be a quality of peremptory primary-process thought in Rapaport's description (*42*).

That hearing one's spoken thought is usually assumed by the speaker to be a necessary accompaniment of his thinking aloud is suggested by the fact that he begins to shout when he cannot hear himself. Changes of voice quality in different situations are suggestive too; for example, the voice flattens in certain circumstances where expression is not necessary, as, for instance, when one is making a veridical report on some aspect of the environment. Many of our artificially voice-deafened subjects in the study to be described below have also remarked that in uttering words they were not sure that they said the "correct word" or if they finished sentences or not; they thought they were making errors in speaking, despite the fact that they knew what they were trying to say. As one subject put it, "I *knew* what I wanted to say, but did I say it?" Again, I am not suggesting that the reduction of the voice feedback is a sufficient condition for producing the altered conditions of consciousness in which primary-process and regressed modes of thinking appear; but if we remember that the voice mediates expression of affect and other qualities of control, then a loss in the *signal or monitoring* value of the voice should to some degree produce an isolation from reality that could have reverberations to one's sense of reality and one's qualities of thinking.

The safeguards of auditory feedback.—Since self as audience is an important part of speaking, it is not surprising that nature has provided safeguards for the capacity to hear one's own voice. Hearing of vocalization is made possible by two means of reception : by air-conducted (side-tone) stimulation of the basilar membrane and by bone-conducted vibrations of the sounds generated from the vocal cords. Deafness to side-tone still permits bone-conducted hearing of one's own voice. Bone-conducted hearing is accomplished directly through the bony tissue of the skull. If the ears are plugged—that is, if air conduction is excluded—a vibrating tuning fork with its shank held against the skull above the mastoid process of the temporal lobe can be clearly heard. Sound waves cause the bones of the skull labyrinth to vibrate, producing vibrations in turn on the basilar membrane as in air conduction. The action of sound vibrations in the auditory receptor by bone conduction is much less sensitive than air conduction ; it seems, therefore, from one viewpoint (*48*), to have a purely supplemental function, with the importance reserved mainly for hearing *one's own* voice. This twin arrangement of bone-conducted and air-conducted sound of one's own voice, along with the capacity for subtle variations of sound emission provided by the human vocal apparatus with its larynx and vocal cords, gives man an incomparable instrument of social intercourse and of control of communicated thinking, as well as a means of discharge through the purely muscular capacities provided by the emission of sound.

VOCAL ISOLATION: THE CONSEQUENCES OF REDUCED AUDITORY FEEDBACK

Now we come to a consideration of the effects of experimentally induced vocal isolation. I have said that if hearing one's own voice in the course of speech is important for monitoring communicated thought, then changes in the character of spoken thought may occur if this process is interfered with. We can perhaps encourage the suppression of the self-audience by preventing or reducing the normal auditory feedback of verbal behavior. The matter is intriguing from the standpoint of determining the conditions under which secondary-process thinking gives way in speech to thinking that is more primary-process or 'regressive' in character.

Our approach to this problem follows the paradigm I described of attempting to induce primary-processlike behavior by systematically undermining functional supports of reality testing—that is, by impairing sensory conditions that are ordinarily supportive to such functions in secondary-process thinking. If something is known about the functions that insure reality-oriented thinking, regressive changes are to be expected when these functions are deprived of their appropriate, supportive background levels of stimulation. In such circumstances secondary-process thinking could be disturbed; given certain other contingent conditions, e.g. a weakening of defenses and heightened sensitization to drive-organized ideation, then thinking may bear the imprint of what is released from inhibition or produce an exaggerated emphasis upon defensive or restraining forces that have remained intact. Those drive-organized ideations ordinarily checked by optimally functioning defenses are then perhaps in a better position to impose themselves upon consciousness.

With these considerations in mind, my colleague Dr. David Wolitzky and I and some of our students have been engaged recently in investigating the generalized effects upon spoken thought of a sharp reduction in the auditory feedback of one's own voice—a condition of relative vocal isolation

There are a variety of ways of interfering with auditory feedback: (*a*) complete or relatively complete reduction of the feedback; (*b*) intensification of the feedback, as for example by plugging the external auditory meatus; (*c*) a delay of the auditory return—the well-known condition of delayed auditory feedback; (*d*) accelerated auditory feedback; (*e*) conflicting auditory feedback, that is, when the bone-conducted auditory return is in conflict with a synchronous side-tone auditory feedback. Disturbances are likely to vary in these different circumstances, but for the present we are studying mainly the first condition—a wholesale reduction of the auditory return of one's own voice *during the act of speaking*. If it is true that communicated or spoken secondary-process thinking is rendered difficult by the elimination of feedback from one's own voice, it becomes a matter of considerable interest to know how in these circumstances the course of *associations* is affected.

The technique we have been using for reducing feedback is one that was employed by Mahl (*38*) and consists of masking the speaker's voice by a band of white noise that is fed into earphones. Admittedly, there is no easy way of eliminating the safeguard of bone-conducted sound; and masking the voice by noise, for all the problems it raises in confounding the effects of noise and feedback reduction, is the most practical procedure we have so far been able to devise. The white noise has an intensity level of 100 decibels, which subjects have found tolerable after a brief adaptation period. In such circumstances subjects cannot hear themselves even when shouting—and many of them indeed soon begin to shout. The subject is alone in a small chamber, on a couch in a semi-reclining position with his feet up, facing a screen in front of him on which various stimuli are exposed from the adjoining experimenter's room. The experimenter appears in the subject's room after each test; the earphones are removed during instructions for the next test. Each subject is tested in the normal and masking conditions within a single session. The order of conditions, as well as the sets of stimuli of each condition, are varied among subjects in a design which calls for each subject to be his own control. The tasks given to the subjects include the following: *imagery,* following each exposure of two surrealist paintings by DeChirico (each picture is exposed for 10 seconds, followed by a 3-minute response period) ; responses to one achromatic and one colored Rorschach card exposed continuously, again with responses limited to a 3-minute period; *free association* to four words, each presented visually for 5 seconds, and a 2-minute response limit to each.[2]

Our subjects, fifteen so far, are mainly actors with whom we have had a long acquaintance. They have been subjects for us in studies of the effects of LSD-25 (*35*) and of sensory isolation (*13, 14*). We know a good deal about them, and, when all of our data are in, we intend to relate their productions under our conditions of vocal isolation to the knowledge we have accumulated about them in previous studies.

I have described some of the main conditions of the study because it is evident to us that, although vocal masking seems to be a critical factor in producing the effects we are observing, there are a number of equally critical variables that must be taken into account before we can be comfortably certain of the specific contribution of the auditory feedback variable. The loss of auditory feedback may gain its critical status by virtue of the context of stimulation and subject. The noise accompaniment is important, a matter we will return to, not least for its possible effects upon the arousal level of the organism. The combination of noise *and* loss of feedback may be conducive to producing a *feeling of isolation,* abetted by the relatively darkened room, a factor known from other studies to be conducive to a more relaxed, passive, reverie-like state of consciousness (*5, 29, 31*). Moreover, we do not know the effects that changes of voice intensity itself—some subjects shout—may have on the quality of thoughts expressed.

Since the study is in progress I cannot give a detailed account of the effects produced under these conditions, except to cite the more prominent currents that have already appeared in the results and to indicate certain dimensions of response along which striking differences occur among subjects. I must also limit my account to the verbal aspects of thought. Obviously, this is only part of the picture; voice qualities as well as words mediate meanings and thoughts, and the changes in respect to voice are surely among the most dramatic in the spectrum of effects.

---

[2]One of the few studies of experimental deafness is Hebb's (*19*). He studied the reactions of several subjects who went about their usual activities for a three-day period with their ears occluded. Although the effects resemble those of our study in some aspects, there is a vital difference between the experiments. Hebb's procedure occluded air-conducted sound but left bone-conduction intact. Thus, own-voice stimulation was very likely exaggerated in his subjects. The critical feature of our procedure was precisely in the masking of bone-conducted hearing. Here obviously is an important comparison of conditions to be made in future study.

A majority of the subjects are more productive under vocal isolation. It is interesting that this seems to be as true of the extremely inhibited subjects as of the borderline, tenuously controlled subjects of the sample. The increased productivity is not, however, itself indicative of loosened control, or, for that matter, of imaginative content either; productiveness and imaginativeness do not necessarily go hand in hand. Exaggerated controlling efforts can also appear within this context. Thus, one of our subjects, extremely guarded and sparing in expressiveness, gave many more responses under vocal masking but with a strikingly exaggerated negation tendency in which time and again assertion was countered by negating qualifiers. A few samples: "I don't think my mother likes X, but I see her anyway"; "Her friend called me and asked me to his house for dinner; luckily I refused." The word *fangs,* which usually brings forth a host of popular-level aggressive associations, was initially perceived by this subject as "franks"; even when the word was finally perceived correctly it elicited only farfetched excursions to pleasant reminiscenses of Paris and of horseback riding in Central Park.

Most subjects have reported that their imagery tended to be livelier and more vivid under vocal masking. One is reminded of similar tendencies under conditions of sensory isolation (*13*). Perhaps relevant to this is the fact that some of the subjects reported that they experienced an isolative retreat into their own thoughts, a reaction they associated in later interviews with both the noise and the vocal isolation from their own voices.

Thus far, analyses of the subjects' images are further along than those of the Rorschach responses. Images are scored for a variety of contents and for formal characteristics of language and speech. Drawing upon content categories worked out for the Rorschach by Holt (*23*), we scored the images for *drive-references*—that is, for ideational contents suggestive of the component sexual drives: oral, anal, exhibitionistic-voyeuristic, as well as aggressive. The classification provides for more blatant, directly drive-related expressions, and more socially acceptable, toned-down expressions. In addition, there are scoring categories for references to remote events in time or space, for intense spatial experiences of vista or three-dimensionality, for expressions of strangeness and irreality, for reminiscence-like references to childhood experiences or memories that intrude upon the images, and for bodily sensations—all of these comprising a group that in our opinion is indicative of a reverie-like loss of distance in the images; we refer to this group as *'loosened ego boundaries.'* Other category groups indicate *vividness* of the imagery experience; and others *'explicit affect'* reports. Then there are a number of categories referring to responses that seem to carry moral overtones, expressions of guilt, punitive and retributive actions, illegality, Biblical and religious references—we call this group *'superego manifestations.'*

Editing tendencies in speech are also an important basis for scoring. One group of categories—*'speech editing'*—includes adjacent repetitions of words and phrases; incomplete sentences; aborted words or sentences changed in midstream; hesitant word completions (for example, "she was mour. . . . mourning"). Occurrence of word-whiskers—*"uhs" and "ahs"*—was made a separate category, because Mahl (*38*) found it to be uncorrelated to other "speech disturbance" categories. A third group of categories that we call *'language editing'* includes qualifying expressions (e.g., "I think," "perhaps") and a variety of forms of negation (e.g., "but," "do not," and positive assertions followed by expressions of negation).

We find a substantial increase in the number of drive-related contents among imagery responses under vocal masking. Although raw, blatant, or intense drive expressions have appeared principally in our more tenuously controlled subjects, there is a tendency even among the relatively coarctated subjects for drive expressions of a more socially acceptable, toned-down, or derivative level to occur more frequently under vocal masking conditions. There are also substantial increases in the frequency of responses categorized as 'loosened ego boundaries'; more frequent expressions of affect; and an increase in indications of vividness of imagery. Along with these trends is a particularly intriguing tendency for drive expressions to appear in a context of moral coloring, of "judgment," "retribution," "appeal," and "guilt." This trend is of interest in relation to the intimate link between superego and the "auditory sphere" argued by Isakower (*24*) and others (*6*).[3] The appearance of superego-tinged responses may range from harsh, punitive preoccupations in our borderline subjects, to more toned-down, abstract preoccupations with "responsibility" and "values" which characterize the protocol of an inhibited subject. There are considerable individual differences in these trends, but the general increases noted appear to be reliable and characteristic.

Where the effect of vocal masking is clearly *not* unidirectional is in the responses that comprise the editing categories. Since the three groups of editing indicators behave similarly in the comparisons we have made, I will consider them here for the sake of convenience in a single grouping of *'speech-language editing.'* A number of interesting trends appear. Some subjects show intensified editing under vocal masking; others actually show a marked decrease—their speech proceeds less interruptedly. However, there appears to be a systematic basis for these varying effects of vocal masking upon editing: Whether editing is likely to increase or not under vocal masking is strongly associated with degree of increase in the frequency of drive references under

[3]E.g., Fenichel: ". . . the sensations that form the basis of the superego begin with the auditory stimuli of words. Parental words of admonition, encouragement, or threat are incorporated by way of the ear. Thus the commands of the superego as a rule are verbalized. . . . accordingly, a person's relation to language is often predominantly governed by superego rules" (*6*, p. 107).

vocal masking. In those subjects for whom vocal masking produces more drive-content in the responses, editing is *intensified*. Subjects who showed the fewest indications of constraints upon the flow of speech were those who also showed the smallest increase of drive-contents in the images. It would appear that the reins on speech are held less tightly by subjects for whom drive expression is not very insistent under conditions of vocal masking. None of the other categories affected by vocal masking showed such stable co-variation with drive content.

Our analysis of the Rorschach responses is incomplete, but a trend is discernible similar to that seen in the imagery responses. Of the ten subjects whose Rorschachs have been scored, eight show an increase in the number of drive-related content scores under vocal masking.

By and large, it is our impression so far that the general effects of vocal masking described above appear in subjects in a pattern of responsiveness that is consistent with the knowledge we have about their characterological qualities of impulse-control and defense. There have been few surprises in this respect.

You can get a relatively good idea of contrasting reactions to vocal masking, and of the conformity of these reactions to character trends, in the results of two of our subjects. One of the subjects was described in a diagnostic workup as a "narcissistic character disorder with conspicuous schizoid features, reaching borderline proportions, and noteworthy hysterical tendencies." He is further described as having "important underlying phobic features with strained and brittle counterphobic defenses. His thinking can become loose, flighty, arbitrary, and peculiar." This subject had also proved to be one of the most reactive subjects to lysergic acid-25, showing under the drug a great deal of regression, visual distortion, inappropriate affect, and bodily preoccupation. In the vocal masking conditions, when he cannot hear his voice, he quickly loses distance from the stimuli, projecting himself into the circumstances he pictures in his images ("I am in the picture") ; the protocol contains synesthetic-type responses, perseverations, explosive, sexually and aggressively colored affects, confabulations, perceptual fluidity, phobic responses, scenes of punishment and retribution, macabre and bizarre imagery having an oral incorporative, leechlike quality. His voice became loud and had a pressured, urgent intensity. Afterwards his face was flushed ; his whole manner suggested that he had experienced a considerable alteration of consciousness. The Rorschach cards also unloosed a torrent of bizarre and violent imagery. Here are some typical responses: "like a rocket taking off" ; "a woman's vagina with blood" ; "it looks like a raw flesh, like someone had an accident and the flesh is bare under the skin" ; "two mouths, like parts of faces as if about to kiss, the two mouths look alike, could be men kissing or women kissing because the two mouths look so much alike." "I see a time thing with sand running out as if time is running out." On another card two men were seen pulling at a woman, "trying to split her down the middle—splitting the seam," to which he adds, "like the *world* was pulling the woman apart in two directions." His responses under normal conditions are qualitatively consistent with these, but they are nowhere nearly so fluid and so wide-open as in the vocal masking condition.

A contrasting but equally distinctive effect of vocal masking appeared in one of our more inhibited subjects, described in the diagnostic work-up as a "moderately well integrated, inhibited obsessive-compulsive character structure whose main defenses are of a constricting and inhibiting kind." Under vocal masking he, too, became more productive. Along with the broadened scope of fantasy, however, many reminiscence responses going back to childhood, and heightened coloring by drive-related ideation, there also appeared exaggerated efforts to keep all these tendencies in check—for example, by undoing and negation responses of the kind described earlier; by an editing tendency that took the form of changing the direction of a word or of a sequence of words in the middle of a sentence; by efforts to put drive-related material into a context of priority, or with elaborate qualifiers erected around the drive-expressive responses. The changes in vocal quality were equally dramatic and consistent in this subject. His voice moved down into the lowest basso registers; speech became slowed, his words drawn out and prolonged like "my-y-y," with many sighs, pauses, and word-whiskers (ubiquitous "uhs" and "ahs" around the words). It is interesting that both subjects said later they were not aware of the changes in their voices. Both also reported they were disturbed less by the masking noise than by not being able to hear their voices, and it seems that in contrasting ways they were making an effort to compensate for this, in the one case by shouting, in the other case by emphasizing the low sound frequencies which would, to a certain extent, escape some of the masking range of frequencies in the white noise band.

We are far from understanding the shifts along many dimensions that seem to be occurring as a result of our experimental variations. The results are thus far an embarrassment of riches, which only more subjects, more experience with the technique, and a variety of experimental controls will enable us to classify and understand. However distinctive may be the effects of vocal isolation, it must be admitted that it is too early to conclude with certainty that the marked reduction in auditory feedback from one's voice is the sole factor in fashioning the changes that occur in the forms and qualities of voice and verbalization. Alternative explanations and qualifying considerations implicit in the experimental design still need to be ruled out. There is, first of all, the issue of vocal isolation being achieved by means of a masking *noise*. The subjects were not really deafened—they heard noise, and the noise was very much part of the situation. That is why I have been careful to speak of the situation as one of being "isolated from one's voice" rather than of "deafness." On the other hand, if there is reason to think that the noise is importantly involved in the effects, it is also our impression that it gains in importance precisely because it is associated with reduced vocal feedback. In the combination of the masked voice and the background of undifferentiated noise we may be creating a peculiarly *isolative* condition that is conducive to a wavering of controls and weakened reality-testing. The combination of reduced informative feedback from voice and monotonic sensory background of the noise, acting together, could have produced an occasion for intensified defense via vocal qualities and forms of language and for increasing the potentiality of peripheral lines of thought and of drive contents breaking through to awareness.

More definite and varied conclusions await further controls. There is of course the question of how much of the effect will be replicated under conditions where noise *alone* is present without impairing feedback. There is also the important issue of whether a situation of air-conduction or side-tone deafness but intact bone-conducted hearing (i.e., no noise accompaniment) will produce similar effects.

In respect to response analysis, moreover, much more attention will have to be given to vocal qualities *per se* in future studies. "The voice," in Baldwin's and Levin's words, "is a marvelously sensitive upsetometer! Voices quiver as the larynx tightens, the tongue trips over itself, there are long pauses while the mind is blank, thoughtless beginnings must be made sensible by awkward circumlocutions, and so on" (*2*). Such manifestations of speech are a very vital part of the controlling and expressive processes of communicated thought. How much of this is monitored by the hearing of one's own voice remains to be seen.

It is time to summarize. It makes a difference whether secondary-process thinking occurs in the context of overt speech or not. The difference is in the syntax of voiced communication, which is carried not only by words but by the expressive, communicative, and concealing capacities of the voice. Speech is an auditory affair as well as a motor-linguistic one, however, in which the speaker is also his own audience, with nature providing strong guarantees that the speaker will hear his own voice. It is possible that these guarantees assert the importance of a background of uninterrupted auditory feedback from one's own voice for monitoring spoken thought, for inhibiting peripheral lines of thought that otherwise would bear down on conscious purposeful thinking; it is a condition that normally may help to ensure synchrony between the logic of thought and its communication through speech. If sensory feedback is generally an important vehicle for maintaining a sense of reality and for making possible the testing of reality, then the auditory return to self as listener is perhaps also an indispensible medium for preserving these functions in communicated thinking. Thus, one avenue to regressive tendencies of communicated thought would be the disruption of this supportive, informative feedback from one's own voice. Our experiments, accordingly, have been concerned with what will happen to thinking when the monitoring function is thus impaired and yet the person still has to communicate—talk aloud—his thoughts.

Our conclusion, then, is simply this: A radical reduction of the normal auditory input from one's own voice against a background of undifferentiated white noise has disrupting effects upon behavior, producing an increase of drive-related contents into thought and a concomitant intensification of editing tendencies in speech. The conditions, generally, are conducive to ego-regressive tendencies including a movement toward primary-process varieties of thinking as well as exaggerated defensive and controlling emphases in thought processes.

I cannot conclude without a passing remark upon the possibility that vocal masking may have some future usefulness as a technical adjunct in therapy. In the same sense that the couch is not itself the basis of therapeutic change but provides an important condition for, or encouragement to, the appearance of ordinarily suppressed undercurrents of thought, so associations under conditions of vocal masking may, with some patients and in carefully selected circumstances, be similarly useful. In promoting a widened orbit of associations it may be therapeutically advantageous for a patient to 'freely associate' without being allowed to hear what he is saying. With some patients it might be a condition for promoting willingness to say aloud thoughts not otherwise easily expressed; for others it may, like the couch, be an occasion for intensifying defensive maneuvers. Of course, just as the decision to put a patient on the couch is not to be taken lightly, so would there have to be similar caution about using vocal isolation. We are, of course, far from the degree of understanding that would justify such application to therapy at this time.

REFERENCES

1 Allport, G. *Pattern and Growth in Personality.* New York, Holt, Rinehart & Winston, 1961.

2 Baldwin, A. L., and Levin, H. "Pride and Shame in Children." In *Nebraska Symposium on Motivation,* edited by M. R. Jones. Nebraska, Univ. of Nebraska Press, 1959.

3 Brown, E. L. "Human Performance and Behavior during Zero Gravity." In *Weightlessness—Physical Phenomena and Biological Effects,* edited by E. T. Benedikt, New York, Plenum Press, 1961.

4 Cherry, C. *On Human Communication.* Massachusetts, Technology Press; and New York, Wiley, 1957.

5 EAGLE, M. Personality correlates of sensitivity to subliminal stimuli. *J. nerv. ment. Dis. 134:*1–17, 1962.

6 FENICHEL, O. *The Psychoanalytic Theory of Neurosis.* New York, Norton, 1945.

7 FISKE, D. W., AND MADDI, S. R. *Functions of Varied Experience.* Illinois, Dorsey, 1961.

8 FREUD, S. "Notes upon a Case of Obsessional Neurosis" (first published in 1909). *The Standard Edition of the Complete Psychological Works of Sigmund Freud,* edited by J. Strachey, Vol. X. London, Hogarth and The Institute of Psychoanalysis, 1953, pp. 155–318.

9 FREUD, S. *The Origins of Psychoanalysis: Letters to Wilhelm Fliess, Drafts and Notes, 1887–1902,* translated by E. Mosbacher and J. Strasberg; edited by M. Bonaparte, A. Freud, and E. Kris. New York, Basic Books, 1954.

10 GERATHEWOHL, S. J. "Effect of Gravity-Free State." In *Environmental Effects on Consciousness,* edited by K. E. Schaeffer. New York, Macmillan, 1962, pp. 73–85.

11 GIBSON, J. J. "Perception as a Function of Stimulation." In *Psychology: A Study of a Science,* edited by S. Koch. Vol. I. *Sensory, Perceptual and Physiological Formulations.* New York, McGraw-Hill, 1959, pp. 456–501.

12 GLOVER, E. *On the Early Development of Mind.* New York, Int. Univ. Press, 1956.

13 GOLDBERGER, L. "The Isolation Situation and Personality." In *Proceedings of the IV International Congress of Applied Psychology,* edited by G. S. Nielsen. Vol. II. *Personality Research.* Copenhagen, Munksgaard, 1962.

14 GOLDBERGER, L., AND HOLT, R. R. "Experimental Interference with Reality Contact: Individual Differences. In *Sensory Deprivation,* edited by P. Solomon, P. E. Kubzansky, P. H. Leiderman, *et al.* Cambridge, Harvard Univ. Press, 1961.

15 HANRAHAN, T. S., AND BUSHNELL, D. *Space Biology: The Human Factors in Space Flight.* New York, Basic Books, 1960.

16 HARTMANN, H. *Ego Psychology and the Problem of Adaptation* (first published in 1939), translated by D. Rapaport. New York, Int. Univ. Press, 1958.

17 HEBB, D. O. "The Problem of Consciousness and Introspection." In *Brain Mechanisms and Consciousness,* edited by J. F. Delafresnaye. Springfield, Charles C Thomas, 1954, pp. 402–417.

18 HEBB, D. O. *A Textbook of Psychology.* Philadelphia, Saunders, 1958.

19 HEBB, D. O., HEATH, E. S., AND STUART, E. A. Experimental deafness. *Canad. J. Psychol. 8:*152–156, 1954.

20 HELD, R., AND HEIN, A. V. Adaptation of disarranged hand-eye coordination contingent upon re-afferent stimulation. *Percept. mot. Skills 8:*87–90, 1958.

21 HELD, R., AND SCHLANK, M. Adaptation to disarranged eye-hand coordination in the distance-dimension. *Amer. J. Psychol. 72:*603–605, 1959.

22 HELSON, H. "Adaptation Level Theory." In *Psychology: A Study of a Science,* edited by S. Koch. Vol. I. *Sensory, Perceptual and Physiological Formulations.* New York, McGraw-Hill, 1959, pp. 565–621.

23 HOLT, R. R., AND HAVEL, JOAN. "A Method for Assessing Primary and Second-

ary Process in the Rorschach." In *Rorschach Psychology,* edited by Maria A. Rickers-Ovsiankina. New York, Wiley, 1960, pp. 263–315.

24 Isakower, O. On the exceptional position of the auditory sphere. *Int. J. Psycho-Anal. 20:*340–348, 1939.

25 James, W. *Principles of Psychology.* London, Macmillan, 1890.

26 Klein, G. S. "On Inhibition, Disinhibition, and Primary Process in Thinking." In *Proceedings of the IV International Congress of Applied Psychology,* edited by G. S. Nielsen. Vol. IV. *Clinical Psychology.* Copenhagen, Munksgaard, 1962.

27 Kohler, I. Die methode des bulleversuchs in der wahrnehimungspsychologie mit bemerkungen zur lehre der adaptation. *Z. exp. angew. Psychol. 3:*381–387, 1956.

28 Kohler, I. On the structuring and transformation of the perceptual world (1951). Translated by H. Fiss. *Psychol. Issue 3*(4): Monograph 12, 1964.

29 Kubie, L. S. The value of induced dissociated state in the therapeutic process. *Proc. Roy. Soc. Med. 38:*681–683 (section of psychiatry, pp. 31–33), 1945.

30 Kubie, L. S. "Psychiatric and Psychoanalytic Considerations of the Problem of Consciousness." In *Brain Mechanisms and Consciousness,* edited by J. F. Delafresnaye. Springfield, Charles C Thomas, 1954, pp. 444–467; see also p. 421.

31 Kubie, L. S., and Margolin, S. A physiological method for the induction of states of partial sleep in securing free associations and early memories in such states. *Trans. Amer. Neurol. Ass.,* 1942, pp. 136–139.

32 Lashley, K. S. "The Problem of Serial Order in Behavior." In *Cerebral Mechanisms in Behavior,* edited by L. A. Jeffers. New York, Wiley, 1951.

33 Lashley, K. S. "Dynamic Processes in Perception." In *Brain Mechanisms and Consciousness,* edited by J. F. Delafresnaye. Springfield, Charles C Thomas, 1954, pp. 422–437.

34 Lashley, K. S. "Cerebral Organization and Behavior." In *The Brain and Human Behavior,* edited by H. C. Solomon, S. Cobb, and W. Penfield. Proceedings of the Association for Research in Nervous and Mental Disease, Vol. XXXVI. Baltimore, Williams and Wilkins, 1958.

35 Linton, Harriet B., and Langs, R. J. Subjective reactions to lysergic acid diethelamide (LSD-25). *Arch. gen. Psychiat. 6:*352–368, 1962.

36 Loewenstein, R. Remarks on the role of speech in psychoanalytic technique. *Int. J. Psycho-Anal. 37:*460–468, 1956.

37 Luria, A. R. *The Role of Speech in the Regulation of Normal and Abnormal Behavior.* New York, Liveright Publishing Corp., 1961.

38 Mahl, G. F. Sensory factors in the control of expressive behavior: An experimental study of the function of auditory self-stimulation and visual feedback in the dynamics of vocal and gestural behavior in the interview situation. Proc. Sixteenth Int. Cong. Psychol., 1960. *Acta psychol., Amsterdam 19:*497–498, 1961. (Abstract.)

39 Miller, G. A. *Language and Communication.* New York, McGraw-Hill, 1951.

40 Ostwald, P. F. "Human Sounds." In *Psychological and Psychiatric Aspects*

of Speech and Hearing, edited by D. A. Barbara. Springfield, Ill., Charles C Thomas, 1960, pp. 110–137.

41 Oswald, I. *Sleeping and Waking.* Amsterdam, Elsevier Publishing Co., 1962.

42 Rapaport, D. On the psychoanalytic theory of thinking. *Int. J. Psycho-Anal. 31:*161–170, 1950.

43 Rapaport, D. Review of "Cybernetics," by Norbert Weiner. *Psychoanal. Quart. 19:*598–603, 1950.

44 Skinner, B. F. *Verbal Behavior.* New York, Appleton-Century-Crofts, 1957.

45 Smith, K. U. *Delayed Sensory Feedback and Behavior.* Philadelphia, Saunders, 1962.

46 Smith, K. U., and Smith, W. M. *Perception and Motion: An Analysis of Space-Structured Behavior.* Philadelphia, Saunders, 1962.

47 Stone, L. *The Psychoanalytic Situation.* New York, Int. Univ. Press, 1961.

48 Von Bekesy, G., and Rosenblith, W. A. "The Mechanical Properties of the Ear." In *Handbook of Experimental Psychology,* edited by S. S. Stevens. New York, Wiley, 1951.

49 Weiner, N. *Cybernetics.* Massachusetts, Technology Press; and New York, Wiley, 1948.

50 Zangwill, O. "Speech." In *Handbook of Physiology,* edited by J. Field, A. W. Magoun, and V. E. Hall. Vol. III. *Neurophysiology.* Washington, D.C., Amer. Physiol. Soc., 1959, pp. 1709–1722.

51 Zubek, J. P., and Wilgosh, L. Prolonged immobilization of the body: Changes in performance and in the electroencephalogram. *Science 140:*306–308, 1963.

FOURTEEN

The Organismic State Associated with Dreaming

FREDERICK SNYDER, M.D.

It might be argued that Freud's insights into the meaning of dreams were the most important not only of his lifetime, as he stated, but of our entire intellectual era—directly from them came that new perspective which has vastly enriched so many aspects of human understanding. The topic of this paper, however, neither arises directly from the perspective of psychoanalysis nor contributes directly to the psychological understanding of dreams. Rather, it is concerned with dreaming as a biological phenomenon.

To those who have pondered the relationship of mind and body dreaming has been of unique interest from antiquity. Conjecture whether its physical basis is the same or different from that of waking psychic life dates from Plato, who localized rational thoughts and perceptions in the head but placed that part of the soul concerned with dreaming in the liver. As the history of this question has been traced, by the scholarship of Evarts, from the writings of Plato to the contributions of contemporary neurophysiology (*28*), the trend of thinking has been to assume that the same central structures are involved in both dreaming and waking perception—i.e., the primary visual cortex. Yet, this does not permit the generalization that the functional state of the brain as a whole is the same, and even within the modern era there have also been those who inferred a basic difference in the underlying physiological mechanisms. In the first chapter of the "Interpretation of Dreams" (*34*) Freud quoted from Fechner's *Elemente der Psychophysik:*

> If the scene of action of psychophysical activity were the same in sleeping and waking, dreams could, in my view, only be a prolongation at a lower degree of intensity of waking ideational life, and moreover, would necessarily be of the same material and form. But the facts are quite otherwise. . . . It is as though psycho-

logical activity had been transported from the brain of a reasonable man into that of a fool.

Fechner referred here to the infantile, primitive quality of dreaming ideation, and I assume that Hughlings Jackson (*43*) had similar considerations in mind when he wrote:

> Suppose a man is asleep and dreaming: for this double psychical condition of two opposites, there is a corresponding double physical condition, also of two opposites, of the highest level; there is loss of function, of, I will suppose, the highest "layer," answering to the negative part of the sleeper's mental condition and there are increased activities of the uncontrolled lower layers which answer to the mentation of his dream.

Although these ideas are highly relevant to our present concerns, many years were to elapse before experimental techniques could be brought to bear upon them. Freud chose to dismiss the possibility of giving Fechner's statement an anatomical or physiological interpretation, and in the meantime he dared to pursue his unique inspirations. As later elaborated in the conception of the primary process, he proclaimed that those same primitive and infantile forces so obviously manifest in dreams actually pervade the entirety of psychic process. Thus, although not addressing himself directly to the physiological problem, Freud's insight into the profound importance of dreaming as a subject for scientific inquiry greatly deepened the implications of that problem; psychoanalysis offers the faith that, to whatever extent we can understand how the brain produces its private world of nightly visions, at the same time we will fundamentally advance our knowledge of the organismic basis of all mental life.

Knowledge of the relationship between brain function and psychic experience may still fall short of testing Fechner's inference, yet I propose to elaborate a theme previously suggested (*84*)—that experimental studies over the past decade do begin to define a unique physiological state distinct both from sleeping, in the usual sense, and from waking; and that in man, at least, dreaming is the experiential aspect of that state.[1] It is the further burden of my paper that, even though our awareness of the psychodynamic significance of dreams has provided much of the remarkable impetus for these studies, this hitherto unsuspected biological state is of great interest, and perhaps of importance, quite aside from the relationship to dreaming. Yet even if the ultimate biological significance of this third state should prove to be divergent from the influences which have nurtured its investigation, our indebtedness

---

[1]This in not intended as a systematic review of developments in the experimental study of sleep and dreaming, which has been done much more comprehensively elsewhere (*22, 23, 58*). Even in elaborating this particular point of view concerning these developments, I give greatly unbalanced emphasis to those studies I know best—my own and my colleagues'.

to psychoanalysis would be no less. In an important sense, this is an instance in which physiology, too, has been enriched by psychoanalysis.

DISCOVERY OF THE RAPID EYE MOVEMENT STATE[2]

Dreams are among the most elusive and subjective of our experiences, yet this discussion can begin with some very simple observations which anyone can repeat at home on his children, his wife, or the pet cat. These most obvious phenomena were unobserved until 1952 and probably would not have been noted then if it were not for the perseverance of a young graduate student who found it impossible to define a "blink" (*4*). Eugene Aserinsky, working in the physiology laboratory of Dr. Nathaniel Kleitman at the University of Chicago, had been tediously watching infants for almost a year trying to test some assumptions about the frequency of eye blinking during wakefulness and sleep. The difficulty was that these infants did all sorts of strange things with their eyes, and Aserinsky concluded that the "blink" was operationally indefinable. To proceed with his thesis he was driven to reformulating the problem in terms of counting any eyelid movements over the course of the infants' sleep cycle. When he did this he made an intriguing discovery: there were times during the infants' sleep when the eyelids were quiescent, strikingly contrasted with other times when they were in active movement. Those periods when eyelid movements occurred were also marked by diffuse bodily movement, whereas the eyelid quiescent periods were times of complete repose. Watching very intently by now, Aserinsky found that these two states alternated in approximately equal intervals, and with quite constant periodicity of about 60 minutes throughout the infants' sleep (*6*).

Aserinsky and Kleitman were quick to look for the same phenomena during the sleep of adults and found that they were unmistakably and invariably present, although different in certain respects to be mentioned later (*5, 7*). Use of the electroencephalogram permitted remote monitoring and revealed that the eyelid movements were actually due to rapid movements of the eyes themselves underneath. Still more intriguing, during those periods of sleep when they occurred there was an equally striking change in the EEG rhythms. The well-known sleep pattern of high-voltage slow waves with sleep spindles was replaced during the rapid eye movement (REM) periods by a low-voltage irregular pattern without spindling, very similar to that of the activated waking state. This is illustrated from records taken in our own laboratory in Figure 14.1. The same pattern had been previously noted during sleep and described by various names, but the regular periodicity of its

---

[2]In keeping with Dr. Oken's topic, this heading might have been "The Importance of Operational Definitions."

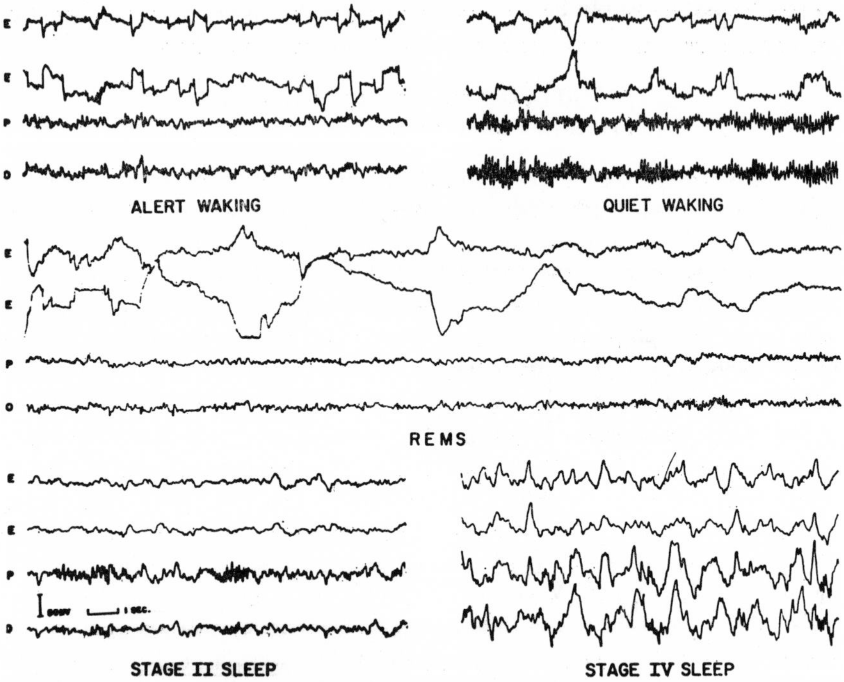

Fig. 14.1.—Human EEG and REM patterns during waking, sleep and REMS. All recordings with reference to both earlobes; electrode placements: *E*=lateral to each eye, *P*=parietal, *O*=occipital. In the REMS EEG note the complete lack of spindling or K complexes and the resemblance to that of alert waking.

occurrence (as shown in Figure 14.2) and its constant association with burst of rapid eye movements had not been observed.

THE RELATIONSHIP OF REM PERIODS TO DREAM RECALL

This unique pattern of physiological events led Aserinsky and Kleitman to surmise that dreaming might be taking place at these times, and in the first test of this correlation their subjects recalled dreams in 74 per cent of the awakenings during REM phases of sleep and in only 7 per cent of the non-REM phases. In the interval since then, and especially during the last five years, this relationship has been examined in many laboratories, and Table 14.1 summarizes some of the more systematic studies which have tested it.

It is apparent that the various investigators have used varying criteria for deciding whether a given response should be considered a positive instance of dream recall. Even when these criteria are similarly worded, they are sufficiently vague that there might be considerable latitude in applying them.

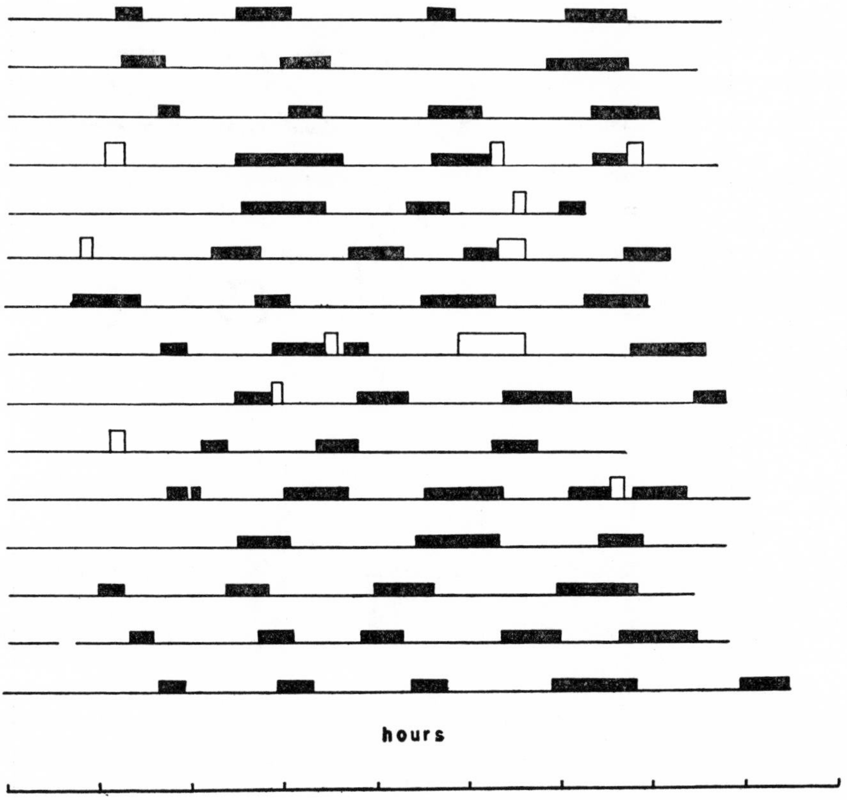

Fig. 14.2.—Periodicity of REMS in uninterrupted human sleep. Examples selected at random of the occurrence of REMS over entire nights of uninterrupted sleep in fifteen young adult subjects. Solid bars = REMS; open bars = waking; single line = non-REMS sleep.

Moreover, neither the nature of the subject samples nor the experimental conditions were uniform among these studies.[3] Despite these discrepancies there is complete agreement among the studies that dream recall is much more frequently elicited from REM sleep.

Should we expect a perfect correlation, there are two faults which we would find with this evidence: first, that dream recall is not always associated with awakenings from REM sleep; and, second, that it is sometimes associated with non-REM sleep—in some of the studies very frequently indeed. The first problem should not trouble us. Dream memories are notoriously evanescent, and we ask a great deal of the sleep-fogged brain that it be in-

[3]Systematic study of the effects upon dream recall of the many possible variations in experimental conditions is just beginning (*81, 97*).

TABLE 14.1

Study and ref.	No. subj. nights	No. subj.	Criteria of dream recall	REM awakenings		NREM awakenings	
				No.	% dream recall	No.	% dream recall
Aserinsky and Kleitman (*7*)	14	10	Definite recall of dream content; detailed dream descriptions	27	74	23	7
Dement (*19*)	18	10	Vivid recall of content	51	88	19	0
Dement and Kleitman (*25*)	61	9	Coherent, fairly detailed description of dream content	191	79	160	7
Wolpert and Trosman (*97*)	51	10	Detailed recall of complete drama	54	85	37	0
Goodenough *et al.* (*35*)	48	16	A dream recalled in some detail	91	69	99	34
Jouvet *et al.* (*51*)	15	4	Not specified	20	60	30	3
Snyder (*83*)	46	16	Content recalled in some detail	148	62	89	13
Wolpert (*96*)	20	8	Not specified	67	85	21	24
Kremen, Series II (*60*)	9	9	Subject's impression of having been dreaming, regardless of content recall	28	75	29	12
Rechtschaffen *et al.* (*74*)	30	17	Some specific content	186	86	96	23
Foulkes (*32*)	57	8	Specific content, either with sensory imagery or altered identity or physical setting	108	82	136	54
Orlinsky (*68*)	240	25	Any specific content	502	86	406	42
Snyder and Hobson	43	10	Recall of complex visual imagery with some progression of events	206	72	114	13

Both figures and criteria of dream recall were not always presented in precisely the same form by the authors, and therefore in some cases the selection shown here is based upon my own reading of the reports.

stantly mobilized to capture and transmit these fleeting phantasms. Some subjects are able to do this almost unfailingly, whereas others rarely succeed. It is fortunate that the first subjects studied by Aserinsky and Kleitman were not examples of the latter. I need not labor the point that this is a highly charged interpersonal situation: the experimenter manipulates the subject's body, watches over his sleep, repeatedly jolts him out of it, and then expects him to divulge his most private experiences. There are a number of comments indicating that this is more similar to a clinical relationship than to an aseptically controlled laboratory procedure (*57, 92*). We should not be concerned that dream recall does not always result; it is all the more remarkable that under these experimental conditions it is forthcoming so consistently.

The second problem—why dream recall ever arises from non-REM sleep and why this happened so frequently in some of the studies—is a more troubling one and has been the subject of much recent controversy among the workers in this field. If we define dreaming as any sort of mental activity during sleep, then it now seems probable that there is no dreamless sleep. However, there is agreement that the reports arising from non-REM sleep are generally quite different from those of REM sleep. This has been systematically studied by a number of investigators, including those who report a high incidence of dream recall from non-REM sleep (*32, 54, 74*). The results of these studies agree that the mentation recalled from non-REM sleep is much less elaborate, vivid, or visual than that recalled from REM sleep, and much more like thinking about contemporary events. Although there are rare instances when this is not the case, the non-REM sleep recall is typically a mere fragment, vague and thoughtlike.

Do we refer to any sort of mental activity remembered from sleep when we speak of our dreams? Aristotle clearly distinguished between dreaming and other kinds of mental activity during sleep,[4] and the same distinguishing characteristics were emphasized by Freud in the first chapter of his masterwork, where he extracted the consensus of many previous authors concerning the psychological attributes of dream ideation (*34*). The essential difference upon which all authorities agreed was that thought activity of the waking state takes place in concepts, whereas dream thoughts are expressed as perceptual, primarily visual, images—i.e., dreams are hallucinations. Of course, hallucinatory imagery also occurs in the hypnogogic and many other conditions; dreaming has the additional attribute that constructed out of these images are complex situations which have a narrative development: they are

[4]Nor should the true thoughts, as distinct from the mere presentations, which occur in sleep (be called dreams). The dream proper is a presentation based on the movement of sense impressions, when such presentation occurs during sleep, taking sleep in the strict sense of the term" (*3*).

dramas, and the dreamer is a passive audience to them. The enumeration of these characteristics seems to be as much a definition of the dream as Freud cared to offer, though he himself did not always adhere to it. A totally different use of the word might prove more fruitful, but it is most pertinent that those empirically derived criteria which distinguish the experiences reported from REM sleep are highly congruent with this older definition.[5]

Definitions are arbitrary and imperfect, and there is always the danger that we will define away the very essence of the living phenomenon which interests us. From this standpoint there is much to recommend the approach used by Kremen (*60*) ; he simply instructed his subjects to employ their own subjective criteria as to whether or not they had been dreaming, regardless of whether they remembered the content of their experience. The correlation he found is still not perfect, but it would be naive to expect a better correlation between physiological and psychological phenomena under these conditions; the relationship between the EEG patterns of sleep and the recognition of having been asleep probably would be no better. Much more could be said about the evidence for this relationship, but I will go on now to the further studies which it has stimulated. Even if future investigation can, in some fashion, establish conclusively that dreaming takes place at times other than those now identified, the proposition that dreaming is associated with the physiological pattern described has demonstrated its heuristic value.

The fact that dreams are recalled with this degree of predictability when subjects are awakened during the regular occurrence of the REM pattern does not prove any inherent relationship between the two. It could be argued, for example, that this pattern looks like 'light' sleep, and it is not surprising that people are more capable of recall, or confabulation, when aroused from it. As we shall see, the assumption that this is 'light' sleep is controversial; but, beyond this, much painstaking work by Dement and his associates has been devoted to demonstrating that there is a much more specific correspondence between the physiological events and the content of the dreams recalled.

This is indicated by a high correlation between the subjective duration of the elicited dreams and the length of the REM periods prior to awakening; by the fact that fragmented dreams were more likely to be remembered if the period had been broken up by major body movements; and by the in-

---

[5]For the purposes of this discussion we have examined some of our latest experimental material in terms of these few explicit criteria. Transcriptions of reports obtained after awakening from both REM and non-REM sleep were rated blindly by an investigator who had not been involved in the experimental procedure itself. Reports were labeled as dreaming or not dreaming on the basis of whether they conveyed a complex, visually experienced situation which had undergone some progression or unfolding. The results of this test are summarized in the last entry of Table 14.1. Since these are stringent criteria, the percentages obtained from both REM and non-REM awakenings are relatively low.

corporation of subawakening stimuli into the dream plots (*26*). These experiments indicated that the temporal course of the dream experience at least roughly parallels the duration of the specific physiological pattern, but a much more precise correspondence came from relating the complex patterns of eye movements to the dream imagery which the subject remembered. It was first demonstrated that REM periods with minimal ocular activity are associated with passive dreams, whereas frequent and large eye movements are associated with active dreams (*26*). Other investigators, who were initially skeptical of this correlation, have since confirmed it (*11*), and it is further supported by a recent study in our own laboratory (*39*).

The earlier study (*26*) also attempted a more difficult test by comparing the last action in the hallucinated visual experience with the direction of the very last activity prior to awakening. In this series the correspondence between the two was clear in 74 per cent of instances; for example, when the last reported dream activity was picking up an object from the floor, the last eye movement was downward. A still more rigorous test of the same hypothesis depended upon the ability of an experimenter to predict the direction, timing, and sequence of REM's with only the subjects' dream reports as data (*76*). When dream recall was vivid, this kind of prediction was successfully accomplished by independent judges in 75–80 per cent of instances. It would be extremely difficult to explain these results except by assuming that the eye movements directly reflect the events of the dreamer's hallucinatory experience and that this experience unfolds concomitant with the physiological events.[6]

VEGETATIVE CHANGE DURING THE REM PERIODS

The distinguishing physiological characteristics of the REMS[7] are not limited to the EEG and eye movement patterns but encompass a broad constellation of physiological changes. Present knowledge of the extent of this pattern is limited only by our ingenuity in devising techniques of physiological measurement compatible with undisturbed sleep. This means that in humans we are virtually restricted to those variables which can be studied from the body periphery, but among almost all of these thus far studied significant differences have been found in the REMS as compared with the rest of sleep.

---

[6]Should it seem incredible that such striking phenomena had not been observed earlier, I shall digress occasionally to indicate that various aspects of the REMS had indeed been noted or predicted much earlier. With regard to the eye movements, G. T. Ladd introspected in 1892 that during dreaming "the eyeballs move gently in their sockets, taking various positions induced by the retinal phantasms as they control the dream (*61*).

[7]The abbreviation REMS will be used throughout to refer to this entire constellation of physiological changes. The *S* may stand for 'Sleep' or for 'State,' according to the reader's preference.

The psychoanalytic view of dreaming posits that this is a mode of discharge for some of the most intense and primitive aspects of our emotional beings. With this in mind, we have found it especially interesting to examine those vegetative functions which might be most expressive of affectful events. In their original study Aserinsky and Kleitman found that respiratory rate averaged 20 per cent higher and pulse rate 10 per cent higher during REM periods in human subjects than during non-REM (NREM) sleep just before or after (*5, 7*). Kamiya reports changes in the same direction, but of lesser magnitude (*54*). Our own studies have confirmed the increases in mean respiratory and heart rate, but we have been much more impressed by the variability of these functions during REM sleep (*83*). With the onset of the REM periods respiration especially became extremely erratic and irregular in both amplitude and rate (as shown in Figure 14.3), though it is only the

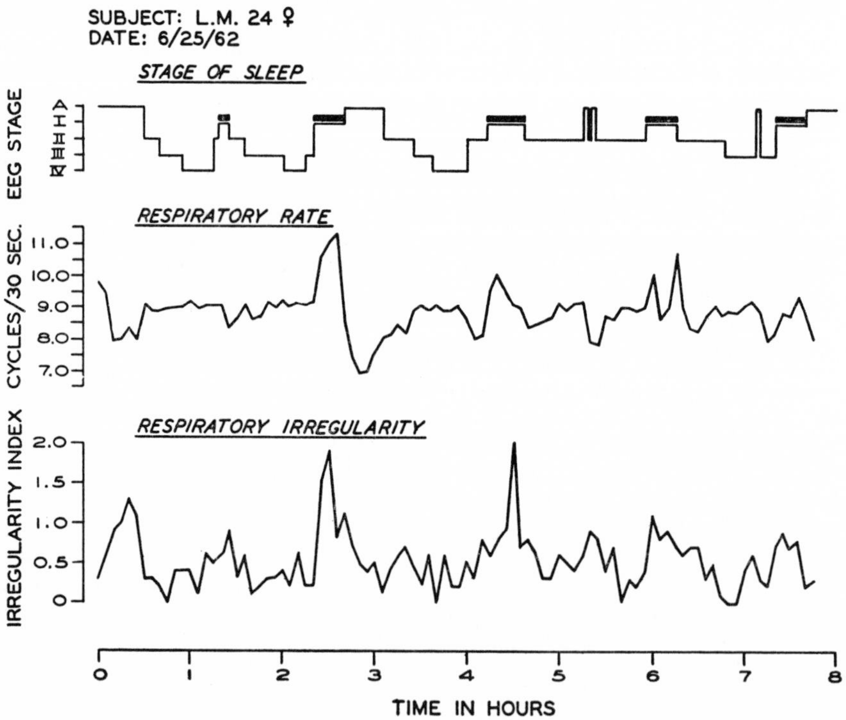

Fig. 14.3.—Respiratory rate and irregularity in uninterrupted sleep. Curves are based upon continuous 30-second counts of respiration throughout the night. The irregularity index is the average successive difference, obtained by summing the differences from one 30-second count to the next over 5-minute samples and dividing by N-1. Solid bars in upper diagram=REMS. (No implication concerning 'depth' of sleep is intended by this manner of diagramming the sleep cycle.)

latter that we have studied quantitatively. In my first attempts to quantify this increased variability I compared the average deviations of respiratory cycle lengths over five-minute intervals of REM and NREM sleep. This proved to be a happy, even though arbitrary, choice of measures, since it distinguished almost absolutely between the two states within individual subject nights as illustrated in Figure 14.4. Jouvet and his colleagues in France had

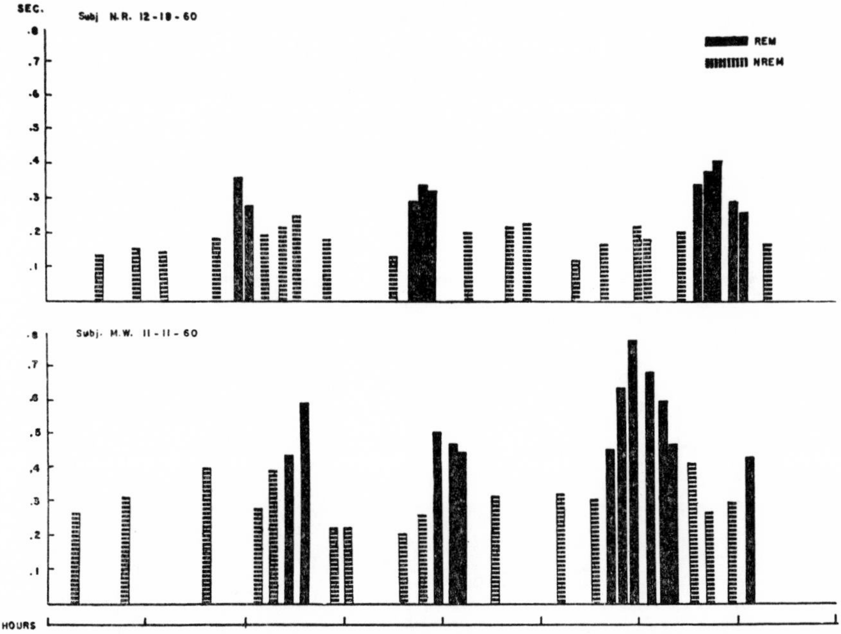

Fig. 14.4.—Respiratory variability in sleep (average deviations of cycle durations in 5-minute random samples). Each bar represents a 5-minute sample of sleep which was free of gross body movements. Within such samples all respiratory cycles on the polygraph record were manually measured, the average deviations obtained in mm., and these converted to seconds (paper speed 10 mm./sec.).

independently noted the respiratory variability in humans (*51*), and it has since been confirmed in a number of laboratories (*22, 75, 80*). As a diagnostic index respiration has the advantage that it can be made audible, and the occurrence of dreaming can be guessed about simply from the pattern of amplified breath sounds. However, since there are also transient periods of respiratory irregularity during NREM sleep, this would not be a highly reliable indicator, and it is only by the laborious measurement and comparison of 5-minute time samples of the written record that it becomes one. Nevertheless, there are frequent episodes of very rapid or markedly irregular respiration during the REM periods such as can never be found during the rest of sleep; for reasons which I shall soon mention, these are particularly favorable times to elicit dream recall.

Since respiration is under the control of both vegetative and voluntary nervous systems, it has an unusual repertoire of variations which have long been utilized by poets and novelists to express subjective reactions. When we turn to purely vegetative phenomena, such as the heart rate, we can expect much less variation. Even so, the average heart rate during the REMS is consistently higher than during the rest of sleep, and this is largely owing to the fact that there are frequent but transient periods of marked acceleration. Once again, irregularity is the most salient feature of the heart rate during the REMS, as shown in Figure 14.5

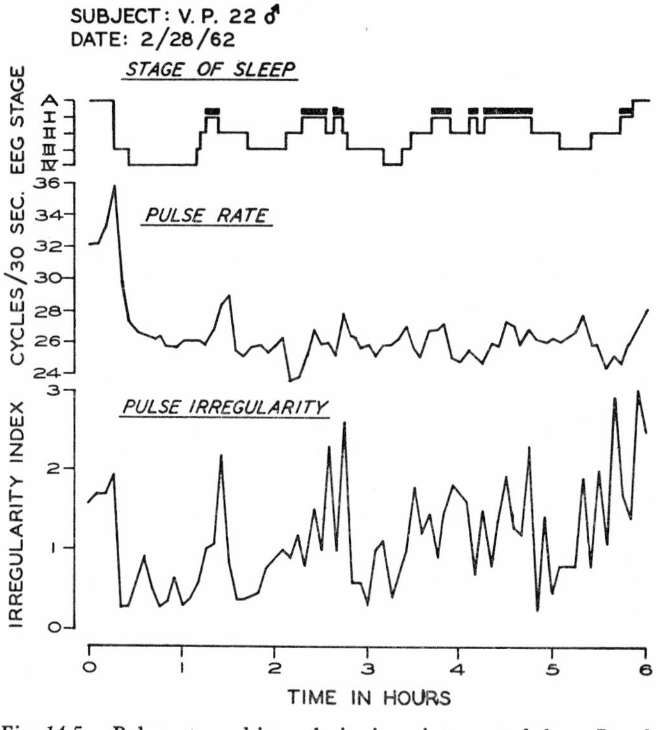

Fig. 14.5.—Pulse rate and irregularity in uninterrupted sleep. Based upon 30-second pulse rate counts throughout the night. In this case also the irregularity index is the average successive differences from one 30-second count to the next.

The measurement of blood pressure during human sleep is a peculiarly difficult problem, both because the positional changes seriously alter the measure and because any available technique will cause some discomfort to the subject. We have recently arrived at a method which, we believe, minimizes these difficulties and has enabled us to obtain records of systolic blood pressure at 1-minute intervals throughout entire nights of human sleep (*86*). In a systematic study of blood pressure, together with heart and respiratory rates (*87*), we obtained curves such as the one illustrated in Figure 14.6. There is a rapid decrease in systolic level beginning prior to

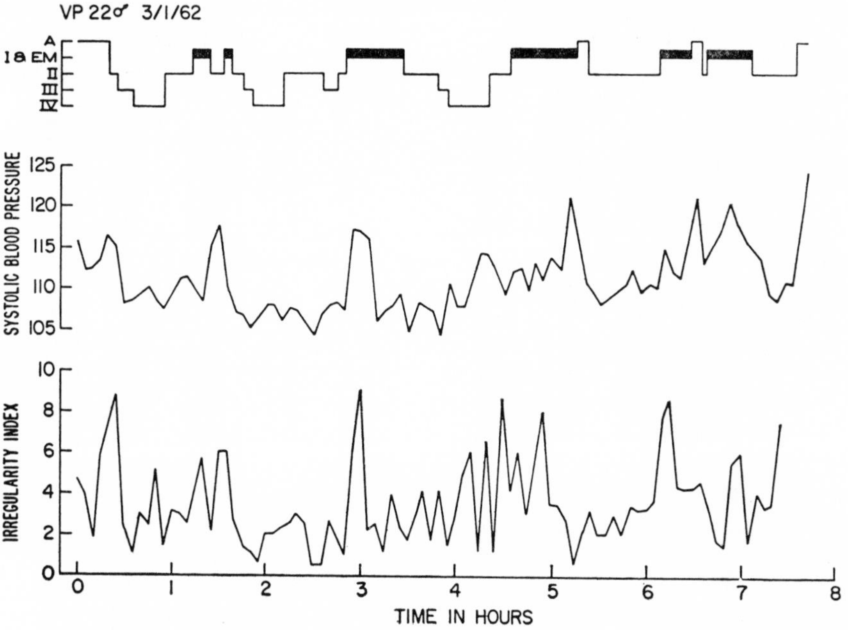

Fig. 14.6.—Blood pressure and irregularity during uninterrupted sleep. In this case curves are based upon once-a-minute determinations throughout the night, and the irregularity index is the average successive differences over 5-minute samples.

sleep onset and reaching its trough within the first one or two hours, after which there is a gradual and irregular upward trend throughout the rest of the sleep period. Aside from numerous and transient elevations which accompany gross body movements or brief arousals, the variability of the systolic level within NREM sleep takes the form of minor oscillations around a relatively stable baseline. Against this background there are reasonably predictable changes of two kinds which occur during the REM periods. In 69 per cent of instances there was at least a small increase in mean systolic level as compared with the previous 20 minutes of sleep, and in 79 per cent the level was higher than that during the subsequent 20-minute periods. Over-all, the average increase in systolic blood pressure during REM sleep was only 4 per cent, but this was consistent in that eleven of twelve subjects showed higher mean levels during this stage than in the others. Again, the marked and erratic variability of systolic blood pressure during REM sleep was the most significant finding. Calculating this in terms of the successive differences from one minute to the next, within 5-minute samples, we arrived at an over-all average increase of 50 per cent for systolic blood pressure variability during the REMS. As shown in Figure 14.7, these changes, like those in respiration

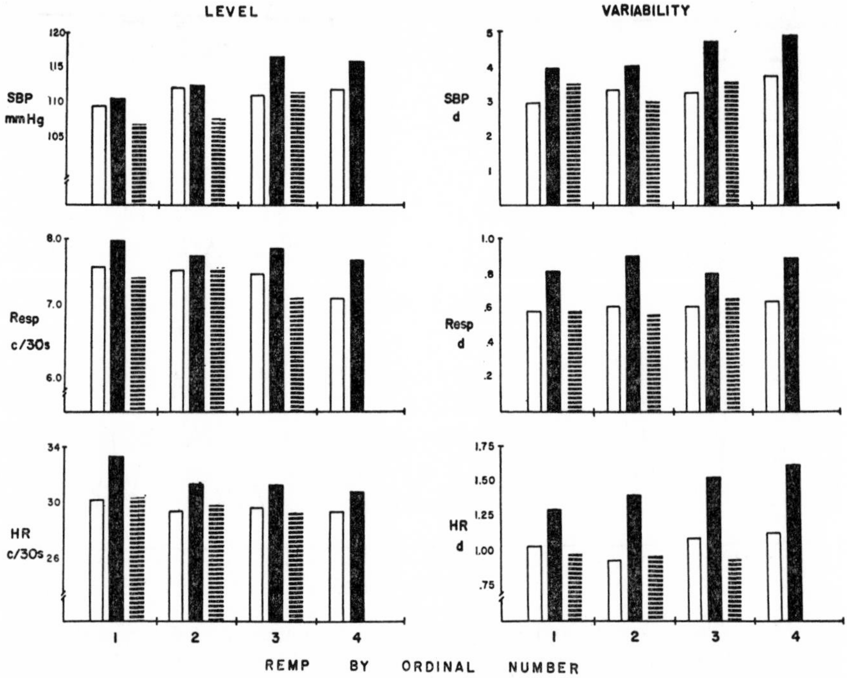

Fig. 14.7.—Blood pressure, respiration and heart rate in uninterrupted sleep. Represents mean levels and variability of systolic blood pressure, respiration, and heart rate in all night records of twelve subjects during successive REMS periods (solid bars) and periods of 20 minutes just prior (open bars) and 20 minutes just after (hatched bars; ref. *87*). Again, the variability index is the average successive difference over 5-minute samples. In each case the variability measure distinguishes more clearly between the REMS and surrounding sleep, and in the case of systolic blood pressure and heart rate this is more conspicuous in the later REMS periods.

and pulse rate, were much more consistent and conspicuous for the third and fourth REM periods of the night than for the first and second, suggesting that REMS is not always entirely the same phenomenon.

Such changes in blood pressure would probably be related to changes in peripheral vascular tone. We had observed such vasomotor changes, as have others (*93*), even prior to obtaining the blood pressure measures; but for technical reasons they are more difficult to demonstrate consistently. If one records the pulsations of the peripheral vessels of the hands with a finger plethysmograph, there is a marked waxing and waning of pulse amplitude during the REMS, periods of constriction often accompanying particularly active bursts of eye movements, respiratory irregularity, and blood pressure elevation. Since this vasoconstriction would involve an average decrease in blood flow, it is probably the same phenomenon which is reflected in the lowering of finger skin temperature which we have observed as a regular concomitant of the REM periods.

In view of the wide fluctuations of other autonomic functions, one might expect significant changes in basal skin resistance or in the psychologists' old favorite—the galvanic skin response. Reports concerning this are conflicting. Hawkins *et al.* (*37*) found that, instead of a hypothesized fall in basal skin resistance, there was a rise during REMS. This contrasts with another report (*54*) that there is no consistent change in basal skin resistance in relation to the REM periods, and our own experience is in agreement with this. There are formidable technical difficulties in recording of basal skin resistance over such long durations and under the conditions of these studies, and the last word on the matter must await their solution. It is clear, however, that there are no consistent drops of basal skin resistance in REMS, as we would expect if it were simply light sleep or partial arousal. A number of observers have also noted that spontaneous galvanic skin responses are much less frequent during REMS than during the surrounding sleep (*80*).

Although the situation with regard to skin resistance is still unclear, it is otherwise evident that REMS is markedly different from the rest of sleep in terms of the behavior of autonomic functions. It is characteristic of NREM sleep that these functions manifest a low and stable level of activity, whereas in REMS they show a most striking and unpredictable flux and change.[8] This is illustrated from typical 5-minute curves of respiration, heart rate, and systolic blood pressure in Figure 14.8.

Marked changes in various functions, as well as in eye movement patterns, tend to occur together, but this is not invariably the case; and the over-all intercorrelation of changes in these measures tends to be low. Indeed, a

---

[8]This is another instance in which there have been isolated observations in the past which were not pursued. In 1923 MacWilliams (*64*) reported that disturbances of blood pressure indicated the occurrence of dreaming, as did accelerations and irregularities of heart action and respiration. Even though MacWilliams did not have EEG monitoring, and one might question the validity of his blood pressure measures done after awakening, I have no doubt that he was observing the same striking phenomena that we have studied. MacWilliams related his report to the high incidence of cardiovascular catastrophes during sleep, and this is an aspect of considerable medical importance which deserves much further investigation.

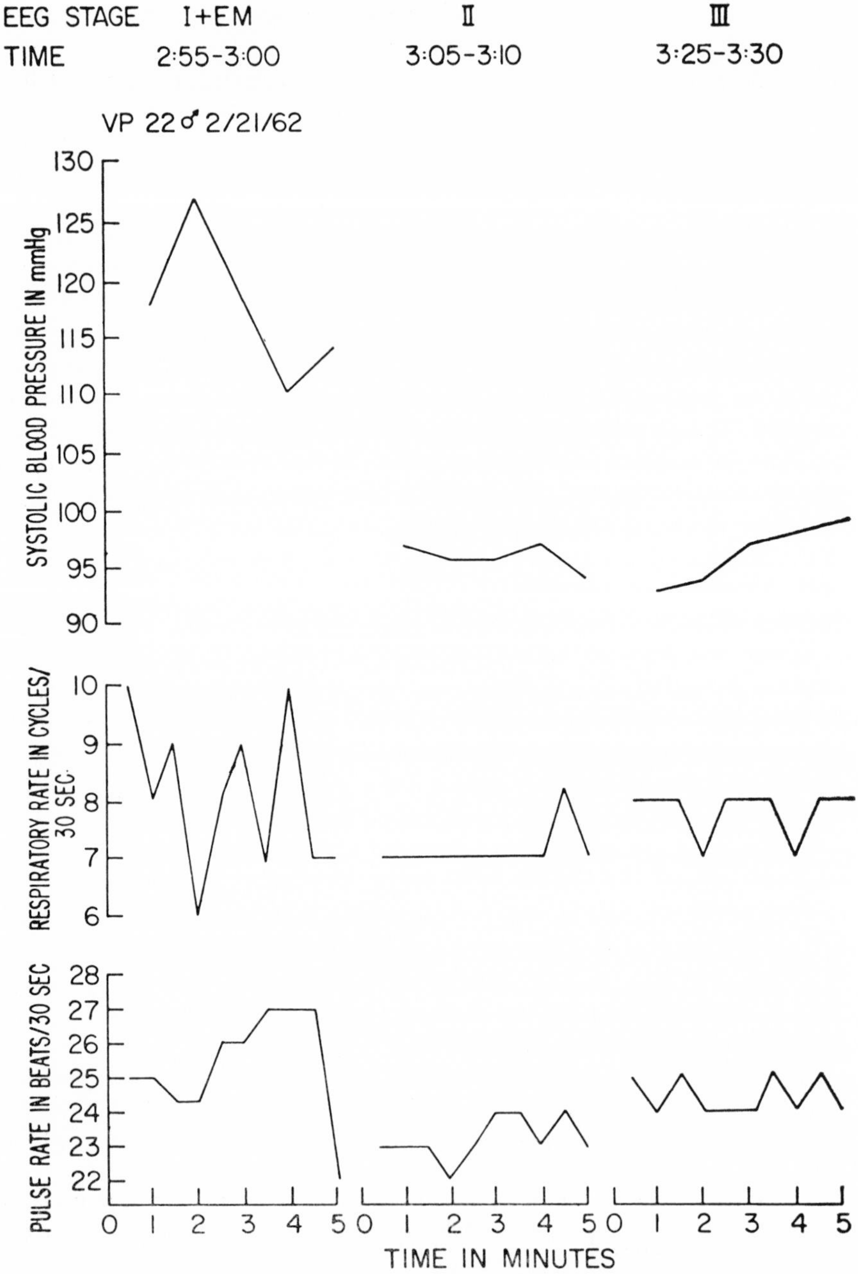

Fig. 14.8.—Blood pressure, respiratory rate, and pulse rate in 5-minute samples of uninterrupted sleep. This is to illustrate in detail the typical differences between REMS and the rest of sleep in terms of the short-term variability of autonomic functions. In the case of blood pressure this is based upon 1-minute determinations, while respiration and heart rate counts were made every 30 seconds.

great many patterns of change occur, and it is tantalizing to think that this patterning is a physiologic code from which we might learn much more about the dream experience as it occurs, and about somatic participation in subjective states generally.

Our attempts to demonstrate such parallels have not been entirely discouraging but yield nothing like the close correspondence found between the dreamer's visual experience and the patterning of eye movements. As I shall soon mention, there are good reasons to wonder whether the marked vegetative irregularity during the REM state has anything to do with the content of the dream experience; but, if one assumes that it does, there are also good reasons why it might prove difficult to demonstrate such a relationship. If such changes reflect emotional experience, current knowledge provides little indication of what specific changes to expect in relation to specific emotional states (*88*). On the other hand, they might also reflect the physical exertions or the vividness of the dream experience, to mention just a few possibilities. It poses a further difficulty that such changes are rarely such discrete events as are the eye movements, any more than the subjective features are as discrete as changes in visual fixation.

If our experimental subjects frequently experienced extremely emotional dreams or "nightmares," we might still expect to find some gross differences between the concomitant physiological patterns and those of more pallid dreams. Unfortunately, such dreams are rarely forthcoming under the conditions of these studies. The few instances when they have occurred yield only anecdotal support, and we must be wary of such evidence in dream research.

In one instance during the course of an unrelated study the respiratory and heart rates were seen to accelerate remarkably during the course of an REM period. The change was so unusual that the subject was abruptly awakened after a few minutes, even though this was not part of the experimental design. He then reported a very vivid and frankly sexual dream which had resulted in seminal emission just prior to awakening.

The majority of dream reports obtained in the laboratory tend to be less spectacular. Perhaps this is true of dreams generally, and we tend to remember only the occasional, more interesting ones from which we awaken.

For these reasons, thus far there have been few systematic attempts to relate the physiological characteristics of the REM periods to the nature of the dream experience. Shapiro *et al.* (*80*) have recently confirmed an earlier observation of my own (*83*) that dream recall is more vivid from those REM periods with greater respiratory irregularity, but pilot attempts to find relationships with specific aspects of dream content have not been promising. In a renewed attack upon this problem (*39*) my colleagues and I have recently concentrated on one particular variable, the respiratory record, and within this upon the short-term events which can be discretely identified. Against the background of generally heightened variability there are a number of such patterns that stand out, such as those illustrated in Figure 14.9.

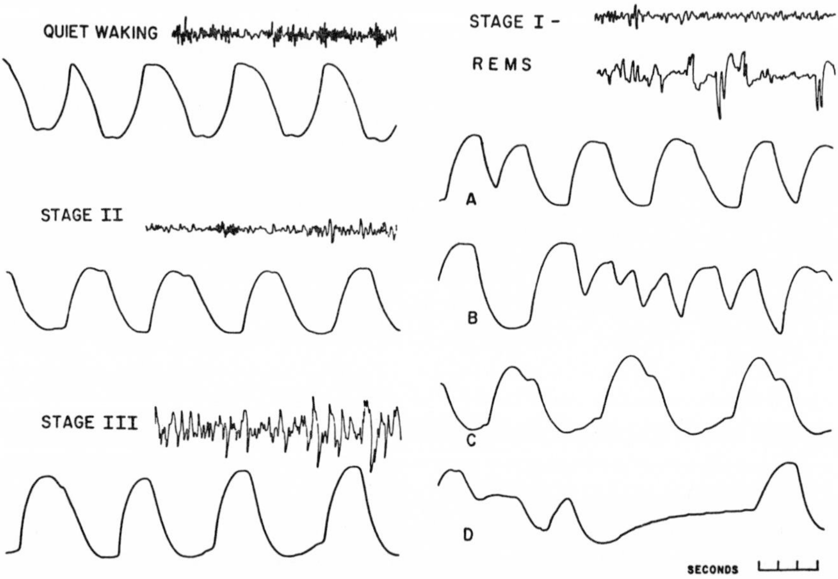

Fig. 14.9.—Characteristic patterns of human respiratory rhythm in REMS as compared with sleep and quiet waking. Under Stage I–REMS: *A*=General irregularity; *B*=transient acceleration; *C*=transient slowing; and *D*=Apnea.

At times, for brief periods the respiration becomes very rapid or very slow, quite often there are long apneic pauses, and frequently there are episodes of particularly marked irregularity. The dreamer was awakened as quickly as possible when such events occurred; he had been previously instructed to focus his attention upon the very last events of the dream experience prior to awakening. The dream content reported was rated on ten-point scales for vividness, emotionality, and physical activity by one of us who has no knowledge of the corresponding respiratory record, whereas the respiratory samples for each subject were divided into categories of high, medium, and low rates and high, medium, and low variability. The analysis of these data is still incomplete but thus far indicates that dreams rated high in emotionality, physical activity, or vividness do tend to obtain from awakenings immediately after periods of rapid or irregular respiration. Since there is a strong tendency for the three content ratings to co-vary (i.e., highly emotional dreams are usually very active and involve much physical activity), the data from this study are too meager to reveal more precise relationships. For the present we can conclude merely that there is some parallel between these physiological measures and the over-all 'intensity' of the remembered experience.

THE REM STATE AS A BASIC BIOLOGICAL FUNCTION

We have seen that to a degree, at least, the physiological changes during the REM state do seem to reflect the psychological experience of the dreamer and could be explained as reactions of the body to hallucinatory experience which happened to be occurring. It would not be surprising if a cat confronted with a mouse, or a hallucination of a mouse, had activation of his EEG pattern, considerable eye movement, and rather marked autonomic variations. This evidence would not necessarily support the claim that dreaming is one aspect of a distinctive organismic state. Such a contention must rest on other evidence, most conclusively provided by neurophysiological studies during the past few years. However, before we had any knowledge of these studies in this country I stated (*83*):

> Its inexorable regularity is scheduled periods over the course of the night, every night, in every individual, and the occurrence of the same physiological pattern in an as yet undetermined number of species other than our own, all contribute to the impression of a very basic, lawful, and by inference, a highly important biological function.

The findings of Aserinsky and Kleitman were first confirmed and extended by William Dement, who had taken part in the original studies while still a medical student and has since made a most singular contribution to the majority of developments which have followed. In one of his early studies with Kleitman (*24*), Dement described in detail the extremely predictable cycle of EEG and EM events during undisturbed human sleep, which has since been substantiated by a host of investigators. I would estimate that the total series of subjects studied by various investigators now numbers in the thousands, and that the number of nights they have been studied is many times that; yet I know of not a single exception to the rule that normal human subjects, provided they have sustained periods of sleep, have manifested the regularly recurrent cycle of REM periods in every instance.

As illustrated in Figure 14.2, this random assortment of records from our own laboratory illustrates the degree of the regularity and the degree of variability of the periodically recurrent REMS. To be sure, this cycle of events is not as regular as a mechanical clock, since individual REM periods can vary from five minutes to as long as 70 minutes. They sometimes fail to occur at the expected time, but this rarely happens except early in the night, and then under conditions of unusual fatigue or in younger subjects. We have been particularly interested in pathological states associated with disturbed sleep where exceptions to the rule might be expected, such as hallucinating schizophrenics (*59*). Others have also studied schizophrenics (*19, 31, 70*), as well as depressions (*69*) and borderline states (*31*). The basic pattern of events is essentially the same in all these situations, although there may be minor but important variations which we have hardly begun to understand.

The original observations of human infants did not include electrophysiological recordings, but it has now been shown in several laboratories (*18, 75*) that the same clearly distinguishable pattern of events is present from the first day, indeed from the fourth hour of extra-uterine life.

THE REM STATE IN ANIMALS

Not only does the regularly recurrent pattern of the REM state appear to be universally and invariably present in human beings, but it is also found in a nearly indistinguishable form in other mammalian species. Dement was the first to describe the association of periodically recurrent, low-voltage EEG patterns with bursts of rapid eye movements in the sleeping cat (*20*).

The same observations have since been made in many laboratories and in all of the species yet studied: the dog (*82*), monkey (*91*), rat (*13, 65, 89*), rabbit (*30*), sheep (*44*), goat (*78*), and chimpanzee (*1*). I believe we have made the latest addition to this list by studying the opossum (*85*). The opossum is an extremely primitive mammalian form, considered to have changed very little since the earliest days of mammalian evolution. Like Winnie the Pooh, the opossum is a creature of very little brain or intellect; next to surviving sleeping is the thing he does best, and happily for us he prefers to do that during the day. Yet electrical patterns of his cerebral activity are not grossly different from our own, as shown by Figure 14.10. In the active waking state he has a low-voltage irregular pattern, usually quite obscured by muscle artefact, with a rhythmical 6–7 per second pattern from the hippocampus; asleep he shows a high-voltage slow-wave pattern. Periodically during sleep the EEG pattern changes abruptly to a low-voltage irregular rhythm, with a conspicuous 6–7 per second theta pattern from hippocampal derivations. Both the cortical and the hippocampal patterns are indistinguishable from those of the alert waking state, aside from the greater amount of muscle artefact obscuring the latter, yet the animal is behaviorally asleep and unresponsive to external stimulation. As illustrated in Figure 14.11, this pattern recurs with marked regularity, at intervals of about seventeen minutes throughout the sleep period, and takes up from 22 to 44 per cent of the total sleep time. It is associated with marked irregularity of respiration and heart rate and scattered rapid eye movements, though eye movements are not such a prominent part of the pattern as they are in man, monkey, or cat. On the other hand, twitches of the ears, vibrissae, and snout muscles

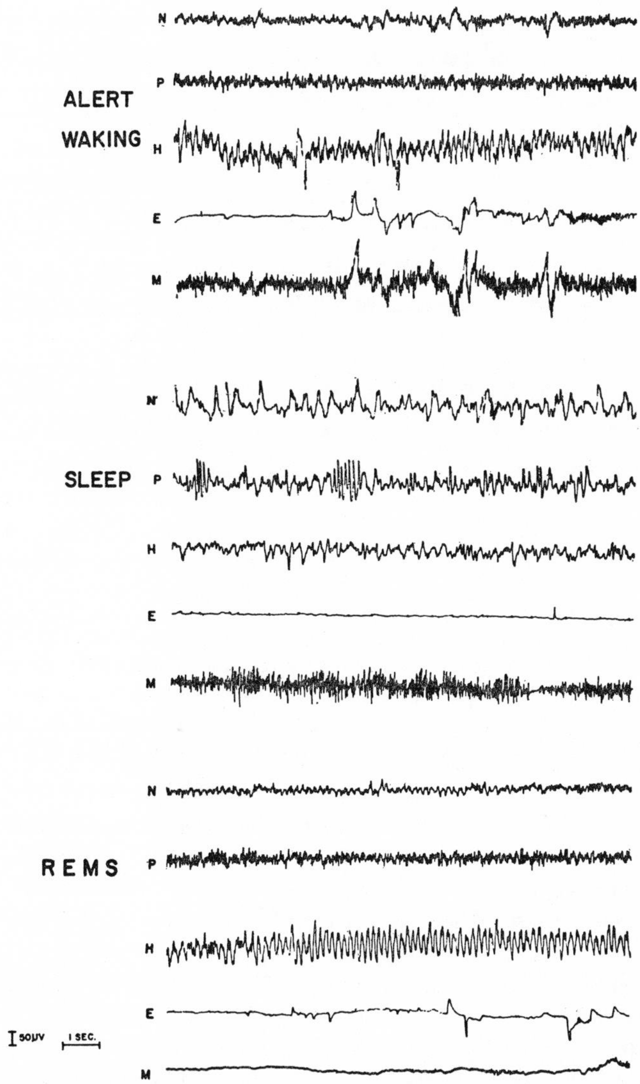

Fig. 14.10.—Polygraph records of waking, sleep, and REMS in the Virginia opossum. *N*=neocortex; *P*=pyriform cortex; *H*=hippocampus; *E*=eye movement; *M*=muscle activity. Note the very striking hippocampal theta rhythm and the complete cessation of muscle activity during REMS.

are obvious, as are movements of the digits. Occasionally there are penile erections, licking and mouthing activities, or gross movements of the extremities or tail.

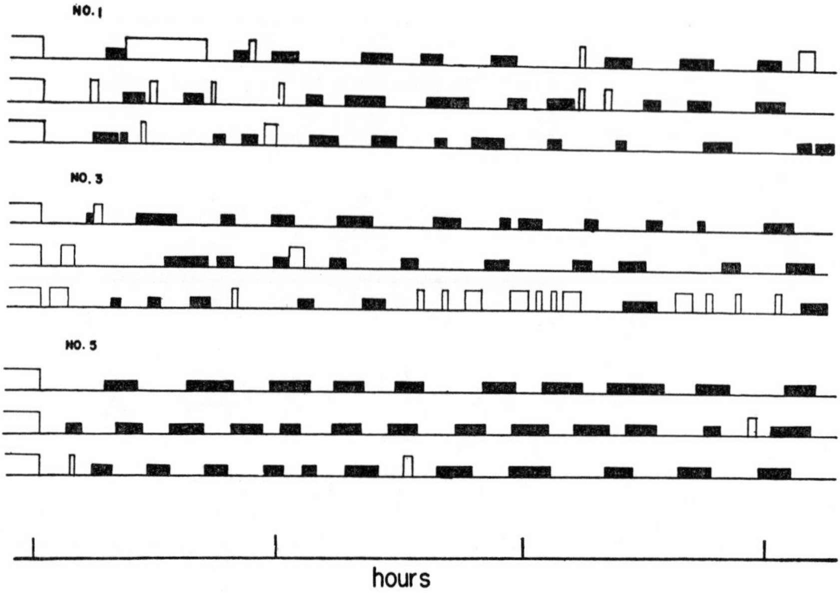

Fig. 14.11.—Diagrammatic representation of sleep cycles in the Virginia opossum. Represents portions of three separate recording sessions from each of three opossums. Solid bars=REMS; open bars=awakening; single lines=non-REMS sleep. Note that REMS tends to be absent during periods of disturbed sleep.

MOTOR MANIFESTATIONS OF THE REM STATE

This brings us to still another aspect of the REM constellation—that of its motor manifestations. It is fundamental to the psychoanalytic theory of dreaming that motor discharge of tensions is replaced by hallucinatory discharge. The REMS abides by this rule, but not completely. The very active but circumscribed and abortive body movements seen in the opossum are a characteristic of this state in all the forms studied. Although not nearly so prominent in human adults, they are still an easily observable part of the pattern, taking the form of occasional twitches at the corners of the mouth and isolated movements of the fingers and wrists.[9] Wolpert has studied these hand movements electromyographically (*96*). You may recall that in the newborns first studied by Aserinsky it was noted that the REM phase was associated with a great deal of motor activity, and this has

[9]Why should these localized motor manifestations be part of the REM pattern, whereas more gross motor effects are not? This question was pondered by Bradley in 1894 (*12*), who noted that movements of the lips and tongue or fingers are common during dreaming, but asked, "Why when we strive to move in dreams do we not always move?" Answered Hughlings Jackson: "Perhaps this inability accords with the hypothesis that large movements (those especially engaged in locomotion) are but little represented in the highest level" (*43*). We can offer no better explanation today.

been confirmed by a more recent study; in newborns there is almost continual evidence of athetoid stretching, smiling, grimacing, brief vocalizations, fine tremors of the limbs, and sucking (*18, 75*). In the light of Freud's view that dreaming begins as hallucinatory gratification of early oral needs, it is particularly interesting that sucking activity appears to be an integral part of the REM process.

Systematic study has shown that the amount of body movement during the REMS is a function of maturation (*75*); from the high level in infancy there is a gradual diminution through the developing years, and it is only in late adolescence that it assumes the adult level.

There is still one further component of the REMS constellation, and this one cannot be explained by the notion that the physiological pattern simply reflects the hallucinatory experience. It was first found in the cat that throughout the REMS period there is an abrupt and complete cessation of tonic muscle activity in the dorsal neck muscle (*45*). Because of the typical posture of sleep in cats this is behaviorally apparent when the head drops and the animal becomes completely flaccid. The same manifestation is clearly present in the opossum, and there is a human counterpart in that the anterior throat muscles do not relax completely until the REM periods, when their muscle potentials are abruptly diminished (*9*). Roffwarg *et al.* (*75*) have made the same observation in the human infant. Of particular interest in this regard is a recent study of Hodes and Dement of reflex responses of the calf and plantar muscles to percutaneous electrical stimulation of the tibial nerve in human subjects (*40*). These reflexes were moderately reduced in sleep, but during the REMS periods they were dramatically and completely abolished. It is still uncertain whether such an effect might be due to an active inhibitory process from higher centers or the reduction of a tonic facilitatory barrage, but it is clear that these localized, monosynaptic responses of spinal elements are very different during this state than during sleeping or waking, and that the loss of tonic muscle tone is a characteristic feature of the REMS in both animals and man.

SPECIES AND INDIVIDUAL VARIATIONS

The components of the REM constellation which we have thus far been able to observe of measure from outside the body can be summarized as follows:

EEG ACTIVATION

RAPID EYE MOVEMENTS

AUTONOMIC VARIATIONS:

increased irregularity and, generally, average level

MOTOR EFFECTS:

disappearance of postural tone; activity of mimetic musculature and distal extremities

All of these same components, but no others, have been found in all the forms in which they have been studied—from opossum, to cat, to newborn infant, to adult human. There are certain differences among these species, just as there may be among individuals. The pulse rate tends to lower during this state in the cat (*46*), as does the blood pressure (*16, 55*); but this is not consistently so, any more than they are consistently elevated in the human. There are species differences in the duration of the cycles and the percentage of the total sleep time taken up by this state. Table 14.2 attempts to summarize our present knowledge of such differences. Such comparative data eventually may reveal phylogenetic trends with respect to the REMS, but for the present there is little that can be said along these lines. The most consistent intraspecies parameter appears to be the cycle duration, the interval from the beginning of one REM period to the beginning of the next; but the significance of the interspecies variations in this measure is by no means clear. It might be interpreted that phylogenetically more primitive forms have shorter cycles, but it would be more compatible with present in-

TABLE 14.2
Normative Data on Sleep Cycle in Various Species

Species	Authors	Average REMS (minutes)	Average cycle (minutes)	% REMS of total sleep
HUMAN				
(1) Adult	Composite*	14	90	20
(2) Neonate	Roffwarg *et al.* (*75*)	?	50–60	60
(3) MONKEY	Weitzmann (*91*)	4.5	?	16
(4) CAT				
Adult	Dement (*20*)	10	20	50
	M. Jouvet (*46*)	10–15	10–30	20–60
Neonate†	D. Jouvet *et al.* (*45*)	10	25–30	100
(5) SHEEP				
Adult	D. Jouvet & Valatx (*44*)	?	?	2.5
Lamb	D. Jouvet & Valatx (*44*)	4.5	20–30	10
(6) RAT	Michel *et al.* (*65*)	4–7	5–10	15–20
	Swisher (*89*)	1–15	10	10–15
(7) OPOSSUM				
Adult	Snyder (*85*)	5	17	22–44

*These figures represent approximations based upon our own experience together with that of many others.

†The state which alternates with REMS in the newborn kitten is interpreted as waking on the basis of behavioral manifestations. The EEG pattern is the same in both states, and REMS is identified by rapid E.M., cardio-respiratory changes, and disappearance of muscle activity.

I am indebted to Dr. J. Allan Hobson for extracting this information from the scattered literature.

formation that this is a function of body size or metabolic rate. Among the forms thus far studied, the shortest cycles are found in the rat, which is the smallest but not the most primitive.

Data concerning the percentage of REMS in the total sleep time is less consistent either within the observations of a single laboratory or in the case of the cat, among various studies. It does seem that this percentage ranges higher in the cat or in the opossum than in the human; but for the monkey or the rat it is slightly lower, and for the sheep much lower. It is possible that the wide variations in percentages observed simply reflect the varying effects upon sleep of our experimental procedures.

Meaningful comparisons among species or within a species must await much more additional information about factors which influence the relative duration of the REMS. The clearest of such factors at present is age. Roffwarg *et al.* (*75*) have found that the percentage REMS is high in infancy, taking up about half of the total sleep time, lower in childhood, then gradually rises at puberty to the young adult level, and remains fairly stable until it gradually declines with old age. Similarly D. Jouvet *et al.* have reported that in the newborn kitten REMS is the only form of sleep (slow-wave sleep develops later [*45*]); and that in the lamb there is a dramatic reduction in this percentage from 10 to 2.5 at the time of weaning (*44*).

It is a question of great psychiatric interest whether the amount of REMS can be affected by stress or anxiety, but information relevant to this point is still meager. Fisher and Dement (*31*) have studied five borderline patients, who had a mean percentage REMS time of 26.5 per cent as compared with 19.8 per cent for a group of eleven normal control subjects in the same age group studied in the same laboratory. One of these subjects precipitously developed an acute paranoid psychosis, at which time his percentage REMS jumped to 50.1 per cent, and the first REM period, lasting for two and a half hours, began at the very onset of sleep. The authors point out, however, that this first long period was not altogether typical of the REMS from the electroencephalographic standpoint, and we might therefore question whether this instance was really such an extreme departure from usual percentage REMS as it appears to be. By contrast, a study of very disturbed, hallucinating schizophrenics (*59*) did not reveal REMS percentages significantly deviant from those typically found in normals. This area deserves much further systematic study both in clinical situations and in experimental animals.

From a more naturalistic point of view we have observed in the opossum that when sleep is disturbed, as indicated by frequent awakenings, the percentage REMS tends to be low. In humans this may explain the common observation that the percentage for subjects' first nights in the laboratory setting tend to be lower than for subsequent nights. On the other hand, following sleep deprivation also, percentage REMS has been found to be lowered in humans (*10*). This has not yet been systematically studied in other species.

REMS AS A SPECIFIC DEPTH OF SLEEP?

It is initially assumed that REMS represented a state of light sleep in the human, and it is now being widely assumed that it represents deep sleep in the cat. I first questioned the simplicity of this assumption for the human when I found that arousal thresholds to sound stimuli are extremely variable in this state as compared with the rest of sleep, and that at times they are higher than they are during the periods of high-voltage slow-wave sleep on the same night (*83*). Williams *et al.* have since done some studies which are most relevant to this question. When subjects were trained to press a lever whenever they heard a repeated auditory stimulus, responses continued throughout sleep but ceased almost entirely during REMS (*94*). This is similar to the results obtained in the cat and support the interpretation that REMS is deep sleep. However, more recent work by the same investigators suggest a very different interpretation (*93*). If the subjects learned that failure to respond to the stimulus resulted in their being rudely awakened, responses continued throughout REMS at a higher level than they do in the rest of sleep. Moreover, when they were trained to respond differentially to two different tones of the same intensity, the accuracy of their discrimination was greater during REMS. These studies seem to suggest that we can respond to external stimuli during REMS if sufficiently motivated, and can do so selectively, but that ordinarily we are too preoccupied with more important internal events to do so.

Although it is possible that the same considerations might apply to the cat, as Grastyan has speculated (*36*), other evidence makes this seem unlikely. Reports are quite consistent that awakening thresholds to auditory stimuli, as well as to direct electrical stimulation of the reticular formation, are typically twice as high during this state as during the rest of sleep (*8, 46, 77*).[10] Taken together with certain differences in the EEG patterns, as well as the lowering of blood pressure and pulse rate reported for the cat, this suggests that there may be important species differences in the manifestations of REMS, and perhaps in its significance as well. Despite these discrepancies, the numerous points of coincidence from the findings in adult humans, newborns, and the lowliest mammals all make it very farfetched to suppose that this is not basically the same organismic state. To assume, however, that a particular quality of 'sleep depth' is its most distinctive characteristic may be very misleading.

Many of those who have studied these phenomena most extensively now

[10] A very recent report indicates that this is not the case in the chimpanzee (*1*).

take the position that it is meaningless to think of this state as a specific level of sleep depth; rather, it appears to be a qualitatively different state from the rest of sleep (*23, 48, 95*). There is a good reason, therefore, why a particular 'depth' of sleep should not be used to designate it, and perhaps we should avoid the term 'sleep' entirely.[11]

DREAMING IN ANIMALS

Whether this organismic state is associated with anything like the human psychic experience of dreaming when it occurs in human neonates or in opossums is, of course, beyond speculation. Yet, we should not beg the question of dreaming in animals. Since antiquity many observers of animal behavior have had no doubt that higher mammals, at least, are capable of dreaming (*38*). Their conviction is based upon those same behavioral manifestations which distinguish the REMS from the rest of sleep.[12]

If we are not unduly wedded to our various anthropomorphic views about the purpose of dreaming, there is no *a priori* reason to deny the possibility of some form of this hallucinatory state to any living creature capable of complex perceptual activity. There is recent evidence of pattern vision in newborn infants (*33*), and it is obvious that even the opossum has complex perceptual activity, although it may be less visual than auditory and olfactory. Although Freud found no occasion to include the dreams of animals within his theory, he did make oblique reference to the possibility of their existence when he wrote (*34*):

> I do not myself know what animals dream of. But a proverb, to which my attention was drawn by one of my students, does claim to know. "What," asks the proverb, "do geese dream of?" and it replies: "Of maize!!" The whole theory that dreams are wish fulfillments is contained in these two phrases.

Since we certainly cannot assume that newborns or opossums do not dream,

---

[11]It is an indication of the newness of this field that it is still plagued by a great deal of terminological confusion. Each laboratory has its own terms for the pattern of events I have described. In humans it has been called Stage I with EM, REM sleep, 'light sleep,' and I have been so brash as to call it 'dreaming sleep.' In animals it was originally called 'activated sleep' by Dement, then paradoxical or rhombencephalic or archi sleep by Jouvet, 'deep' sleep by many, Stage IV by some, 'rapid' sleep by myself, 'low voltage fast' sleep and 'desynchronized sleep' by still others. If it is a state essentially different from both sleeping and waking then we are in need of a comparable term. I have none to suggest, and the abbreviation 'REMS' used throughout this discussion is a most unsatisfactory expedient.

[12]Lucretius wrote, "Thus you will see stout horses, even when their bodies are lying down, yet in their sleep sweat and pant without ceasing and strain their powers to the utmost as if for the prize, or as if the barriers were thrown open. And often during soft repose the dogs of hunters do yet all at once throw about their legs and suddenly utter cries and repeatedly snuff the air with their nostrils, as though they had found and were on the tracks of wild beasts; and after they are awake often chase the shadowy idols of stags, as though they saw them in full flight, until they have shaken off their delusions and come to themselves again" (*62*).

then it is still possible that the constellation of physiological changes in the REMS may simply be consequences of hallucinatory experience. We have already considered many reasons why this is unlikely. We turn now to studies involving the depths of the brain and its experimental manipulation, which, I believe, demonstrate that this is not the case.

NEUROPHYSIOLOGICAL EVIDENCE

The hitherto unnoticed REMS in the cat has elicited intensive neurophysiological investigation throughout the world, but nowhere has this been more fruitful than in the laboratory of Michel Jouvet and his associates at the University of Lyon (*46–48, 50*). By recording from implanted electrodes this group first demonstrated that REMS can be distinguished by typical changes in the electrical activity of regions of the brain other than the cortex. The rapid, low-voltage activity is also found in the diencephalon and mesencephalic reticular formation, in contrast to slow waves and spindles during the remainder of sleep. Most strikingly, during REMS the dorsal hippocampus shows a slow, rhythmical, 5–6 per second pattern, similar to that seen during active arousal in the waking state. This has been confirmed in the cat by several investigators (*14, 36, 71*), as well as in the rat (*13*) and dog (*82*); and, as mentioned previously, we have found an identical hippocampal rhythm conspicuously present in the opossum. Finally, at the level of the pontine reticular formation a spindling rhythm of 6–8 per second is found during REMS.

After extending the physiological definition of the state in this manner, the Lyon group proceeded to study the effects of various experimental lesions, which I have schematically summarized in Figure 14.12.[13]

It was shown that after total removal of the cerebral cortex slow-wave activity no longer appeared in the diencephalon or mesencephalon, indicating that this pattern comes from the cortex; but all the same manifestations of REMS still continued to recur periodically.[14] If the eye movements and autonomic changes were simply consequences of the hallucinatory state, as might have been assumed, then it would have to be postulated that they resulted from some crude residuals of perception in the decorticate animal.

This possibility became entirely untenable with the next experimental step. When the cats were sectioned through the anterior border of the mesencephalon, structures in front showed continuous slow-wave and spindle activity, and those behind the section had continuous low-voltage, fast patterns; yet the REMS still recurred periodically, as indicated by rudimentary eye movements, typical cardiorespiratory changes, suppression of muscle

[13]Dr. Jouvet has allowed me to take this liberty with his classical studies, but responsibility for erroneous or misleading impressions is my own.

[14]Although the eye movements tended to be more regular and rhythmical.

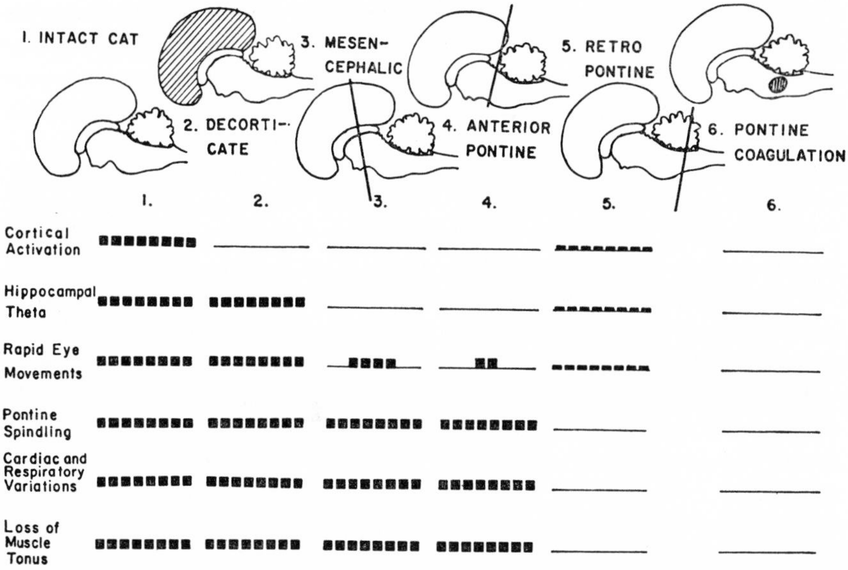

Fig. 14.12.—Schematic summary of Jouvet studies on the neuro anatomical mechanism of REMS. Heavy dashed lines indicate presence of the particular manifestation as part of the recurrent REMS. (In the retro pontine preparation it might be expected that the mechanism would be intact except for its vegetative and muscular components, but since such preparations exhibit spontaneous vertical eye movements even during wakefulness, and the activity of the brain rostral to the section is permanently and unspecifically activated, additional indications will have to be found before this point can be clarified. The uncertainty concerning this preparation is indicated by the thin dashed line.)

tonus of the neck, and the characteristic pontine spindling. The same was true when sections were made in the middle of the mesencephalon or at the anterior border of the pons, except that eye movements no longer appeared. However, if the section was made just behind the pons, no residuals of the REM pattern remained, suggesting that cerebral structures indispensable for the periodic appearance of the REM state must be situated at the level of the pons. This was confirmed when circumscribed lesions in the pontine reticular formation eliminated the recurrent REM periods while the slow phase of sleep, as well as normal activation after arousal, still continued.[15]

Thus it was established that the occurrence of the REMS depends upon certain nuclei[16] in one of the most primitive portions of the brain and that most of its typical manifestations are essentially independent of higher

[15]This has been substantiated in at least one other laboratory (*71*).

[16]The critical structures are identified as the nucleus pontis caudalis, the posterior part of the nucleus pontis oralis, and the superior central nucleus of Bekhterev.

nervous function. This is hardly more surprising than Plato's locating the source of dreaming in the liver! It is a long leap from the cat to the human, but there is now good reason to believe that the underlying mechanism is the same. Jouvet *et al.* (*53*) have studied five cases of clinically decorticate persons in whom the recurrent periods of REMS still persisted, distinguished by rhythmical eye movements, supression of hyperactive muscle tonus, and typical cardiorespiratory alterations. Conversely, in two decerebrate patients with destruction of the pontine reticular formation, the REMS did not occur.

The mechanism which triggers the REMS appears to be an intrinsic function of the lower brain stem. It is possible to produce sustained periods of this state in the cat by one or two seconds' stimulation of the pontile reticular formation, provided this is done during slow sleep. However, it is never possible to trigger several periods successively—a recovery interval of 15–30 minutes must elapse. This fact, together with the effects of atropine in abolishing the REMS, or eserine in prolonging it, has led Jouvet to postulate the existence of a local neurohumoral mechanism in the pons as the periodic triggering mechanism.

To explain Jouvet's findings, the muscular, cardio-respiratory, and eye movement components of the REMS would have to be directly integrated at the brain stem level; yet this fact must be reconciled with evidence that to some extent the patterns of eye movement or respiratory activity come to reflect the hallucinatory experience, which obviously involves the highest levels of brain function. Actually this poses no new problem, since these same brain stem functions are modulated by cortical influences in the waking state also. We can only assume that there must be ascending pathways for the activation of higher centers and descending pathways for the modulation of the brain stem functions by higher centers.

Demonstration of the role of the ascending mid-brain reticular activating system in mediating waking arousal has been one of the major achievements of modern physiology. Jouvet and his co-workers have found that lesions of the reticular formation at the level of the midbrain tegmentum, which prevent the cortical activation of waking, have no effect on the cortical hippocampal activation of the REMS. On the other hand, lesions of the septum, subthalamic area, and of the region of the ventral mesencephalon at the level of the interpeduncular nucleus, which have no effect on waking activation, completely eliminate the cortical and hippocampal activation of the REMS. These lesions would all interrupt a circuit linking certain nuclei at the level of the pontile reticular formation to the limbic system (*67*), and Jouvet speculated that this might be the crucial ascending pathway. However, a recent study of Carli *et al.* (*17*) disputes this possibility and suggests instead that this conduction system is widely scattered throughout the midbrain. In any event, it is clear that the pathway involved is different from that implicated in the cortical activation of waking, and this is further argument that the REMS is distinct from waking, or even partial waking, as many had earlier thought of it.

Further evidence that this is the case comes from studies on the effects of stimulation of the reticular activating system on cortical activation. From the earliest studies of the REMS it has been noticed that the cortical arousal response (K complex), present throughout sleep, is completely absent during the REMS (*24*). Using microelectrodes to study the activity of single neural units in the mesencephalic reticular formation of the cat, Huttenlocher (*41*) has shown that activity in the cochlear nucleus and primary auditory cortex in response to click stimuli remained essentially the same in quiet waking, 'slow wave sleep,' and the REMS. In the mesencephalic reticular formation, however, activity was moderately depressed during 'slow wave sleep,' and almost completely suppressed during the REMS. Furthermore, Rossi *et al.* (*77*) have reported that thalamic and brain-stem stimulations which produce cortical EEG synchronizing responses during slow-wave sleep are completely ineffective in doing so during the REMS. Yet, if the cats were given intravenous barbiturates while in the midst of the REMS, cortical EEG synchronizing responses to thalamic stimulation were again evident. These authors interpreted their results to mean that in the REMS there is an active inhibition of the reticular activating system, which can be released by the depressing effects of barbiturates on the central nervous system. Again, these findings for the cat may not apply to anthropoids. Adey *et al.* (*1*) recently reported that averaged evoked responses to midbrain reticular stimulation in the chimpanzee do not drop out during REMS. Comparable to the findings of Williams *et al.* (*95*) for the human, these evoked responses in the chimpanzee are of a configuration similar to that of waking, but of lower amplitude.

Even while those mechanisms which mediate interactions with the environment may be inhibited there is equally impressive evidence that the REMS is characterized by marked intensification of activity within the nervous system. Huttenlocher (*42*) has found that single units of the mesencephalic reticular formation generally show more spontaneous activity during 'slow wave sleep' than during quiet waking but that these rates were dramatically increased during the REMS, often to as much as 10–40 times those of waking. Using the same techniques of chronically implanted microelectrodes, Evarts (*27*) has reported that single neurons in the primary visual cortex of the cat typically have a 70 per cent higher rate of discharge during the REMS than during sleep with EEG slow waves. This is in agreement with the finding of Arduini (*2*) that spontaneous activity of large populations of cortical pyramidal tract neurons decreases during slow-wave sleep but is as high or higher during REMS as it is during the fully awake state. In these studies, as in Huttenlocher's, activity tended to occur in bursts associated with the movements of eyes, vibrissae, and extremities.

Thus, a rapidly growing body of evidence indicates that there is intensive neuronal activity within the nervous system during REMS dramatically different from that during the rest of sleep and comparable only to the kind of function found during the highly aroused waking state. Confirmation for this view is now coming from another source, the study of cortical blood flow during various behavioral states. Kanzow *et al.* (*55*) have found that cortical blood flow during the REMS increases 30–50 per cent over that during the rest of sleep, changes similar to those which they had earlier demonstrated in states of aroused, waking attention.

It would seem plausible that the primitive brain stem mechanism responsible for triggering REMS would have its primary connections with older portions of the cerebrum such as the limbic system, as Jouvet has suggested. I have previously summarized certain evidence independent of that related to REMS for postulating that these structures might be especially involved in dreaming (*84*). In addition, there is reason for suspecting that the hippocampus is a crucial link between the primitive brain-stem triggering mechanism and cerebral cortical participation in REMS. It has been noted that electrical stimulation of the hippocampus during this state results in its disappearance and the resumption of slow-wave sleep (*36*). This implies that the cortical activation of REMS may be mediated through the hippocampus or, as Grastyan suggests, may result from elimination of a hippocampal inhibitory mechanism. The effects of bilateral ablation of the hippocampus on the cortical activation of REMS would be of great interest in this regard but, to my knowledge, has not yet been studied. Taking into consideration the distinctive psychological characteristics of dreaming and the accumulating evidence that limbic structures are uniquely implicated in the mechanisms of primitive emotion, memory, and sleep itself (*63, 66, 72*), it is not farfetched to assume that further studies of limbic system participation in the REMS may provide the crucial test of Fechner's premise.

In the light of the evidence thus far assembled the opinion of Fechner that "the scene of action of psychophysical activity" must be different, or that of Hughlings Jackson that there is "increased activity of the uncontrolled lower layers' answering to the primitive mentation of the dream," begins to seem highly prophetic. Yet this picture is far from complete. The evidence argues most strongly that REMS is a different biological state from the rest of sleep, but it distinguishes much less clearly between this state and waking. It is true that both motor and sensory modes of interaction with the external environment are drastically altered in REMS as contrasted with waking and that the brain-stem mechanisms involved are markedly different, but it might still be possible that the functional organization of higher brain activity is essentially the same in these two states. Even though the conditions for their functions are very different, it is possible that the same cerebral processes which are stimulated by sensory input from the environment during waking are set in motion by the intrinsic pontine triggering mechanism during REMS. The gross patterns of electrical activity recorded from either the cerebral cortex or the hippocampus are remarkably similar in waking and in the REMS, so that the answer to this question must await a much more refined definition of waking brain function as well as that during REMS.[17]

Some of the observations I have mentioned are still awaiting publication, and many of them have yet to be confirmed; yet enough are firmly established that we may be confident of the following:

Universally and with regular periodicity, throughout mammalian life the physiological and certain of the behavioral characteristics by which we now identify sleep are abruptly interrupted and replaced by a qualitatively very different constellation of events. In contrast to the low and stable level of function during sleep, during these regularly recurrent periods most functions show a high and widely fluctuating level of activity. Exceptions are those functions which mediate interaction with the external environment, and certain of these undergo complete cessation. The neural mechanism of these events is distinctly different from those of sleep or waking and involves more primitive mechanisms. In adult humans, at least, there is good evidence that, concomitant with some periods, there is a distinctive experiential state which we know as dreaming. In my opinion these observations categorize an organismic state, of the same order, yet different from both sleeping and waking.

THE FUNCTION OF REMS

As Dr. Weiner pointed out in Paper 2, in the biological framework we are always concerned about the function or purpose of an event. What, then, is the function of REMS? I must preface the few comments I can offer about that by saying that I really have no idea and have no indication that anyone else does either. In an evolutionary context the answer to this question must take the form of an explanation how the particular event serves

---

[17]In a very recent study (*29*) Evarts found that average discharge rates of single pyramidal tract neurons in the cerebral cortex of the monkey are similar during REMS to that of waking, but that the temporal pattern of spontaneous activity is entirely different. During waking the discharges are regular, becoming sporadic during slow-wave sleep, and still more sporadic during REMS. Although it would be unwarranted to generalize that other elements of the cortex behave in the same fashion, such studies of single neuron activity in unanesthetized, unrestrained primates illustrate the degree of technical refinement now being applied to this problem.

the preservation of the species; but just as there is no possible explanation of biological purpose for life itself, so it is that some of its most basic aspects tend to defy such explanation. The function of sleep is still problematical, and we have known about that much longer than we have known about the REMS. It may be anthropormorphic to assume that sleep or dreaming must have a purpose in maintaining waking life; it might as well be argued that waking life, involving essential interactions with the environment, has developed for the purpose of sustaining existence in the other states of being. Studies of the activity patterns of rats in captivity indicate that they spend 80 per cent of their daily lives in sleep (*15*); more casual observations of our opossums suggest that the percentage is at least that high. Why do we assume that such creatures sleep to live, rather than live to sleep, or to dream?

The data are still fragmentary and do not extend to infra-mammalian forms, but there is some basis for the hypothesis that REMS is relatively more important in older phylogenetic stages. In the opossum the percentage of sleep taken up by REMS is usually much greater than that ever found in normal humans, and probably much greater than the percentage of waking, at least under the conditions of captivity. This conforms with the physiological evidence suggesting that the REMS is an archaic and, perhaps in man, an atavistic state of existence. Such a hypothesis is still better supported at present by the evidence from earlier ontogenetic stages both in humans and in animals. D. Jouvet *et al.* (*45*) have reported that in the newborn kitten the REMS is the only observable form of sleep—slow-wave sleep develops later. It follows that we must now attempt to determine whether or to what extent REMS occurs in mammals still *in utero,* in premature infants, or in infra-mammalian forms.[18]

Whatever the function of that state there is reason to believe that it is a necessary and vital one. Dement's studies of "dream deprivation" (*21*) are undoubtedly familiar to you and need no elaboration here. The physiological effects of "dream deprivation" have now been confirmed in cats (*49*) as well as in humans (*84*).[19] Equally relevant are the findings of Jouvet and Mounier (*52*) that cats chronically deprived of REMS by means of pontine lesions showed marked behavioral changes (ravenous appetites and a kind of waking activity which suggested that they were hallucinating), together with progressive tachycardia which ended in death.

There are several observations now in the literature which temporarily

[18]Although the technical difficulties are formidable, we hope to be able to approach this problem by studying the pouch young of the opossum.

[19]I have previously expressed my misgivings about assuming that it is the deprivation of dreaming itself rather than the interruption of the physiological function which produces these effects (*84*).

simply add to the mystery of the REMS. Sawyer and Kawakami report that, following coitus or artificial vaginal stimulation in the estrous rabbit, there is a period of a few minutes to one-half hour of a drowsy state, associated with high-amplitude slow waves and sleep spindles, which then gives way abruptly to a state of further behavioral depression concomitant with cortical activation and a rhythmical 8 per second pattern from the hippocampus (*79*). This latter state, which appears to conform in detail with the REMS, is claimed by the same authors to be reproducible by low-frequency electrical stimulation of the hypothalamus, olfactory bulb, septum, hippocampus, and amygdala, as well as by injection of certain pituitary hormones (*56*). Equally intriguing, D. Jouvet and Valatx find that in the lamb there is an abrupt diminution in the percentage of REMS from 10 to 2.5 per cent coincident with weaning and the onset of rumination (*44*).

Such reports suggest that the REMS may be related to two other rather important biological functions, those of sex and nutrition. There are other reasons for interest in the relationship of REMS to alimentation, such as the sucking of infants during REMS, or the increased appetites of Jouvet's cats with pontine lesions, or of some of Dement's "dream deprived" subjects. In one of their original papers Aserinsky and Kleitman gave major emphasis to the fact that the cycles of ocular motility in infants were generally even fractions of interfeeding intervals on self-demand feeding schedules (*6*). In other words, after every four or five REM periods the infants awakened clamoring to be fed instead of going through the next REM period. This is also evident in some of the more recent observation of Roffwarg *et al.* (*75*) who noted that awakenings in infants almost always take place at the onset of REM periods.

Do such observations suggest that the REMS has relevance for psychoanalytic dream theory? Since that issue could be discussed much more knowledgably by many of those present and has been dealt with elsewhere (*31, 90*), I shall confine myself to a few closing remarks about it. If anyone should insist upon the notion that the four-hour-old infant is hallucinating a breast which it has never seen, I would object; but what we now know of the REMS is certainly not incompatible with Freud's premise that dreaming begins as the hallucinatory gratification of elementary needs, primarily oral in nature. In the broadest sense everything that has been learned during the past decade about the REMS seems to complement remarkably Freud's insights concerning the integral relationship of dreaming to basic biological forces. It is an exciting prospect that further study of REMS may lead to additional knowledge of those biological wellsprings.

There is a strong temptation to venture immediate translations of these physiological findings into the parlance of psychoanalytic theory, but I believe that this temptation should be resisted. The concepts and constructs of that theory evolved out of the necessity to account for the unique data obtained from application of the psychoanalytic method, and it is my impression that they were successfully achieved only after, or to the extent that, Freud was able to free himself of those neurological preconceptions which Dr. Holt has detailed so well. In the history of science there must be many such parallel situations in which interest in one area of observation stimulates the exploration of another; yet the full development of the second area would be burdened and misdirected by confinement to the theoretical mold of the first.[20] Like the discovery of psychoanalysis, the discovery of the REMS can be credited to the fact that there was an individual sufficiently free of theoretical preconceptions to see what others had overlooked. The phenomenon of the REMS is still unfolding before us. At this point we can suspect that it is an organismic state of basic importance but cannot forsee what its ultimate biological significance may prove to be, or in what direction it may lie.

REFERENCES

1 Adey, W. R., Kado, R. T., and Rhodes, J. M. Sleep: Cortical and subcortical recordings in the chimpanzee. *Science 141:*932, 1963.

2 Arduini, A. Differences in cortical activity during desynchronized sleep and arousal. *Proc. of 22nd Int. Cong. of Physiol. Sci.* (Leiden) *1:*464, 1962.

3 Aristotle. "On Dreams." *Great Books of the Western World,* edited by R. M. Hutchins. Vol. VIII. Chicago, Encyclopaedia Britannica, Inc., 1952.

4 Aserinsky, E. Personal communication to the author.

5 Aserinsky, E., and Kleitman, N. Regularly occurring periods of eye motility and concomitant phenomena during sleep. *Science 118:*273, 1953.

6 Aserinsky, E., and Kleitman, N. A motility cycle in sleeping infants as manifested by ocular and gross bodily activity. *J. appl. Physiol. 8:*11, 1955.

7 Aserinsky, E., and Kleitman, N. Two types of ocular motility occurring in sleep. *J. appl. Physiol. 8:*1, 1955.

8 Benoit, O., and Bloch, V. Seuil d'excitabilite reticulaire et sommeil profond chez le chat. *J. Physiol., Paris 52:*17, 1960.

9 Berger, R. Tonus of extrinsic laryngeal muscles during sleep and dreaming. *Science 134:*840, 1961.

10 Berger, R., and Oswald, I. Effects of sleep deprivation on behavior, subsequent sleep and dreaming. *Brit. J. Psychiat. 108:*457, 1962.

11 Berger, R., and Oswald, I. Eye movements during active and passive dreams. *Science 137:*601, 1962.

12 Bradley, F. H. On the failure of movement in dreams. *Mind 2:*441, 1894.

13 Brugge, J. F. Hippocampal activity in the unrestrained rat. (Abstract.) *Fed. Proc. 22:*No. 2, Part 1, 1963.

14 Cadilhac, J., Passouant-Fontaine, T., and Passouant, P. Modifications

[20]The plea which Rapaport made in behalf of psychodynamics (*73*) is equally applicable in the present instance.

de l'activité de l'hippocampe suivant de divers stades du sommeil spontané chez le chat. *Rev. neurol. 105:*171, 1961.

15 Calhoun, J. B. Personal communication to the author.

16 Candia, O., Favale, E., Guissani, A., and Rossi, G. F. Blood pressure during natural sleep and during sleep induced by electrical stimulation of the brain stem reticular formation. *Arch. Ital. Biol. 100:*216, 1962.

17 Carli, G., Armergol, U., and Zanchetti, A. Electroencephalographic desynchronization during deep sleep after destruction of midbrain-limbic pathways in the cat. *Science 140:*677, 1963.

18 Delange, M., Costan, P., Cadilhac, J., and Passouant, P. Les divers stades du sommeil chez le nouveau-né et le nourrisson. *Rev. neurol. 10:*271, 1962.

19 Dement, W. C. Dream recall and eye movements during sleep in schizophrenics and normals. *J. nerv. ment. Dis. 122:*263, 1955.

20 Dement, W. C. The occurrence of low voltage, fast electroencephalogram patterns during behavioral sleep in the cat. *EEG clin. Neurophysiol. 10:*291, 1958.

21 Dement, W. C. The effect of dream deprivation. *Science 131:*1705, 1960.

22 Dement, W. C. *Eye Movements during Sleep. U.S.P.H.S. Symposium on the Oculmotor System,* edited by M. B. Bender. Hoeber, New York, 1961. In press.

23 Dement, W. C. An essay on dreams. Paper presented at Le Roue et les Societes Humaines, Royaumont, June 1962.

24 Dement, W. C., and Kleitman, N. Cyclic variations in EEG during sleep and their relation to eye movements, body motility, and dreaming. *EEG clin. Neurophysiol. 9:*673, 1957.

25 Dement, W. C., and Kleitman, N. The relation of eye movements during sleep to dream activity: An objective method for the study of dreaming. *J. exp. Psychol. 53:*339, 1957.

26 Dement, W., and Wolpert, E. The relation of eye movements, body motility, and external stimuli to dream content. *J. exp. Psychol. 55:*543, 1958.

27 Evarts, E. V. Activity of neurons in visual cortex of cat during sleep with low voltage fast EEG activity. *J. Neurophysiol. 25:*812, 1962.

28 Evarts, E. V. "A Neurophysiologic Theory of Hallucinations." In *Hallucinations,* edited by L. J. West. New York, Grune & Stratton, 1962.

29 Evarts, E. V. Temporal patterns of discharge of pyramidal tract neurons during sleep and waking in the monkey. *J. Neurophysiol. 27:*152, 1964.

30 Faure, R. La phase "paradoxale" due sommeil chez le lapin. *Rev. neurol. 106*(2):190, 1962.

31 Fisher, C., and Dement, W. Studies on the psychopathology of sleep and dreams. *Amer. J. Psychiat. 119:*1160, 1963.

32 Foulkes, W. E. Dream reports from different states of sleep. *J. abnorm. soc. Psychol. 65:*14, 1962.

33 Frantz, R. Pattern vision in newborn infants. *Science 140:*296, 1963.

34 Freud, S. "The Interpretation of Dreams." *Standard Edition of Complete Psychological Works of Sigmund Freud,* edited by J. Strachey, Vol. IV. London, Hogarth, 1953.

35 Goodenough, D. R., Shapiro, A., Holden, M., and Steinschriber, L. A

comparison of "dreamers" and "nondreamers": Eye movements, electroencephalograms, and the recall of dreams. *J. abnorm. soc. Psychol. 59:*295, 1959.

36 Grastyan, E., and Karmos, G. A study of a possible "dreaming" mechanism in the cat. *Acta physiol. Acad. Sci., Hung. 20:*41, 1961.

37 Hawkins, D. R., Puryear, H. B., Wallace, C. D., Deal, W. B., and Thomas, E. S. Basal skin resistance during sleep and "dreaming." *Science 136:*321, 1962.

38 Hediger, H. *Studies of the Psychology and Behavior of Captive Animals in Zoos and Circuses.* New York, Criterion Books, 1955.

39 Hobson, J. A., Goldfrank, F., and Snyder, F. *Respiration and Mental Activity in Sleep.* In preparation.

40 Hodes, R., and Dement, W. C. Abolition of Electrically Induced Reflexes (EIR's or "H Reflexes") During Rapid Eye Movement Periods of Sleep in Normal Subjects, 1963. In preparation.

41 Huttenlocher, P. R. Effects of state of arousal on click responses in the mesencephalic reticular formation. *EEG clin. Neurophysiol. 12:*810, 1960.

42 Huttenlocher, P. R. Evoked and spontaneous activity in single units of medial brainstem during natural sleep and waking. *J. Neurophysiol. 24:*451, 1961.

43 Jackson, J. H. *Selected Writings of John Hughlings Jackson,* edited by James Taylor. New York, Basic Books, 1958.

44 Jouvet, D., and Valatx, J. L. Étude polygraphique du sommeil chez l'agneau. *C. R. Soc. Biol., Paris 156:*1411, 1962.

45 Jouvet, D., Valatx, J. L., and Jouvet, M. Étude polygraphique du sommeil du chaton. *C. R. Soc. Biol., Paris 155:*1660, 1961.

46 Jouvet, M. "Telencephalic and Rhombencephalic Sleep in the Cat." In *The Nature of Sleep,* edited by G. E. W. Wolstenholme and M. O'Connor. Boston, Little, Brown & Co., 1961.

47 Jouvet, M. Recherches sur les structures nerveuses et les mécanismes responsables des differentes phases du sommeil physiologique. *Arch. Ital. Biol. 100:*125, 1962.

48 Jouvet, M. Sur l'existence d'un systeme hypnique ponto-limbique ses rapports avec l'activite onirique. Physiologie de L'Hippocampe. *Colloq. Int. Cent. nat. Rech. sci.,* No. 107, p. 297, 1962.

49 Jouvet, M. Personal communication to the author.

50 Jouvet, M., and Michael, F. Reserches sur l'activite electique cerebrale au cours du sommeil. *C. R. Soc. Biol., Paris 152:*1167, 1958.

51 Jouvet, M., Michel, F., and Mounier, D. Analyse electroencéphalographique comparée du sommeil physiologique chez le chat et chez l'homme. *Rev. neurol. 103:*189, 1960.

52 Jouvet, M., and Mounier, D. Effets des lésions de la formation réticule pontique sur le sommeil du chat. *C. R. Soc. Biol.,* Paris *154:*2301, 1960.

53 Jouvet, M., Pellin, B., and Mounier, D. Etude polygraphique des differentes phases du sommeil au cours des troubles de conscience chronique (comas prolonges). *Rev. neurol. 105:*181, 1961.

54 Kamiya, J. "Behavioral, Subjective and Physiological Aspects of Sleep and Drowsiness." In *Functions of Varied Experience,* edited by D. W. Fiske and S. R. Maddi. Homewood, Ill., Dorsey Press, 1961.

55 Kanzow, E., Krause, D., and Kuhnel, H. Die vasomotorik der hirnrinde in den phasen desynchronisierter EEG-aktivitat im naturlichen schlaf der katze. *Pflüger's Arch., ges. Physiol. 274:*593, 1962.

56 Kawakami, M., and Sawyer, C. H. Induction of behavioral and electroencephalographic changes in the rabbit by hormone administration or brain stimulation. *Endocrinology 65:*631, 1959.

57 Keith, C. R. Some aspects of transference in dream research. *Bull. Menninger Clin. 26:*248, 1962.

58 Kleitman, N. *Sleep and Wakefulness.* Revised edition. Chicago, Univ. of Chicago Press, 1963.

59 Koresko, R. L., Snyder, F., and Feinberg, I. "Dream Time" in hallucinating and non-hallucinating schizophrenic patients. *Nature 199:*1118, 1963.

60 Kremen, I. Dream reports and rapid eye movements. Unpublished doctoral dissertation. Harvard Univ., 1961.

61 Ladd, G. T. Contribution to the psychology of visual dreams. *Mind 1:*299, 1892.

62 Lucretius. "On the Nature of Things." *Great Books of the Western World,* edited by R. M. Hutchins. Vol. XII. Chicago, Encyclopaedia Britannica, Inc., 1952.

63 MacLean, P. D. New findings relevant to the evolution of psychosexual functions of the brain. *J. nerv. ment. Dis. 135:*289, 1962.

64 MacWilliams, J. A. Blood pressure and heart action in sleep and dreams. *Brit. med. J. 2:*1196, 1923.

65 Michel, F., Klein, M., Jouvet, D., and Valatx, J. Etude polygraphique du sommeil chez le rat. *C. R. Soc. Biol., Paris 155:*2289, 1961.

66 Milner, B. Modifications de la memoire aprés lésions hippocampiques bilatérales. Physiologie de L'Hippocampe. *Colloq. Int. Cent. nat. Rech. sci.,* No. 107, 1962.

67 Nauta, W. J. H. Hippocampal projections and related neural pathways to the midbrain in the cat. *Brain 81:*319, 1958.

68 Orlinsky, D. E. Psychodynamic and cognitive correlates of dream recall. Unpublished doctoral dissertation. Univ. of Chicago, 1962.

69 Oswald, I., Berger, R. J., Jovamillo, R. A., Keddie, K. M. G., Olley, P. C., and Plunkett, G. B. Melancholia and barbiturates: A controlled EEG body and eye movement study of sleep. *Brit. J. Psychiat. 109:*66, 1963.

70 Passouant, P., *et al.* Etude EEG du sommeil chez un groupe de schizophrenes. *Rev. neurol. 104:*246, 1961.

71 Passouant, P., and Cadilhac, J. Les rhythmes theta hippocampiques au cours du sommeil. Physiologie de L'Hippocampe. *Colloq. Int. Cent. nat. Rech. sci.,* 1961.

72 Passouant, P., and Cadilhac, J. La place de l'hippocampe dans l'organisation fonctionnelle du cerveau. *J. de Psychologie 4:*379, 1962.

73 Rapaport, D. "Consciousness: A Psychopathological and Psychodynamic

View." In *Problems of Consciousness,* edited by Abramson. New York, Josiah Macy, Jr., Foundation, 1951.

74 Rechtschaffen, A., Verdone, P., and Wheaton, J. Reports of mental activity during sleep. *Canad. Psychiat. Ass. J. 8:*409, 1963.

75 Roffwarg, H., Dement, W., and Fisher, C. Preliminary observations on the sleep dream pattern in neonates, infants, children and adults. In *Problems of Sleep and Dream in Children,* edited by E. Harms. Monographs on Child Psychiatry, No. II. New York, Pergamon, 1964.

76 Roffwarg, H. P., Dement, W., Muzio, J., and Fisher, C. Dream imagery: Relationship to rapid eye movements of sleep. *Arch. gen. Psychiat. 7:*235, 1962.

77 Rossi, G. F., Favale, E., Hara, T., Guissani, A., and Sacco, G. Researches on the nervous mechanism underlying deep sleep in the cat. *Arch. Ital. Biol. 99:*270, 1961.

78 Ruckebush, Y., and Bost, J. Activite corticale cours au de la sommolence et de la rumination chez la chevre. *J. Physiol., Paris 54:*409, 1962.

79 Sawyer, C. H., and Kawakami, M. Characteristics of behavioral and electroencephalographic after-reactions to copulation and vaginal stimulation in the female rabbit. *Endocrinology, 65:*622, 1959.

80 Shapiro, A., Goodenough, D. R., Biederman, I., and Sleser, I. Dream recall and the physiology of sleep. *J. appl. Physiol. 19:*778, 1964.

81 Shapiro, A., Goodenough, D. R., and Gryler, R. B. Dream recall as a function of method of awakening. *Psychosom. Med. 25:*174, 1963.

82 Shimazono, Y., Horie, T., Yanagisawa, Y., Hori, N., Chikazawa, W., and Shozuka, K. The correlation of the rhythmic waves of the hippocampus with the behavior of dogs. *Neurol. Med. Chir. 2:*82, 1960.

83 Snyder, F. Dream recall, respiratory variability and depth of sleep. Paper delivered at Roundtable on Dreams Research, Annual Meeting of the American Psychiatric Ass., May 1960.

84 Snyder, F. The new biology of dreaming. *Arch. gen. Psychiat. 8:*381, 1963.

85 Snyder, F. Electroencephalographic Sleep Patterns in the Virginia Opossum. In preparation.

86 Snyder, F., Hobson, J. A., and Goldfrank, F. Blood Pressure Changes During Human Sleep. *Science 142:*1313, 1963.

87 Snyder, F., Hobson, J. A., Morrison, D. F., and Goldfrank, F. Changes in Respiration, Heart Rate and Systolic Blood Pressure in Relation to Electroencephalographic Patterns of Human Sleep. *J. appl. Physiol. 19:*417, 1964.

88 Sternbock, R. A. Assessing differential autonomic patterns in emotions. *J. Psychosom. Res. 6:*87, 1962.

89 Swisher, J. Activity, electroencephalogram, and observed behavior of the sleeping rat. Unpublished master's thesis. Univ. of Florida, 1961.

90 Trosman, H. Dream research and psychoanalytic theory of dreams. *Arch. gen. Psychiat. 9:*27, 1963.

91 Weitzmann, E. D. A note on the EEG and eye movements during behavioral sleep in monkeys. *EEG clin. Neurophysiol. 13:*790, 1961.

92 Whitman, R. M., Kramer, M., and Baldridge, B. Which dream does the patient tell? *Arch. gen. Psychiat. 8:*277, 1963.

93 WILLIAMS, H. L. Personal communication to the author.

94 WILLIAMS, H. L., HAMMOCK, J. T., DALY, R. L., DEMENT, W. C., AND LUBIN, A. Responses to auditory stimulation, sleep loss and the EEG stages of sleep. *EEG clin. Neurophysiol. 16:*269, 1964.

95 WILLIAMS, H. L., TEPAS, D. I., AND MORLOCK, H. C., JR. Evoked responses to clicks and electroencephalographic stages of sleep in man. *Science 138:*685, 1962.

96 WOLPERT, E. A. Studies in psychophysiology of dreams. II. An electromyographic study of dreaming. *Arch. gen. Psychiat. 2:*231, 1960.

97 WOLPERT, E. A., AND TROSMAN, H. Studies in psychophysiology of dreams. *Arch. Neurol., Chicago 79:*603, 1958.

FIFTEEN

The Problem of the Eczema-Asthma Complex: A Developmental Approach

SHELDON T. SELESNICK, M.D.
AND ZANWIL SPERBER, PH.D.

Our purpose is to formulate a set of theoretical propositions describing how psychodynamic and physiological factors may work together to account for eczema, asthma, or combinations of the two. As medical problems, both eczema and asthma are phenomena well known to practicing physicians. General practitioners, pediatricians, or specialists in dermatology, allergy, and, less frequently, psychiatry have occasion to work therapeutically with children suffering from these illnesses. Depending on the background of the practitioner, the treatments recommended can be strictly physical—focused on alleviating symptoms (e.g., by coal tar applications, bronchodilators) or on preventing future recurrences (dietary restrictions, allergic desensitization). For other cases the treatment may be exclusively psychological, whereas for still others a combination of physical and psychological treatment is pursued in a more or less integrated fashion.

Like many problems in the field of psychology, the conceptual division into exclusive dichotomies—e.g., nature versus nurture, or psychic versus somatic—represents an arbitrary conceptualization which often sets the researcher on an energetic march up a blind alley in pursuit of a nonexistent quarry, *the* cause. We do not, in our theorizing, propose that the "cause" of eczema or asthma is either psychological *or* somatic. We are in agreement with authors such as *Sulzburger* (*49*), who described the atopic or allergic

Funds for this research were made available to the Department of Child Psychiatry, Mount Sinai Hospital, Los Angeles, California, by the Cheerful Helpers for Handicapped Children.

aspects of eczema-asthma, and with Marmor *et al.* (*27*) who propose that, when there is constitutional compliance, psychological forces can feed into, maintain, or intensify the illness.

Recent psychosomatic studies of asthmatic children bear on this point of view. Purcell *et al.* (*32*) have demonstrated that some children with chronic, severe asthma are steroid-dependent. They stand out in sharp contrast to other youngsters, who present equally serious cases clinically, but clear up without steroids when placed in a therapeutic environment away from their homes. Typically, for the steroid-dependent children, the parents' descriptions of the child and of the parent-child relationships revealed fewer signs of pathology.

Further data from an extensive study were recently presented by Jeanne Block (*4*). Block defined two groupings of children who could not be discriminated on the basis of clinical signs of asthma but who had significantly different scores (above or below the median) on a scale measuring the hereditary-constitutional potential for allergic disease. A team of psychologists and psychiatrists examined the personalities of the parents of the children, the parental relationships, the parent-child relationships, and studied the childrens' personalities without knowledge of the allergic scale scores. The two groups presented strikingly different psychological patterns. The low allergic children were found to be more anxious and insecure, and the parental relationship and the parent-child relationship indicated many more stress points.

The research by both Purcell and Block was designed to elucidate the characteristics of groups at the ends of a continuum. At one extreme the constitutional loading for the allergic illness is heavy, and clearly definable psychological tensions are not apparent; but psychic forces may serve to trigger transient exacerbations of the symptoms. At the psychological extreme of the continuum the constitutional factor appears to provide an available path for expressing tensions, whereas fluctuations in psychodynamic forces are most closely related to variations in the symptomatology. In most cases there is a complex interaction involving substantial weightings of both psychological and constitutional factors.

Our interest in the problem of the eczema-asthma complex follows from a realistic concern with a serious medical problem. The incidence of asthma is 23 cases per 1000 population, and approximately 6000 deaths due to asthma occur annually in the United States (*30*). Eczema, one of the illnesses of the allergic diathesis, is often found in association with asthma. The data cited by Dees (*9*), Glaser (*15,* p. 7), and Rapaport *et al.* (*33*) indicate that probably 50–60 per cent of cases having infantile eczema eventually develop asthma; an additional 20 per cent develop some other form of respiratory allergy (e.g., rhinitis, hay fever, etc.). In only 34 per cent of a series of 276 cases of asthma studied by Glaser (*15,* p. 9, table V) was there an absence of prior allergic symptomatology. Thus, since eczema is one of the most common prodroma of asthma and since infantile eczema is frequently diagnosed, although there are few reliable statistics on the incidence of asthma in the infant (*8*) it appears that a detailed study of the course of eczema in association with asthma will provide valuable data concerning the epidemiology of a devastating illness.

For the past five years the Child and Family Study Center of Mount Sinai Hospital has been studying the eczema-asthma complex in the preschool-age child in relation to familial dynamics (*28, 29, 42, 44*). Most of this work has involved intensive clinical research with a small number of youngsters and their families. All families undergo detailed diagnostic workups: separate interviews with the mother and father conducted by social workers to elicit a complete family history; depth-oriented psychiatric interviews with both the parents and the child; psychological testing of the child and his parents; and a home observation by the nursery school teacher. Once in the therapeutic-research program, the child is observed in the therapeutic nursery school for five mornings a week and is also seen in psychotherapy. Both parents are seen in psychotherapy, and the mother also participates in a weekly mothers' group meeting conducted by the nursery school director (*2*).

Of the initial group of ten families studied intensively, the preschool-age child in seven instances was referred with asthma. Five of these youngsters had previously had eczema. Three children were referred with eczema and no history of asthma; two of them eventually developed asthma. We have since added six more families to our clinic series and have accumulated less extensive data from eighteen nonclinic allergic families studied in a pilot investigation by more rigorous, specifically focused data-collection methods (*45*).[1] Our presentation is based on our own experiences, examined in the light of the psychological and medical literature.

The purpose of the theory is to establish a rationale which can account for the following patterns of symptoms clinically observed in the eczema-asthma complex:

1. The child with chronic eczema.
2. The asthmatic child who had transient eczema or no eczema.
3. The child with chronic eczema who also develops asthma.
4. The child with remitting eczema and no asthma.

THE CHILD WITH CHRONIC ECZEMA

Developmental notes.—The human condition is one of social interaction. The human neonate is a diffusely organized, globally responding, helpless

---

[1]We are indebted to Max Benis, M.D., and Jesse Younger, M.D., of the Allergy Department of the Southern California Permanente Group for furnishing cases for this study.

organism who, for a protracted period, will be dependent for sheer survival on the protection and nurture provided by adults. As Spitz (*47,* pp. 255–56) has pointed out in his description of the infant:

. . . no organization is demonstrable in its psychic apparatus. It is only toward the second half of the first year that a central steering organization, the ego, is gradually developed. During the whole period of which we are speaking, i.e., the first year of life, this ego remains rudimentary. It would be completely inadequate for self-preservation were it not complemented by an external helper, a substitute ego as it were, to whom the major part of the executive, defensive and perceptive funcions are delegated.

As an inevitable by-product of receiving nurturing care, the child experiences some patterned social stimulation (*52,* p. 36). As adults attend to the infant, they invest every observable behavior and physiological response the neonate makes with communicative significance. Spitz has also noted the infant's responses ". . . are manifested more or less indiscriminately, reminding one of overflow phenomena; it is difficult to assign the earliest responses to either the somatic or the psychological field, as they occur mostly in such a manner as to express the characteristics of both psyche and soma" (*47,* p. 257). Following Spitz, we reinterpret the oral stage to de-emphasize the classical psychoanalytic focus on the specific sensitivity of the mouth and lips as *the* zone used by the infant to perceive the world. We are much more impressed with the wide variety of stimuli, internal and external, which can lead to a sense of discomfort, and by the totalistic way in which the infant's body responds to discomfort.

The skin, as the encompassing envelope, is the boundary between the neonatal organism, with its internal sources of sensory stimulation, and the external world, with its interpersonal and physical sources of stimulation. The skin participates intimately in the reception and communication of "messages" expressing the state of the neonatal organism. When the young infant is uncomfortable, his entire body reflects his tension. His skin changes color and temperature, and loses or gains moisture; his extremities thrash, and his body writhes. The neonatal respiratory apparatus also participates in the response to tension. As part of the pattern of motor movements lungs contract, forcing air out through lips and mouth tightened by facial muscles under tension. This produces a characteristic vocal pattern of "discomfort sounds," universal across all language groups (*24,* pp. 16–17).

These first vocal sounds are not signals emitted with an intent to communicate. They are part of a global pattern expressing the state of discomfort of the infant and can clearly be discriminated from the softer, less nasal, vaguer "comfort sounds" (*24,* p. 18). Since sounds are more easily perceived at a distance than are the other elements in the pattern expressing discomfort, they are readily available as signals to which the adult can respond differentially.

The regular and cyclical nature of the infant's crying (*34*) suggests that the most frequent source of tension arises from gastrointestinal tensions associated with hunger. The infant, however, is not selectively focused. Keeping in mind the evidence provided by Wolff,[2] we assume that the specific oral contact, with breast or bottle, will not be reacted to with specific sensitivity and pleasure. For the infant to be completely soothed, the total organism expressing stress must be taken into account by the comforting adult. This requires that the baby be touched and cuddled as well as fed.

To the degree that the parent actually provides only minimal social stimulation, the infant has less diversified social experiences. In research with rats, Levine *et al.* (*23*) demonstrated that animals who received handling in their earliest periods of life have an earlier maturation of the adrenocortical response to stress. Laboratory animals, in a relatively deprived environment, are less efficient in their adaptive response to stress than are either laboratory animals provided with varied stimuli, or wild animals (*35*). Sternberg and Zimmerman (*48*) presented suggestive evidence that the adult eczematous patient might also be deficient in his ability to respond to stress with adrenocortical mechanisms. As we shall see, eczema frequently develops in infants who are deprived of soothing tactile contact. If we can assume that as infants the eczematous adults studied by Sternberg and Zimmerman received limited handling, then there would exist a relationship between skin sensory deprivation, adrenocortical insufficiency, and chronic eczema.

Based on early communication disturbances, there exists another relationship—that between chronic eczema and serious psychiatric states. M. M. Lewis (*24*) notes that the universal comfort and discomfort sounds shared by infants of all language groups begin to vary as a result of the differential response of the child's parents. These early variations are the precursors of a developmental sequence leading ultimately to learning one's "mother tongue." Irwin and his students (*5, 16, 17, 18*) have shown that, even in the first years of life, the lack of social stimulation results in fewer and less varied vocalizations. If the baby is to learn how to communicate more selectively by means of language, he must first receive a response to his initial expressive utterances and a relationship which will stimulate him to imitate sounds.

The psychologically distant parent provides a minimum of such experiences. If the social deprivation is extreme and continues long enough, a

[2]Wolff (*56*, footnote, p. 113) has shown the neonate can perceive selectively for only approximately 30 minutes of the entire day during the period when he is awake, alert, but quiet.

barrier develops which prevents the child from expressing his feelings to others or from understanding the language by which others attempt to express thoughts and feelings to him. Such a deficit in the ability to communicate is compatible with the high proportion of serious psychopathology observed to coexist with a history of infantile eczema by some investigators. Bergman and Aldrich (*3*) followed up a series of eczematous patients all of whom had experienced the onset of eczema before their third year of life. As young adults 64 per cent of the patients, many of whom still had eczema, were found to have serious psychopathology. Schizophrenia, paranoid reactions, and passive aggressive personality disorders were dramatically evident in this series selected *only* by the criteria of severe infantile eczema.

The child who has not had the opportunity to develop more mature and efficient ways for getting close to other humans would be more prone, physiologically and psychologically, to utilize immature modes of communication, e.g., the skin, to express needs and tensions than would be an adequately stimulated infant.

Psychophysiological notes on the child with chronic eczema.—Initially in our work with eczematous and asthmatic youngsters, five observers (a nursery school teacher, psychologist, pediatrician, psychiatrist, and social worker) wrote free-style descriptions of all the nursery school children at that time. There were no guiding hypotheses to bias the reporters. Striking was the consistency with which each observer, in characterizing the three eczematous children, independently described their immaturity.

For his parents, the child's inability to handle age-appropriate tasks was no issue; they expected little in the way of achievement. Although superficially the parents appeared to relate to each other harmoniously, exploration of their individual dynamics revealed a great deal of latent discord. The parents tended to avoid and deny any expression of disappointment in each other. One or both of the parents utilized the child's eczema as a means of maintaining distance from the other. For example, the parents slept in different rooms, one sleeping with the child in the parental bed while the other occupied the child's bed—the rationale being that in this way the child could be cared for and his scratching could be prevented. The child's eczema served as an important support to the defensive structure of the family; the skin became the organ through which the child could be infantilized, while emphasis on skin care continuously modified parental interaction.[3] In each case, there was an overstroking of the child's skin as a reac-

[3]We are not alone in finding cases of chronic eczema where the pattern of parent care involves excessive contact. Marmor *et al.* (*27*) have noted that, where there is a strong family history of eczema, parents may react to skin rashes in their young children with excessive preoccupation and contact. Woodhead (*57*) has reported a series of 26 cases of infantile eczema which remained chronic. In most of these cases either

tion formation against unconscious rage at the youngster. A fourth case of eczema, which recently came to our attention, is presented to illustrate some of these considerations:

Anita R., age 3½, had had severe eczema for four months at the time her parents brought her to the clinic. There was no allergic history in the family. Her speech and behavior were so retarded that she was considered to be either autistic or mentally backward. Our studies, however, revealed that the child was neither schizoid nor retarded. Mrs. R. had been overprotected continuously by her own mother and recalled that the only time she was spanked was when she played "too far away from home." Her greatest satisfaction was from gaining the position as mother's favorite, which was accomplished by obeying her mother's every wish. In compliance with her mother's desire, she married a Dutch naval officer, who took her to America, away from her home in Holland. She has always regretted having married and left her mother. Mrs. R. overprotected and infantilized Anita in much the same way as she was treated by her mother. In fact, she, like her mother, took the child into her bed and forced the father to sleep elsewhere. She did not allow the child any show of independence or opportunities for exploration. Mrs. R. unconsciously feared the child would wander away from home into foreign lands and be victimized by a husband as had occurred in her own life. The desire to keep the child away from her peers went to such lengths that she had not taught her the English language.

At the time that the child first developed her ezcema, the mother noted that she was masturbating. This upset her because she had been told by her own mother that this was an evil practice. The mother's identification with the child was a hostile one: unconsciously, she wanted to be the child in the family and resented that her husband paid so much attention to Anita. Anita's father was a meticulous, compulsive individual who also opposed the child's explorative interests. He believed that if a child got into too many things she would become dirty, which was dangerous.

The parental communication was concerned mainly with the child. Even before the onset of eczema, they both continually patted and overstroked her skin.

In contrast to our findings based on the *preschool child,* which indicated that the already eczematous skin was overcontacted, are studies by many other investigators. These reports indicate that eczema in *infants* occurred when there was marked maternal neglect or avoidance of skin contact because of either underlying hostility or fortuitous circumstances (*27, 38, 47, 54*). The question now arises why *avoidance of skin contact with the infant* can result in the same pathology as *overhandling of the eczematous skin of the older child?*

Rosenthal's comprehensive article on the pathogenesis of eczema in infants, when mothers avoid contact with the skin, is particularly illuminating in this regard. He points out that in these infants there is "inadequate counter-balancing of unpleasant skin experiences with pleasant ones" (*39,* p. 450), so that the skin is more reactive to irritants from external sources.

---

mother or father or both spent long periods of time preoccupied with the child's skin. The family structure might have facilitated their preoccupation with the child. Statistics on birth order reveal that 80 per cent of the children were either the youngest or the only child in the family.

Kepecs and Robin (*20*) emphasized that gentle touching of the infant's skin eventually provides an inhibitory effect on stimuli entering through pain receptors: "Phylogenetically, pain is the most primitive sensation. Anatomically, it is carried by unmyelinated or fine myelinated fibers. Touch is phylogenetically of more recent origin and is transmitted by large myelinated fibers. Touch seems to have an inhibitory effect on pain. In its absence, pain perception becomes more primitive and intense." As with other functions of the nervous system, later acquired systems have an inhibitory effect on those of earlier origin. According to Rosenthal, painful stimuli injure the prickle cells in the epidermis. Destroyed cell contents become part of the tissue fluid, which increases osmotic pressure locally and "sucks adjacent tissue fluid to the area." Epidermal vesicles are formed and constitute the initial pathology of the eczematous lesions. Rosenthal explains that the extension of the lesions occurs because of the stimulation of pain receptors which serve overlapping epidermal areas ". . . retrograde stimuli which pass along pain fibers, reach terminals immediately adjacent to the destroyed cells" (*39*). Rosenthal considers vesiculation an adaptive response which protects the tissue by insulation from further painful stimuli.[4] Although vesiculation dilutes "pain substances" which may have been liberated by the injury, the increased osmotic pressure and the antidromal impulses lead to an extension of the eczematous lesion to adjacent skin areas. The initially protective response thus eventually leads to a maladaptive result.

When overstimulation or overmanipulation of the eczematous skin is a reaction formation to the unconscious motivation to injure, it is possible to assume that the handling will be rougher and thus be perceived as pain. This will maintain the pathogenic mechanism. Furthermore, as Kepecs, Robin, and Munro (*21*) demonstrated, repetitious stroking, even without unconscious hostile motivation, ultimately acts as an irritating stimulus. Therefore, repeated overcontact not only may maintain an eczematous lesion but theoretically can initiate defensive vesiculation as described by Rosenthal. Our studies were in the older, already eczematous child, in whom we could not directly observe the mother-infant relationship which may have been instrumental in producing eczematous lesions; but our findings do suggest psychological factors by means of which the lesions were perpetuated.

[4]Freud anticipated that it was of utmost importance to estimate the manner in which organisms deal with adverse stimuli when he wrote, "For the living organism, protection against stimuli is almost a more important task than reception of stimuli. . . . Beneath the common protective barrier, the sense organs, which essentially comprise arrangements for the reception of specific stimuli . . . also possess special arrangements adapted for fresh protection against an overwhelming amount of stimulus and for warding off unsuitable stimuli" (*14,* cited in Rosenthal [*39,* p. 444]; also see Pribram's discussion of "gating" in Paper 5 of this volume).

Vesiculation, a physiological mechanism for insulating against pain, may be a primary pathogenic factor even in eczematous children who have a low loading of allergic predisposition (the case of Anita R.), or it may contribute synergistically to promote eczema in infants with a high allergic potential.

Excessive contact or harsh stimulation of the skin may not emanate from the parents but from the child. In these cases the chief factor is the utilization of the skin lesion as an outlet for psychic expression, which results in excessive scratching and exacerbation of lesions. In several cases recently studied we were struck by the fact that there was a deep-seated desire on the part of the parents to inhibit the eczematous child's assertiveness. In the case example just described, Anita was not permitted to express aggression motorically, and the child turned the aggression toward her own body, scratching the skin lesions.

The psychoanalytic literature has called attention to the fact that the guilty child frequently releases guilt feelings by gouging at skin lesions (*42*, p. 192). A pattern resulting in skin hypercathexis was noted in older children who had eroticized relationships with their mothers. Excessive skin contact by these mothers was perceived by these children as painful, owing to the concomitant guilt, and the children frequently scratched at their lesions for self-punitive reasons, especially when they were in the presence of the seductive mother. Yet another well-known pattern occurs in the child who uses his eczema to gain secondary attention from his solicitous parents. Whenever the parents prepare to leave, the child scratches himself vigorously. The parents are then forced to remain to prevent further injury to the child's skin. The infantilized child thus initiates a sequence which reinforces his infantilism.

We assume that the eczematous child who has chronic eczema has been involved in a situation with the mothering person in which (*a*) there has been insufficient contact or excessive stimulation of the skin, or (*b*) there has been a hypercathexis of the skin arising from a need of the child to release inhibited aggression or discharge guilt feelings.

The patterns just described would contribute to an understanding of later psychopathological disturbances, described by various authors, in patients with chronic eczematous lesions. The mother-child relationship which is characterized by avoidance might result in a schizoid personality described by Bergman and Aldrich (*3*). Spitz (*47*) has presented developmental test data showing that insufficient maternal handling of the eczematous baby leads to a pattern of behavior, already identifiable in babyhood, which could be considered a precursor of schizoid withdrawal. Spitz found that mothers of eczematous babies avoided contacting them as a defensive reaction to their (clearly evidenced) unconscious hostility. The babies were retarded on measures of learning (memory and imitation) and also retarded in their social relations.[5]

The mechanisms leading to a hypercathexis of the skin can also help us to understand the exhibitionistic individual who displays himself to obtain attention and affection, as described by Alexander (*1*). The overprotected and overstimulated child could become the passive-dependent personality, as seen in the children of our nursery school (*28, 29*). The child whose aggression has been inhibited by the parent, and who turns that aggression toward himself, might become a masochistic personality so often associated with neurodermatitic patients (*6, 22*). The depressive personality has been described as resulting from guilt associated with erotic overstimulation from the maternal object (*10,* p. 391).

THE ASTHMATIC CHILD WHO HAD TRANSIENT ECZEMA OR NO ECZEMA

Developmental notes.—The skin is an inefficient and primitive mode for communicating needs and expressing tension. Children from ages 2 to 4 are encouraged to communicate in a more mature way by talking. Between the ages of 18 months and 36 months there is a rapid acceleration in language usage. Children move from verbal responses of one word to the use of three- to four-word sentences (*26*). Parents of the three-year-old will usually begin to expect more mature methods of communication by words rather than by acts. The transition to more mature language occurs during a period in which the child is also more assertive and is striving to achieve semi-autonomy.

Available data (*31*) indicate that three years is indeed a peak age for the onset of asthmatic symptoms. French, commenting on the choice of organ in psychosomatic diseases, and referring especially to asthma, stated that the organ which appears most under *tension at the moment of frustration* is the one likely to develop the symptom (*12,* p. 45). We assume that the behavior in transition is behavior potentially under stress. For any youngster the point of transition to a more mature mode of communication involving sentences and complex thoughts puts stress on the vocal-respiratory apparatus. As will be pointed out, parents of asthmatics not only encourage but demand more adult behavior, thereby putting additional stress on the vocal respiratory

[5]Spitz provides a thoughtful discussion of the interpersonal process necessary if a baby is to develop the capacity for social relatedness. "If the mother avoids touching her baby, she makes it impossible for her child to identify with her. . . . In the process of psychological development in the course of the first year the child acquires its ego with the help of numberless identifications with its mother which are made possible through the sensory experiences offered by her. Among the most important of these, if not *the* most important are the tactile experiences which include both superficial and deep sensitivity (*47*).

apparatus, which for the allergic child is already vulnerable physiologically.

Psychophysiological notes on the asthmatic child.—Edoardo Weiss, in 1922, after analyzing one asthmatic adult patient, postulated that asthmatic episodes are precipitated upon separation from the mother (*53*). French and Alexander and their co-workers conducted a psychoanalytic study of 27 cases of adults and children with asthma (*13*). They concluded that these patients were unable to resolve their dependency upon their mothers and experienced anxiety whenever there was a *threatened* separation from her. They proposed that the asthmatic attack represented a call for the mother in order to gain gratification of dependency yearnings which, prior to the asthmatic attack, appeared unobtainable. They concurred with Weiss's suggestion that the asthmatic wheeze thus represented a "repressed cry for the mother." Alexander observed that sounds emanating from a child who attempts to suppress his cry are similar to the frank asthmatic wheeze. Alexander further stressed that when a patient confesses his guilt feelings to his mother or to his therapist, he re-establishes a "dependent attachment" to the mother, and asthmatic attacks are often aborted (*1*). Alexander concluded his chapter on asthma by stating: "It is possible that the sensitivity to the 'separation' trauma and to allergens frequently appear together in the same person and are parallel manifestations of the same basic constitutional factor" (*1*).

However, in our studies (*28, 29, 42, 44*) we noted that the asthmatic child is particularly vulnerable to separation because of an earlier life pattern in relation to the mother. Mothers of asthmatic children frequently had disappointing relationships with their own mothers and very often questioned their capacity to render maternal care. Their feelings of inadequacy as mothers are frequently reinforced by ungratifying relationships with their husbands, in which there is often open conflict. The asthmatic child, as a consequence, does not receive a secure sense of support from his mother. Instead, he is encouraged to erect defenses (particularly a façade of pseudo-maturity) against the wish for dependency gratification. We were struck by the fact that frequently there are isolated areas in which the mother "bootlegs" dependency gratification to the child. For example, the nursery school child may still be permitted to use a bottle. The degree of support that the asthmatic child does receive allows the defense of pseudo-maturity to continue. When the minimal support is endangered, as with threatened detachment from the mother, the defense is ineffectual, and often the onset of asthma occurs (*29*).

Many investigators of the dynamics of asthma have discussed the importance of separation anxiety as a factor precipitating asthmatic attacks (*7, 13, 19, 28, 29, 37, 42, 46*).[6]

---

[6]Some investigators object to the separation anxiety formulation. Arguments pro and con have previously been discussed by Selesnick (*42*).

A dramatic example of the importance of separation anxiety in the precipitation of an asthmatic attack came to our attention most recently when a mother had an intensive dependent attachment to her therapist. As part of a research project, her asthmatic youngster had been treated psychotherapeutically while attending our nursery school and had completely recovered. The child's graduation precipitated the mother's fear of losing her therapist. She told the caseworker that she would like to have her youngest child brought into the nursery school. She knew that, since this child did not have a psychosomatic illness or obvious psychological problems, it was unlikely that the child would be accepted in our nursery school program. That same evening she became infuriated at her youngest child and told him to go to his room and not to come out. Heretofore, this form of punishment had not been utilized. While the child was in the room by himself, he developed his first attack of asthma. When the mother told the therapist about the asthma, she could barely disguise her delight. She requested the child's admission to the school and also that she might continue her treatment.[7] The mother's separation anxiety in regard to the therapist resulted in a deliberate effort on her part to alienate herself from her child. It was as though she knew the specificity theory and applied it to bring about a crisis in a child's life which would precipitate asthma.—(*43*)

More recently we emphasized that the child's fear of separation is not exclusively related to the fear of estrangement from the actual mother (*28*). Initially, the attachment to the mother or her substitute is the strongest bond in the early years of a child's life. Eventually, the child most fears severance from the internalized image of the mothering person. The child's internal perception of his mother may in many respects differ from the actual person the mother has become. Still later, the child fears severance not from the mothering person but from the father or any other strongly cathected object such as a dear friend, or even an animal. When threatened with estrangement from these objects he suffers intense separation anxiety, an experience which, in our studies, almost always preceded asthmatic attacks (*42*).

Recent research with animals on the problem of imprinting provides an intriguing lead to an explanation of the asthmatic child's sensitivity to alterations in his relationship with important adults. In Scott's analysis entitled "Critical periods in behavioral development" (*40*), he points out that given a condition of emotional arousal the young developing organism becomes strongly attached to the individual with whom he is in contact for a considerable period of time. When the relationship of the young organism to the adult is 'troubled'—i.e., where there is stress imposed on the young organism by the adult—the emotion aroused is more intense and the relationship to the adult becomes stronger.

Thus, in a study by Fisher (*11,* cited by Scott [*40*]), a group of puppies was sometimes punished and sometimes rewarded by kind treatment, the reward and punishments being distributed in random fashion. This group showed the most attraction and dependency behavior with respect to the

[7]The request was not granted. Instead, the mother's fear of termination was examined. The child has had no further asthmatic attacks.

experimenter, compared with groups of puppies that were always rewarded or consistently punished. The haphazard distribution of rewards and punishments in the study with puppies represents an experimental paradigm for the pattern of behavior provided a child by an ambivalent parent. There is evidence from our own studies of asthmatic children that the mother is highly ambivalent about her relationship to her child. Sometime in his childhood the asthmatic's mother begins to provide love 'conditionally.' The child perceives that, if he is to receive affection, he has to meet certain maternal demands for performance. These demands are set up to meet his mother's need rather than his own.

Rogers (*36*) has suggested that a person is free to expand his potentialities and develop his personality resources best in an interpersonal context where, by and large, he is receiving 'unconditional regard.' In contrast, where the regard is more conditional, he is subjected to incongruent pressures. His own needs and interests are in conflict with those imposed by his parents. Rather than a free expansion of his personality, a heightening of tension and a defensive constriction result.

The asthmatic child perceives that his relationship to the critical adult is not secure but rather is contingent on the success of his efforts to meet the adult's standards. As demonstrated by the level-of-aspiration experiment of Little and Cohen (*25*), the standards the asthmatic mother sets for her child are often not easy to meet. In comparison with mothers of normal children, the asthmatic child's mother was significantly more prone to raise her aspiration level well above the child's performance level.

An illustrative case follows:

Carl was a 3½-year-old asthmatic child whose real parents did not have an allergic history. At two weeks of age he was adopted into a family where the parents' natural son, a ten-year-old, had been asthmatic since early childhood. The adoptive mother was extremely impressed by Carl's precocity and was involved in his level of performance. On the day scheduled for his diagnostic interview, the mother called seeking to cancel because "He has a slight cold and may not perform as well as he really can." She was extremely proud of his ability to communicate verbally and emphasized that he made very few mistakes in diction. When the psychiatrist commented on Carl's mature speech pattern his mother said: "He has not had speech training, I merely would specify a word and ask him to repeat it until it was correct." This mother had hoped to become a professional singer, but her own mother discouraged this ambition by continually criticizing her improper diction. Carl's father denied his own dependency yearnings and projected this defense on to his child whom he felt should be the model of the independent individual like himself. He also emphasized the child's excellent ability to communicate verbally.

The parent who loves conditionally is one who loves ambivalently. The child becomes focused on the ambivalent parent and sensitive to the threatening implications of that parent's attitudes. Consequently, the parent-child relationship is chronically at a state of high emotional arousal. Any anticipation of an actual separation exerts an additional pressure on the sensitive relationship.

Correlations between conflict and pathogenesis are not as clearly worked out as they are for eczema. In their discussion of asthma, Wittkower and White (*55*) have suggested that an antigen-antibody reaction triggers the release of acetylcholine and histamine. On the other hand, stimuli arising in the cerebral cortex may influence the hypothalamic nuclei, which also cause the release of acetylcholine, histamine, and 5-hydroxytryptamine (p. 185). Alexander has suggested that short-term emergencies activate the sympathetic nervous system, whereas the parasympathetic nervous system is implicated in those affects which imply a long-term survival threat. Is it possible that conditions of love implying the wish for the child to mature quickly engenders a fear, over a protracted period, of loss of maternal protection? In time, it may be possible to connect these affects and ideations with the arousal of the parasympathetic nervous system. At present, correlations between neurogenic, psychogenic, and biochemical processes involving the bronchi have not been established.

THE CHILD WITH CHRONIC ECZEMA WHO ALSO DEVELOPS ASTHMA

We have discussed clinical findings about the eczematous child by using a general theoretical perspective which attempts to delineate factors which could perpetuate the eczematous lesions. Unfortunately, there are too few reports describing the child with eczema which also examine the family relationships at the point of onset of asthma.

In the three cases of eczema we studied (*29*) the pattern of care provided by the parents did not reveal frank avoidance of the child. Instead we observed excessive preoccupation with the child's skin, which served to defend the mother against her hostile wishes. The mother herself did not always provide the excessive contact but supported familial arrangements which permitted others to do so. Of course, it is conceivable that when these children were infants, before we had the opportunity to observe the mothers, the hostility manifested itself through maternal avoidance. In describing the mothers of eczematous children, Spitz (*47*) also noted an anxious, hovering concern about the child, often coupled with an inhibition in touching the child. He labeled this pattern of mothering "hostility garbed as manifest anxiety."

We were impressed by the fact that, when two of our eczematous children began to become assertive, they had their first asthmatic attack. The order of conflict in the one eczematous child who did not develop asthma was different from that of the two eczematous children who later developed asthma. In the former the struggle was in the service of obtaining infantile dependent gratifications. He never encountered the conflict over assertiveness and showed little indication of phallic aggressiveness (*29*). In the two eczematous children who developed asthma the conflict involved an attempt to achieve a degree of autonomy which in effect modified the more regressive aspect of the relationship to the mother.

The pressure for maturity can originate from the mother who feels overburdened by the child whom she has babied, and reacts to his toddling or other signs of autonomous development as a signal that she can rid herself, at long last, of a heavy responsibility. She may precipitously give up her former mode of infantilization and encourage the child to premature development. The child who has been excessively infantilized in the past is most unprepared to develop suddenly a mature stature. If he is induced, too quickly, to express himself communicatively by vocalization, then there will be undue stress on the communicative organs which are unprepared for such activity (French [*12*], p. 45). Obviously, a vocal symptom such as stuttering could develop, but in a child allergically predisposed asthma would be more likely to occur. Furthermore, if precipitously urged to be aggressive, the child who feels hostile to his mother may fear that by asserting himself he will alienate her. The consequence would be anxiety over separation. Conceivably, difficulties in expiration, a process involved in wheezing as well as in talking, might result.

Although the mother may suddenly exert pressure on the child to become independent, there will be a time lag in which he still reacts to the attitude of a formerly infantilizing mother whom he has internalized:

> The mother of a 6-year-old eczematous youngster who was in therapy suddenly decided that she had been inappropriately babying him. Many times previously he had been denied permission to go swimming. On this occasion when the child asked for permission, his mother said, "You are a big boy, of course you can go." On the way to the pool, the child had an asthmatic attack. In his therapy hour the next day, the boy confessed that he felt his mother really would be angry at him if he went swimming. He feared he would alienate his mother as he conceived of her—i.e., the internalized prohibitive mother. Previously the condition set by his mother for love was "Be a baby." Now she suddenly implied "Be a man."

The infantilized eczematous child who develops asthma finds himself subjected to the additional pressure resulting from a double-bind situation. The internal image demands that he be immature, whereas the external dictum is "Grow up and be a man right now."

THE CHILD WITH REMITTING ECZEMA AND NO ASTHMA

There are data suggesting that fluctuations in the physiological threshold of sensitivity to irritation can account for the commonly observed course of eczema. The infant in the first 6 to 8 months of life has tender and immature skin which readily reacts to heat, wet diapers, and other irritants, with transient rashes and lesions. Studies of sensitivity to experimentally controlled irritation, conducted by Kepecs *et al.* (*21*), reveal that both normal and constitutionally allergic (atopic) babies are very sensitive to irritating stimuli in their first year of life. By the end of the first year the normal baby's threshold for irritation rises. In contrast, the threshold for atopic babies remains low, and they continue to be highly sensitive to irritating stimuli until 3 years. The data of Kepecs *et al.* (*21*), relating the course of sensitivity to irritating stimuli to the age of the child, account for the frequent remissions of eczema between 3 and 4 years of age on a constitutional basis. Between the ages of 3 and 4 the sensitivity of atopic youngsters drops sharply, until by age 4 it is equivalent to that of normal, nonallergic children. From 4 to approximately age 10, the graph describing variations in sensitivity to irritating stimuli are congruent for both normal and atopic youngsters.

From the above considerations we presume that the baby who has infantile eczema which does not go on to a chronic state of eczema or neurodermatitis beyond the age of 3 or 4, is the child who has *not* been exposed to excessive physical contact from adults or to the psychogenic factors which produce a hypercathexis of the skin or evoke a pattern of excessive self-stimulation.

A constitutional disposition for a low threshold makes an atopic youngster highly vulnerable to irritating stimuli. Even when the parents of the very atopic child provide close, soothing contact, it would be difficult to prevent episodes of eczema between 2 and 3 years of age. Eczematous lesions which continue beyond 4 years of age appear to require the order of psychodynamic input we have described.

When parents can communicate more rather than less unconditional regard and permit the child to express aggressiveness without placing a premium on it, our theory would predict that the psychogenic factors for initiating a transition to asthma would also be absent.

RESEARCH IMPLICATIONS OF THE THEORETICAL SPECULATIONS

Our theoretical outline poses a number of questions pertinent to a better understanding of the eczema-asthma diathesis, which could be, but has not yet been, studied empirically.

Given the emphasis on the relationship between a transition to more mature verbal communication and the onset of asthma, the small number of babies having asthma attacks in the first year of life pose a challenge. Do the first attacks occur around 7 to 9 months of age, the period when babies discriminate between mothers and "strangers," often reacting with apprehension to the latter (*41,* Fig. 5, p. 13, p. 22)?[8] Do attacks actually occur in circumstances when the baby is left in the care of a "stranger"? Some babies have first attacks at a younger age, or in psychologically more neutral circumstances. Do these infants have a very strong constitutional disposition for asthma—e.g., would they have high scores on the allergic potential scale (*4*)?

Previously, we noted the lack of empirical research, or even of clinical case reports, dealing with the transition from eczema to asthma and the associated psychodynamic events. Do parents of children who have made the transition to asthma exert stronger pressures on the child to be independent than parents of children who continue to have chronic eczema? Are asthmatic children more prone to be self-assertive, involved in achievement strivings, and more sensitive to separation anxiety than their eczematous peers? To answer these questions we have begun to study a nonclinic series of 3- to 6-year-old asthmatic and eczematous children in their own homes. We observe the child as he responds to the challenge of a psychometric test and as he plays with dolls representing his family constellation. We also interview and administer questionnaires to his parents exploring, among other questions, the parents' attitudes toward achievement and perception of the child's maturity.

What are the conditions of familial interaction which maintain the eczematous child's symptoms even during a chronological period when the increased threshold to irritation is conducive to remission? We have been struck by the psychological distance which characterizes the parental relationship, paradoxically coupled with their perception of the marital relationship as harmonious, as described earlier. In many cases there was *de facto* separation. The ready acceptance of a situation leading to a lack of emotional contact between the parents seems to be compatible with observations of an incapacity to relate to the infant. According to the literature, the incapacity to contact the baby is a fundamental problem of the mother of the eczematous child. We are currently interviewing mothers and fathers of eczematous children and control groups of parents of asthmatic and normal children. Our theory leads us to predict that a higher order of psychological distance will characterize the relationship of parents of the eczematous children.

Our theory has incorporated formulations relating the experience of separation anxiety to the asthmatic attack. Is the problem of separation a specific conflict area for the asthmatic? Can the occurrence of asthmatic attacks be related to the presence or absence of separation threats? Currently, in the Psychiatric and Psychosomatic Research Institute of Mount Sinai Hospital, adult patients with various psychosomatic illnesses, including asthma, are being shown commercial movies. The films were selected to represent,

[8]It would be most valuable if reliable statistics were finally available on the rate of incidence of initial asthmatic attacks during the first year of life.

dramatically, psychodynamic tension areas hypothesized to be specifically relevant to different psychosomatic problems. Thus, asthmatic patients see films where themes involving separation are prominent. The asthmatic patient also sees control films involving conflicts other than separation, and control groups with other psychosomatic illnesses also see the movies portraying separation themes. As the subjects watch the films, recordings are made of respiratory and autonomic responses to stress. We expect the asthmatic patients' response will indicate specific sensitivity to the separation theme.

Is separation anxiety a particularly critical problem for the asthmatic child? Is not separation a universal threat for all preschool-age children, with the tension discharged in a variety of ways by nonasthmatic children? We intend to examine those intervals in the asthmatic child's life when he is not having attacks. We will analyze the dynamic material provided by detailed reports of the therapeutic work with parents and child. We predict a relative absence of threat concerning separation from the cathected object in those periods when the asthmatic child is not having symptoms.

Turning to the detailed protocol of the nonasthmatic children in our clinic nursery school, we will determine periods of high and low symptom manifestation and see whether the changes in the child's symptoms co-vary with separation occurring in his life (parent's business trips, therapist's vacations). We would not expect the nonasthmatic child to be as sensitive to separation experiences as is the asthmatic child.

In our work with children we are planning to monitor therapy hours, using a light transistorized biometric device which can be worn by the child to pick up and transmit dyspnea, rhonci, rales, and wheezing. Thus we will have a condition for an interpersonal experiment where specific separation stresses can be introduced into the interaction and respiratory signs assayed.

Are we correct in assuming that a significant source of stress in the asthmatic child's relationship with his parent arises from the tendency to grant love and support only on the condition that the child's accomplishments meet certain standards? We are currently testing the role of 'conditional regard' by administering parental attitude scales to the mothers and fathers of 3- to 6-year-old asthmatic, eczematous, and normal children. These scales which were developed by Torgoff (*50, 51*) measure the parents' tendency to be 'achievement-inducing,' or 'independence granting.' As conceptualized by Torgoff, achievement-inducing parents assume that children learn in response to pressure from an external agent. By asking parents to specify the age at which the child should accomplish certain tasks, the scale establishes the parents' tendency to push the child in a prescribed direction. The independence-granting parent "lets go," permitting the child to assume responsibility for his own activity and to make his own decisions. If independence-granting is coupled with a warm interest in the child, the parent will communicate a sense of support and respect for the child's capability to act autonomously. On the other hand, achievement-inducing presents a conditional demand on the child to excel in order to placate the parent. We, therefore, anticipate significant differences in the response of parents of asthmatic, eczematous, and normal children.

Further empirical research is suggested by our analysis of the early conditions of parent-child contact with the onset of infantile eczema which becomes chronic. If we examine the mental hospital population of chronic schizophrenic patients—process rather than reactive—would there be an unusually high incidence of eczema? Would there be a significantly lower incidence of asthma in these patients?

An ideal research program for testing a developmental theory would provide an opportunity for longitudinal study of parental *behavior* with their children, as well as the study of their attitudes and reports of family life. It would be feasible to define a group of parents with a strong allergic diathesis and a control group of parents who do not have a constitutional predisposition to produce allergic children. By starting with the parents during the last trimester of pregnancy, and then following the child and family for the first six years, many questions about conditions leading to the onset and perpetuation of eczema, transition to asthma, and the relationship of these symptoms to the course of development of verbal communicative skills could be elucidated.

In conclusion, we believe that a developmental orientation to the eczema-asthma complex, emphasizing the maturity level of communication and the interpersonal role of 'conditional regard,' provides a fruitful basis for understanding the transition from eczema to asthma and poses questions which can be answered by empirical research.

REFERENCES

1 Alexander, F. *Psychosomatic Medicine.* New York, Norton, 1950.

2 Augenbraun, Bernice, Machtinger, Paula, Lavine, P., and Pearce, Ruth S. Casework treatment in a therapeutic nursery school. *Soc. Casew.,* Dec., 1963.

3 Bergman, R., and Aldrich, C. K. The natural history of infantile ezcema: A follow-up study. Paper presented at the Meeting of the American Psychosomatic Society, Atlantic City, New Jersey, April 27–28, 1963.

4 Block, Jeanne. Are psychosomatic syndromes homogenous: Evidence supporting a differentiated approach. Paper presented at the Meeting of the Society for Research in Child Development, Berkeley, California, April 10, 1963.

5 Brodbeck, A. J., and Irwin, O. C. The speech behavior of infants without families. *Child Develpm. 17:*145–156, 1946.

6 Cleveland, S. E., and Fisher, S. Psychological factors in the neurodermatoses. *Psychosom. Med. 18:*209–220, 1956.

7 Coolidge, J. C. Asthma in mother and child as a special type of intercommunication. *Amer. J. Orthopsychiat. 26:*165, 1956.

8 Dees, Susan C. Development and course of asthma in children. *Arch. Dis. Childh. 93:*228–233, 1957.

9 Dees, Susan C. Asthma in infants and young children. *J. Amer. Med. Ass. 175:*365–369, 1961.

10 Fenichel, O. *The Psychoanalytic Theory of Neuroses.* New York, Norton, 1945,

11 Fisher, A. E. Unpublished doctoral dissertation, Pennsylvania State Univ., 1955.

12 French, T. M. "Physiology of Behavior and Choice of Neurosis." In *Studies in Psychosomatic Medicine,* edited by F. Alexander and T. M. French. New York, Ronald Press, 1948.

13 French, T. M., and Alexander, F., *et al.* Psychogenic factors in bronchial asthma. Parts I and II. *Psychosom. Med. Monogr.,* Vol. I, No. 4, Washington, D.C., National Research Council, 1941.

14 Freud, S. *Beyond the Pleasure Principle.* London, Hogarth, 1950.

15 Glaser, J. *Allergy in Childhood.* Springfield, Ill., Charles C Thomas, 1956.

16 Irwin, O. C. Infant speech: Speech sound development of sibling and only infants. *J. exp. Psychol. 38:*600–602, 1948.

17 Irwin, O. C. Infant speech: The affect of family occupational status and of age on sound frequency. *J. speech hear. Disord. 13:*320–323, 1948.

18 Irwin, O. C. Infant speech: The affect of family occupational status and of age on the use of sound types. *J. speech hear. Disord. 13:*224–226, 1948.

19 Jessner, Lucie, Lamont, J., Long, R., Rollins, Nancy, Whipple, Babette, and Prentice, N. Emotional impact of nearness and separation for the asthmatic child and his mother. *Psychoanal. Stud. Child. 10:*353–375, 1955.

20 Kepecs, J. G., and Robin, M. Studies in itching. II. Some psychological implications of the inter-relationships between cutaneous pain and touch systems. *Arch. Neurol., Chicago 76:*325–340, 1956.

21 Kepecs, J. G., Robin, M., and Munro, Clare. Tickle in atopic dermatitis: Interference with the organization of a pattern response. *Arch. gen. Psychiat. 3:*243–251, 1960.

22 Klaber, M. M. Manifestations of hostility in neurodermatitis. *J. consult. Psychol. 24:*116–120, 1960.

23 Levine, S., Alpert, M., and Lewis, G. W. Infantile experience in the maturation of the pituitary adrenal axis. *Science 126:*1347, 1957.

24 Lewis, M. M. *How Children Learn to Speak.* London, Harrap, 1957; New York, Basic Books, 1959.

25 Little, Sue W., and Cohen, L. D. Goal setting behavior of asthmatic children and of their mothers for them. *J. Pers. 19:*376–382, 1951.

26 McCarthy, Dorothea. "Language Development in Children." In *Manual of Child Psychology,* 2nd edition, edited by L. Carmichael. New York, Wiley, 1954.

27 Marmor, J., Ashley, M., Tabachnic, N., Storkan, Margaret, and McDonald, F. The mother-child relationship in the genesis of neurodermatitis. *Arch. Derm., Chicago 74:*599–605, 1956.

28 Mohr, G. J., Selesnick, S., and Augenbraun, Bernice. "Family Dynamics in Early Childhood Asthma: Some Mental Health Considerations." In *The Asthmatic Child,* edited by H. I. Schneer. New York, Hoeber, 1963.

29 Mohr, G. J., Tausend, Helen, Selesnick, S., and Augenbraun, Bernice. Studies of eczema and asthma in the preschool child. *J. Amer. Acad. Child Psychiat. 2:*271–291, 1963.

30 Mustacchi, P., Lucia, S. P., and Jassy, Liliana. Bronchial asthma: Pattern of morbidity and mortality in the U.S., 1951–1959. *Calif. Med. 96:*196–200, 1962.

31 Peshkin, M. M. Intractable asthma of childhood: Rehabilitation at the institutional level with a follow-up of 150 cases. *Int. Arch. Allerg. 15:*91, 1959.

32 Purcell, K., Bernstein, L., and Bukantz, S. C. A preliminary comparison of rapidly remitting and persistently "steroid-dependent" asthmatic children. *Psychosom. Med. 23:*305–310, 1961.

33 Rapaport, H., Falk, M., and Adler, D. The allergic index. *Ann. Alerg. 18:*179, 1960.

34 Rebelsky, Freda, Nichols, Irenea, and Lennenberg, E. H. A study of infant vocalization. Paper presented at the Meeting of the Society for Research in Child Development, Berkeley, California, April 10–13, 1963.

35 Richter, C. T. Part I: Domestication of the Norway rat and its implication for the study of genetics in man. Symposium on "Light from animal experimentation on human heredity." *Amer. J. hum. Genet. 4:*273, 1952.

36 Rogers, C. R. The necessary and sufficient conditions of therapeutic personality change. *J. consult. Psychol. 21:*95–103, 1957.

37 Rogerson, C. H., Hardcastle, D. H., and Guduid, K. A. A psychological approach to the problem of asthma and the asthma-eczema-prurigo syndrome. *Guy's Hosp. Rep. 85:*289, 1935.

38 Rosenthal, M. J. Psychosomatic study of infantile eczema: Mother-child relationship. *Pediatrics 10:*581–592, 1952.

39 Rosenthal, M. J. Neuropsychiatric aspects of infantile eczema: Special reference to the role of cutaneous pain receptors. *Arch. Neurol., Chicago 70:*428–451, 1953.

40 Scott, J. P. Critical periods in behavioral development. *Science 138:*949–958, 1962.

41 Scott, J. P. The process of primary socialization in canine and human infants. *Monogr. Soc. Res. Child Develpm. 8:*No. 1, 1963.

42 Selesnick, S. "Separation Anxiety and Asthmatic Attacks Related to Shifts in Object Cathexes." In *The Asthmatic Child,* edited by H. I. Schneer. New York, Hoeber, 1963.

43 Selesnick, S., Alexander, F., and French, T. M. "Psychoanalysis Integrated and Expanded." In *Science and Psychoanalysis,* Vol. VII, edited by J. Masserman. New York, Grune and Stratton, 1964.

44 Selesnick, S., Friedman, D. G., and Augenbraun, B. Psychological management of childhood asthma. *Calif. Med. 100:*406–411, June, 1964.

45 Sperber, Z., and Weinberger, P. E. The independence granting and achievement inducing attitudes of fathers and mothers and their children's intelligence

test performance. Paper presented at the Meeting of the Western Psychological Association, Santa Monica, California, April 18, 1963.

46 Sperling, M. The role of the mother in psychosomatic disorders in children. *Psychosom. Med. 11*:377–385, 1949.

47 Spitz, R. A. The psychogenic diseases in infancy: An attempt at their etiologic classification. *Psychoanal. Stud. Child 6*:255–275, 1951.

48 Sternberg, T. H., and Zimmerman, M. C. Stress studies in the eczema-asthma-hay fever diathesis. *Arch. Derm., Chicago 65*:392–398, 1952.

49 Sulzburger, M. B. "Atopic Dermatitis." In *The Eczemas,* edited by L. J. A. Loewenthal. London, E. & S. Livingstone, 1954.

50 Torgoff, I. Parental developmental time table. Paper presented at the Annual Meeting of the American Psychological Association, Washington, D.C., August, 1958.

51 Torgoff, I. Synergistic parental role components: Application to expectancies and behavior; consequences for child's curiosity. Paper presented at the Annual meeting of the American Psychological Association, Chicago, Illinois, August 1960.

52 Von Bertalanffy, L. A biologist looks at human nature. *Scient. Monthly 82*:33–41, 1956.

53 Weiss, E. Psychoanalyse eines falles von nervoesem asthma. *Int. Z. Psychoanal. 8*:440, 1922.

54 Williams, D. H. Management of atopic dermatitis in children: Control of the maternal rejection factor. *Arch. Derm., Chicago 63*:545–560, 1951.

55 Wittkower, E. D., and White, K. L. "Psychophysiologic Aspects of Respiratory Disorders." In *American Handbook of Psychiatry,* Vol. I, edited by S. Arieti. New York, Basic Books, 1959, pp. 693–694.

56 Wolff, P. H. Observations on newborn infants. *Psychosom. Med. 21*:110–118, 1959.

57 Woodhead, Barbara. The psychological aspect of allergic skin reactions in childhood. *Arch. Dis. Childh. 21*:98–104, 1946.

SIXTEEN

Psychic Energies in Health and Disease

MORTIMER OSTOW, M.D.

The need for a quantitative factor in psychologic and psychiatric theory derives not from the fallacious idea that only that which can be measured can be treated scientifically, or from the fact that it is easier to handle quantitative than qualitative variables, but from the fact that the observation of human behavior creates an impression of a continuously varying intensity factor of some kind. It is evident from Freud's earlier writings that he was at first more concerned with quantitative than with dynamic factors. The *Project for a Scientific Psychology* dealt with "quantity theory" (*5*). In early published papers (*4*) he spoke of a "sum of excitation." At the same time, he seemed to regard affect as equivalent to, or immediately derived from, this hypothetical excitation. Subsequently, the idea of this quantitative factor became crystallized in the concept of psychic energy.

In attempting to work out a system of psychodynamics Freud attributed both inner origin of motivation and displaceability of impulse to an energetic entity which affected the vicissitudes of drives. At the same time he elaborated the concept of psychic energy in a somewhat different direction. Not only were individual impulses each endowed with a sum of excitation, but the ego itself depended upon a supply of psychic energy for its function. The ego could distribute and discharge the energies conveyed to it by the id. It could also retain some of these energies for its own activities. In fact, if it was deprived of its energies, the ego's performance was seriously impaired (*10*). On the other hand, when the ego was flooded with more energy than it could conveniently handle, its function was seriously disrupted (*12*). Although Freud claimed an independent existence for these psychic energies, he did relate them to sexual hormones and to other humoral elements (*7, 14*). It should not be overlooked that Freud anticipated that, when therapeutically effective anti-psychotic drugs became available, they would achieve their effectiveness by influencing the distribution of psychic energies.

My own interest in this field was kindled by my experience during the past ten years with the anti-psychotic drugs. It has been my impression that the states that they produce correspond to states of libido deficiency and libido excess as these were described by Freud. From my observations (*15*) I inferred that tranquilizers act to diminish the ego's supply of libido, whereas energizers act to increase its supply. On the basis of this assumption I was able to devise clinical criteria for estimating the level of the ego's energy supply; to elaborate and extend the psychoanalytic theory of energetics; to devise a system for selecting drugs and for monitoring their effects; and to suggest a method for combining drug therapy with psychoanalysis and psychotherapy.

It is my intention to demonstrate the clinical usefulness and far-reaching implications of the energy concept in describing the natural history of mental illness in general; in predicting and understanding some of the specific forms of symptomatic behavior; and in accounting for some of the changes in behavior and temperament which we normally encounter as we observe individuals traversing the secular life cycle. Let me emphasize that these generalizations and speculations are based upon clinical observation of spontaneous developments in mental illness, the effects of psychoanalytic therapy, and the effects of repeatedly administering and withdrawing psychically active drugs to patients under daily scrutiny. There can be no doubt that even the most purely psychic kind of energy that we can imagine must be based upon some organic substrate, or probably upon a whole system of organic substrates. I have discussed elsewhere (*15*) the possible contributions made by the globus pallidus, sex hormones, pituitary hormones, other steroids, and catechol and other amines. It is my impression that the concept of psychic energy will provide the most direct link between psychic function and the physiology of the brain.

THE NATURAL HISTORY OF MENTAL ILLNESS

From a long-range point of view one may say that mental illness follows a characteristic course which, after its initial phase, is determined largely by the course of the ego's libido supply. The latter, in turn, is determined by the psychic changes brought about by the illness, by the growth and aging of the individual, and by other influences which we shall discuss below. This concept obviously resembles Freud's early concept of the *aktual neurosis*. The latter is an illness caused by an excessive accumulation or deficiency of libido (*6, 10*). Freud included anxiety neurosis, neurasthenia, and hypochondria, and subsequently (*10*) suggested that some cases of melancholia might also belong in this group of illnesses. These conditions, in which there is a serious deviation of the ego's libido supply, became the nucleus upon which or around which psychoneuroses crystallized. The latter were pathologic conditions determined by the interplay of dynamic forces. In recent decades little attention has been given to *aktual neuroses* in the psychoanalytic literature, but I believe that a close study at the present time of these and related conditions will permit important advances in psychoanalytic theory and practice.

Let us review several phases into which I have arbitrarily divided the typical course of mental illness. The reader should note that these phasic variations and the syndromes that accompany them cut across all the various nosologic entities. In other words, each phase may be found at one or another time in most diagnostic conditions. What determines the kind of illness into which the patient breaks down is the nature of his ego weakness, probably determined constitutionally. Energetic fluctuations determine when and whether a breakdown occurs and the subsequent course of the illness. Among the various symptoms that one encounters in mental illness, some are determined by the unique developmental experiences of the individual, others by constitutional predisposition, others by the interplay of dynamic forces, and still others by the energy state prevailing at the time. Most symptoms, however, are determined by several or all of these influences acting together.

Phase I: The phase of conflict.—Every mental illness of adult life begins with a reactivation of the oedipal conflict. This, in turn, is brought about by a disequilibrium between impulse and defense. When oedipal influences threaten to override the defenses which normally contain them, there follows a mobilization of primitive emergency defenses including regression. As a result of this regression, the oedipal conflict now becomes overlaid and complicated by infantile conflicts which had remained more or less latent for years. Symptoms are created by the classical mechanism of condensation of impulse, defense, and punishment. Even as the symptoms are being formed, the ego attempts to accommodate itself to them and in this way produces some of the secondary manifestations of mental illness.

Phase II: The phase of libido plethora.—In some patients the discharge of energies by the production and maintenance of symptoms may stabilize the psychic economy for a shorter or longer period. In many other patients symptom formation fails to stem the generation of a libido surplus or even to absorb a significant amount of libido. The libido, which is continuously generated by the blocked impulses, spills over into the ego.

When it is thus endowed with an excess of libidinal energies, the ego exhibits certain characteristic changes. One sees at first a sense of vigor, of vitality, of euphoria. As the libido level rises further, the patient may complain of a feeling of being driven, and this feeling is often associated with anxiety. Overactivity and overtalkativeness appear commonly. After an initial period of facilitation, intellectual functions then go on to deteriorate. Sleep is at first reduced and then becomes impossible. Finally, the patient becomes excited, irritable, and belligerent.

There are also characteristic changes in the manifestations of drive and drive derivatives. First, the patient describes an increased genital erotism. As this becomes more intense, genital performance becomes impaired. Neurotic or psychotic symptoms are then invoked to handle the increased erotic excitement. We observe an intensification in the pursuit of love objects. The increased drive intensity ultimately creates a threat to the ego, and therefore it invokes an intensification of defense. Defenses which operate by modifying the aim of the instinct fail to deal with this intensified drive and give way to more desperate defenses which act to increase the distance of the subject from the love object. In other words, they attempt to create detachment from the love object either by intrapsychic maneuvers or by physical maneuvers or by both. We observe frequently, too, that under the influence of a plethora of libido the patient tends to identify with his mother in her maternal role. For example, we often encounter fantasies of or wishes for pregnancy; we observe a concern for others as though they were helpless children who require gifts, care, and protection. Finally, as a result of the patient's objectlessness, and as a result of his identification with mother, the patient's libido is turned back entirely upon himself, and we see manifestations of pathologically intense narcissism with the well-known delusions of omnipotence and omniscience. These delusions are also partially determined by a need to deny the consequences of severe impairment of ego function—namely, impotence, in its general as well as its genital sense, and confusion.

If the patient is in analysis he sees his analyst not as a parent, but rather as a contemporary companion; at a later stage as a suitable object of erotic desire; still later as a child who does not understand. The patient then identifies with the psychoanalyst in the latter's parental role. Ultimately extreme narcissism compels the patient to abandon the analyst as an object altogether and to see him as a frustrator and unwelcome threat.

Phase III: The phase of depletion of libidinal energies.—At some point in the development of libido plethora a correction is likely to ensue. This correction may induce a swing of libido level back to or past normal. As the plethora subsides and as ego functions recover, the patient feels evident relief. The relief is often accompanied by fantasies of rebirth.

However, events are often not so simple. The corrective depletion and the apprehension of further depletion often evoke anxiety, since the ego is actually as helpless in the face of inadequate libido as it is in the case of excess libido. As a result of this anxiety, the patient attempts to resist depletion by invoking clinging, pregenital, aggressive, anaclitic impulses. In other words, the process of depletion often induces a paradoxical state of hypermotivation in which we see symptoms similar to those of the plethora phase. I believe that the large majority of neurotic patients seeking help, and therefore probably more than half the patients in long-term psychotherapy and psychoanalysis, are properly assigned to this phase of depletion hypermotivation.

What are the characteristics of the ego in this state? We observe a fluctuation in the speed and range of ego activities. Projections and identifications exist together or alternate. There is an evident regressive libidinization of sublimated activities. In this state the patient tolerates isolation badly. Any abrupt increase in the threat of depletion may induce an attack of anxiety, either free-floating or attached to some percept.

We observe the following characteristics of the drive activity: In the first place there is an intensification of all drive activities, direct and derivative, object-related and narcissistic. We encounter a regression to oral and anal interests. However, we observe that drives are anaclitic rather than pure, and filial rather than parental. The patient clearly prefers familiar objects to strange objects, which he avoids phobically. (When the anaclitic drive is so great as to evoke anxiety, the directions of preference and aversion may be defensively reversed.) Any of the well-known neurotic or psychotic syndromes may be invoked to deal with this paradoxic hypermotivation.

The behavior of the patient in this state often creates the impression that there is a psychosomatic, centripetal stream drawing objects and materials closer to the patient. We see a craving for stimulation, a clinging and a clutching, a tendency to addiction, to bulimia, and to constipation.

In patients in this state we encounter readily visible evidence of superego activity. The patient often seems to attempt to appease the superego along with one or more parent figures. Guilt feelings may prevail, and the patient deals with them by efforts to make restitution. When such religious interests are caricatured in the psychotic states that are often created by paradoxic hypermotivation, the older psychiatrists spoke of "pietism."

If the patient is in analysis we observe a classical transference—i.e., the patient sees the analyst as though he were one of his parents. This transference establishes an anaclitic relation to the analyst.

Phase IV: The phase of libido deficiency.—At times the depletion process may carry too far, the corrective actions may become exhausted, or they may be frustrated. In any of these cases the pregenital emergency libido subsides, and the patient is left with an impoverished ego. This ego impoverishment may achieve expression in any of a number of classical, clinical syndromes: neurasthenia, hypochondria, depression, melancholia, some forms of schizophrenia and of *post-partum* psychosis.

As a result of the impoverishment of the ego there is a decrease in the speed and range of ego activities, an impairment of all ego functions including apperception, memory, thought, and action. The patient cannot tolerate demands for attention, for affection, for work, or for response of any kind.

We see little or no evidence of the existence of libidinal drives. There is neither direct libidinal activity nor derivatives of libido. On the other hand, aggressive tendencies prevail, because aggressive instinctual pressure is increased either absolutely or relatively. Whatever little libido is seen finds expression in pregenital aims. Because there is so little libido, what remains is concentrated exclusively upon the self, so that we find an unyielding narcissism.

Homologous to the centripetal stream of the state of paradoxic hypermotivation is a centrifugal stream in the state of libido deficiency. The patient avoids objects, he complains of a sensation of pulling on his extremities, and he rejects and ejects through his orifices. He tolerates no demands, whether for love or for work, and responds to such demands aggressively.

Perhaps the most distressing feature of the state of libido deficiency is the sense of inner pain which it creates. This pain colors all psychic activity in the state of depletion so that all experience becomes painful, all anticipations are pessimistic, all narcissism becomes hypochondria, and death seems to be preferable to life. It is this pain which is the proximate cause of suicide when that occurs.

In the state of libido deficiency superego influence appears openly. It would seem as though the state of impoverishment is interpreted by the ego as an indication of abandonment by the superego, just as continuing discomfort is interpreted by the infant as an indication of abandonment by his mother. A struggle ensues between the ego and the superego in which the ego protests this abandonment and expresses hatred for the anaclitic love object. Simultaneously or alternately, the ego accepts the superego's accusations and confesses and anticipates punishment.

When such a patient is in analysis or in psychotherapy we find that narcissism, the preoccupation with the inner pain and with the superego, all make the patient intolerant of the psychoanalyst. The occasional fleeting attempt to cling to the therapist may be ascribed to residual anti-depletion clinging.

If one is to take seriously the idea that energetic changes can influence the manifestations of mental illness so powerfully as this scheme seems to suggest, then one must attempt to arrive at some understanding of the mutual interplay between dynamic and energetic influence. Obviously, dynamic forces can bring about energetic changes. For example, repression of impulses can produce frustration, a consequent damming up of libido, and ultimately a state of plethora. Again, retreat from the object as a technique of defense can induce depletion of the ego. Further, a rejection by the anaclitic love object can frustrate and thus terminate a state of paradoxical hypermotivation so that the patient slips into a syndrome of definitive libido deficiency. On the other hand, the influence of energetic states over dynamic forces is made clear in the foregoing description of the various syndromes, each respectively characteristic of an energy state.

The power of these energy states to evoke specific constellations of dynamic forces is tellingly revealed by the following clinical observation. Occasionally we observe that a given energy state is first dissipated and then at some subsequent time recurs, either spontaneously, as a result of some psychotherapeutic intervention, or as a result of drug therapy. When such an event occurs the identical dynamic content which accompanied the first appearance of this energy state recurs in the second. For example, a man may entertain a specific delusion in a state of paradoxic hypermotivation. An energizing drug under such circumstances will undo the state of paradoxic hypermotivation and restore the energy level to within a normal range. The delusion will then disappear, and the patient will seem to acquire insight into the delusional, that is, the unreal character of his belief. If now the drug is discontinued, this state of paradoxic hypermotivation is likely to recur, and with it once more the original delusion. In other words, the patient accepts the delusion appropriate to his abnormal energy state and rejects the insight appropriate to the normal energy state. We may conclude that the recurrence in adult mental illness of the energy states of childhood serves as a powerful influence for the regressive induction of the dynamic constellations of childhood.

Let me illustrate this point by discussing the feeling of guilt. The feeling of guilt is, I believe, constantly associated with libido deficiency. Libido deficiency often follows a real transgression. For example, the misbehavior may lead to some misadventure, or it may lead to punishment, or it may elicit a self-punitive superego response. Under these circumstances, the guilt seems appropriate to all observers. On the other hand, libido deficiency may also occur in the course of illness—e.g., melancholic depression. In that case, the guilt that accompanies the deficiency seems inappropriate, and if extreme we consider it delusional. In other words, guilt is regularly associated with libido deficiency, but it is not necessarily associated with misbehavior when the latter is not followed by libido deficiency. But if the feeling of guilt does not mean actual guilt—i.e., responsibilty for transgression—then what does it mean? Because the feeling of guilt is constantly associated with the state of libido deficiency; because it is frequently accompanied by acts of confession, restitution, and by resolutions to improve oneself and one's behavior (that is, by acts that would seem calculated to appease a parent); because the feeling of guilt is frequently accompanied by a sense of being observed and being criticized—therefore, I would infer that the sense of guilt represents a desire to be reunited and reconciled with the supporting, protecting, parental love object. Thus the sense of guilt does not express the influence of the superego; rather, it represents a desire by the ego to find favor with the parent or his superego representative. One may say that the sense of guilt represents the child's cry for his absent parent (*13*). It is invoked in adult life by regression to a state of helplessness due to libido deficiency which first existed in childhood.

CYCLIC VARIATIONS OF THE EGO'S LIBIDO SUPPLY

During the course of the life span, cyclic changes occur in the physiology of the organism, many of which are reflected in cyclic fluctuations in the ego's libido supply. These should be noted by the psychiatrist not only because they influence vulnerability to and symptoms of mental illness, but also because they give rise to certain fluctuations in behavior and temperament which we expect in the normal individual.

Let us consider first the circadian cycle—i.e., those changes that repeat cyclically every 24 hours. I have no data which apply to the circadian cycle in the normal. However, we do know that there are circadian cyclic fluctuations in metabolic processes, hormone secretion, work output, appetite, and the need for rest. One can readily imagine that these changes determine or relate to cyclic fluctuations in the ego's libido supply, fluctuations all within limits of normal variability.

In illness some evident cycles can be discerned and clearly associated with drug administration and with ego libido states. Among the most striking are disturbances of sleep. Early morning awakening, hypersomnia, and sleep interruptions such as nightmares, sleepwalking, and jumping up from sleep are phenomena all characteristic of states of libido deficiency or of anti-depletion hypermotivation. On the other hand, in manic states created by libido plethora or paradoxical hypermotivation, there is a refusal to sleep. Related to these sleep disturbances is the phenomenon of nocturnal eating. Many patients in a state of mild anti-depletion hypermotivation become overwhelmed by an almost irresistible craving to eat at night either before sleep or during a sleep interruption. Many patients in states of mild to moderate libido deficiency but without much reactive hypermotivation, especially when this state is maintained by energizing drugs, become overwhelmed by a torpor suggesting narcolepsy every afternoon, sometime between 3 and 6 P.M.

The problem of circadian fluctuations in ego libido does not lend itself easily to study in the practice of psychoanalysis. Yet I believe that much of the cyclic variation in mood, temperament, disposition, and level of activity which we take for granted may relate to cyclic variations in the ego's libido content.

One would expect, *a priori,* that the menstrual cycle would be accompanied by coordinate fluctuations of ego energies. For example, Benedek (*1*) found sufficiently consistent changes in her analytic material to permit her to guess relatively well at the date of ovulation. Moreover, in many women one can easily discern a regular and clear-cut premenstrual syndrome indicating mild libido deficiency with perhaps little or no reactive hypermotivation.

One may, in a sense, consider the entire life span of the individual from birth, or perhaps from conception to death, as a single wave in a recurring cycle. One may call such a cycle a secular cycle. I believe that the ego libido fluctuations during the secular cycle deserve much attention, since I believe that they relate significantly to such things as vulnerability to mental illness and manifestations of mental illness. They also relate to certain aspects of pathologic behavior. Let us consider, for example, vulnerability to mental illness, disregarding, of course, those mental illnesses which are the direct consequences of acquired physical damage to the brain. It seems to me that there is a peak of vulnerability during the decade between 15 and 25 years. Illness at this time is often associated with turmoil and agitation. It may take the form of schizophrenia, of neurosis, or of psychopathy. During the next decade and a half there are fewer initial episodes of mental illness, and many of those who have recovered from a first attack earlier remain in remission. Between the ages of 40 and 55, a second peak of vulnerability occurs. Illness beginning or recurring at this time may be associated either with turmoil and agitation or with inertia. In the first group we may find schizophrenia, manic-depressive psychosis, or melancholia with agitation. In the second group we find inert melancholia, hypochondria, and neurasthenia. The syndrome which is called psychopathic behavior is a phenomenon of the decade between 15 and 25. Relatively little occurs after 25, and there is almost none after 40. After the age of 55 there seems to be a constant and increasingly strong tendency toward the development of melancholia.

Suicide attempts occur most frequently, I believe, at the two periods of maximum vulnerability. At the earlier peak, more women than men attempt suicide, and at the later peak more men than women. Accomplished suicides are more common among older people than among younger people. Men succeed in their suicide attempts three times more frequently than women, and women fail three times as often as men (*2*). These cyclic changes in vulnerability to mental illness and propensity to suicide depend, in my opinion, on fluctuations of the ego's libido content. This opinion finds support in the fact that in the successful administration of anti-psychotic drugs age may be used as a criterion for selection as successfully or more successfully than symptom complex and diagnostic category. Specifically, energizers are probably indicated much more frequently than tranquilizers. Tranquilizers are probably most effective during the 15- to 25-year peak and thereafter. I have had no experience with the use of antipsychotic drugs among children, but *a priori* I would expect energizers to be more useful than tranquilizers. When tranquilizers are effective outside the 15- to 25-year period they will be even more effective when combined with energizers. Even during the 15- to 25-year peak, many patients who seem to respond well to tranquilizers will do even better when tranquilizers and energizers are given together.

Since I believe that tranquilizers achieve their effect by reducing the ego's libido supply and energizers act to augment it, the response of a syndrome to the administration of these drugs indicates whether we are dealing with a deficiency or a plethora of libido. From such observations I infer that there is probably a regular sequence of change of the ego's libido content during the secular life cycle. As a first approximation one may guess that the sequence runs something like this: During childhood the available libidinal energies consist almost exclusively of anaclitic, pregenital energies. Aggressive energies are also available to the child almost from the beginning. During adolescence and early adult life a new stream of libidinal energy develops and gives rise to the genital impulses of adult life. These genital energies may reach a maximum potential at about 20 and probably begin to subside after 35. Thereafter, the upward thrust of genital energies declines continuously while the downward pull of depletion grows; but even while the genital energies prevail most vigorously, a reservoir of pregenital anaclitic libido remains available and is drawn upon freely whenever the genital supply fails. However, after a given point, perhaps the fourth or fifth decade, this pregenital supply begins to subside too. Thereafter, mental illness seems to be associated with less turmoil than before.

If this hypothetical construct is correct, then certain clinical consequences follow. In early adult life there seems to be a special susceptibility to plethora states. On the other hand, I have observed often enough that, when psychic maturation is interrupted by failure to develop satisfactory object relations, genital libido is not evolved, and depletion and deficiency states appear even in adolescence and early adult life. After 35 there is an increasing susceptibility to depletion and deficiency states. Anti-depletion clinging seems to be more vigorous before the age of 45 or 50 than after, and this difference seems to be more striking among women than among men. There is probably a statistical sex difference in the age versus libido supply curve which may be reflected in the differential incidence of mental illness in the two sexes at different ages.

However, these secular changes in libido supply influence not only the phenomena of mental illness but also many aspects of normal behavior. We expect these secular variations in the following features of the human personality: ambition, sexual drive, competitiveness, temperament, readiness for adventure, relative preference for the strange and new as opposed to the old and familiar, interest in the future as opposed to the past, attitude toward religion, creativity, and the phenomenon of deferred obedience. This last phenomenon, to which Freud called attention (*8*), refers to the fact that defiance of the father which may have existed during childhood or early adult life gives way to obedience at some subsequent period. We may assume that defiance is favored by the evolution of genital libido, which brings about a termination of the period of childhood obedience. When genital libido subsides, the tendency to obey prevails once more. A positive inclination toward religion probably follows a similar time course.

I conclude that cyclic changes of the ego's libido supply affect certain normal aspects of personality function and create special vulnerabilities to mental illness.

REGULATION OF THE EGO'S LIBIDO CONTENT

The biologic cycle changes, circadian, menstrual, and secular, constitute only one set of factors which determine the ego's libido content at any given time. Other influences also affect the libido level powerfully. Of these I have been able to discern a few.

Constitutional endowment, I believe, plays an important role in determining the stability of the ego's libido content; that is, some children seem to be born with more difficulty in regulating the level of ego libido than others. This constitutional factor determines, then, not the actual level of ego libido at any given time, but rather its responsiveness to cyclic biologic pressures, physiologic stress, and psychic experience. To the extent that susceptibility to the melancholic type of illness and suicide can be inherited, the inheritance may proceed by the transmission of defective libido-regulating mechanisms. Such a hypothesis is not inconsistent with current ideas that what the gene actually transmits is only an enzyme-regulating mechanism. The organic substrate of whatever it is that we call libido must include enzyme regulation within its structure.

Experience with psychosis has led me to conclude that the integrity of the ego is essential for any kind of fine regulation of the ego's libido content. In other words, an intact ego seems to retard fluctuation, to limit the volatility of the ego libido level. Once there has been psychotic detachment from reality, or even an hysterical dissociation of a significant portion of the ego, the libido level swings widely and easily. In psychosis, the ego's libido level responds much more quickly and sensitively to drugs than it does when the ego is intact. Therefore, regulation of the libido level during psychosis is more delicate and more difficult than it is before definitive detachment from reality has taken place.

What are the depleting influences which we commonly encounter? We may consider first a group of factors which, taken together, can perhaps best be labeled bad hygiene. Inadequate sleep quickly creates a state of libido deficiency. For example, I believe that the so-called dream-deprivation experiments of Fisher and Dement (*3*) are actually sleep-deprivation experiments. In their subjects, as well as in subjects who have been clearly and forthrightly deprived of sleep, manifestations of libido deficiency or paradoxic hypermotivation occur promptly. Malnutrition of any kind creates libido deficiency, and so do most metabolic disturbances. During physical illness we commonly encounter the deficiency syndrome, though generally with little reactive hypermotivation. Physical exhaustion generally creates libidinal exhaustion. Acute intoxication—for example, with alcohol—disrupts the ego's function but does not produce a definite libido deficiency syndrome. On the other hand, chronic intoxication does seem to create a deficiency state.

Perhaps the two most common and most powerful of the depleting influences, other than organic, are loss of love object and narcissistic blow. Object loss may be brought about by defection of the person loved. The loved individual may disappoint the subject, he may become ill, or he may die. The result is the same in each case.

A situation more familiar to us in mental illness is that in which the subject turns away from the object as a result of one inhibiting influence or another. The position of narcissism to which the subject retreats after abandoning the object may be partial, as in neurosis, or complete, as in psychosis. In the latter instance there is a complete detachment from the world of reality. The loss of object is just as effective a trigger for libido depletion whether it is brought about by the initiative of the subject, by the initiative of the object, or by fate.

Much study has been devoted recently to the effects of prolonged isolation upon psychic function. It is my impression from the reports I have seen that, where isolation is prolonged and especially when it is associated with anxiety, both paradoxical hypermotivation and the deficiency syndrome play a part in determining the resultant effect upon the individual.

Any experience which acts as a blow to one's narcissism acts powerfully and almost instantaneously to reduce the ego's libido content. Mutilation of the body by accident or disease, physical or mental disability, failure in some important line of endeavor, criticism by others, may each, at one time or another, exert a depleting influence.

Under certain circumstances one experience may create a combination of impressions of object loss and narcissistic blow at the same time. For example, if the principal love object withdraws his love and attacks and degrades, the subject simultaneously suffers the loss of the love of the object and the loss of his own self-esteem. Similarly, superego protest can create the impression of the loss of the protecting love of the superego and an attack upon self-esteem. The protest may be incurred by a violation of superego standards or by success guilt, by *hubris*.

What factors exert a repleting influence upon the ego's libido content?

We may first list organic factors. There is no doubt that one can raise the ego's libido content by administering certain drugs which we call energizers. These include primarily monoamine oxidase inhibitors and iminodibenzyl derivatives. Certain hormonal and other steroid substances may exert a similar energizing effect, but here our data are barely suggestive. Even if this effect does exist, I suspect that the administration of such substances for increasing the availability of libido to the ego is much trickier than the use of energizing drugs. Finally, in at least one instance, it has seemed to me that genital irritation caused by cystitis has seemed to create the manifestations of libido plethora.

On the whole it seems to me that repleting influences are harder to produce than depleting influences. Although the loss of love object, or more precisely the loss of the love of the object, is a potent depleter of libidinal energies, its converse, the opportunity for object love, probably exerts a repleting effect but one which is less compelling. In other words, it seems to me easier to bring about depletion by robbing an individual of the love that he seeks than to induce a repletion by tempting him with a love object.

Again, just as narcissistic disappointment serves a depleting function, so narcissistic satisfaction seems to do the opposite. Success and triumph, especially when these are confirmed by the admiration of others and when they do not incur superego protest, invigorate the ego. The presentation of new opportunities for conquest promises success and may induce at least a temporary inspiration.

When an individual earns the approval of the superego, for example as a result of success in some ordeal, he benefits from the combined effect of narcissistic satisfaction and the superego equivalent of object love.

Sometimes the existence of a demand can act to make libidinal energies available to the ego that would not otherwise be present. For example, an individual who otherwise has little energy available for the routine activities of daily life may find that, when confronted with an emergency, he can rise and contribute to it large quantities of effort. Similarly, young children and weak and helpless adults possess a kind of appeal which can make available to the observer supplies of libido. However, in each case after the demand passes the libido supply which it induced quickly subsides. On the other hand, if the demand requires efforts or powers beyond the capacity of the individual, it may exert a depleting rather than a repleting effect.

I should like to emphasize specifically that the superego possesses the power to provide and remove libidinal energies just as though it were an external love object. It is possible that in some individuals the superego is the more powerful, and in others the external object exerts a greater effect. The superego derives on the one hand from the incorporated images of the parents, and on the other hand from social and cultural influences. We should expect then, and I believe that the expectation is reasonable, that community support for an individual exerts a repleting effect.

On some occasions, observing patients in a state of moderate depletion, I have had the impression that there has been a spontaneous recovery, a spontaneous repletion which arose from no specific influence that I could detect. I have wondered accordingly whether there might be some automatic corrective device which prevents excessive excursions either in the direction of plethora or deficiency and maintains a kind of homeostasis of the ego's libido content. Even if we grant that in some instances there may have been unconscious repleting forces that I have missed, nevertheless I suspect that at least in some of these instances the repletion was not determined by psychic events. The rebirth fantasy that often accompanied these automatic shifts can be understood as the consequence of the correction of the libido excess or deficiency, rather than its cause.

There are three areas of psychic involvement which exert a continuing influence, now depleting, now repleting, upon the ego's libido content. These are self-esteem, family life, and life within the community.

Freud (*9*) suggested that self-esteem derives from three sources: a residue of infantile narcissism; the fulfillment of the ego ideal; and the satisfaction of object libido. In practical terms this means that self-esteem is a function of, among other things, the degree with which one achieves compliance with the idealized image of oneself with respect to one's appearance, capacity, and performance. One's estimate of the closeness of this compliance is strongly reinforced by, but is not completely dependent upon, the admiration of others. One powerful source, then, of self-regard is work. Work satisfies the superego, it evokes admiration from individuals and from the community. At the same time one has the impression that work also discharges libido and thus discourages an excessive accumulation of libido within the ego. Unfortunately, we are dealing with a difficult area in which theoretical speculations are not readily verifiable by clinical observation. We assume that, when certain forms of mental activity are blocked, innervation passes to physical organs—e.g., in hysteria and catatonia. If that is true, then both psychic and physical activity draw motivational support from the same pool. From this we infer that the motivational pool may be drained by either physical or psychic activity. Aside from the drain, or wholesome effect, caused by the work, success at work repletes the ego whereas failure depletes the ego. Awareness of a threat of depletion may evoke extravagant efforts to reinforce one's self-esteem by extreme efforts at self-improvement, efforts in occupational activity, as well as in the area of sexual success. It is this phenomenon that is responsible for the commonly observed "overwork" that so often precedes a breakdown. The need to sustain self-esteem in desperate situations may also give rise to a belligerent determination to avoid and turn away criticism. The inability to tolerate criticism is characteristic of individuals struggling to sustain the ego's energy level against a perceived, powerful depleting tendency.

Family life is a second area which serves simultaneously as a great source and a great sink of libidinal energies. In this essay I shall attempt no more than a schematic introduction to the subject. Optimally, we expect young adults to enter the marital relation out of an impulse to love in a giving, caring way. As these adults age, the genital, libido pressure begins gradually to decline, and periods of depletion become more frequent and more profound. Therefore the relation between the husband and wife changes over the years to a dependent, anaclitic one in which each asks for affectionate support from the other. It is not that this aspect of the relation is entirely absent during early years; but it becomes more frequent and more constant as time goes by. Much of the pathology of marriage, I believe, can be understood in terms of a disturbance of the libidinal economic equilibrium between the two partners.

Obviously, the sexual relation plays a central role in the marital libido economy, both creating disturbances in the economy when it is itself disturbed and indicating their presence even when the source of the disturbance lies elsewhere. Normally we assume that the desire for coitus in young adults arises from the pressure of the genital libido. We assume also that the level of genital libido is temporarily diminished by the sexual act. However, pregenital, anaclitic energies may also achieve expression in genital excitement and desire. For example, erotomania, more often than not, is driven by pregenital, anaclitic energies mobilized by impending or actual depletion. When sexual activity is driven by pregenital energies, we find that the preorgastic excitement tends to combat the depletion and is therefore eagerly pursued and elaborated, often into perversions. In such instances, however, after the orgasm, there is a profound letdown which presents in men as depression, guilt, and self-condemnation, and in women as an increase rather than a decrease in desire, clinging, weeping, and eagerness to repeat the act or else as degradation of herself and her partner. Early morning, upon awakening, is usually the period of lowest libido supply. There are individuals who prefer intercourse in the morning, and in most cases it is the repleting power of this sexual experience that they seek.

Let me give two examples to illustrate these points I have made about the relation of sexual behavior to the libidinal economy. A young man reported, "My wife asked me whether I was coming into her bed. I did and we had intercourse. I enjoyed it but I felt that I was using her. I awoke in the morning with an erection and I masturbated. I had had a dream that night in which I thought, 'You can revitalize an old building with electricity. I put my penis into an electric outlet to be charged up.' "

This man made his living by improving old buildings. In analysis we learned that this activity gave expression to his childhood wish to cure his mother of her chronic illness which had kept her away from him for long periods when he was a child. Not only did the buildings represent his mother, they actually belonged to her. Among the relevant associations to the dream was a memory that in childhood he liked to stick his finger in electric sockets and he enjoyed the painful shock. Recently it had seemed to him that his penis was longer or more sensitive than usual.

In this instance it is clear that the coital act was exploited for the purpose of securing revitalization or repletion of energies. Actually it neither satisfied him nor accomplished the repletion he desired. Therefore he was forced to seek gratification a few hours later, in the morning, upon awakening. It is my tentative impression that the morning erection with which some men awaken at times stems from this effort to secure repletion by genital activity. Compulsive masturbation can be explained as the consequence of the following cycle: Depletion–compensatory sexual excitement–masturbation–further depletion–further sexual craving–masturbation, and so on.

The next example will illustrate the differing meaning of coitus in states of libido deficiency. A young woman reported on Thursday:

> I feel better today. For a change I'm not so depressed. We had intercourse on Tuesday night. After the orgasm I started a crying jag again. I cried much stronger after he had his orgasm. I was left with such an empty feeling.
>
> I did well on my trip yesterday. Last night after I came home he wanted to have intercourse again. This time I didn't cry after it. The first thing that came to my mind was about my plans for this summer. I told him, "I'm going to do a great job." On my plane trip home yesterday, I had fantasies of seeing people vomit. I guess without my career I'm nothing. I started thinking last night about giving dinner parties. I've been able to avoid overeating too.
>
> On Tuesday night I had a dream. A man was trying to kidnap or kill me or do something. I was rescued or ran away.
>
> Suddenly I feel as if I can conquer the world. It's as if I'm two people. I felt a strange feeling of contempt for one of my neighbors who visited this morning. It semed to me last night that my mother-in-law looked shabby.

When I had seen this patient on Tuesday, it was clear that she was suffering a mild libido deficiency syndrome. That night she seemed to welcome intercourse for some relief. However she felt a strong letdown after orgasm, both hers and her husband's, and she wept. This behavior was not uncommon for her in a state of libido deficiency. This unpleasant experience was followed promptly by a dream which indicated her resentment against her husband who had failed to satisfy her, and her wish to escape to a homosexual relation with her mother. The latter detail does not appear in this dream, but it does appear in other dreams which start the same way. On the following day, in another city, she achieved a minor professional success, and this improved her self-esteem to the point of creating a mild plethora with elation. The mild plethora induced a wish to give, to feed, to entertain, represented by her wish to give dinner parties. There was great enthusiasm for her future. Complementing her increased self-esteem, she felt contempt for others. Sexual intercourse under these circumstances now meant a means of giving pleasure to her husband and reinforcing satisfaction with herself. It was now satisfying and invigorating rather than disturbing. The plethora also canceled her need to incorporate, to overeat, and even reversed it, thus creating a tendency to vomit as well as to give. This example illustrates the fact that coitus can be used in the services of pregenital as well as genital needs.

The parent's relation to his child strongly influences the parent's libido level. The appearance and cries of the newborn infant exert an invigorating effect upon the parent. When the parent's libido supplies are meager, the stimulation which the infant provides constitutes a demand which cannot be met. Under such circumstances, the effect of confrontation by the infant is not a mobilization of libido supplies but rather a depletion or deficiency syndrome. Of course these influences play especially strongly upon the mother, but the father too is affected by them. These circumstances often create what amounts to a *post-partum* disturbance in the father.

To a lesser but still important extent all young children constitute at the same time a drain upon the parents' libido supplies and a stimulus for the evocation of supplementary supplies. Illness or a failure or misbehavior on the part of the children evokes emergency energies in the parents, energies which are required to cope with the problem. On the other hand, these also constitute a narcissistic blow to the parent and as such may exert a depleting effect. Often the parent responds initially by rising to the occasion, but when emergency action is no longer needed, a sharp decline ensues. For example, a schizophrenic woman (X.N.Z.), in partial remission, learned that her 11-year-old son was having so much difficulty at school that he was asked not to return. She received the information with shock and attempted at first to ascribe the difficulty to the school authorities. To her this news meant that she had transmitted her illness to him and that she had caused his illness by her failure as a mother. Also, ever since she was a child she had suffered from guilt that she was in some way responsible for her older brother's chronic schizophrenic illness. The idea that her child was mentally ill and required treatment revived this old guilt. Following the initial shock she busily involved herself in making arrangements for the child's treatment, in smoothing the difficulties at school, in arranging for transfer to another school, and in arranging for tutoring. These were plainly emergency supplies and seemed to me to have the characteristics of paradoxical hypermotivation. However, after three or four months, when treatment was well established and when satisfactory provision had been made for transfer to another school, she began to show a progressively deepening deficiency syndrome, progressing to a schizophrenic melancholia. This state was quickly dissipated by means of an energizing drug.

The child's libido supply, of course, depends heavily upon his relation with his parents. Since I have almost no experience in this area, the following remarks are based only upon conjecture. The young child's libido supplies consist almost exclusively of anaclitic energies. They are devoted probably entirely to securing and holding the parent's love and concern. For the young child the love of the parent is its only protection against depletion. In the course of maturation the child comes to find self-love, to a certain extent a satisfactory substitute for the love of his parents. Where an effective superego is established, it acquires the power of the parent to elicit and sustain libidinal energies. Thereafter the superego becomes an important and powerful regulator of the ego's libido content. One has the impression at times that condemnation by the superego is sufficient to empty the ego of its libidinal energies. Similarly, the superego's favor seems to possess the power of adding to the ego's energies. The ego takes cognizance of this power of the superego when, in a state of depletion, it performs acts which can only be interpreted as efforts to appease the superego.

As the child grows into and through adolescence, he acquires genital energies. This genital libido establishes genital primacy. That is, the genital organs and, more specifically, the genital organs in their reproductive function become the definitive carriers of the instinctual drive. Other erotic zones are often called into play, but only in the service of the reproductive desire and only to supplement the functions of the genital organs themselves. These same libidinal energies tend also to lead the adolescent away from the first objects of his love, his family, to strange or unfamiliar objects. This transition from familiar to unfamiliar objects may evoke separation anxiety. Such separation anxiety may, at least in some instances, be caused by exclusive dependence of the libido supply upon the presence of the mother. Anticipation of separation from mother then promises a drop in libido supply, and this prospect itself may provoke anxiety. On the other hand, the persistence of separation anxiety through adolescence and into early adult life inhibits the evolution of mature genital energies and leads to an inhibition of adult activities, to clinging and immaturity. In contrast to this, I should assume that the successful consummation of genital reproductive activities would lead in a circular fashion to a further elaboration of libidinal energies. In other words, the ego's genital libido supply seems to be encouraged by the successful discharge of this libido and discouraged by persistent frustration. When this frustration does occur, the threats of libido depletion which characterized childhood persist and continue to motivate childhood patterns of clinging to familiar objects.

However, the child's clinging to the parent for libidinal sustenance employs not only erotic modes. When these fail to secure an adequate response, the child may turn against the parent in anger and direct toward him aggressive energies which are intended to supplement the frustrated libidinal ones. We often see the same sequence in adults who are, in regression, clinging to the object as they did when they were children. At first there is an affectionate approach and, when the latter is frustrated, anger. The crucial difference is that, whereas the mother will respond to a young child's anger with more vigorous efforts to satisfy him, the adult lover or spouse will soon lose patience and turn against the aggressive clinger. By his anger, then, the latter succeeds only in driving away the disappointing love object. However, since the mother tolerated these attacks when the patient was a child, the patient cannot understand why his current love object should behave differently.

The capacity of clinging libido to mobilize aggressiveness becomes evident again in sibling relations. Primarily and initially rivalry with other sibs may be considered an aspect of anaclitic clinging to the parents for sustenance. When the sib threatens to encroach upon the child's supply of nourishing material and affection, the clinging love for the parent is supplemented by aggressiveness toward the rival. Subsequently, the sibs themselves may partially overcome their rivalry and form groups in which some act as parents toward the others. Freud, for example (*11*), pointed out that one variety of homosexuality may derive from an individual's conquest of his rivalry toward a sibling of the same sex.

It would be a mistake to neglect the influence of the community upon the individual's libido level. Because the organized community is to the individual the successor, the heir of his family as he saw it in childhood, it can provide supporting affectional ties. These ties include the affection of the other members of the community, incorporation of the individual into the corpus of the group—e.g., by ritualized forms of identification—and, finally, approval by the leader of the group. But the individual must pay for this group support. He is required to exhibit loyalty to the group, for example, by detaching himself from competing groups. He is expected to sacrifice those of his personal interests which compete with the interests of the group. He is expected also to abstain from sexual gratification with other members of the group, except with the group's specific approval, and then under severe restrictions.

The group serves as a competitor in some respects to the adult family of the subject. In this competition it enjoys certain advantages. Those individuals who find sexual contact anxiety-provoking or difficult find the nonsensual relations of the group more comfortable. Most groups demand relatively little from the individual, and often those demands are scaled to the capacity of the individual. Within the group sublimated homosexual relations are encouraged. The continuity of the group in time promises immunity from losing the supporting love object. For these reasons it becomes necessary for the individual to distribute both his emotional investments and his expectations for support between the community and the family.

One should note, however, that not every group can offer effective libidinal support to the individual. The group's capacity to offer this support depends upon its own morale. This, in turn, is a function of the morale of the individual members of the group, of the integrity of the group organization, of the presence and effectiveness of tradition as a unifying factor; and it is also a function of the prestige and power of the leader.

At the beginning of this essay I described some typical clinical states which were determined by libido supply. I went on, then, to discuss some of the determinants of libido supply. Let me now conclude by describing three different processes through which the psyche shifts from one state of libido supply to another. Consider, first, the shift from pregenital, anaclitic, clinging hypermotivation of depletion threat to a definite libido deficiency syndrome. This shift may be brought about by physical or mental exhaustion, as a result of disappointment by the anaclitic object, as a result of the individual's turning away from the object as he does in neurosis or psychosis, as a result of a critical attack by the object, as a result of a narcissistic blow, or as a result of the administration of a tranquilizing drug. All these may at one time or another cause movement from paradoxical hypermotivation to definitive deficiency. When this change occurs we see a relatively abrupt cessation of libidinal activities and derivatives of libidinal impulses. At the same time we often observe an increase in manifestations of the aggressive instincts. The individual tends to detach himself from his love objects and from all objects. Ultimately, all the residual libido is directed toward the self, as are the aggressive instincts. This last state of affairs creates hypochondria and a wish for death. The move toward the deficiency state is also characterized by the appearance of pessimism and depression and by a shift from centripetal to centrifugal tensions.

Under other circumstances this pregenital clinging hypermotivation of the depletion state gives way to a mild deficiency rather than the profound definitive deficiency described above. We see such an event when depleting influences are removed, such as external pressures or demands or tranquilizing medication which was given in doses sufficient to threaten depletion. This state of affairs may also be induced by reinforcing repleting tendencies. For example, a crucially important love object or a psychotherapist may provide affectionate emotional support. Some affectionate or vocational gratification would exert a similar influence. Again, an energizing medication may be administered in doses sufficient to terminate the depletion threat but not sufficient to undo the deficiency completely. Under these circumstances we observe a termination of extravagant libidinal activity and of accompanying aggressive activity. More specifically, we see a weakening of the clinging interest in objects. At the same time, there appear a number of narcissistic repleting activities. These include masturbation, bulimia with obesity, mild addictions, mild discontent with oneself, and a tendency to hypersomnia.

Finally, let us consider the shift from pregenital anaclitic clinging hypermotivation to true genital motivation. This is a rather subtle change which we ordinarily consider merely improvement or remission. Those instances which are sufficiently dramatic to come to our attention are probably pathologic exaggerations of what must otherwise be considered a normal process. One encounters such caricatures of this process most commonly in the occasional patient who recovers spontaneously from melancholia only to pass directly into mania. The same process may occasionally be brought about by the inadvertent or deliberate administration of an excessive amount of energizing drug. The normal, more limited advance may be assumed to occur when one or more of the pregenital hypermotivation activities become successful in terms not only of achieving its immediate goals but also of alleviating the threat of depletion. Under such circumstances there may seem to be a promise of further success and gratification. The object relation imperceptibly changes its character from clinging activity to more adult drives. Adherence to the old and familiar gives way to an adventurous pursuit of the strange. (This change, however, must be distinguished from something which looks like it—i.e., a defensive, phobic turning away from the anaclitic object to a strange object.) Dependent attitudes are discarded in favor of supporting attitudes. The pregenital orientation gives way to a genital orientation. Sublimations become more complete. Aggressiveness subsides. It almost seems as if the pregenital hypermotivation provided a shower of kindling sparks which suddenly found a combustible material and ignited it to self-sustaining flame. Psychically the individual gives evidence of fantasies of rebirth and of identification with one or the other of his parents. One may perhaps compare this sequence to the sequential transition from pregenital foreplay to genital intercourse.

SUMMARY

In this essay I have tried to elaborate and develop further the concept of the ego's libido content as a variable quantity which exerts a considerable influence on the tenor of normal activities and on the natural history of mental illness. Specifically, I have presented a revised account of the phases of mental illness in terms of this aspect of libido theory. I have attempted to relate libido level to certain cyclic aspects of life, including among these circadian, menstrual, and secular cycles. Moreover, I have enumerated and discussed briefly certain of the principal determinants of the ego's libido level—that is, depleting and repleting influences which are encountered in daily life and in psychiatric therapy.

The importance of this theory is that it permits a more rational use of drug therapy, both alone and in combination with psychoanalysis and psychotherapy; it relates classical psychoanalytic theory more meaningfully to clinical observation; it permits more accurate clinical prediction; and it affords a more rational basis for devising therapeutic programs.

REFERENCES

1 Benedek, Therese. An investigation of the sexual cycle in women. *Arch. gen. Psychiat. 8:*311–322, 1963.

2 Dublin, L. I. *Suicide.* New York, Ronald, 1963.

3 Fisher, C., and Dement, W. Studies on the psychopathology of sleep and dreams. *Amer. J. Psychiat. 119:*1160–1168, 1963.

4 Freud, S. "The Neuro-Psychoses of Defense" (first published in 1894). *Standard Edition of the Complete Psychological Works of Sigmund Freud,* edited by J. Strachey, Vol. III. London, Hogarth, 1962.

5 Freud, S. "The Project for a Scientific Psychology" (first published in 1895). *The Origins of Psychoanalysis: Letters to Wilhelm Fliess, Drafts and Notes, 1887–1902,* edited by M. Bonaparte, A. Freud, and E. Kris. New York, Basic Books, 1954.

6 Freud, S. "Sexuality in the Aetiology of the Neuroses" (first published in 1898). *Standard Edition,* Vol. III. London, Hogarth, 1962.

7 Freud, S. "Three Essays on the Theory of Sexuality" (first published in 1905). *Standard Edition,* Vol. VII. London, Hogarth, 1963.

8 Freud, S. "Totem and Taboo" (first published in 1912–1913). *Standard Edition,* Vol. XIII. London, Hogarth, 1955.

9 Freud, S. "On Narcissism: An Introduction" (first published in 1914). *Standard Edition,* Vol. XIV. London, Hogarth, 1957.

10 Freud, S. "Mourning and Melancholia" (first published in 1917). *Standard Edition,* Vol. XIV. London, Hogarth, 1957.

11 Freud, S. "Certain Neurotic Mechanisms in Jealousy, Paranoia and Homosexuality" (first published in 1922). *Collected Papers,* Vol. II. London, Hogarth, 1955.

12 Freud, S. "Inhibitions, Symptoms and Anxiety" (first published in 1926). *Standard Edition,* Vol. XX. London, Hogarth, 1959.

13 Freud, S. "Civilization and Its Discontents" (first published in 1930). *Standard Edition,* Vol. XXI. London, Hogarth, 1961.

14 Freud, S. *An Outline of Psychoanalysis,* translated by J. Strachey. New York, Norton, 1949.

15 Ostow, M. *Drugs in Psychoanalysis and Psychotherapy.* New York, Basic Books, 1962.

INDEX OF NAMES

SUBJECT INDEX

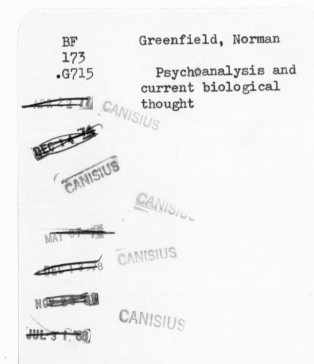